Hampshire Field Club & Archaeological Society: M

Sparsholt Roman Villa, Hampshire
Excavations by David E Johnston

By David E Johnston & Jonathan Dicks
with a Foreword by Professor Martin Biddle

with contributions by

Denise Allen, Tom Blagg, Kayt Marter Brown, Garrard Cole, Steve Cosh,
David Peacock, Susan Scott, Rachael Seager Smith, Ian Sims,
Nick Stoodley, Richard Ward, Peter Warry, David Williams & Hugh Williams

illustrations by

Mike Brace, Steve Cosh, Colin Coward, Jonathan Dicks, Vicki Harrison,
S E James, David E Johnston, D S Neal & Graham Scobie

Published by the Hampshire Field Club & Archaeological Society
in co-operation with English Heritage

HAMPSHIRE FIELD CLUB MONOGRAPH 11

Published by the Hampshire Field Club & Archaeological Society

This monograph is published with the aid of a grant from English Heritage, to whom the Field Club and publishers extend their grateful thanks.

Publication by the Hampshire Field Club does not imply that this body endorses the views expressed; the factual content and the opinions expressed herein remain the responsibility of the authors.

© Hampshire Field Club & Archaeological Society 2014

ISBN 978-0-907473-12-1

Edited by Nick Stoodley & David Allen

Produced for the Society by 4word Ltd, Bristol
Printed by T J International Ltd, Padstow, Cornwall

CONTENTS

LIST OF ILLUSTRATIONS v

LIST OF TABLES viii

ACKNOWLEDGEMENTS ix

ABSTRACTS x

FOREWORD *by Professor Martin Biddle* xiii

Chapter 1	INTRODUCTION	1
	Summary	1
	Structure and aims of the report	1
	The site and its setting	2
	Archaeological background	2
	Previous investigations	6
	The excavation project	6
	Excavation and recording methodology	7
	Outline of the site	10
Chapter 2	THE IRON AGE (Site L)	12
	Introduction	12
	Phasing	12
	Results of the excavation	12
	Overview	18
Chapter 3	THE AISLED BUILDINGS (Sites A & F)	20
	Introduction	20
	Results of the excavation	20
	Overview	38
Chapter 4	THE MAIN HOUSE (Site D)	41
	Introduction	41
	Results of the excavation	41
	Overview	58
Chapter 5	THE BARN (Site C)	59
	Overview	63
Chapter 6	THE HALL (Site G)	64
	Overview	68
Chapter 7	THE COURTYARD	71
	The Courtyard wall	71
	The entrance to the Courtyard	73
	The interior of the Courtyard	75
	Overview	76
Chapter 8	DISCUSSION	82
	The Iron Age period	82
	The Romano-British period	84

SPECIALIST REPORTS

Chapter 9	POTTERY	90
	The Iron Age pottery *by David E Johnston*	90
	The Romano-British pottery *by Rachael Seager Smith and Kayt Marter Brown*	94
Chapter 10	THE MOSAICS *by Steve Cosh*	113
	Main House	113
	Aisled Building	114
	Discussion	114
Chapter 11	CERAMIC BUILDING MATERIAL *by Rachael Seager Smith and Kayt Marter Brown*	121
	Introduction	121
	Methodology	121
	Results	121
	The ceramic roofing material *by Peter Warry*	123
Chapter 12	THE WALL PLASTER	128
	Introduction	128
	Wall plaster *by Susan Scott*	128
	Petrographic examination of wall plaster samples *by Ian Sims*	130
Chapter 13	ANALYSIS OF CONCRETE AND MORTAR SAMPLES *by Ian Sims*	132
	Summary	132
	Introduction	132
	Methods of treatment	132
	Results	134
	Discussion	137
	Conclusions	138
Chapter 14	THE COINS *by Hugh Williams*	139
Chapter 15	THE FINDS	141
	The metalwork *by Nick Stoodley*	141
	Roman glass *by Denise Allen*	156
	Loomweight *by David E Johnston*	160
	The objects of bone *by Nick Stoodley*	161
	Stone objects	164
	The querns *by David E Johnston*	164
	The column *by Tom Blagg*	165
	Flint *by David E Johnston*	166
Chapter 16	BONE	167
	The human skeletal remains *by Garrard Cole*	167
	The faunal remains *by Richard Ward*	175
Chapter 17	REFERENCES	189
INDEX		195

LIST OF ILLUSTRATIONS*

a: David E Johnston	xii
1: Location of Hampshire in the United Kingdom and Sparsholt in Hampshire	1
2: Location plan showing the villa, Route 45a and sites referred to in the Introduction (drawn by NS & MB)	3
3: Location plan showing the villa and Route 45a (drawn by DEJ)	4
4: Aerial photograph showing the 'ride' cutting through the site (1968, Army School of Aviation)	5
5: The Barn showing the typical Wheeler box-type excavation (photographed 1968)	7
6: Aerial photograph of Site L under open-area excavation (Army School of Aviation)	8
7: The Site and site codes (drawn by DEJ, redrawn by MB)	9
8: Aerial photograph of the Aisled Buildings under excavation (Army School of Aviation)	11
9: Plan of Iron Age enclosure (drawn by DEJ)	13
10: Iron Age and Roman ditches (drawn by DEJ)	14
11: Iron Age and Roman ditches (drawn by DEJ)	16
12: Iron Age storage pits (drawn by DEJ)	17
13: Site plan of the Aisled Buildings (drawn by DEJ, modified by JD)	21
14: Grave discovered next to the south foundation trench (photographed 1972)	22
15: Plan of AB I's baths (drawn by JD, based on original by CC)	23
16: AB I plunge bath below AB II (photographed 1972)	24
17: Plan of the entrance to AB II (drawn by JD, based on original by CC)	25
18: Entrance to AB II in the eastern wall (photographed 1971)	25
19: North wall of AB II showing change in method of construction (drawn by JD, based on original by CC)	27
20: Plan of the western section of the south wall of AB II (drawn by JD, based on original by CC)	27
21: Plan of original part of the north courtyard wall and the side entrance (drawn by JD, based on original by DEJ)	28
22: Column base set into the western gable wall (photographed 1971)	28
23: Mosaic in Room 12 (photographed 1971)	29
24: Section through Room 13 floor layers and partition wall (drawn by JD, based on an original from a site note book)	29
25: Plan of the hearth built into the south wall of Room 19 (drawn by JD, based on an original from a site note book)	30
26: Oven 1 in Room 19 (drawn by VH)	31
27: Oven 2 under Oven 1 in Room 19 (drawn by VH)	32
28: Hearth in Room 23	33
29: Plan of bath suite in AB II (drawn by JD, based on an original by CC)	34
30: View of the bath suite in AB II looking west (photographed 1972)	35
31: View of T-shaped corn drier, stoke hole and baths (photographed 1972)	36
32: Room 16, two large grog-tempered storage jars	37
33: Hypocaust under the *tepidarium* looking south (photographed 1972)	37
34: View of the tiles used in the construction of the steps into the bath in Room 18 (photographed 1972)	39
35: View of the steps into the plunge bath in Room 18 (photographed 1972)	39
36: Outline plan of Phase 1 House (drawn by JD)	42
37: Outline plan of Phases I and II of the House (drawn by JD)	42
38: Example of an ashlar cornerstone (photographed 1972)	43
39: Plan of the south-east corner of the original building and Room 2 (drawn by JD, based on a sketch in a site note book)	43
40: View of the tessellated floor of the corridor of the Main House (photograph by Jonathan Erskine)	44
41: Section through floor of the corridor (drawn by VH)	44

LIST OF ILLUSTRATIONS

42: View of the tessellated floor in Room 2 of the Main House (photograph by Jonathan Erskine)	46
43: Section through floor layers of Room 2 (drawn by VH)	46
44: Fireplace built into the wall of Room 4 (photographed 1969)	47
45: Plan of Room 5 (drawn by JD, based on original by CC)	48
46: Rooms 5 and 6 (photographed 1969)	49
47: Plan of Room 6 (drawn by JD, based on original by CC)	50
48: Room 7 floor layers (photographed 1969)	51
49: Plan of Room 9a and Room 11 (drawn by JD, based on original by CC)	51
50: Plan of Room 10 (drawn by JD, based on original by CC)	52
51: Possible hearth in Room 10 (photographed 1966)	53
52: Hearth and butt joint of the corner of the north wing (drawn by JD, based on a sketch in a site note book)	53
53: Part of the border of the mosaic in Room 11 (photographed 1967)	54
54: Section through hypocaust flues in Room 11 (drawn by JD, based on original by DEJ)	54
55: View of Room 11 showing hypocaust box flues (photographed 1967)	55
56: Plan of Roman ditches and pits in the vicinity of the Main House (drawn by JD)	56
57: Section through Pit XX (drawn by DEJ)	56
58: Section of Ditches I and IV at the junction with the north wall of House (drawn by DEJ)	57
59: Outline plan of the Barn (drawn by JD)	60
60: General view of the Barn under excavation, looking west (photographed 1969)	61
61: North-east corner of Room 21 (photographed 1969)	61
62: Junction of the wall of the Barn with the Courtyard wall (Drawn by JD)	62
63: The north-west corner of the Barn showing the abutted Courtyard wall (photographed 1969)	62
64: The blocked entrance to Room 21, looking south (photographed 1969)	63
65: Outline plan of the Hall (drawn by JD)	65
66: Detailed plan of the Hall (drawn by CC)	66
67: North-west corner of the Hall (photographed 1970)	67
68: Tiled hearth against the wall of the Hall (photographed 1970)	67
69: Plan of the oven in the Hall (drawn by VH & DJ)	68
70: Post-excavation view of the oven (photographed 1970)	69
71: 'Grave' of infant burials (photographed 1970)	69
72: Site plan showing area enclosed by the Courtyard Wall (drawn by JD)	72
73: Outline plan of the eastern Courtyard Wall (drawn by JD, based on original by DEJ)	73
74: Eastern wall under excavation (photographed 1968)	74
75: South-west corner of the Courtyard Wall (photographed 1965)	75
76: Plan of the junction of the Courtyard Wall and the Main House (drawn by JD, based on a sketch in a site note book)	76
77: Plan of the eastern end of the north wall of the Courtyard (drawn by JD)	77
78: Excavated entrance looking south (photographed 1969)	78
79: Plan of the entrance to the Courtyard (drawn by DEJ)	79
80: Section through the entrance (drawn by JD, based on original by CC)	79
81: View of the crater and the top of the well shaft (photographed 1969)	80
82: The Phase II Villa layout (drawn by JD)	81
83: The Phase III Villa layout (drawn by JD)	81
84: Comparative Iron Age sites (drawn by MB and NS)	83
85: Comparative Romano-British sites (drawn by NS)	85
86: Coin loss pattern comparisons with rural villas	89
87: Coin loss pattern comparison with Winchester	89
88: Iron Age pottery (drawn by DEJ)	93
89: Romano-British pots 1–15 (drawings by S E James)	109
90: Romano-British pots 16–35 (drawings by S E James)	110
91: Romano-British pots 36–45 (drawings by S E James)	111
92: Romano-British pots 46–60 (drawings by S E James)	112
93: Sparsholt plan of main building showing mosaics (artwork by S R Cosh)	115
94: Sparsholt Room 2 (painting by S R Cosh)	116
95: Sparsholt Room 1 (detail) (painting by S R Cosh)	116

LIST OF ILLUSTRATIONS vii

96:	Sparsholt Room 7 (painting by D S Neal)	118
97:	Sparsholt Room 11 (painting and reconstruction drawing by S R Cosh)	119
98:	Sparsholt Room 12 (painting by S R Cosh)	120
99:	Sparsholt Room 12, probable reconststruction (artwork by S R Cosh)	120
100:	*Imbrex* fragment with a pre-firing incised graffito (drawing by S E James)	122
101:	Type 5 *tegula* showing inserts into flange (Photograph P Warry)	125
102:	Left, cut-away with residual flange remaining; right, flange absent (Photograph P Warry)	125
103:	Flange dimensions grouped by cut-away lengths	125
104 and 105:	Size distributions of Type 7 *tegulae* from all recorded sites	126
106:	Small finds 1–9. Copper alloy	146
107:	Small finds 10–14. Iron	148
108:	Small finds 15–27. Iron	150
109:	Small finds 28–36. Iron	152
110:	Small finds 37–50. Iron	154
111:	Glass cup (SF 570)	156
112:	Small finds 1–10. Glass	158
113:	Loomweight (SF 655)	160
114:	Small finds 1–6. Bone	162
115:	Column	165
116:	Flints 486 and 489	166
117:	Sample K SPLOT inhumation (photographed 1972)	169
118:	Sample A F27 *in situ* (photographed 1972)	172
119:	Overall species representation shown as percentages of the Number of Individual Specimens	177
120:	Percentage of bone survival for main domesticates based on overall MNI	178
121:	Age stages of domesticates determined from complete mandibles recovered	179
122:	Wear stages of loose M3s for cattle and sheep/goat recovered	179
123:	Survivability curves for the major domesticates based on epiphyseal fusion noted from the remains	180
124:	Sex plot for cattle metacarpals and metatarsals	180
125:	Distribution of deer species as NISP of total Cervus specimens	181
126:	Distribution of different bird species found as percentage of total bird NISP	183
127:	Tri-plot (ox, sheep/goat, pig) by King (1989) with Roman and Iron Age Sparsholt	185
128:	Tri-plot (ox, sheep/goat, pig) with King (1984) original data	185

Key for abbreviations:
MB (Mike Brace); CC (Colin Coward); JD (Jonathan Dicks); VH (Vicki Harrison); DEJ (David E Johnston); NS (Nick Stoodley)

* photographed by David Johnston unless stated otherwise

LIST OF TABLES

1:	Number of Iron Age sherds by pit	18
2:	Dimensions of Iron Age storage pits	18
3:	Sparsholt Iron Age fabric types compared to local sites	90
4:	Sparsholt Iron Age form types compared to local sites	91
5:	Romano-British fabric totals	96
6:	Romano-British vessel forms assigned to specific types	97
7:	Romano-British vessel types from each site correlated with fabric	99
8:	CBM types by fragment count	121
9:	Dimensions of complete CBM pieces	122
10:	*Tegulae* dimensions	123
11:	Contextual data for roofing material	123
12:	Size analysis of all Sparsholt Type 7 *tegulae*	127
13:	Plaster sample received	131
14:	Summary of results of scanning electron microscopy and microanalysis of plaster	131
15:	List of the concrete and mortar samples collected	133
16:	Observations from plane surface and hand specimen examination	135
17:	Observations and determinations from thin section examination	135
18:	Composition of seven selected concrete samples as determined by the acid-dissolution technique	136
19:	Size distributions of the insoluble aggregates	136
20:	The colour changes observed after heating for one hour at temperatures in the range 100–800°C	137
21:	Metalwork divided by category (%= of that particular metal)	141
22:	Quantities of metalwork at villas investigated by the Danebury Environs Roman Project (no./%)	142
23:	Chilgrove 1 & 2, types of ironwork	142
24:	Material by building/area	143
25:	Ironwork by category and by building/area	144
26:	Ironwork from Pit XX	145
27:	Bone artefacts by site	161
28:	Initial bone assemblage summary	167
29:	Radiocarbon dating summary	168
30:	Sample K SPLOT dental formula	169
31:	Sample F SPDFH, pars basilaris metrics	170
32:	Waldron context concordance	171
33:	Samples H and L MNI values	171
34:	Samples H and L sex determination	171
35:	Sample F SPDFH dental formula	171
36:	Location of Romano-British human bone	172
37:	Sample A F27 pars basilaris metrics	172
38:	Sample A F27 dental formula	173
39:	Residual human bone	174
40:	MNI summary by period	174
41:	Sex determination by period	174
42:	Faunal remains: summary of all species identified on site	176
43:	Overall MNI for animal species on site	177

ACKNOWLEDGEMENTS

The excavation and post-excavation analysis of Sparsholt involved a large number of people over many years. David E Johnston would have wanted to thank personally the many excavation volunteers and the field supervisors who contributed so much to the success of the project. Unfortunately a complete list could not be found and it seems unreasonable to mention only those known to the editors. However, John Carter, Jonathan Erskine, Ian Sims and Geoff Syer were sometime Assistants to David Johnston during the excavation, and there were many Site Supervisors over the years, including John Magilton and Ed Kirkham. A student architect (now the Reverend), Colin Coward was Site Surveyor throughout the eight years of the main excavation. Over the whole period there were three Site Assistants: Sue Turner, Sarah Butler (now Collinson and responsible for illustrating and recording the finds) and Penny Sheffield (now Sheffield Sims).

David's wife, Pamela, must be mentioned for her invaluable support throughout the excavation, when amongst other things she ensured that the diggers' welfare was always a priority.

Permission for the excavation was granted by the Forestry Commission and David Percy was particularly active in arranging permission for the work. The main episodes of excavation were funded by the then Department of the Environment, with support from the University of Southampton Departments of Archaeology and Extra-Mural Studies. The Hampshire Field Club launched a successful appeal to save the mosaic (cover: Room 7, Main House) and members of the public gave generously. The follow-up excavation in 1985 was funded by the University of Southampton Department of Extra-Mural Studies.

The majority of the site drawings were done by Colin Coward, while the final site drawings are the work of David Johnston, Jonathan Dicks and Vicki Harrison. The abstracts were translated by Christine Burls (French) and Jörn Schuster (German).

The specialist work involves a group of reports written, or commissioned, by David and there has been no attempt to revise these because it would only have delayed the publication of the monograph. A number of groups of finds had only received preliminary analysis and arrangements were made to commission these reports. The contributors to the post-excavation analysis are listed on the Title page and the various specialists are thanked for their contributions to the monograph, especially those who gave freely of their time. In particular, Dr Ian Sims and his colleagues at RSK Environment Ltd are acknowledged for undertaking a scientific analysis of the wall plaster. Richard Ward studied the animal bones for his MSc (Southampton University) and revised his thesis for the monograph. Specialist reports on the pottery, ceramic building material and metalwork could not have been completed were it not for generous grants from Hampshire County Council and Winchester City Council. English Heritage financed the publication costs.

We are grateful to Steve Cosh, Barry Cunliffe and Tony King for reading and commenting on various sections of this text. Robin Isles and Helen Rees (Winchester Museums Service) are thanked for providing access to the Sparsholt archive, often at very short notice. Dave Allen (Hampshire County Council) and Dick Selwood (Hampshire Field Club) are warmly acknowledged for their advice and practical assistance throughout the preparation of the monograph.

Jonathan Dicks and Nick Stoodley

ABSTRACT

Sparsholt villa is located 6 km to the east of the *civitas* capital of Winchester and belongs to a small group of villas in southern England that have benefitted from a relatively complete excavation. It is a type-site for Hampshire villas of comparable plan and is an important site in the Iron Age and Romano-British sequence for central Hampshire.

At the end of the 19th century an archaeological excavation uncovered an unusually well-preserved series of remains, but the full significance of the site was only revealed through the investigations conducted by David E Johnston. In 1965 David undertook an evaluation that demonstrated the presence of a range of well-preserved buildings and resulted in a further seven seasons of excavation. The villa began as a single rectangular aisled building of the mid to late 2nd century; during the following century the site evolved into a courtyard villa and in the early 4th century it witnessed a significant series of alterations before being abandoned in the latter part of the century. In addition, a ditched enclosure, with occupation from the Middle to the Late Iron Age was also examined.

This report describes the excavations, presenting details of each building while outlining the chronological development of the villa complex. In the Discussion Sparsholt is assessed against the backdrop of Roman Hampshire and the social and economic background of the villa is considered. A series of specialist reports, which include the pottery, mosaics, wall plaster, small finds and the human and animal bones, are provided.

RÉSUMÉ

La villa romaine de Sparsholt se trouve 6 km à l'est de la capitale de civitas de Winchester et fait partie d'un petit groupe de villas situées dans le sud de l'Angleterre ayant bénéficié de fouilles relativement complètes. C'est un site de référence pour les villas du comté de Hampshire ayant une disposition similaire, qui tient une place importante dans la chronologie Âge du Fer – période Romano-Britannique du centre du Hampshire.

Dès la fin du 19e siècle, des fouilles archéologiques y avaient dévoilé une série de vestiges relativement bien conservés ; toutefois, la véritable importance du site n'a été mise en évidence qu'en 1965 par les recherches menées par David E. Johnston, lors d'une évaluation qui a démontré la présence d'un ensemble de bâtiments bien conservés, donnant lieu à sept saisons de fouilles supplémentaires.

A l'origine, la villa était composée d'un seul bâtiment rectangulaire doté de travées et datant de la fin du 2e siècle ; au cours du siècle suivant, elle a évolué pour devenir une villa à cour centrale, puis a connu au début du 4e siècle une suite d'importantes modifications avant son abandon vers la fin de ce siècle. Par ailleurs, un enclos fossoyé présentant des vestiges d'occupation datés du milieu à la fin de l'Âge du Fer a également été étudié.

Ce rapport décrit les fouilles et présente les détails de chaque bâtiment en résumant le développement chronologique de l'ensemble de la villa. Une série de rapports de spécialistes, comprenant la céramique, les mosaïques, les enduits muraux et le petit mobilier ainsi que les os humains et animaux, est aussi incluse. Dans le chapitre final, Sparsholt est évaluée dans le cadre chrono-culturel du Hampshire Romain, et le contexte social et économique de la villa est étudié.

(Traduction: Christine Burls)

ZUSAMMENFASSUNG

Die Villa von Sparsholt liegt 6 km östlich des civitas-Hauptortes Winchester. Sie gehört zu einer kleinen Gruppe südenglischer Villen, die nahezu vollständig ausgegraben werden konnten und ist der namengebende Fundort für Villen mit vergleichbarem Grundriss in der Grafschaft Hampshire. Darüber hinaus ist Sparsholt ein bedeutender Fundplatz für die eisenzeitliche und romano-britische Chronologie in Mittel-Hampshire.

Ende des 19. Jahrhunderts wurden in einer archäologischen Ausgrabung einige erstaunlich gut erhaltene Grundmauern gefunden, aber erst die Untersuchungen von David E. Johnston machten die Bedeutung des Fundplatzes deutlich. In einer 1965 durchgeführten Voruntersuchung gelang David der Nachweis zahlreicher gut erhaltener Gebäude, die darauffolgend in sieben Kampagnen ausgegraben wurden. Die Villa wurde zunächst im späten 2. Jahrhundert n.Chr. als ein rechteckiger, einschiffiger Bau errichtet, der sich dann im folgenden Jahrhundert zu einer Villa mit Innenhof entwickelte, die im 4. Jahrhundert eine Reihe erheblicher Umbauten erfuhr, bevor sie dann gegen Ende des Jahrhunderts aufgegeben wurde. Außerdem konnte auch eine von einem Graben umgebene Einfriedung der mittleren und späten vorrömischen Eisenzeit untersucht werden.

In diesem Band werden die Ergebnisse der Ausgrabungen beschrieben, in dem die Details jedes Gebäudes vorgelegt und in die chronologische Entwicklung des gesamten Villenkomplexes eingeordnet werden. In einer Reihe von Einzeluntersuchungen werden die Auswertungsergebnisse zu Keramik, Mosaiken, Wandverputz, den Kleinfunden sowie den menschlichen und tierischen Resten vorgelegt. Das Schlusskapitel widmet sich der Diskussion Sparsholts vor dem Hintergrund des römischen Hampshire unter Berücksichtigung des sozialen und ökonomischen Umfeldes der Villa.

(Übersetzung: Jörn Schuster)

David E Johnston

FOREWORD

The excavation of the Sparsholt villa over eight seasons from 1965 to 1972 was one of the last triumphs of the age of the local volunteer before the greening of archaeology and the view of excavation as destruction gradually brought research excavation to a virtual halt in the 1980s.

David Johnston was a good excavator who insisted on a standard of excavation which is well demonstrated in many of the photographs of carefully-cleaned flint walls and spreads of fallen flint work which appear in this volume. He was well up to the times and gradually abandoned the box type excavation in favour of open-area excavation as demonstrated by Figure 6 (of the Iron Age area Site L) and Figure 8 (of the area of Aisled Building I and II) which give a clearer indication of David's developed approach to the investigation of the site.

It was indeed one the first villa sites to be extensively excavated in modern times with attention given, as far as was possible, to all its components. As such David's Sparsholt gives us an important glimpse into the rural background of neighbouring *Venta Belgarum* (Winchester), the cantonal capital, only 6 kilometres away. Some chronological comparison between the two is possible.

The small late Middle Iron Age settlement under the Sparsholt Roman villa seems to be approximately contemporary with the use of the 20-hectare Oram's Arbour enclosure at Winchester, both coming to an end after the arrival of fragments of Italian Dressel Type 1A amphorae which arrived probably through Hengistbury Head not much later than about 50 BC.

Roman activity at Sparsholt, seen in the construction of Aisled Building I, did not begin until the middle of the 2nd century AD, long after the erection of the first urban defences of Winchester perhaps in the 80s AD, the construction of the forum and the provision of an aqueduct-fed water supply soon after 100. It was not until the mid to late 3rd century that the Sparsholt corridor row-house was built and the plan of a courtyard villa emerged. The first part of the 4th century was the high-point in the villa's development with additions to the main house and the laying of decorated mosaic floors but within a short season contraction and abandonment set in. This was the period when the population of Winchester, as reflected in a vast increase in the number of burials in its cemeteries, rose sharply and the defences were strengthened, perhaps by the addition of bastions. That there might be some common factor in these contrasting fortunes seems possible.

There are sharp contrasts too with the villa at Twyford, 5 km south-east of Winchester, excavated in part only under very different circumstances in 1958. There occupation began in the Flavian period and lasted until the end of the 4th century, a chronological span matching that of Winchester itself.

The importance of the Sparsholt excavation and its publication is precisely this, that it enables us to make such comparisons. We may well wonder what lies behind the contrasts which seem to begin to appear. They might reflect significant changes in the status of Winchester itself, from civitas capital to late Roman re-distribution centre with a significant military presence, or they may be no more than the physical record of the rise and fall of the fortunes of an individual farming family, the Archers of their day.

This publication of David Johnston's excavation at Sparsholt is thus an important event in our developing comprehension of the Romano-British region. The editors deserve our warmest thanks for their successful completion of what has been a considerable task, and the Hampshire Field Club for including the volume in its now long-running and prestigious monograph series.

Martin Biddle
March 2014

Chapter 1

Introduction

Summary

Sparsholt is a Hampshire village situated to the west of Winchester (Fig. 1). The Roman villa is located 2.25 km to the south-west of the modern village in West Wood, part of Farley Mount Country Park (Fig. 2). In the Roman period the *civitas capital* of Winchester (*Venta Belgarum*) was 6 km to the east, while the Roman road from Winchester to Old Sarum (*Sorviodunum*) was only 650 m to the south. Work on the villa was directed by the late David E Johnston, who for many years was lecturer in the Adult Education Centre, University of Southampton. His excavation of approximately 3 acres (120m by 100m) began with an evaluation in 1965 which demonstrated the presence of a range of well-preserved buildings and resulted in a further seven seasons of investigation (1966–72). The discovery of an almost intact mosaic in the villa's principal residence initiated a fundraising project which enabled it to be conserved. It is now displayed in Winchester City Museum (cover). The villa began as a rectangular aisled building of the late 2nd century; during the following century it evolved into a courtyard villa and in the early 4th century witnessed a series of significant alterations, before being abandoned in the latter part of the century. In addition, a ditched enclosure with Middle to Late Iron Age occupation was also examined. The site is a Scheduled Ancient Monument (HA 163).

Structure and aims of the report

At the time of Johnston's death in 2011 the site remained unpublished. Post-excavation work was underway, particularly on the Iron Age settlement and parts of the villa, while certain groups of finds had been studied and specialist reports written. Generous grants from The Hampshire Field Club, Hampshire County Council, Winchester City Council and English Heritage have enabled the completion of the finds analysis and this report on the excavations. The report is based upon Johnston's manuscripts and archival records. The primary data and finds have been deposited with Winchester Museums Service (Accession number WINCM 2923).

The report consists of 16 chapters. This introduction outlines the background to the project, describes the excavation and recording methodology and provides an overview of the site. Chapters 2–7 summarise

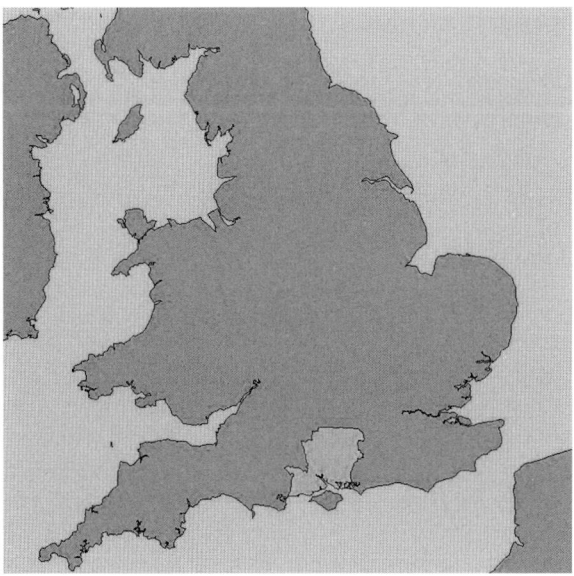
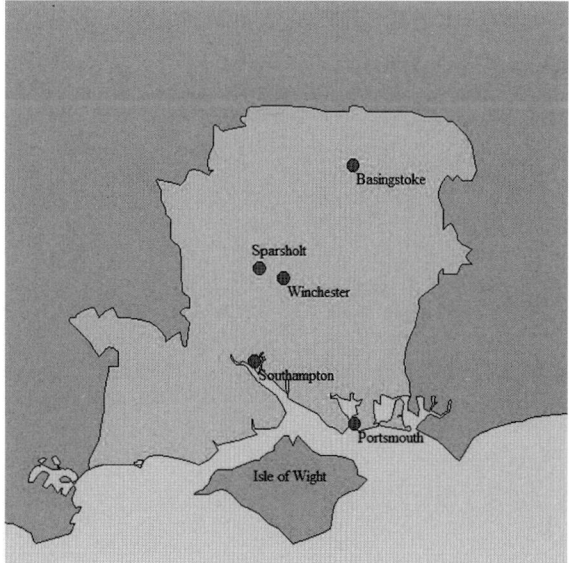

Fig 1 Location of Hampshire in the United Kingdom and Sparsholt in Hampshire

the excavated evidence by area. A Discussion of the evidence follows which aims to answer questions about the chronological development of the site and its social and economic basis, whilst placing it in its local and regional context. The Discussion is followed by the specialist reports (Chapters 9–16). A plan of every structure is provided, in addition to detailed plans and sections of significant features.

The site and its setting

The villa is situated in West Wood (SU 4149 3012) 2.25 km to the south-west of Sparsholt (Fig. 3), on a slight spur at approximately 100 m OD, overlooking a shallow dry valley. The ground falls away gently to the north, affording views of the surrounding countryside. The villa was probably approached by a trackway from the main Roman road (route 45a, Winchester–Old Sarum, Margary 1967, 100–1), some 650m to the south.

West Wood is ancient woodland, now part of Farley Mount Country Park. The place-name Sparsholt is first recorded in 901 as *Speoresholte* (OE spere + holt) 'wood of the spear', which may refer to a spear-trap for wild animals, or a wooded area where spear shafts were acquired, although the first element may be *spearr* 'a spar' or 'rafter' (Mills 1993, 304). This woodland would also have provided fuel and timber, in addition to pannage for pigs.

The local geology is dominated by Cretaceous chalk capped by a thin layer of clay-with-flints (Chatwin 1948). The chalk produces rendzinas and brown calcareous soils which dominate the landscape. The calcareous soils normally have a neutral or alkaline reaction throughout their soil horizon profiles (Courtney & Trudgill 1984) and were ideal for both arable and pastoral farming (Wade-Martins 2004). The chalk slopes of the dry valley to the west would have provided ideal grazing for sheep and goats whilst the more level ground to the south and east could have been cultivated. The area immediately around the villa was probably covered by scrub, not forest (Johnston 1981, 113): the excavation did not find the humus characteristic of an accumulation of rotted leaves.

By 1965 the east-facing slope of the spur was totally obscured by trees, but fieldwork found faint traces of lynchets and the three nearest the site were investigated. The topmost lynchet appears to have been integrated into a track serving the villa: a layer of flints had been laid directly upon the chalk surface and many of them were weathered and worn. A worn 'bank', containing Roman pottery and building materials, apparently formed the lower limit of the track.

In 1988, the course of this track was surveyed and it was shown to connect to the Roman road (Fig. 3). Close to the junction with the road it was identified as a narrow unmetalled terrace some 9 m wide. As it approached the villa it was just a slight scarp, but used the uppermost lynchet, as noted above. No metalling was identified at the entrance to the villa, although a complex of 'wheel-marks' was recognised as traces of solifluxion. The track may have branched here before it passed the north-east corner of the Courtyard, arriving at the entrance to an aisled building and a small gate giving access to the Courtyard. Just outside the north-east corner of the Courtyard a linear feature (Ditch 602), about 1 m wide ran north-west to south-east. Undated, it could have belonged to either an Iron Age or Romano-British field system.

Archaeological background

Unless otherwise stated the information is from the Hampshire Archaeology and Historic Buildings Record (AHBR).

Prehistoric

Evidence of early prehistoric activity in the Sparsholt area is rare. Flint flakes and scrapers of the Palaeolithic period were found 12 km to the north-east at Lainston House and a flint scatter dated to the Mesolithic–Neolithic was recovered during field-walking in the area of Crab Wood (Boismier 1994).

The Bronze Age is represented by burial monuments. A large round barrow lies at a distance of about 1.5 km to the south-east in West Wood. In 1968 it had a diameter of 36 m and a height of 1.8 m. One km south of the villa is a ditched bowl barrow. The mound survives to a height of 2 m and it has a diameter of about 20 m; surrounding the mound is a shallow ditch up to 6 m wide and 0.2 m deep. In 1991 the mound and ditch had a combined diameter of 32 m. It is depicted on a 16th-century manorial map as 'Robin Hode's Barrow' and in 1955 was known locally as 'Skilling's Barrow'. To the north and north east of the villa lie three groups of plough damaged barrows, some surveyed by Grinsell and others visible on NMR photographs. (Grinsell 1938–40, RCAHM(E) Air Photographs SU4232/16,14).

A hilltop enclosure, about 2.5 ha in extent and of probable Iron Age date lies 1.5 km to the south-west of the villa at Farley Mount. Air photographs show that it is roughly circular, with two parallel banks flanking a ditch. On the eastern side a single ditch projecting out approximately 35 m would have guided animals into the enclosure. The interior is divided by a ditched bank which creates an inner enclosure in the north-west corner (Crawford & Keiller 1928). Further west, Ashley Camp (SU 394 301) (Williams-Freeman 1933; Bowen & Fowler 1966, fig. 1) lies just north of the Winchester–Old Sarum Roman road and is a univallate hillfort about which little is known. In contrast, excavations at Little Somborne, 3.75 km north-west of the villa, sampled an enclosure of mainly Middle Iron Age date containing two round houses, granaries and storage pits (Neal 1980). Close by, at Somborne Park Farm, a D-shaped enclosure dating to the Late Iron Age, but with evidence of earlier occupation, has also been investigated (Harding 2010). Three or four km to the north-east of the villa, air photography has

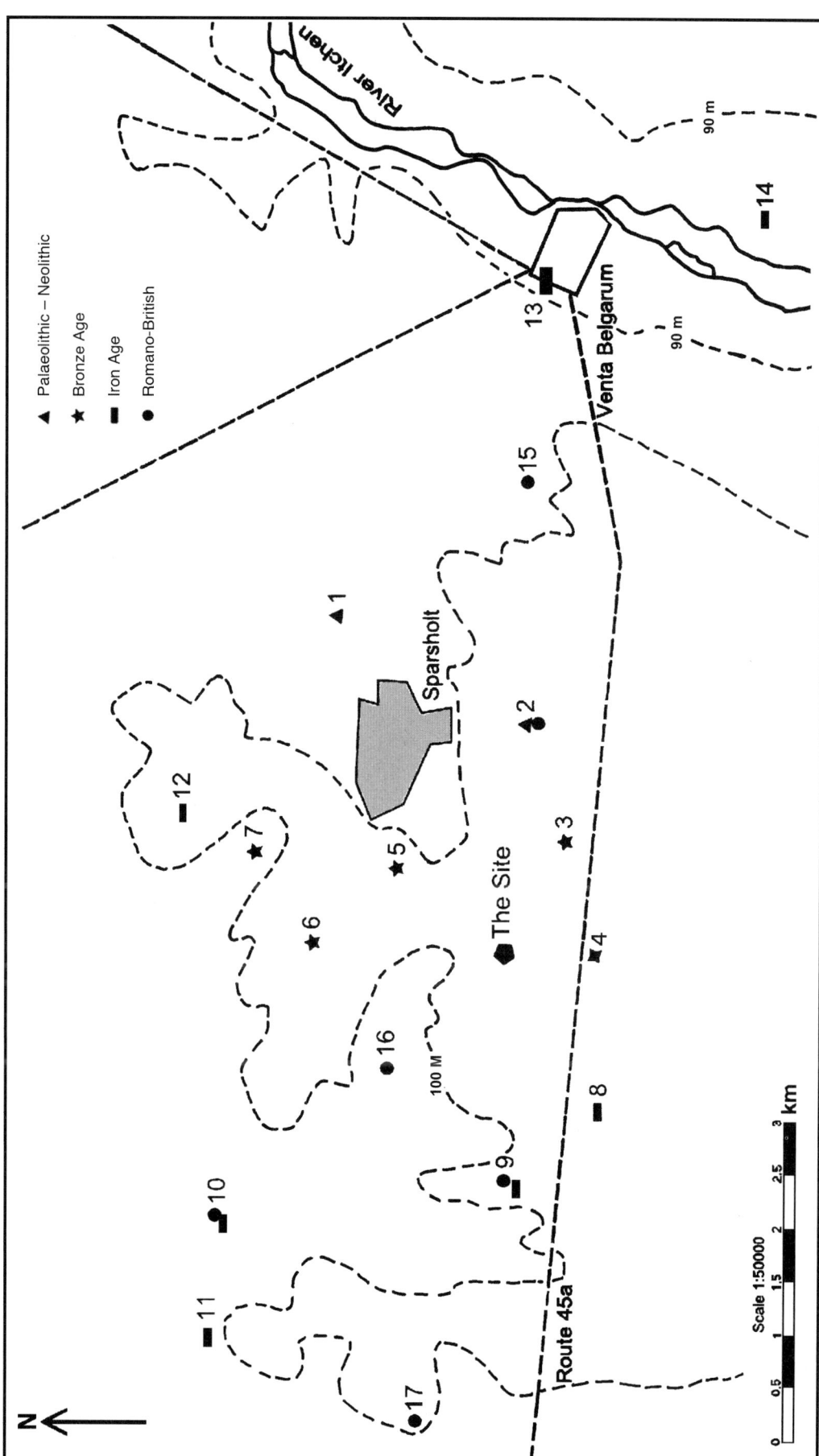

Fig 2   Location plan showing the villa, Route 45a and sites referred to in the Introduction (drawn by NS & MB) 1) Lainston House 2) Crab Wood 3) West Wood 4) 'Skilling's Barrow 5-7) Groups of barrows 8) Farley Mount 9) Ashley 10) Little Somborne 11) Somborne Park Farm 12) Kirton Farm 13) Oram's Arbour 14) St Catherine's Hill 15) Teg Down 16) Great Up Somborne Wood 17) King's Somborne

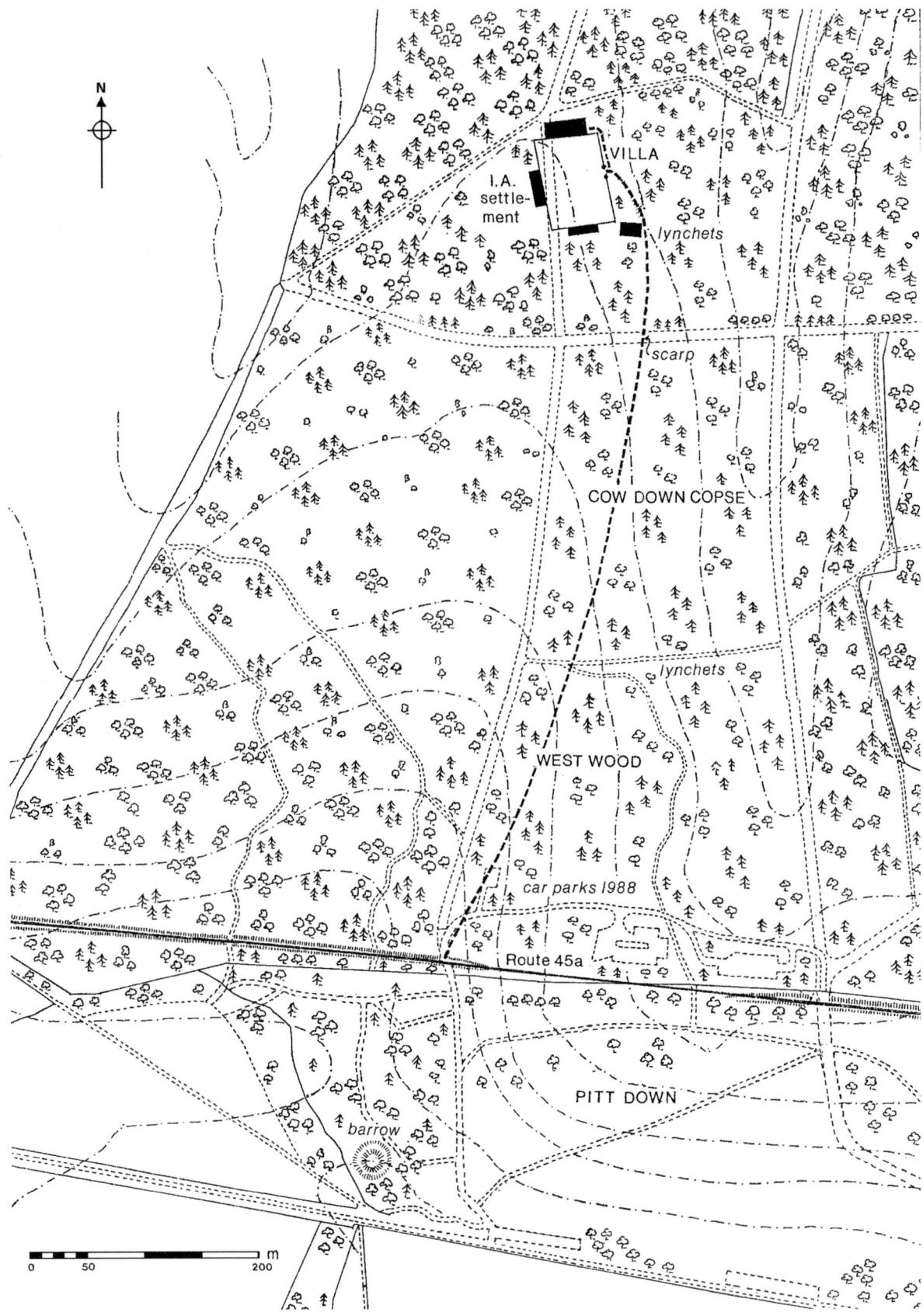

Fig 3   Location plan showing the villa and Route 45a (drawn by DEJ)

Fig 4   Aerial photograph showing the 'ride' cutting through the site (1968, Army School of Aviation)

identified a possible 'banjo' enclosure near to Kirton Farm; finds of pottery and worked and burnt flint have been made in the vicinity. A gas trench excavated in 1958, about 2 km to the east of Sparsholt village, produced two ditches and a pit with Iron Age pottery, while an Iron Age glass bead (aqua in colour) was found close to Sparsholt College. More significant Iron Age sites are found closer to Winchester. The enclosed settlement at Oram's Arbour is 6 km to the east and St Catherine's hillfort is 7 km to the south-east.

Aerial photographs show undated prehistoric field systems to the north of the villa and an associated curvilinear feature (HCC composite aerial photographic plot: AQ2 27–8, CPE/UK/1927:5080, F22 82/RAF/1954:26. 2) extending in a north-east to south-west direction. Pollen evidence indicates that by the end of the Iron Age much of southern England was being exploited for agricultural purposes (Dark & Dark 1997, 94). The evidence shows that the landscape around the villa was no different and had been under the plough for centuries before the Romans arrived.

Roman

Sparsholt villa was located 6 km to the east of the *civitas capital* of *Venta Belgarum* (Winchester) in the tribal area of the Belgae. The Roman road from *Venta* to *Sorviodunum* passes to the south of the villa and in the 19th century it was noted that it 'remains hard and fit for travel' (Jacob 1895, 202).

There is a local, but unsubstantiated, report of Roman building material, which included a quantity of tessellated pavement, being discovered close to Sparsholt village at Mere Court Manor Farm, now Moor Court Farm (Moss 1993, 49; Scott 1993, 87). A small enclosure at Teg Down (4.5 km to the east of the villa) is associated with a field system and has been interpreted as a farmstead.

The aforementioned Ashley Camp witnessed a phase of reoccupation in the Roman period. Pottery and other objects were recovered from the upper levels of the defensive ditch and were also spread throughout the interior. In the 1860s a 'tank' with steps leading into it, presumably a Roman bath, was discovered in the south-west corner of the site.

About 1 km to the north-east of Ashley Camp lies Great Up Somborne Wood where a probable Roman villa has been identified from building material, pottery and coins of mainly 4th-century date (Scott 1993, 85). There are additional records of pottery and other finds from this locality and the site may have extended over a wide area. According to Neal (1980, 142), there is a villa at Up Somborne, which is probably the site in question. To the west of the wood aerial photography has located an extensive system of cropmarks which has been interpreted as a Roman settlement associated with the villa. Aerial photographs also show other ancient, but undated, fields to the south of the wood. A series of rectangular enclosures approached by a linear feature, probably a trackway, have been recognised at the Iron Age site at Little Somborne (Neal 1980, 91, fig. 2). The complex has been identified as a Romano-British settlement.

Excavation and geophysical survey at a site 0.8 km east of King's Somborne (SU 371 310) revealed a series of enclosures and plots dating from the early to late Roman period. One of the enclosures contained a possible structure and 4th-century pottery was found in an oven and a post-hole

Roman activity in the vicinity of Sparsholt villa is also represented by the chance discovery of artefacts. A *sestertius* of Severus Alexander (AD 222–235) was found just to the south, a *denarius* of Caracalla (AD 188–217) was a stray find from Ham Green and a bronze coin of Gallienus (AD 253–268) was found in a rabbit scrape to the east of Sparsholt. In Crab Wood a *denarius* of Philip (AD 244–49) was discovered and, in 1899, twenty sherds of Roman pottery were found, along with bone fragments, suggesting a disturbed cremation burial (Collis 1977, 69–72). Roman finds, in addition to artefacts of medieval and post-medieval date, were recovered by a metal detectorist about 4 km to the north-east. Finally, a coin of Maximian (AD 286–305) was discovered in a garden at Up Somborne.

Post-Roman

Sparsholt has produced little archaeological evidence for the Anglo-Saxon period. The place-name is first recorded in the 10th century and may refer to a spear-trap for wild animals, or to a wooded area where spear shafts were acquired. The closest physical evidence for early Anglo-Saxon activity is a later 5th- to 6th-century inhumation burial accompanied by a shield boss from Mount Down, 1.75 km to the south-west of the villa (Meaney 1964, 97–8), but an evaluation at Sparsholt Allotments recovered evidence of pits, post-holes, and a lynchet or terrace, with several features producing pottery of the 10th–12th centuries.

Previous investigations

The woodland that grew around the villa aided its preservation and protected it from agricultural disturbance, and the existence of ruined buildings attracted the attention of antiquaries. During the 19th century the ruins were prominent enough to be protected by a wooden fence (Jacob 1895, 201). Formal investigations began in 1890 when Winchester's Chief Magistrate, along with several members of the Hampshire Field Club, visited the site (*ibid*). The party was struck by the extent of the buildings as evidenced by the 'almost buried walls'. Plans for an investigation were put in motion and the owners of the area (the Ecclesiastical Commissioners) gave permission. In September 1895, W H Jacob, T W Shore and Norman C Nisbett carried out the first excavation published, albeit briefly, in the *Proceedings of the Hampshire Field Club* (Jacob 1895). The report states that a survey of the site identified 'an undulating surface and foundations in every direction' and that a day's digging produced large quantities of flints of varying sizes, in addition to large roofing tiles and tiles from a hypocaust. 'Very massive walls formed with flints, bedded in mortar and also pieces of worked chalk' were uncovered and one of the walls was excavated 'down to a smooth surface formed on the footing of flints' (*ibid*, 203). No details of the structures, or any other features, are given in the report and the work was referred to as 'experimental excavations', i.e. a trial excavation. Around this time a local gamekeeper found a *denarius* of L Marcus Julius Philippus (104 BC) (*ibid*). Neither the coin nor any of the finds from the excavation have survived, although there is a record that they were sent to Southampton Museum (Johnston 1981, 114).

The next documented investigation took place in April 1961 when Edward Bannister, a Sparsholt resident, and Robert C Turner of Winchester established the location of the site by tracing a line of low banks through the undergrowth (Johnston 1981, 114). They were successful in defining a large rectangle, which was later found to equate with the full extent of the villa Courtyard (*ibid*). The existence of the earthworks was reported to the Field Club whose secretary notified the Ministry of Public Buildings and Works (MPBW) and in August 1962 an investigator was dispatched to make a record (*ibid*).

The excavation project

By 1919 the Forestry Commission had taken over the management of the site and had replanted the area with trees (Fig. 4). It was tree-root damage to the villa and the threat from the proposal to bulldoze a ride through an adjacent area that initiated a formal programme of investigation. In 1965 the MPBW approached David E Johnston, a master in the Classics Department of Raynes Park Grammar School, to supervise an exploratory excavation and evaluation of the site. This resulted in seven years of excavation (1965–72), with an additional season taking place in 1985, under the auspices of the University of Southampton and Hampshire County Council, to resolve several problems that arose during post-excavation analysis.

As a scholar of the Roman period with a particular interest in villas, Johnston had a deep personal interest in the site. When work commenced at Sparsholt, few villas in southern Britain had been investigated in their entirety and the site presented Johnston with the opportunity to undertake a large-scale excavation. The aim was to recover sufficient evidence to reconstruct the plan of the complex, the structure of individual buildings and to outline the

Fig 5 The Barn showing the typical Wheeler box-type excavation (photographed 1968)

chronological development of the site. Although the final report remained unpublished, the dissemination of information through lectures, interim reports and articles (e.g. Johnston 1972, 1981, 2004) ensured that Sparsholt quickly became a type-site for the courtyard villa in central southern Britain.

Excavation and recording methodology

The investigation at Sparsholt began at a time when the favoured approach to excavation was the grid, or box, system devised by Mortimer Wheeler and Kathleen Kenyon. This was popular because stratigraphy was exposed in sections, i.e. the baulks, while allowing layers and features to be recorded in the horizontal plane. The method does present several problems, however, especially when a site consists of numerous features spread out over a relatively large area: the baulks often obscure details and make it difficult to connect layers across the site.

At Sparsholt the method was used over several seasons. A series of $3m^2$ trenches was laid out and excavated by hand (Fig. 5). The 1970 season saw a change in tactics, however. A mechanical digger was used to cut a series of trial trenches across both the Courtyard and the Iron Age site. This change was a response to the need to investigate a large area rapidly and was developed further in 1972 when a machine was used to excavate a large trench over the Iron Age site (Fig. 6). This was effectively an 'open-area' excavation aimed at exposing the plan and structure of the site first identified in 1970.

For recording purposes the complex was divided into individual sites, each being given an alphabetic code (A-L, Fig. 7) which largely corresponded to buildings. The rooms were numbered 1–23 throughout; a new sequence was not started for each building. Roman numerals were used for pits and ditches found on Site L. Within each site, trenches, 'sub-trenches' and baulks were given unique numbers. Greek letters were sometimes used to avoid (or increase!) confusion: on Sites G (The Hall) and F (The Aisled Buildings, east end). Layers (and this term might have been used as a convenience) are numbered within each trench, or area if applicable.

A brief description of the activities was recorded in the trench/area supervisors' note book. In the earlier years these books recorded the different layers, with a brief description and a simple sketch, but for the later seasons they included a statement about the objectives of the excavation and a conclusion.

Pottery and bones were collected in bags, which also recorded the location of the finds: excavation code (SP), site letter (e.g. G) and a bag code which was a unique sequential identifier allocated each day, for example SPGAY. The contents of each bag were

Fig 6   Aerial photograph of Site L under open-area excavation (Army School of Aviation)

recorded in the site 'bag books' as well as in the site note books for each area. In addition, there are lists of bags which detail the finds and give their provenance. The small finds were numbered consecutively throughout the excavation. Although the recording methodology was structured, in the earlier years it did not clearly tie artefacts to features, or identify stratigraphical relationships, which was mainly a consequence of using the grid method of excavating.

A full survey of the area around the site was not possible because of the trees and undergrowth (Figs 3 & 4).

Excavations in 1965

The first year of excavation was 1965. The Forestry Commission cleared the site and a series of trial trenches were dug to determine the extent of the Courtyard walls and ascertain the location of the main buildings. The most spectacular find was an almost intact mosaic from the Main House (Site D), now on display in the City Museum (cover and pp.113–115).

Excavations in 1966

Based on the results of 1965 a programme of annual excavation was implemented, funded by the

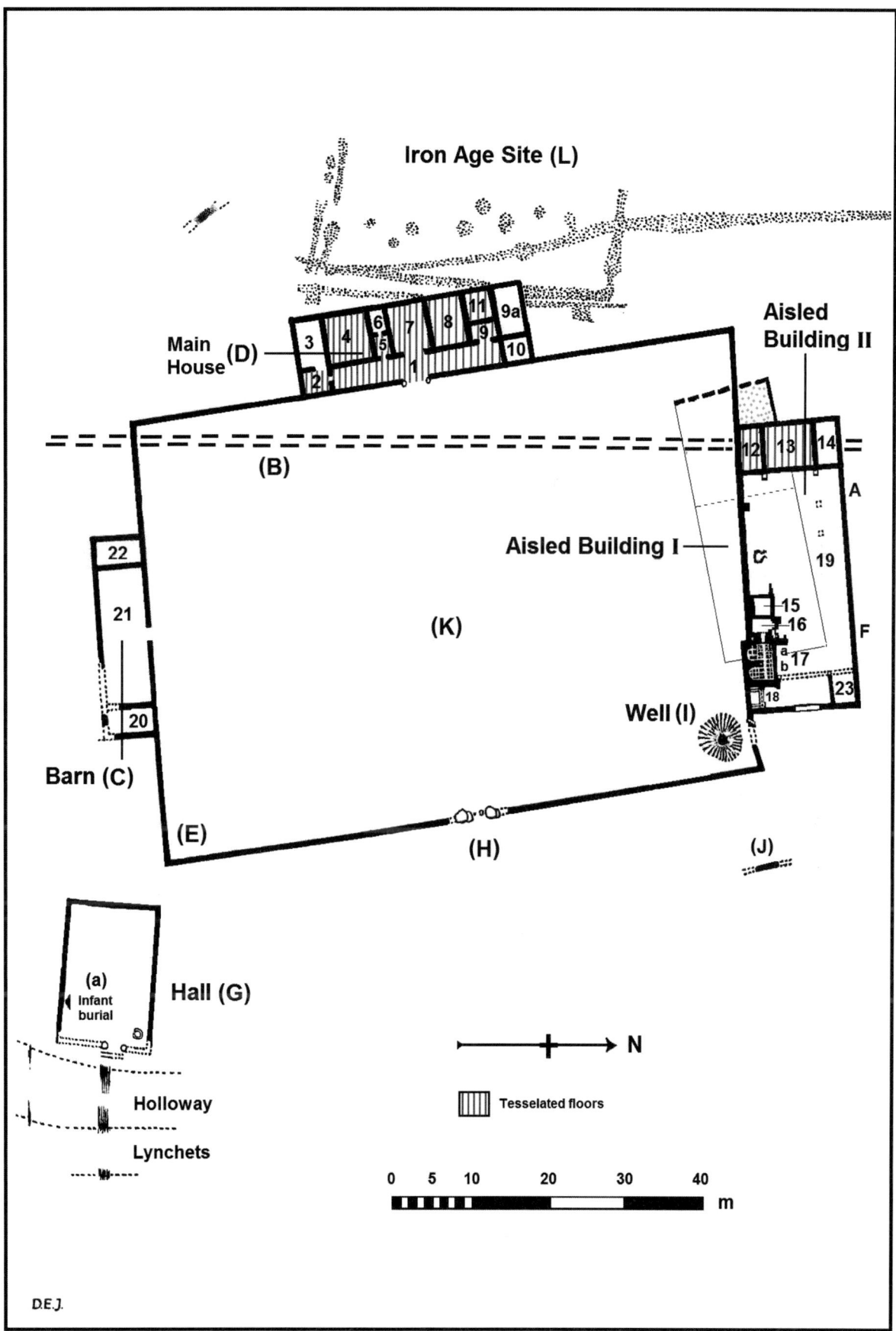

Fig 7   The Site and site codes (drawn by DEJ, redrawn by MB)

MPBW. Each season took place during August and September. In 1966 a grid of 26 trenches (each 3m^2), was excavated over the Aisled Building (Sites A and F) and a grid of 24 trenches (each 2.74m^2), over the Main House.

Excavations in 1967

In the following year, Rooms 9, 9A, 10 and 11 of the Main House were re-examined, plus an area of the Baths in the Aisled Buildings.

Excavations in 1968

The year 1968 saw the excavation of four trenches of varying length, from 3 to 11 m, over a building just to the south of the Courtyard wall (The Hall, Site G), while an exploratory trench was opened to investigate an area outside the Courtyard on its eastern side (Site J). In addition, a trench over 73 m long and 1.5 m wide was opened along the line of the eastern Courtyard wall, and the Well (Site I), first identified in 1966, was re-examined. Twenty trenches were dug over the Barn (Site C), which had first been identified during trial trenching in 1965.

Excavations in 1969

The excavation of the Barn was completed and further work was done on the bath house in the Aisled Building (Fig. 8). Rooms 2, 3 and 7 of the Main House were re-investigated, along with the north-east corner of the building, to establish the relationship between the Main House and the Courtyard wall.

Excavations in 1970

The year 1970 saw further work on the Hall, but the major activity was the excavation of 20 trial trenches across the Courtyard (Site K), and outside its west side (Site L). The trenches (about 0.60 m wide) were excavated using a mechanical digger. No features were recorded within the Courtyard, but several ditches and pits were identified outside it.

Excavations in 1971

The Aisled Building witnessed additional work and an earlier building was discovered beneath it. The investigation of the Hall continued with the opening of a large 13.5 m x 4 m trench which traced the building's north wall.

Excavations in 1972

By 1972 the focus had shifted back to the area west of the Courtyard (Site L) (Fig. 6). A mechanical digger was used to clear the topsoil, allowing area excavation to take place. The investigation of the earlier Aisled Building and its bath house continued, while four trenches associated with the exploration of the Main House were re-opened to establish the relationship between the original building and its south wing.

Excavations in 1985

Johnston returned to Sparsholt for a final time in 1985. The work involved a re-excavation of the later Aisled Building to try to establish the relationship and function of several of the walls within the building.

Outline of the site

The site occupies a small spur of land orientated north–south; to its east is a small dry valley and the location afforded a clear view over most of the surrounding countryside. A ditched Iron Age enclosure was located to the west of the villa. Although several beehive-shaped pits were discovered during excavation, no evidence was found for any structures or buildings.

The villa complex consisted of an Aisled Building, a rectangular Main House and a Barn. These structures were arranged around three sides of a Courtyard and were joined by a wall which also formed the front of each building (Fig. 7). The Hall was situated just outside the south-east corner of the Courtyard. An earlier Aisled Building (AB I) was discovered beneath its larger successor (Aisled Building II). The original north Courtyard wall was aligned with this building and formed an angle with the western wall, enclosing a regular trapezium-shaped area roughly 76 m by 55 m. The rhomboidal plan was created when the successor building was constructed on a different alignment, probably to make the Courtyard more rectangular.

The western limits of Aisled Building I were never established, but in common with its successor it contained a bath house. Dating evidence for the original building was limited, but it was probably constructed during the mid to late 2nd century AD. During the late 3rd century it was replaced by the much larger structure (AB II) whose roof was supported on wooden posts set on stone bases. The western end of the building was extended by the addition of a suite of three rooms, two of which had red tessellated floors, while the third had a mosaic.

The main residential building (the Main House) was probably a single-storey structure, 9 m wide by 30 m long, with a Corridor on the front which originally gave access to a series of seven rooms, one of which was heated by a hypocaust; another room (7) had a geometric mosaic. Several of the other rooms, including the Corridor, had patterned tessellated floors. In the late 3rd or early 4th century pairs of rooms, or pseudo-'wings', were added to both the north and south ends of the building. Walls were constructed from mortared flints, while the internal surfaces were decorated with painted plaster. The roof and the Corridor were covered by Purbeck limestone tiles, but the two rooms at either end were tiled with

Fig 8   Aerial photograph of the Aisled Buildings under excavation (Army School of Aviation)

clay *tegulae* and *imbrices*. Pottery and coin evidence suggest a main period of occupation from the mid 3rd century up to at least the middle of the 4th century AD.

The Barn was a single-storey agricultural building, 16 m long by 5 m wide, constructed of faced flints with a mortar render. Coin and pottery evidence indicate a period of use from the mid-3rd to mid-4th century. The Hall, which was situated just outside the Courtyard, probably comprised a timber frame set on low masonry walls. It was 18 m by 12 m and of a single span. It contained an oven and a small grave with a multiple burial of possibly five neonate skeletons. Dating evidence was limited, but the building may have been occupied after the abandonment of the main villa.

… Chapter 2

The Iron Age (Site L)

Introduction

An Iron Age settlement (Site L), lying to the west of the villa complex, was investigated in 1970 and 1972. In 1970, 20 trenches were machine dug. They were approximately 0.60 m wide and the soil was removed down to chalk bedrock, with features being hand cleaned and recorded. An open-area excavation took place in 1972 with a full investigation of the features previously identified.

The excavation revealed three sides of a rectangular ditched enclosure of unknown extent and the presence of earthworks indicated that it was part of a far larger complex. Twelve pits and an entrance were investigated but no structures or dwellings were identified.

Phasing

Phase 1: pre-enclosure (Middle Iron Age?)
Phase 2: enclosure (Middle–Late Iron Age)
Phase 2b: Pit VIII

The phasing of the pits and ditches has been established through stratigraphic relationships and dated pottery. Two main phases have been identified. The earliest evidence is provided by Ditch III and two pits (IX and XXIII); no diagnostic pottery was found so the features are assigned to Phase 1 because they are stratigraphically earlier than Ditch I. The next activity (Phase 2) is represented by the enclosure ditch (Ditches I and XXI), which is dated to the Middle to Late Iron Age. The pottery also shows that a number of the pits from the interior were contemporary with the creation of this boundary. Post-dating this activity was Pit VIII which cut Ditch I. There is no dating evidence but the absence of securely stratified Roman material suggests that the pit is part of the Middle/Late Iron Age settlement. The pit was subsequently disturbed by a re-cutting of Ditch I, probably in the Roman period. Two of the pits from the enclosure were subsequently modified, i.e. the enlargement of Pit XIII and the possible digging of a new pit (XIV b) over the site of Pit XIVa, but both episodes are undated.

A number of features were stratified beneath the Aisled Buildings (p.20). They were probably part of the Iron Age settlement but could not be securely dated.

Results of the excavation

Ditches
Ditch III

The earliest activity on the site comprised a steep-sided, round-bottomed ditch approximately 1.50 m wide, with a rounded end, running west–east (Fig. 9). It is of unknown length or purpose and its fill contained animal bones. The ditch had been re-cut before being allowed to silt up naturally and its upper fill contained a single bone and three sherds of Iron Age flint-tempered pottery.

Ditches I and XXI

Ditches I and XXI created three sides of the enclosure, Ditch I occupying the east and south sides (Figs 10 & 11). The primary silts of Ditch I probably derived from a bank. Both ditches were steep-sided but of varying dimensions with a rounded bottom. The corners were tightly curved, becoming narrower in the north-east sector. A 4.50 m wide gap in Ditch XXI is interpreted as an entrance. At some point the ditches were re-cut, but only the upper fill was removed (to a depth of 0.46 m). The re-cut was generally V-shaped. The lower fills of Ditch I produced 171 sherds of Iron Age flint-tempered pottery, but the upper fills contained 91 sherds of predominately late 3rd to late 4th century AD date, indicating a Roman period re-cut. Ditch XXI produced 93 sherds of Iron Age pottery, but in its upper fill was a shallow grave containing a female burial. This was C14 dated to the 1st century BC, confirming that by the Late Iron Age (c.100 BC–AD 50) the ditches had silted up and the enclosure had probably been abandoned.

Pits

Inside the enclosure were six Iron Age storage pits (VII, XII, XIII, XIV, XV and XVII), two pits possibly associated with the earlier Ditch III (IX and XXIII), and three shallow hollows which were either natural

THE IRON AGE (SITE L)

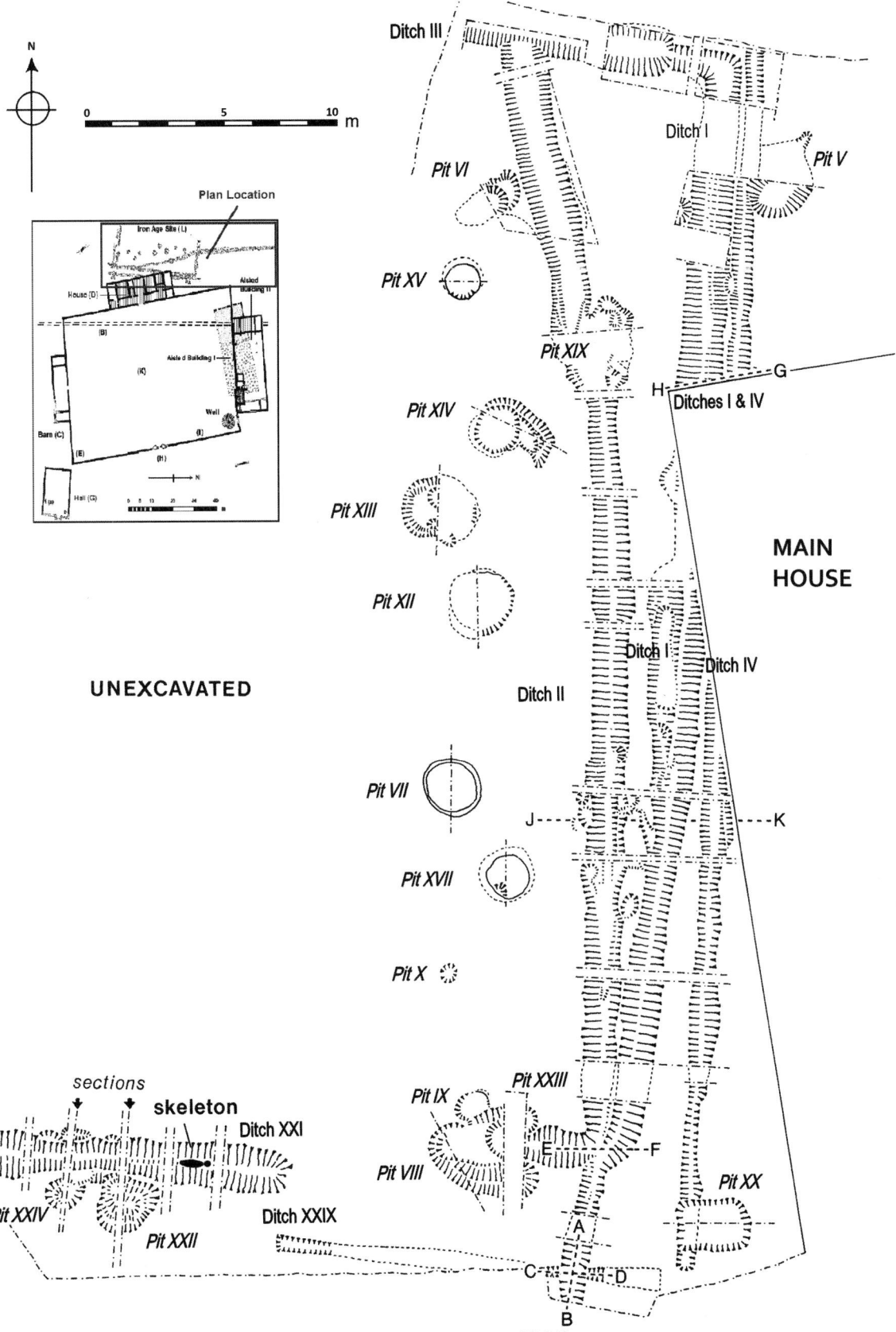

Fig 9   Plan of Iron Age enclosure (drawn by DEJ)

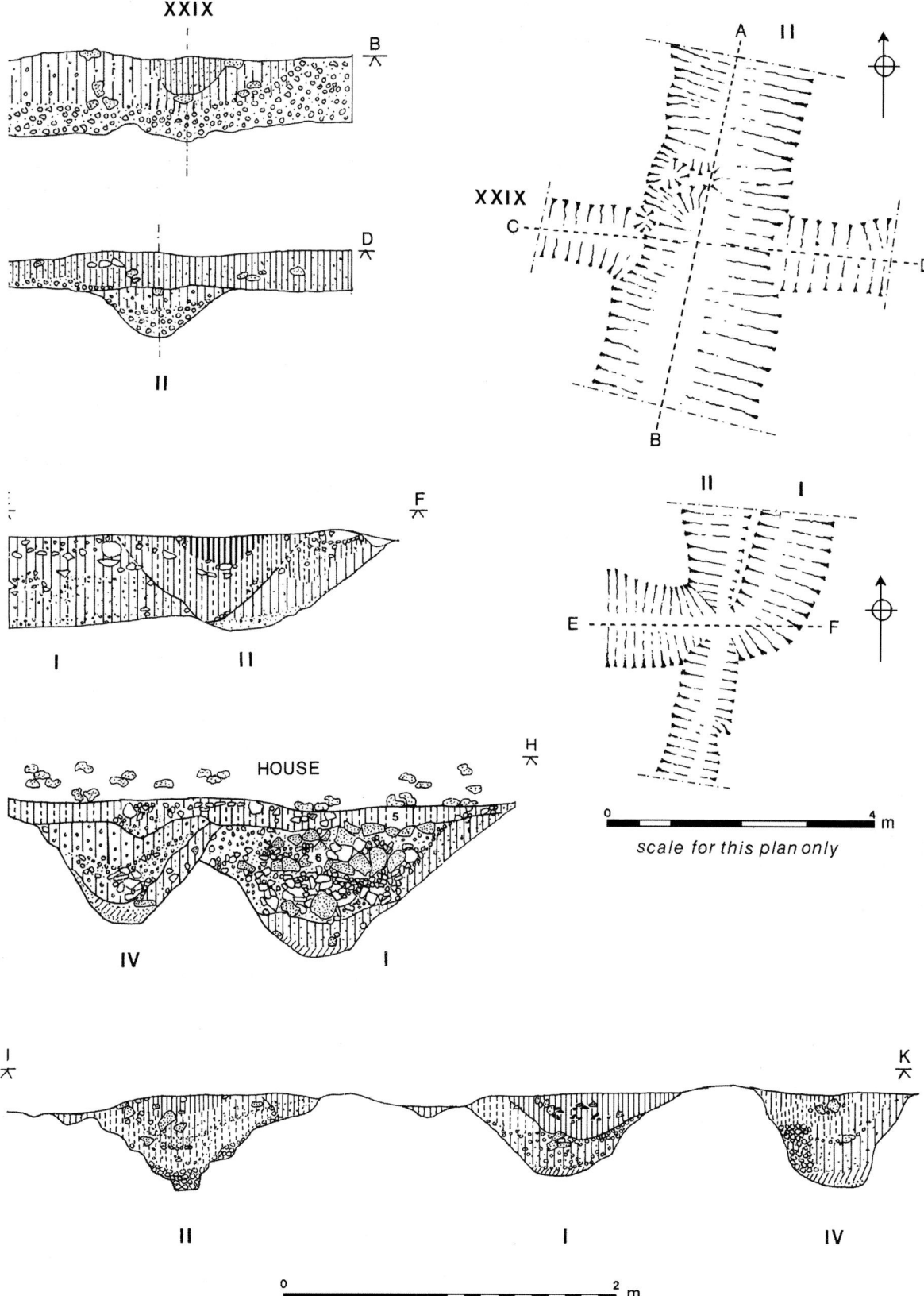

Fig 10   Iron Age and Roman ditches (drawn by DEJ)

geological features or ancient tree throws (VI, X, and XVI). Outside the enclosure were two Roman pits (V and XX) and four natural hollows (XVII, XXII, XXIV and XXV).

Pits IX and XXIII

The two pits were roughly circular and steep-sided. Both were cut by Ditch I and probably predated the enclosure. There was some slight weathering or undercutting on their north faces. The pits did not produce any finds and were not mirrored on the other side of the entrance.

Pit VII (Fig. 12)

This was a steep-sided flat-bottomed pit 1 m in diameter and 0.5 m deep. It may have been of beehive shape; the top had crumbled inwards, probably during deliberate infilling. The lower fills, which contained a mass of closely packed fire-fractured flints, appear to have entered from the north side of the feature. The uppermost layers, however, apparently entered from the south. The two uppermost layers represent the re-use of a partly-filled pit and contained burnt material and a sherd of late 3rd- to 4th-century AD pottery. The lower levels contained 11 sherds of flint-tempered pottery, including a sand-tempered saucepan pot (Fig. 88, no.15), animal bone and antler.

Pit XII (Fig. 12)

This was an almost perfectly circular pit 2.45 m in diameter and 2.40 m deep. The original profile would have been beehive-shaped with a flat bottom, but the narrow opening had been deliberately widened. The complex interleaving of layers suggests deliberate infilling in two stages, with little or no interval between them (conjoining sherds were noted from widely separated contexts). The initial fill, introduced through the narrow opening, formed a convex heap at the bottom; the opening was then widened to form wedges of chalk rubble, while the final fill followed a natural profile. The upper fill produced two sherds of amphora. Ninety sherds of flint-tempered and shell-tempered pottery were recovered from the lower fills. Four layers contained a mass of burnt flints.

Pit XIII (Fig. 12)

This may have been a beehive pit that was subsequently and incompletely enlarged. The original pit was circular in shape and 1.15 m deep. The smooth base showed signs of burning which might indicate fire-cleaning. The bottom 0.60 m of the pit was almost perfectly circular, 1.40 m in diameter, with near vertical sides. On the west side, the top part of the pit had concave sides, while on the east there was a horizontal shelf with large flint nodules. The remainder of the upper side of the pit was almost vertical, probably resulting from an abortive attempt to enlarge it. The west end had signs of unsystematic concave hacking with a small axe-like implement, the only tool-marks from the Iron Age site. The east end had a neat shelf and a straight working face corresponding to the seam of flint. There were three broad phases of fill: rapid silting (11) probably trampled by workers enlarging the pit; natural silting (7) and deliberate backfill (Layers 5 and 2) incorporating much burnt material. The upper layers contained 89 sherds of Iron Age flint-tempered pottery and masses of burnt flints.

Pits XIV (a) and (b)

These were two relatively shallow intersecting pits. The earlier pit (XIVa) was 0.66 m deep and circular, with a maximum diameter of 1.80 m. The chalk base was burnt. The fill contained a large quantity of fire-cracked flints and 18 sherds of predominantly flint-tempered pottery.

Pit XIVb, which cut XIVa, was an irregular shallow depression only 0.53 m deep. There were no finds except for a few bones, and it might have been a natural depression caused by a tree throw.

Pit XV (Fig. 12)

This was a small beehive pit with an aperture of only 1.37 m and a depth of less than 1.0 m. Originally it would have been about 1.40 m in diameter with a narrow opening. It had been deliberately backfilled with burnt flint and clay containing domestic debris including a bronze loop-headed pin (SF 521) and a tiny bronze ring (SF 641). The pit also produced 169 sherds of flint-tempered pottery. A layer of chalk rubble could have resulted from the sides collapsing during backfilling.

Pit XVII (Fig. 12)

This small beehive pit was the most perfectly-shaped on the site; it had an aperture diameter of 1.67 m, a maximum diameter of 1.90 m and a base diameter of 1.77 m. The flat base was 1.27 m below chalk level, suggesting an original depth of 1.70 m. The upper fill contained 115 sherds of Iron Age flint-tempered pottery. A rare feature (and unique on this site) was a miniature beehive-shaped, round-bottomed pit in the floor, dug to a depth of 0.43 m. The fill, of clay and chalk with some charcoal flecks, gave no indication of its purpose. The lowest level was of loose, granulated chalk – the result of burrowing by rodents. The fill produced the remains of at least 17 voles and three shrews, comprising 76% of the rodent bones from the site (192 of 253). The quantity of bones and their differing states of fusion may indicate a nest site (p.182).

Pit VIII (Fig. 11)

This elongated pit, approximately 0.50 m deep, cut into the fill of Ditch I, was subsequently disturbed by

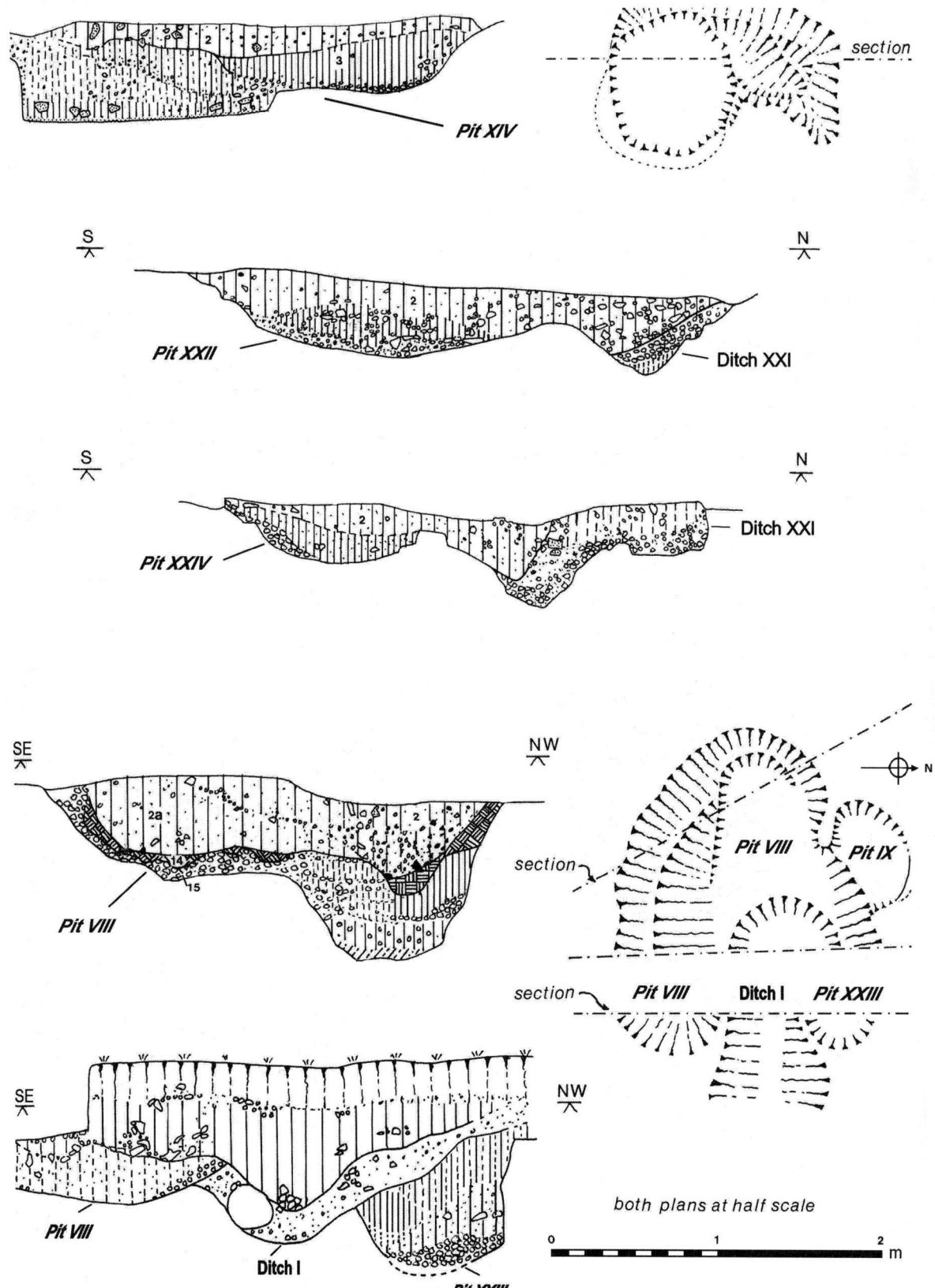

Fig 11 Iron Age and Roman ditches (drawn by DEJ)

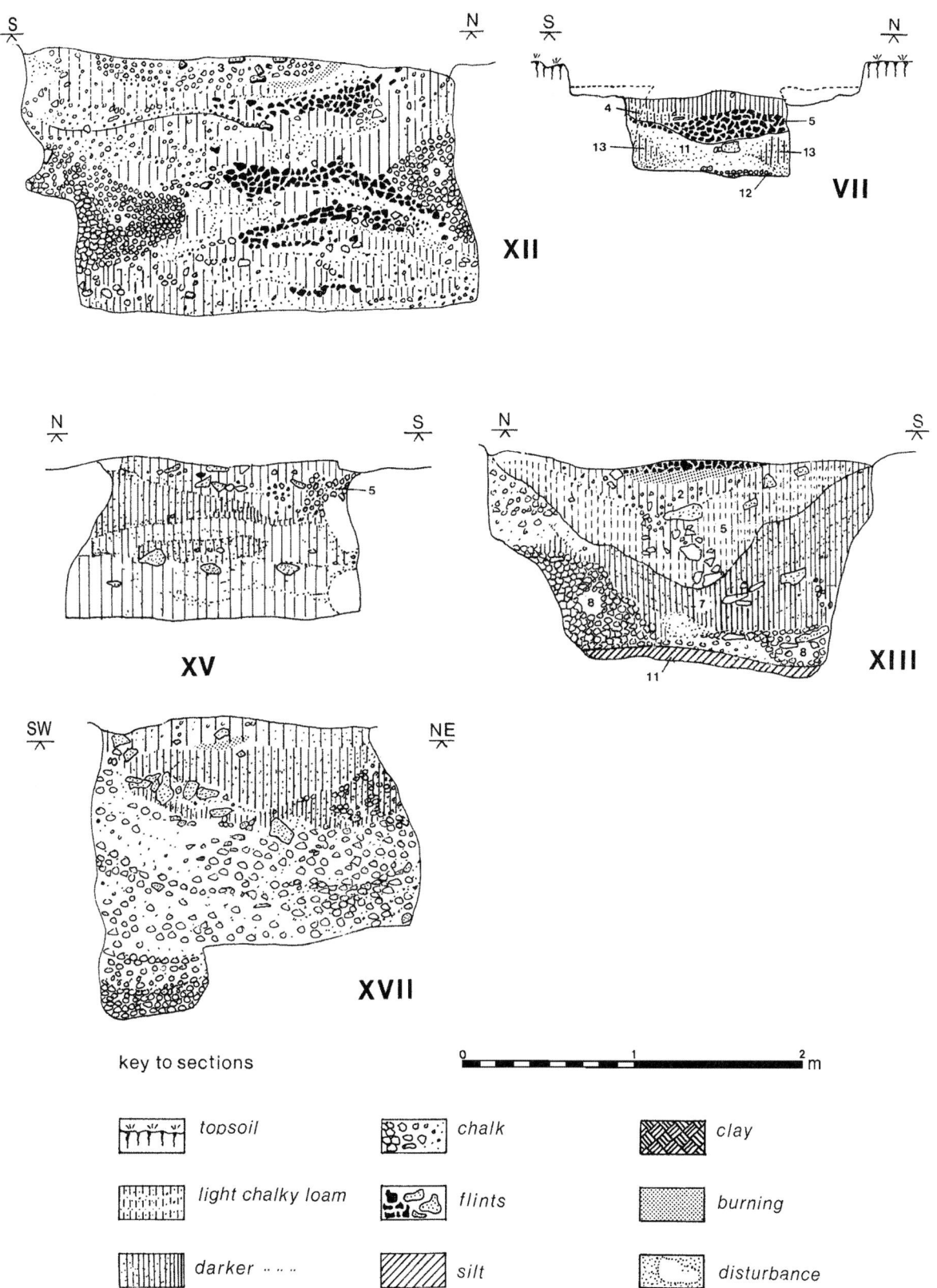

Fig 12 Iron Age storage pits (drawn by DEJ)

the ditch re-cut. Its fill of re-deposited clay and flints was very similar to that of the re-cut and represents natural silting during the Roman period. No pottery was found, but two bronze fragments (SF 429 and 431), one of which might be part of a simple wire bracelet, were recovered. The most significant layer may be a thick and sticky dark brown clay containing very little flint or chalk, carefully smoothed over a layer of clean chalk rubble, possibly the original upcast. Neither layer contained any finds. The feature is interpreted as an enlargement of the partly silted Ditch I to form a clay-lined sump, possibly to collect water.

Pits XXII and XXIV (Fig. 11)

Just to the south of the enclosure was a pair of virtually contiguous pits or scoops that nearly touched the weathered side of Ditch XXI. Pit XXII was 1 m in diameter but only 0.40 m deep. It was filled with re-deposited natural. Pit XXIV was also 1 m wide, but slightly shallower at 0.37 m. The fill was dark brown to black clay with some evidence of burning. Neither feature produced finds.

Overview

Dating evidence

The six pits in the eastern end of the enclosure were well-defined storage pits containing Iron Age flint-tempered pottery, with smaller amounts of sand and shell-tempered ware (Table 1). Pits VII and XV also produced sherds of Romano-British pottery, but the majority were in the upper fills and probably intrusive.

Pit XII contained a flint-tempered sherd decorated with simple vertical striations (Fig. 88, no.4), stylistically similar to 3rd to 1st century BC material from St Catherine's Hill (Cunliffe 2005, 627). In the upper fill of the pit were two large amphora sherds in a hard, smooth sandy fabric, with buff outer and red inner surfaces similar to Italian vessels. Petrological and typological evidence suggests that they are from a Dressel 1 form; a date between 130 BC and the end of the 1st century BC is appropriate (p.94).

Pit XIII contained several sherds in a coarse flint-tempered material with a cordoned and striated decoration (Fig. 88, nos. 9 & 13), similar to pottery from the Iron Age settlement at Worthy Down (Hooley 1928, plate IV).

Pits	Flint-tempered	Sand-tempered	Shell-tempered	Total
Pit VII	10	1		11
Pit XII	66	3	19	88
Pit XIII	86	3		89
Pit XIV	16		1	17
Pit XV	166	3		169
Pit XVII	99	2	9	110
Totals	443	12	29	484

Table 1: Number of Iron Age sherds by pit

Pit XV contained sherds from a saucepan pot and a jar with oblique lines between rows of dots (Fig. 88, nos.2 & 5) in St Catherine's Hill-Worthy Down style. Pit XVII contained a small sherd from a St Catherine's Hill-Worthy Down-style jar (Fig. 88, no.10), another from a Trundle-style pot (Fig. 88, no.12) and another from a Glastonbury ware bowl (Fig. 88, no.16) (p.92).

These various styles of pottery were in use from the Middle Iron Age to the 1st century BC. Both St Catherine's Hill and Worthy Down are only a short distance from Sparsholt, but the Glastonbury bowl and Trundle-style pot were traded over much greater distances. There are also several sherds from a number of distinctive 'saucepan'-type pots, which were particularly prolific and characteristic of the Middle Iron Age in southern England (Gibson 2002, 120).

The evidence indicates that the enclosure was occupied from the mid-4th century BC until the beginning of the 1st century BC. Greater chronological precision may be provided by the size of the pits (Table 2). It has been suggested that smaller pits belong to the 4th century BC, while by the 3rd and 2nd centuries BC they were larger, on average about 2 m deep (Cunliffe 2005, 411). This would indicate that Pits VII and XIV were the earliest, Pits XIII, XV and XVII slightly later, and Pit XII the latest, dating to the 3rd or 2nd century BC.

Pit	Opening diameter	Maximum width	Width at bottom	Depth
Pit VII	0.75 m	1.00 m	0.95 m	0.50 m
Pit XII	2.45 m	2.45 m	2.30 m	2.40 m
Pit XIII	2.25 m	2.30 m	1.40 m	1.15 m
Pit XIV	1.75 m est	1.80 m	1.45 m	0.60 m
Pit XV	1.50 m	1.70 m	1.70 m	0.95 m
Pit XVII	1.50 m	1.80 m	1.70 m	1.30 m

Table 2: Dimensions of Iron Age storage pits

Structural evidence

Only the eastern end of the enclosure was excavated and no evidence of structures or granaries was found. If the site contains such features they are located in the unexcavated area.

Economy

There was no environmental analysis at Sparsholt and it is not possible to know for certain what crops were cultivated. Evidence from the Danebury Environs Project revealed that the main crops throughout most of the Iron Age were spelt wheat and six-row hulled barley (Cunliffe 2000, 172) and this was probably the case at Sparsholt. In common with other settlements, Sparsholt would have been self-sufficient, with the community involved in all stages of crop-production, processing and storage.

More information is available regarding animal husbandry, however, and a stock-rearing economy dominated by cattle and sheep is identified. The evidence comes mainly from animal bone found in the pits. Sheep were more numerous than cattle (p.183-84) and this may indicate the rearing of sheep on site and the slaughtering of them for meat at an earlier age than cattle. A greater proportion of sheep to cattle was also found at the Andover sites of Old Down Farm and Knights Enham (Stoodley 2013), a pattern typical in Wessex (Hambleton 1999, 87). In addition, Sparsholt produced a small amount of pig and a large quantity of roe deer, although most of the latter came from a single animal recovered from Pit XIII.

Ritual

The left hind leg of a cow of around 2–3 years was found at the base of Pit XIII; the bones from the tibia and foot were articulated and the femur, although disarticulated, was in line with the rest. The pit also produced a juvenile roe deer represented by parts of its vertebrae and most of its limb bones, suggesting that the animal had been buried largely intact. The deposition of animals, and in some instances humans, in the basal fills of pits has been recorded on many Iron Age sites. Such 'special deposits' have been interpreted as ritual behaviour, offerings and sacrifices to the gods for a successful harvest or to secure victory in war (Cunliffe 1992, 79; Hill 1995). Examples can be cited from Winnall Down (Fasham 1985), Weston Down, Micheldever (Gibson & Knight 2007, 30) and Knights Enham (Stoodley 2013).

Decline and abandonment

The enclosure was occupied from the mid-4th century BC and abandoned towards the beginning of the 1st century BC. Settlement discontinuity was common at many Middle Iron Age sites in southern England in the 1st century BC and has been attributed to the emergence of a new socio-political regional elite and the establishment of local tribal chiefs (Cunliffe 2005, 141). A Belgic incursion into the Solent region in the decades around 130–100 BC may have been the catalyst for these changes: the arrival of refugees in advance of the Roman conquest in Gaul in the 50s BC would have caused widespread social and economic disruption (*ibid*, 127–35).

Chapter 3

The Aisled Buildings (Sites A & F)

Introduction

Investigation of the Aisled Buildings took place in seven of the eight years of excavation. Initially it was thought that there were two separate structures (A and F) but in 1969 it was confirmed that they were parts of the same building, which resolved itself as Aisled Building II (AB II). In 1971, it was realised that AB II was constructed over an earlier building (AB I) which was on a slightly different alignment (Fig. 13). Further excavation took place in 1985 to investigate questions raised during the post-excavation process.

Evidence for AB I was limited, because most of it was destroyed during the construction of AB II and its full extent was never identified. The surviving foundations indicate that it was at least 30 m long and approximately 12 m wide, with a bath-suite in the south-east corner of the building. AB II was a larger structure, nearly 36 m long and 14 m wide. It also contained a bath-suite in its south-east corner.

Results of the excavation

Features pre-dating the Aisled Buildings

During the excavation six features, four pits and two gullies were found sealed beneath the floor of AB I. They are probably of Iron Age date. All the pits were shallow, about 0.45 to 0.50 m deep and none contained artefacts. The two gullies were irregular in shape, and only one contained Iron Age pottery.

Pit 12 was an irregular shallow pit, 0.45 m deep. Only one quadrant of Pit 14, approximately 0.50 m deep, was excavated. The fill consisted of three layers of re-deposited clay-with-flints and some chalk. Pit 188 contained flint and re-deposited building material. It was probably an Iron Age pit levelled in the Roman period. Pit 206 was about 0.50 m deep and contained a complex fill ranging from pure clay through to mixtures of clay and mortar, to a dark brown matrix possibly containing turves in its lowest layer. It was sealed by burnt material probably representing site clearance for the construction of AB II.

Feature 19 was an irregular gully or scoop. The lower of its two fills contained Iron Age pottery and daub and some charcoal. Feature 56 was a fragmentary ditch or gully cut by the east wall foundation trench of AB I. The trench and wall had subsided slightly into the ditch. When the area was re-excavated in 1985 no sign of the ditch was found to the east of the building.

Aisled Building I

The excavation produced little information for the plan of AB I and crucially no evidence for the internal posts. Its shape and size are consistent, however, with aisled buildings from southern England (Cunliffe 2008). It is estimated to have been just over 30 m in length. At 12 m wide, it could have accommodated a central aisle of 20 Roman feet (about 6 m) and two naves of 10 feet. Large stone column bases were used in the construction of AB II and it is possible that these were salvaged from AB I, which would explain their absence. Aisled buildings are known to have replaced similar structures on slightly different alignments at Castle Copse, Wiltshire (Hostetter & Howe 1997), Dunkirt Barn, Abbotts Ann, Hampshire (Cunliffe & Poole 2008c) and Beddington, London (Adkins & Adkins 1986), to give just three examples.

Foundations and walls

The north wall of the building was laid directly onto the clay-with-flints subsoil. It was approximately 1m wide and had an outer face of flint nodules and an inner face of chalk blocks, while the centre was packed with small chalk pieces. The north-east corner of the building was identified under the floor of AB II and this allowed the eastern limit of the building to be established.

The south wall was only detectable as a foundation trench although the wall formed part of the north Courtyard wall. It was constructed in a shallow trench, 0.90 m wide and 0.10 m deep, filled with compacted chalk. Originally the Courtyard was trapezium-shaped, only becoming rectangular with the construction of AB II.

All trace of the western wall was erased during the construction of AB II, but there were a number of clues, including differential foundation trench width and packing, which showed where the southern wall turned westwards.

THE AISLED BUILDINGS (SITES A & F)

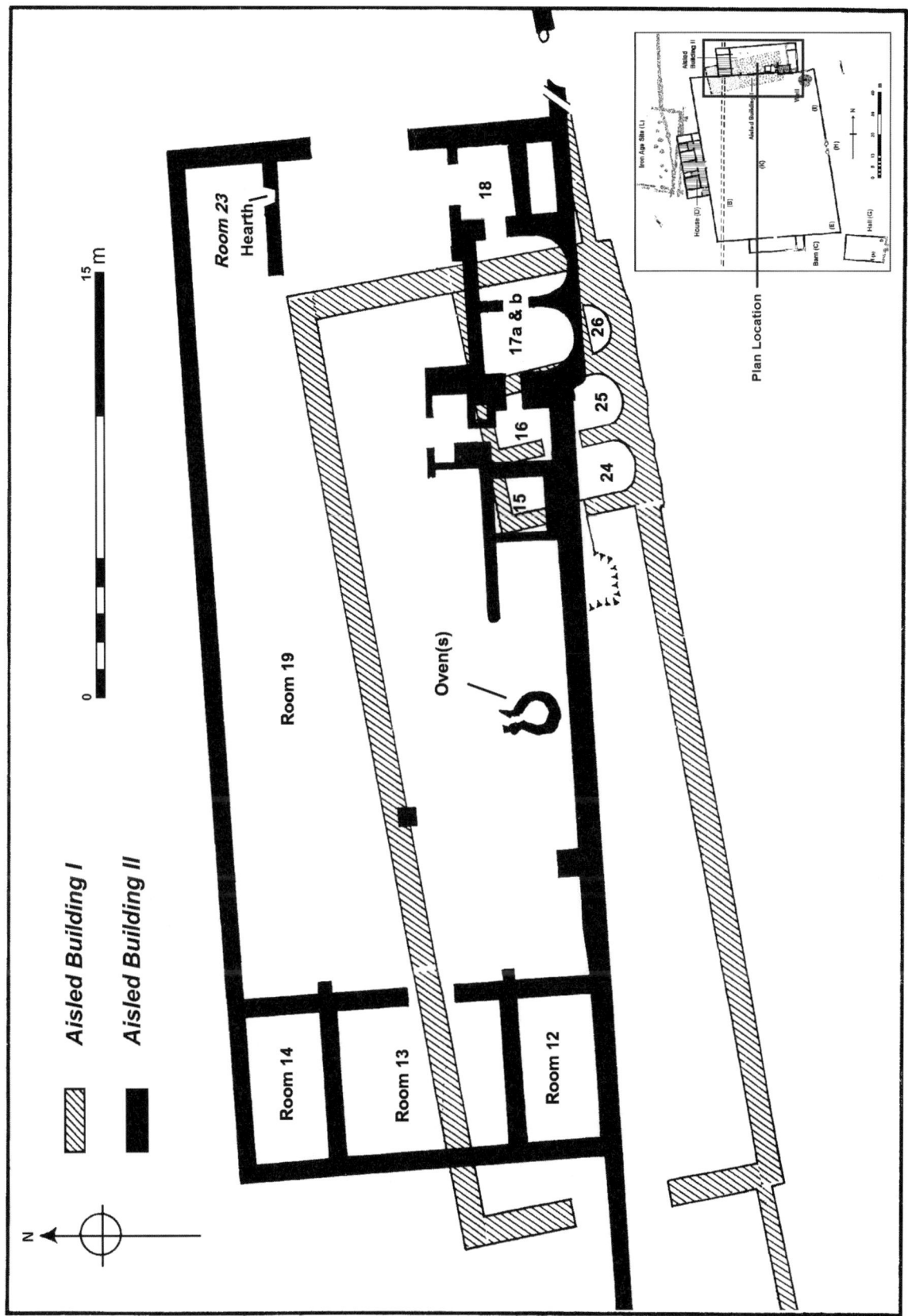

Fig 13 Site plan of the Aisled Buildings (drawn by DEJ, modified by JD)

A shallow, roughly circular grave was discovered next to the south foundation trench (Fig. 14). It contained the remains of a neonate who died at 39–42 weeks gestation (p.172–173). Radiocarbon dating places the burial in the 16th century AD.

The Baths

A simple bath house was situated in the south-east corner of the building. Its walls were constructed entirely of mortared flint nodules. It was demolished during the construction of AB II and the debris was dumped into the hypocaust to create a level surface for the later building. Sufficient remained of the foundations and the hypocaust, however, to identify the floor plan and function of the rooms (Fig. 15).

Room 26

Room 26 contained the lower part of a D-shaped plunge bath, lined with bright red painted plaster. The full dimensions of the room are unknown, but it could have extended east of the plunge bath (Fig. 16). The room may have functioned as the changing room (*apodyterium*) as well as a cold room (*frigidarium*) with cold bath. The northern wall and south-east corner were truncated by the foundations of AB II. The doorway, probably the only entrance to the bath-suite and possibly in the east wall, was defined by a threshold of limestone slabs.

Room 25

This room, 1.75 m by 5.25 m, was defined by its apse and the remains of the wall that separated it from Room 24. It was probably the warm room (*tepidarium*), but no trace of *pilae* were found in the hypocaust pit. Two small rectangular holes might have held wooden posts that supported the floor during construction.

Room 24

Room 24 was positioned at the western end of the bath-suite and was next to the hypocaust stokehole. It had a flint-built apse 1.80 m wide and contained the remains of a single *pilae* aligned with the external flue. This hot room (*caldarium*) would have contained a hot plunge bath.

The date of AB I

AB I was the earliest Roman building on site and pre-dates the Courtyard (p.79). No stratified material was recovered to indicate the date of construction but 73 sherds of imported fine wares, including Central Gaulish Black colour-coated wares (c. AD 150–250), Central Gaulish samian (AD 120–210), and *Moselkeramik* (c. AD 180–250) were probably contemporary with its use. Fifteen fragments of blue-green glass were found in the debris of the two Aisled Buildings. They probably come from bottles dating to the 1st and earlier 2nd century AD. Two unstrati-

Fig 14 Grave discovered next to the south foundation trench (photographed 1972)

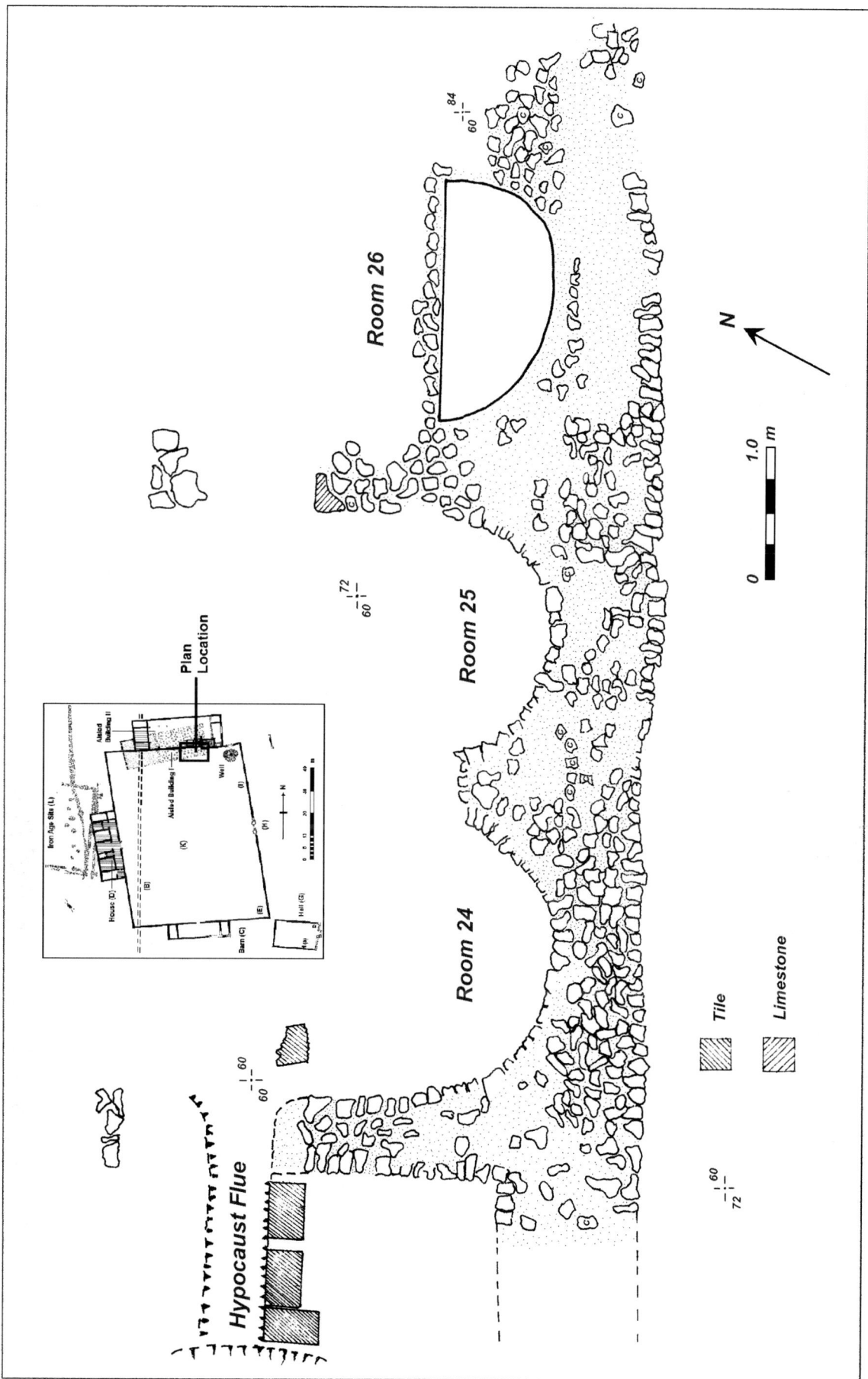

Fig 15 Plan of AB I's Baths (drawn by JD, based on an original by CC)

Fig 16 AB I plunge bath below AB II (photographed 1972)

fied coins (SF 53 and 430) of the late 1st to mid-2nd century were also found in the same area. None of this evidence is conclusive, but it strongly suggests that the building was first occupied during the mid-to late 2nd century AD.

The plunge pool and hypocaust for Rooms 24 and 25 were filled with demolition material and domestic rubbish, including 1,595 g of pottery. A further 633 g were recovered from the stoke hole. The pottery includes New Forest wares, both fine and coarse, south-east Dorset BB1 and late grog-tempered wares, all of which can be dated to the late 3rd and 4th centuries, suggesting a late 3rd century date for the demolition of AB I and its replacement by AB II. There were, however, two sherds from a black, rouletted *Moselkeramik* beaker and a sherd from a Central Gaulish mortarium, which can be dated from the late 2nd to the mid-3rd century.

A very hard-packed chalk and mortar deposit sealed the foundations of the southern wall of AB I. Associated with it was a shattered pot (SPFNX) and six coins (SF 440, 446, 450, 454, 458 and 475). Three are illegible, but the others are of Tetricus I (AD 271–74) or Tetricus II (AD 272–74). All the additional pottery associated with this context (SPFOG, SPFQN, SPFQP, SPFTM and SPFTJ) can be dated to no earlier than the mid-3rd century AD. It is likely, therefore, that AB I was in use from the late 2nd century until its demolition in the late 3rd century.

Aisled Building II

Foundations and walls

Only the lowest courses of the walls of AB II survived, but enough to show that they were substantial and that there were at least two phases of construction. The original walls were set in a 1 m wide and 0.30 m deep foundation trench, packed with chalk and mortar upon which was laid a bed of flint nodules 0.88 m wide creating offsets on either side of the wall. The wall itself was 0.60 m wide, with an outer facing of flint nodules, inner faces of chalk blocks and a filling of chalk. Thin limestone slabs had been used as a string-course. A large, dressed block of Bembridge limestone was found in the north-east corner of the building, and it is probable that all four corners had similar quoins. The south-east corner had been heavily robbed. The building was entered through a large, 3.85 m wide, doorway in the eastern wall. The entrance was delineated by a threshold of limestone slabs set on a foundation of mortared flint nodules (Figs 17 & 18).

The foundations and structure of the north and south walls were similar and both showed a change in construction 27 m from the east end, suggesting that the original construction terminated here (Fig. 19). From this point the walls were not as thick and were less well constructed and represent a western extension. A north-south partition wall foundation trench, 0.90 m wide and 0.30 m deep, was also identified.

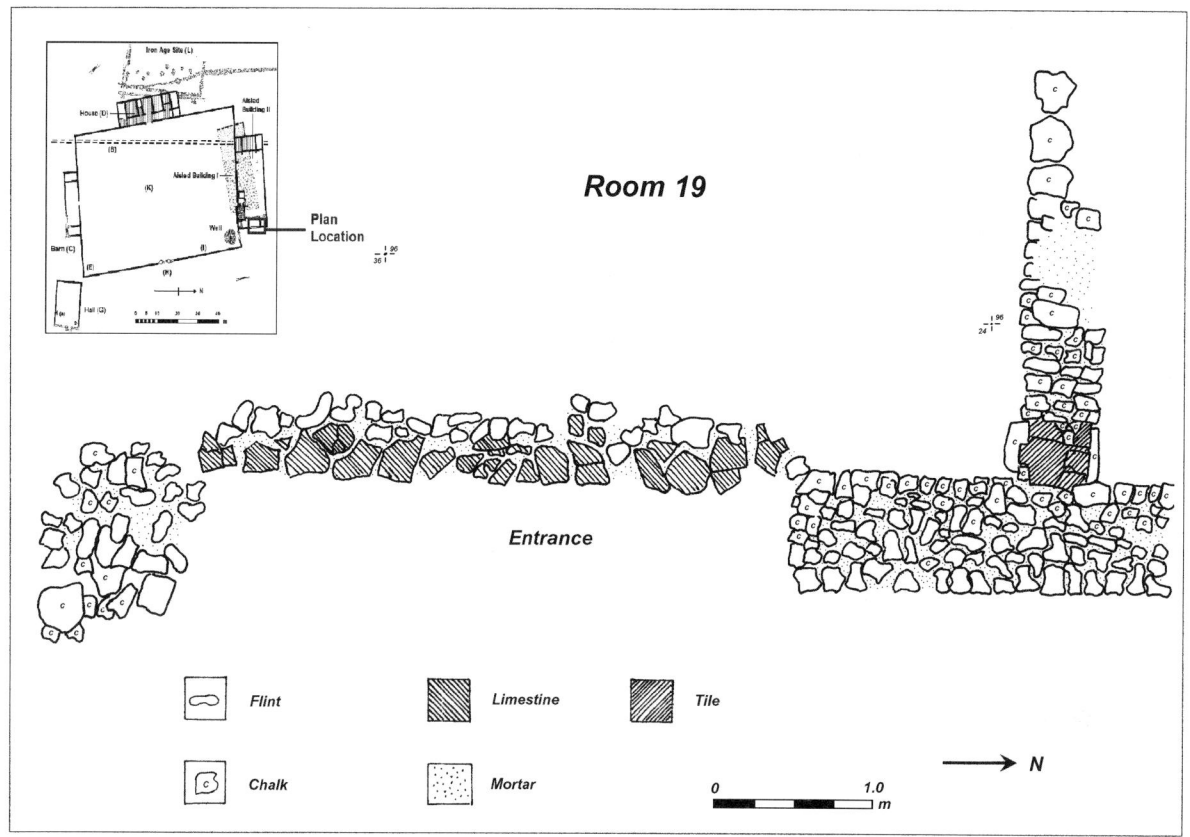

Fig 17   Plan of the entrance to AB II (drawn by JD, based on original by CC)

Fig 18   Entrance to AB II in the eastern wall (photographed 1971)

The partition was 0.56 m wide and built from mortared and shaped chalk blocks inserted after the completion of the extension. Where the north and south walls met the partition wall they showed signs of modification. The west end of the south wall was very different in construction from the east end: the width of the wall was reduced from 0.75 m to 0.65 m and terracotta tiles were used in its construction (Fig. 20). The extended west end of the building created a new suite of rooms (12, 13 and 14) giving the building an overall length of 36 m. A chalk and mortar layer at the west end of Room 19, which extended beneath the partition, was probably levelling laid down after the demolition of the original gable end wall. Red and white wall plaster was found in the demolition rubble and also *in situ* at the west end of the hall.

AB II was laid out on a different alignment to its predecessor and the Courtyard wall was adjusted to accommodate this. The north stretch of the Courtyard wall was demolished and a new one built, making the Courtyard more rectangular in shape. At the east end a small section of the original wall was retained and it is possible that a small gate was inserted between the Courtyard and the entrance to the new aisled building (Fig. 21).

Roof

In its original form, AB II was 27 m long and 14 m wide and it would have had two rows of nine (seven free-standing) substantial timber roof supports 3.50 m apart. Only five of the original stone column bases and two mortar pads were identified, however. Each of these bases was roughly 0.48 m by 0.40 m and 0.27 m thick. Each block had been set on a mortar base (0.10 m thick) in the natural clay-with-flints which left the top 0.12 m proud. The upper faces had been worked to a fine flat surface, and the chisel tooling marks were still visible; the edges were bevelled and chamfered. Four of the bases were set into the gable end walls of the building; the two in the west wall had been incorporated into the new partition wall (Fig. 22). The nave was 7 m wide and the aisles 3.50 m, but the exact nature of the superstructure is unknown. The nave may have projected high above the aisle roofs to allow for clerestory windows. The evidence from the demolition debris suggests that the roof of the nave was covered with limestone hexagonal tiles held in position with nails, while the aisles were covered by ceramic *tegulae* and *imbrices*.

The rooms

The use of a bulldozer to construct a forest ride prior to the excavations destroyed parts of the western end of the building, particularly the south-west corner and Room 12.

Room 12

Room 12 measured 5.18 m by 2.74 m and was divided from Room 13 by a wall built of chalk blocks, butted against the north–south partition wall of AB II. It was not clear whether it also abutted the western gable wall, although this seems probable because the dividing wall between Rooms 13 and 14 was bonded into the external gable wall and the north–south partition wall. This suggests that Rooms 12 and 13 were originally one and their separation probably coincided with the laying of a geometric patterned mosaic, 1.95 m by 2.75 m, which was the latest in a series of floors (Fig. 24). A large portion of the mosaic had been damaged, but sufficient survived (Fig. 23) to identify the pattern (see p.115). It had a coarse tessellated border of red brick and white limestone *tesserae* and several, seemingly random, flint *tesserae*.

Beneath the mosaic was a red mortar floor. This was the same layer encountered in Room 13 (see below), supporting the theory that Rooms 12 and 13 were originally one. There was no clear evidence of a doorway between them, but a gap in the middle of the dividing wall may mark the location. No other features remained *in situ* within the room, but a small stone column (SF 396) was found in the rubble on the mosaic floor.

Dating evidence was restricted to 60 sherds of pottery from the late 3rd to the 4th century AD. The style of the mosaic links it to those in Rooms 7 and 11 of the Main House and suggests that they are contemporary, i.e. early 4th century AD.

Room 13

Room 13, measured 5.18 m by 5.80 m, and was the middle of the three rooms, probably giving access from Room 19 to Rooms 12 and 14 via a 1m wide doorway. Room 13 had a red tessellated pavement and a strip of red, white and black *tesserae* marked the entrance threshold. The *tesserae* were set in a thin chalky material that formed the top layer of a 0.02 m thick bed of mortar. Beneath the tessellated floor was a 0.01 m thick floor of compacted mortar, topped with a surface of crushed red brick (Fig. 24). This was the same bedding identified in Room 12 and a similar compacted red mortar layer was found beneath the mosaic in Room 7 of the house. This may be coincidental or an indication that the floors are contemporary.

The room produced no features and dating evidence was limited to a coin (SF 16) of Constantine II Caesar (AD 317–37) recovered from the tessellated floor and 44 sherds of late 3rd to late 4th century pottery. The pottery evidence indicates that the rooms were in use until at least the middle of the 4th century AD, if not later.

Room 14

This room, 5.18 m by 2.60 m, had simple flooring and no obvious doorway to the hall. In several places a red mortar quarter-moulding sealing the wall and floor junction remained *in situ*, suggesting that the walls were originally plastered. On the floor was a large scatter of the type of nails associated with hexagonal limestone roof tiles and ceramic

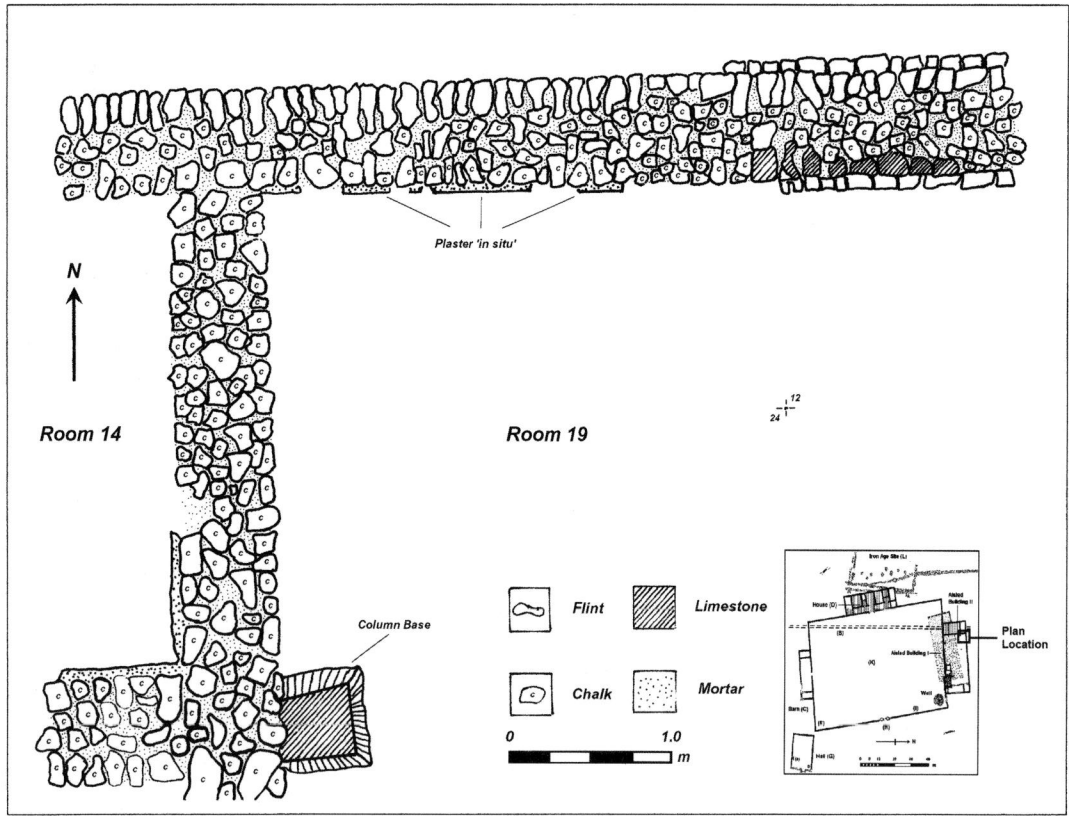

Fig 19 North wall of AB II showing change in method of construction (drawn by JD, based on original by CC)

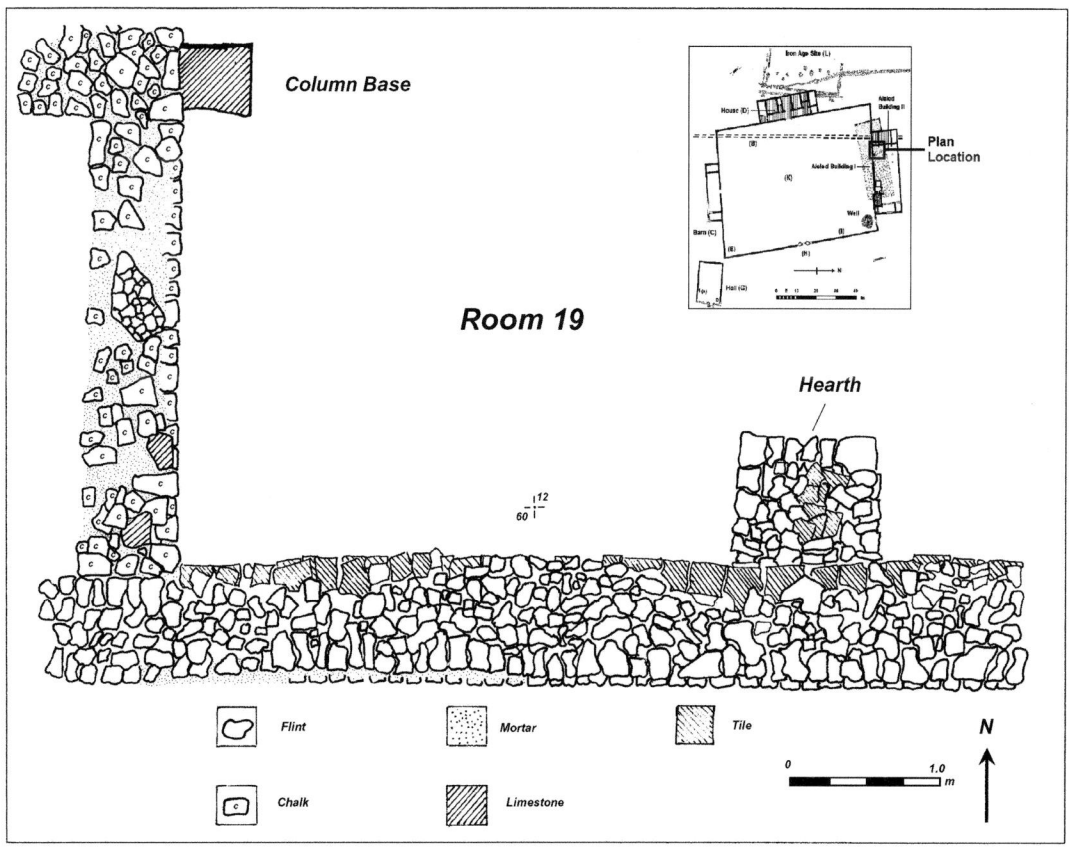

Fig 20 Plan of the western section of the south wall of AB II (drawn by JD, based on original by CC)

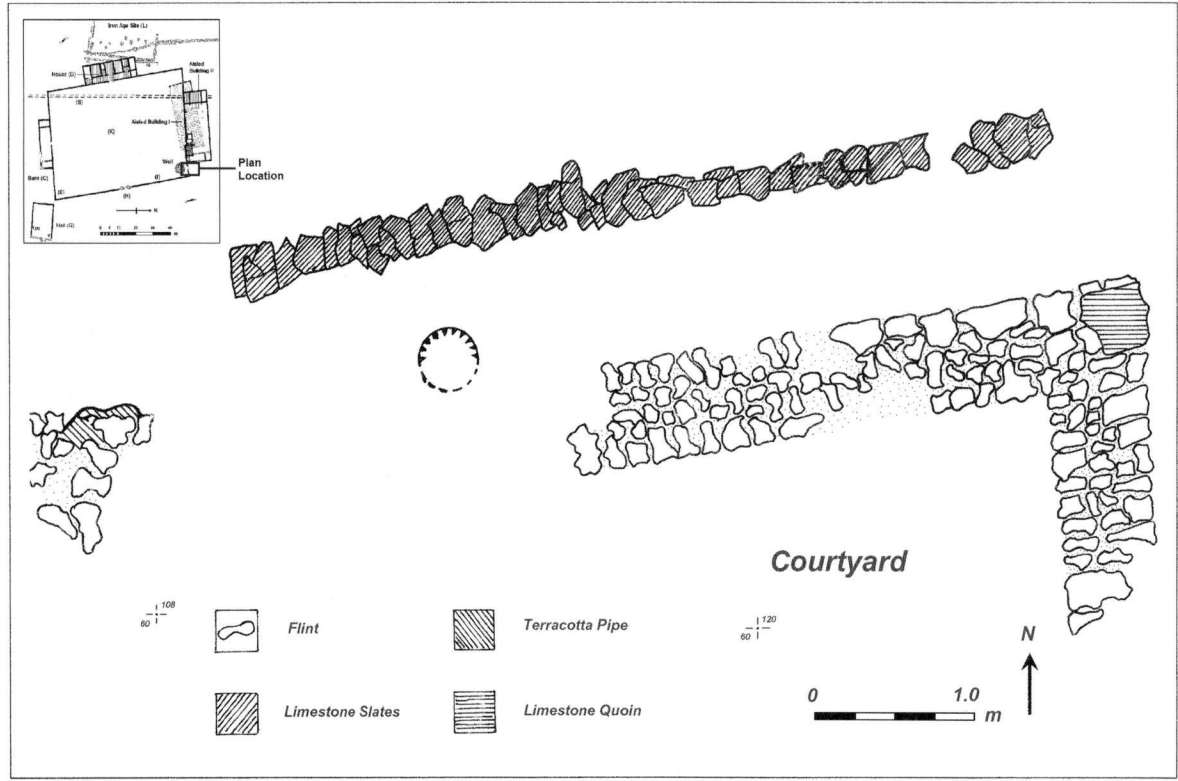

Fig 21   Plan of original part of the north Courtyard wall and the side entrance (drawn by JD, based on original by DEJ)

Fig 22   Column base set into the western gable wall (photographed 1971)

Fig 23   Mosaic in Room 12 (photographed 1971)

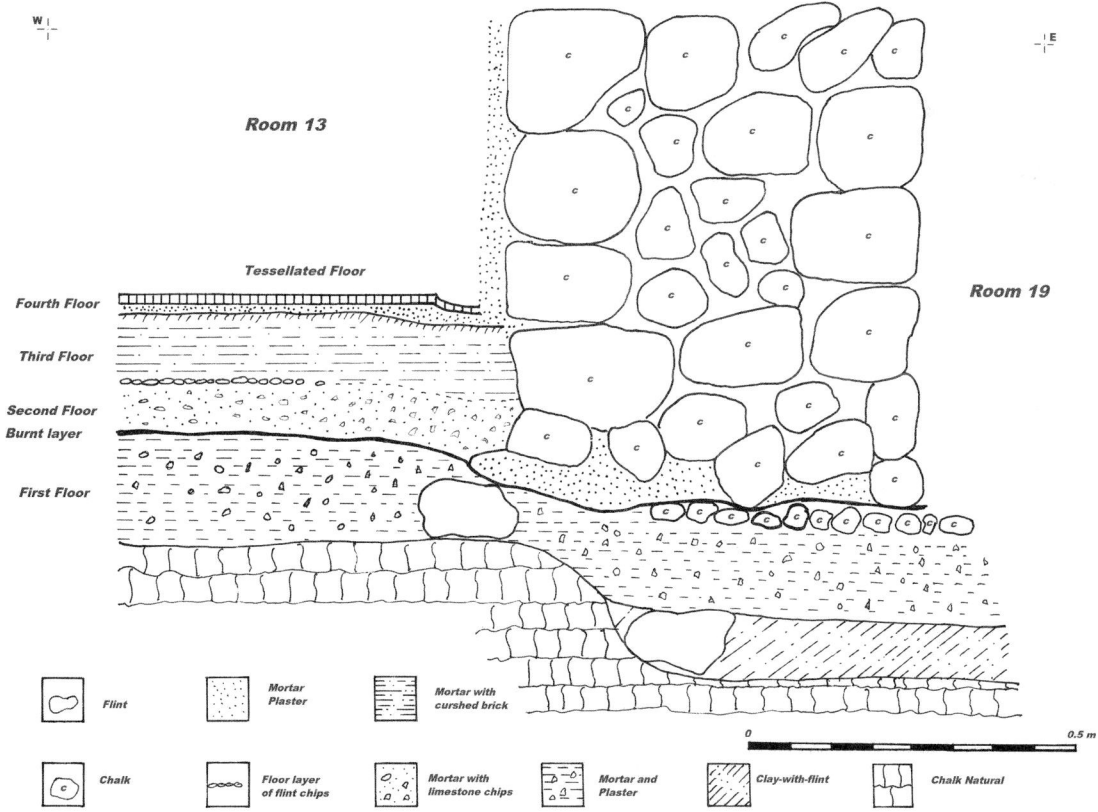

Fig 24   Section through Room 13 floor layers and partition wall (drawn by JD, based on an original from a site note book)

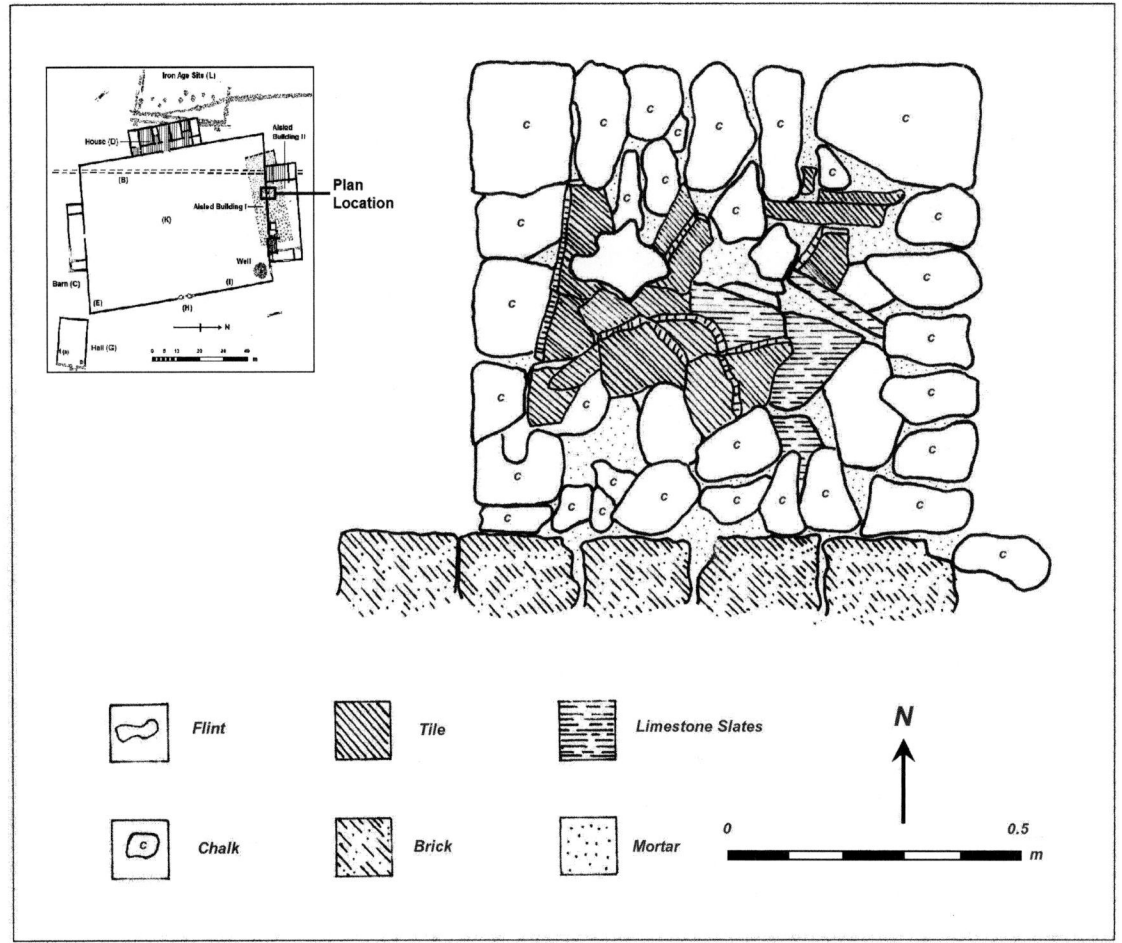

Fig 25   Plan of the hearth built into the south wall of Room 19 (drawn by JD, based on an original from a site note book)

tegulae, possibly evidence of the salvaging of building materials.

A single coin (SF 343), a *follis* of Crispus (AD 317–26), was recovered from rubble within the room. In addition, 137 sherds of late 3rd to late 4th century pottery were recovered. This is consistent with a main period of occupation in the early 4th century.

Room 19

The main 'hall' of AB II was 29 m long and 12.70 m wide, with a large 3.85 m wide door in the eastern wall. It was divided into aisles by seven pairs of roof supports creating a nave 7 m wide with 3.50 m wide aisles. The floor was beaten earth with trodden-in chalk and tiles. This was superseded at the eastern end by a cobbled surface and at the western end by layers of chalk and mortar. The various surfaces suggest that different activities were carried out at either end of the hall.

A hearth was built into the wall near the south-west corner. It abutted the remains of the original flint wall and employed ceramic tiles in a manner similar to the extension of the south wall so it seems likely to have been a later addition. The hearth was roughly square (0.85 m by 0.80 m), made of rectangular chalk blocks, flints and tiles, held together with mortar (Fig. 25); it was probably the base of a much taller feature. The hearth was surrounded by a burnt area and the associated debris contained quantities of oyster and mussel shells, as well as fragments of a large late 3rd to 4th-century New Forest grey ware cooking bowl (SPAb4AU). Other sherds of grey ware were sealed by the construction of the hearth (SPAb4BT) and also incorporated into its fabric (SPAb4BV).

A pair of ovens, one superimposed onto the other, was located between two roof piers in the southern aisle. The later oven (1) had a single flue and oval hearth 0.70 m by 0.80 m and was cut through a chalk and mortar floor into the natural clay-with-flints. It was constructed of chalk blocks, sandstone and flints set in orange mortar. Red ceramic tiles (*tegulae*) lined the oven (Fig. 26) and floor. Oven 1 was full of ash and there were signs of extensive burning, but no cooking debris or dating evidence was found. Sherds from a Fulford (1975) Type 42 New Forest colour-coated beaker (c. AD 300–70) and a G30 New Forest grey ware jar (c. AD 270–350) were recovered from the demolition rubble of the oven. The earlier oven (2) lay directly beneath its

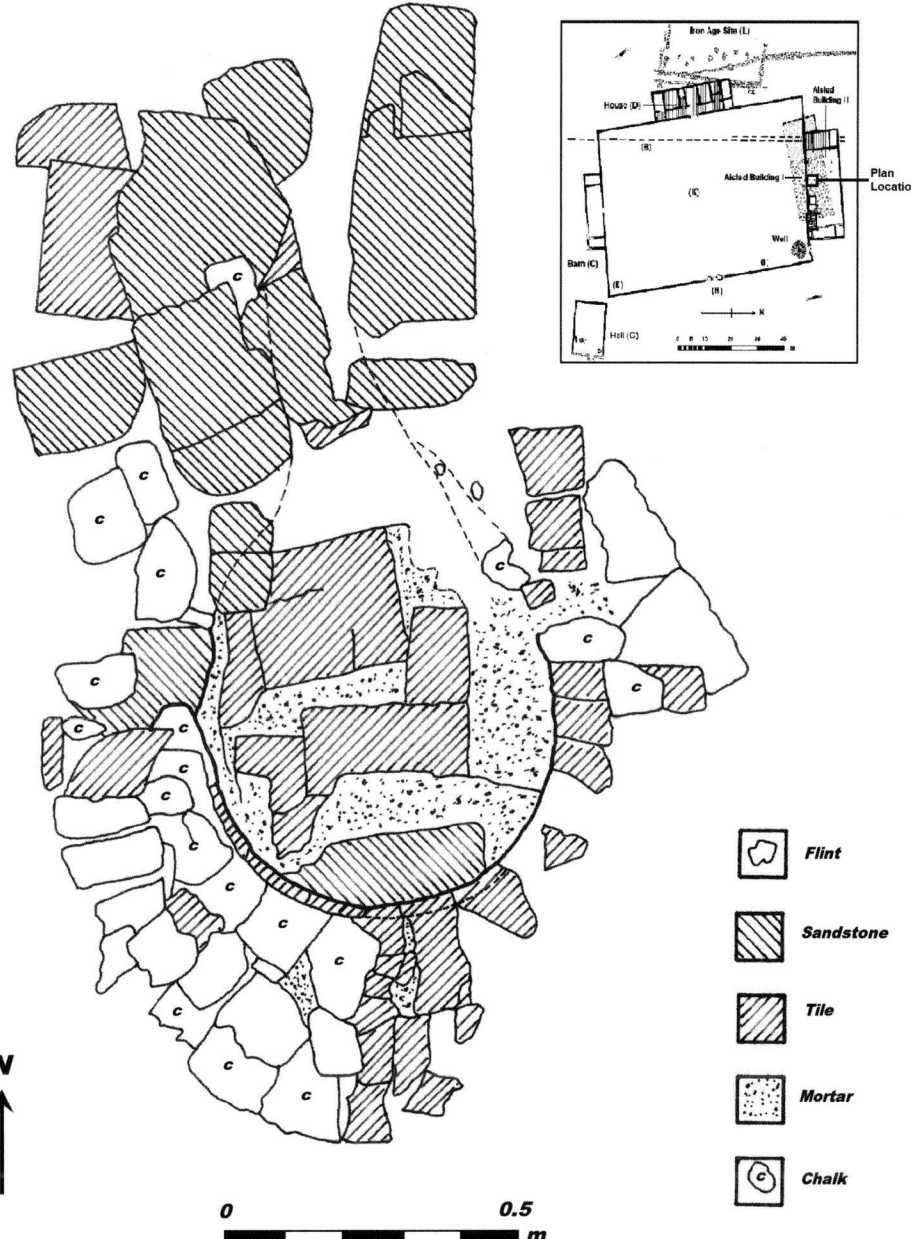

Fig 26 Oven 1 in Room 19 (drawn by VH)

successor and was of a similar construction (Fig. 27). It produced no dating evidence.

Dating evidence for Room 19 was limited. A single denarius (SF 24) of Commodus (AD 180–92), found in the rubble covering the floor at the western end of the hall, was probably residual from AB I. An assemblage of 5407 g of pottery was recovered from the area, all of which can be dated to the late 3rd to late 4th century AD. Several came from New Forest grey ware vessels, including Fulford type G6 bowls, G20 jugs and G30 jars. The New Forest fine wares included a Fulford red-slipped T63 bowl (c. AD 270–400), T27 beakers (c. AD 270–400) and a T87 parchment ware lid (c. AD 320–40); the latter was recovered from an occupation layer on the floor of the hall.

Although Room 19 may not originally have been divided into separate areas, the features within it and the various floors suggest that different functions evolved over the lifetime of the hall. The cooking hearth indicates that the west end was more domestic in nature, while the cobbled floors at the eastern end were possibly laid to house livestock, although there was no evidence of stalling or drainage.

Room 23

Room 23 was in the north-east corner of the building, close to the entrance. It had been created by erecting a wall between two of the roof supports and the gable-end. The partition wall was 0.46 m wide, constructed of chalk blocks and flint nodules mixed in random fashion. The room was associated with a

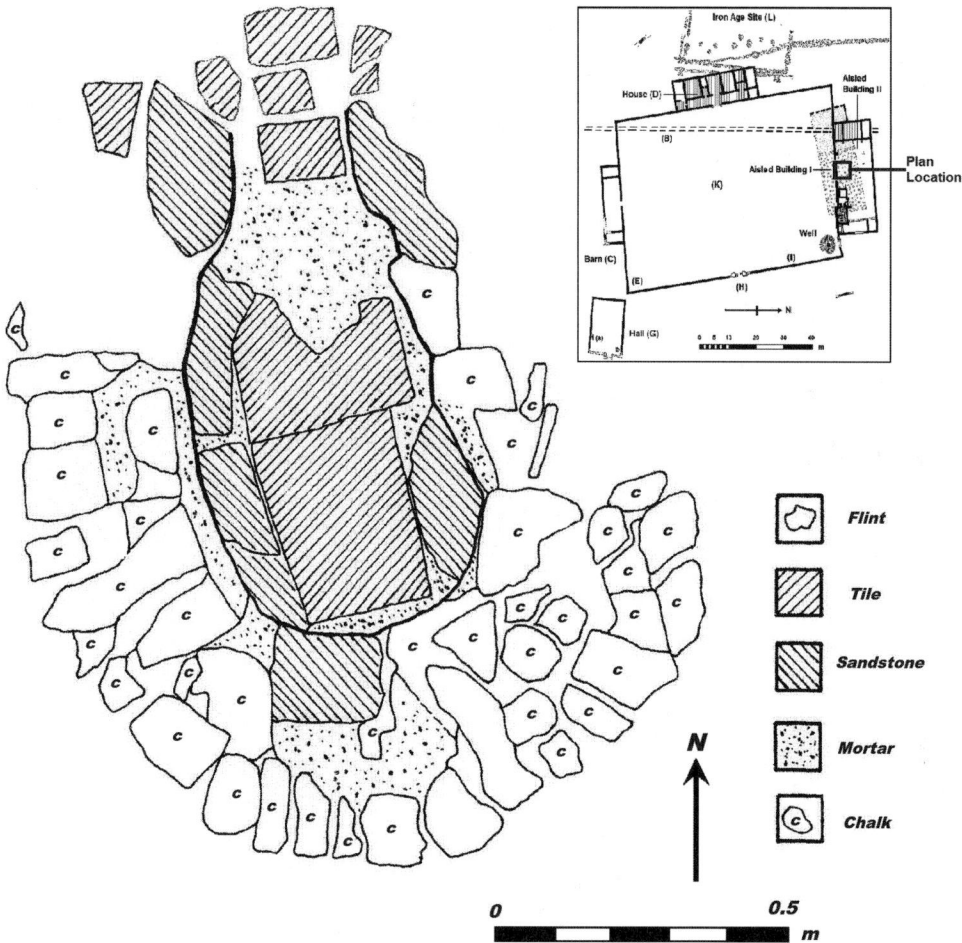

Fig 27   Oven 2, under Oven 1 in Room 19 (drawn by VH)

stone-slab floor 0.13 m above the beaten earth floor that extended throughout the building, showing that it was not an original feature. This room may also have had a domestic function: set into the partition wall was a hearth constructed of tile (Fig. 28), and an earlier hearth, sealed by the partition wall, was contemporary with the earliest earthen floor.

There were 239 sherds of pottery found (3516 g) all of which can be dated to the late 3rd to late 4th century. New Forest and grog-tempered grey wares dominate the assemblage with examples of Fulford Type G30 and G32 jars and a red-slipped Fulford T59 bowl (c. AD 320–400). Also present was a complete south-east Dorset BB1 miniature jar (SF 390) with obtuse lattice decoration (c. AD 270–400+). The stone floor sealed several sherds (SPAg2G, SPAg2AB, SPAg2AE, SPAg2AO, and SPAg2AQ), from the late 3rd to late 4th century AD.

The Bath-suite

The Baths, which were an integral part of the building, were built into the south-east corner of the hall (Fig. 29). They covered four of the aisle bays and were a complete suite comprising a cold plunge bath (*frigidarium* – Room 18), two rooms heated by a hypocaust (the *caldarium* and *tepidarium* – Rooms 17a and b), and the hypocaust stoke area (*praefurnium* – Room 16). An additional 'room' (15) to the west was also heated, but was not part of the bath-suite (Fig. 30).

The outer walls of the bath-suite were constructed from flint, built in a herring-bone style of variable thickness which resulted from the apses of Rooms 17a and b projecting 0.60 m beyond the southern wall. The apses were not outwardly visible however: the wall presented a flat exterior, plastered and painted red. In contrast, the north wall was a double wall with an outer layer of chalk blocks set within a common foundation trench.

The hypocausts of the *caldarium* and the *tepidarium* would have had vertical box flues to create the necessary draught to draw the hot air through the system and while none was found *in situ* there were many broken examples in the rubble. Tufa voussoirs were found in the rubble from the hypocaust chambers, showing that the roofs of both the *caldarium* and *tepidarium* were barrel-vaulted.

Painted wall plaster was also recovered from the demolition rubble and several pieces were still *in situ* within the *caldarium*, *tepidarium* and *frigidarium*. In addition to plain cream there were fragments of multi-coloured panels (p.130). Building material had

Fig 28   Hearth in Room 23

been removed after the abandonment of the building, and demolition rubble and debris filled the hypocausts and Baths.

Room 15

This room, which contained a T-shaped corn drier, was approximately 2 m square and was constructed within the south wall of the building (Fig. 31). The main corn drier flue, neatly vaulted with chalk blocks, and the ventilation shafts had been cut 1.30 m through the infill of Room 24 of AB I and into the natural chalk. The drier was heated through a brick-built *praefurnium* arch that led from the stoke hole in Room 16. Although the masonry showed little sign of intense heat, the floor of the flue had layers of ash and charcoal containing charred grain.

There was no evidence of a doorway to Room 15. The floor above the ventilation shafts consisted of a 0.12 m thick layer of mortar covered by beaten chalk, although much of it had collapsed into the flue along with the vaulting. The unplastered walls of the room, 0.28 m thick, were constructed of rough chalk blocks and random flint nodules.

T-shaped corn driers have been found at many sites including Abbotts Ann (Cunliffe & Poole 2008c, 56–60) and Grateley South (Cunliffe & Poole 2008b, 1–7), both in Hampshire. Analysis of the grain from both sites showed that the structures were used to dry spelt wheat prior to grinding into flour. Both ovens date from the late 3rd to late 4th century AD. At Sparsholt, Room 15 may have been built to take advantage of the already existing stoking area (Room 16). The dating evidence cannot confirm this, however: the assemblage comprises 40 late 3rd to late 4th century sherds consisting of New Forest colour-coated and grey wares including a Fulford 103 mortarium (c. AD 270–350), and late grog-tempered wares.

Room 16

Room 16 was the *praefurnium* for the hypocaust, heating both the bath suite (Rooms 17a and b) and the corn drier (Room 15). Originally it was an open area acting as the stoke hole to the bath-suite hypocaust, but was enclosed when the corn drier was built. Access to the stoke hole was through a narrow (0.45 m) gap in the northern wall, between two stone and brick-built piers which measure 0.58 m by 0.48 m and were probably bases for cold water cisterns supplying the hot water tank (*testudo*), although the tanks and associated pipe work have not survived. The sides of the flue and the *praefurnium* arch (0.60 m wide and 1.45 m long) leading to the *caldarium* hypocaust were intact. This substantial archway had been constructed in two parts, utilising the wall of the *caldarium* and an abutting wall of the stoke hole. The flue was faced with ceramic bricks and *tegulae* placed on chalk block foundations and had a floor constructed from *tegulae*. Part of the flue may not have been arched as the walls were vertical and could have supported a hot water tank, as at Dunkirt Barn, Abbotts Ann (Cunliffe & Poole 2008c, 35).

34 THE AISLED BUILDINGS (SITES A & F)

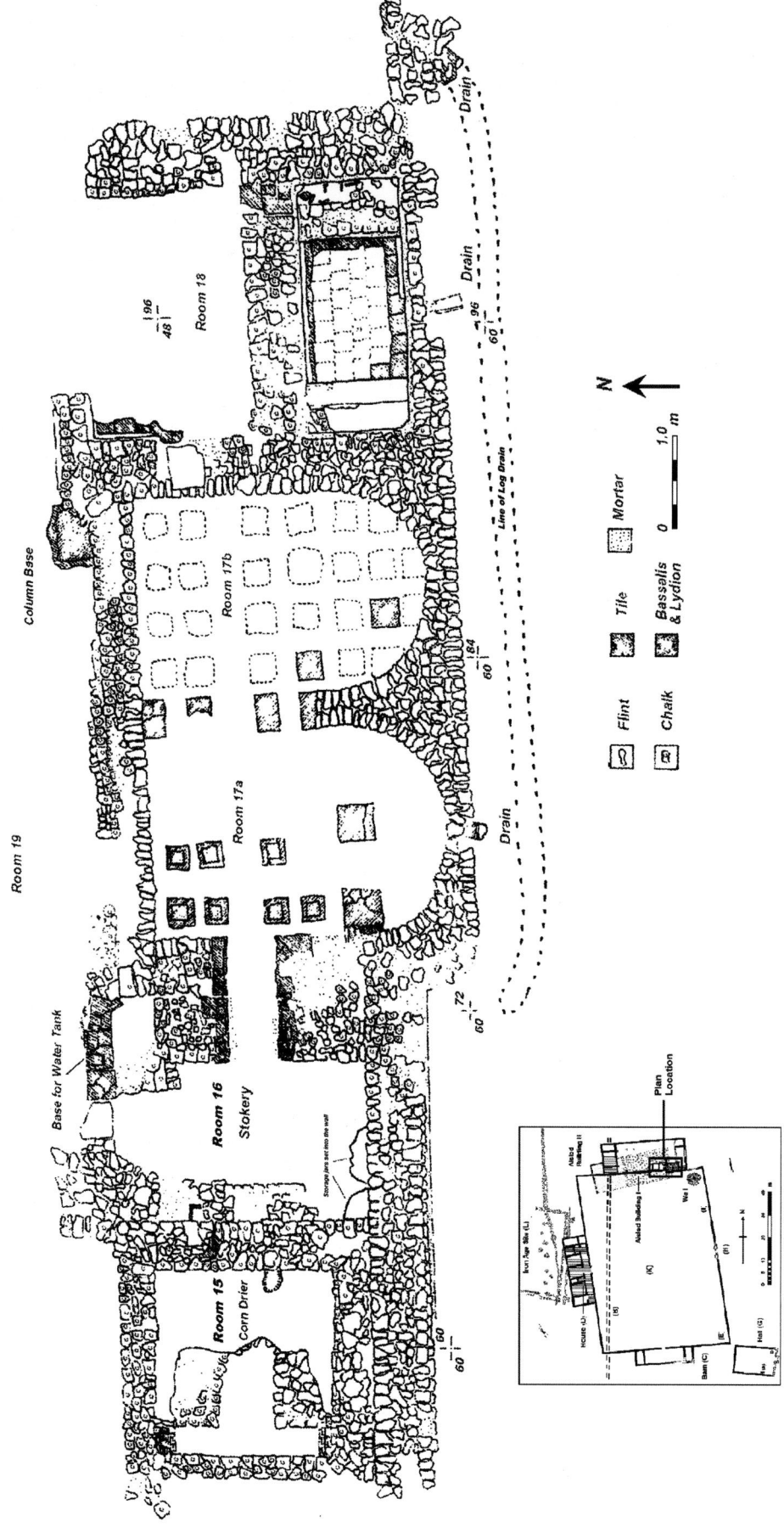

Fig 29 Plan of bath suite in AB II (drawn by JD, based on an original by CC)

Fig 30   View of the bath suite in AB II looking west (photographed 1972)

The floor of the working area had been modified several times. It was dug to approximately 1.20 m below the original floor level to accommodate and allow access to the new flue of Room 15, at the same time giving continued access at a higher level to the existing flue to Rooms 17a–b. The enlargement of the stoke hole had cut through, and largely removed, earlier levels and only a small area remained on the north side, resulting in a step and on the south side a shelf or seat. The lowest level consisted of trampled chalk on which had accumulated a layer of ash and charcoal. This was sealed by a mortar layer containing small flints covered by another layer of ash and charcoal.

Set into and projecting from the southern wall of AB II were two large grog-tempered storage jars which must have been part of the original fabric of the structure (Fig. 32). The bowl of each jar, which had rope-effect outer rims and herring-bone decoration on the interior, was filled with layers of ash. When Room 15 was constructed the easternmost jar was incorporated into the new wall. Pottery recovered from within the jars including sherds from an Oxford red colour-coated mortarium (Young Type C100), the base of a New Forest parchment ware bowl and a large piece of Dressel 20 amphora, suggests that they were used for cooking.

After the building was abandoned the stoke hole was filled with debris that comprised flint nodules, chalk blocks, limestone slabs and ceramic tiles, plus an assortment of late 3rd to late 4th century pottery.

The *praefurnium* arch was blocked by a massive limestone slab and it is unclear whether this was a deliberate act of 'sealing' or an accidental occurrence.

Rooms 17a–b
This double room consisted of a pair of matching apsidal-ended rooms heated by the hypocaust. Access was from Room 18, the *frigidarium*, through a 0.65 m wide doorway in the north-east side of 17b. Both rooms were 2.13 m wide by 3.30 m to the apex of the apse. Room 17a was the *caldarium* and originally had a hot bath in the apse, while 17b was the *tepidarium* (Fig. 33).

The hypocaust had been heavily robbed, but in places the bases of the *pilae* were still *in situ* set in mortar and the position of others was apparent from the 'ghost' impressions of mortar patches preserved in the ash layers. In the north-west corner of Room 17a a stack of five tiles survived to a height of 0.35 m. There was also a set of larger tiles under the floor at the southern end of the apse in 17a, supporting the heated bath. The position of the bath was marked by *pilae* projecting from the walls and green and red painted wall plaster still *in situ* around the curved apsidal end.

Box flue tiles were present amongst the demolition rubble but none was found *in situ* suggesting that they were built onto rather than into the masonry walls. A set of large tiles on the hypocaust floor marked the entrance between the *caldarium* and the *tepidarium*.

Fig 31 View of T-shaped corn drier, stoke hole and Baths (photographed 1972)

Fig 32   Room 16, two large grog-tempered storage jars

Fig 33   Hypocaust under the *tepidarium* looking south (photographed 1972)

A series of six small iron brackets had been driven into the north wall of Room 17a approximately 0.13 m above floor level and a seventh was recovered from the rubble. These brackets, which were too small to retain or secure box flue tiles, could have been used to fasten stone veneer, such as marble, to the wall of the *caldarium*, although no such material was found in the rubble.

The doorway from Room 18 to the *tepidarium* was through the flint partition wall and had a tiled threshold overlaid with *opus signinum* 0.15 m higher than the floor level in Room 17b. This cement pad, which presumably supported more tiles, corresponded with the successive raising of floor levels in Room 18 (see below).

Waste water from the *caldarium* was emptied through a drain in the apse wall formed from two *imbrices* which could have housed a lead pipe. The water would have been channelled to the wooden drain situated in the Courtyard (see below).

Between the *pilae* the floor of the hypocaust was covered with a black sooty layer – ash from the stoke hole. This contained 22 sherds of pottery and a single coin (SF 38), an *antoninianus* of the emperor Victorinus (AD 269–71), which give a general date for the firing of the hypocaust in the late 3rd century. The pottery can be dated to the fourth quarter of the 3rd century, or later, and includes a Fulford Type 53 New Forest colour-coated cup with incised wavy line decoration.

Room 18
The south-east corner of the building contained Room 18, which measured 2.75 m by 3.60 m internally. This room had suffered badly from tree-root disturbance and slippage into the nearby crater caused by the collapse of the Well. It would have served a dual function as a cold room (*frigidarium*), incorporating a cold plunge bath and dressing room (*apodyterium*).

The room was entered through a door in the north wall about 1.50 m wide. The cold plunge bath had been modified three times. The earliest version measured 2.70 m by 1.17 m and was only 0.38 m deep. The base was covered in red ceramic tiles set in thick *opus signinum* cement and the walls were covered in cream-colour painted plaster, the edges of which were sealed with *opus signinum* quadrant fillets. Associated with this phase was a floor of mortar containing crushed chalk. The next stage saw a step added at the eastern end, constructed in part by tiles set on edge (Fig. 34) and rendered with *opus signinum*. There was no matching step to the west, but at the northern end the edge of the bath was tiled at floor level. At the same time the floor was raised by the addition of brown soil containing fragments of *opus signinum* consolidated with a surface of compacted chalk, tile fragments and mortar.

The final modifications saw the addition of double steps, or seats, at both ends of the pool, now 0.86 m deep (Fig. 35). The floor level was raised throughout the rest of the room by laying a new floor of red ceramic tiles on a bed of *opus signinum*. The tiles were laid up to the edge of the bath and thresholds were created by extending the tiles into both the entrance to the room and the doorway into the *tepidarium*.

A gap in the masonry of the east wall and an adjacent *imbrex* is possible evidence for a drain. In addition, a mortar filled inverted *imbrex* passing through the wall contained the impression of a pipe. There was, however, a drain already associated with the bath (see below). The disturbed stratigraphy at this corner of the building made interpretation difficult but another drain at this point would have facilitated the removal of water when sluicing down the tiled floor.

While it was possible to identify the various modifications to Room 18, there was insufficient evidence to date them accurately. Some 123 sherds of late 3rd to 4th century pottery were recovered, mostly from the rubble filling, but the low average sherd weight of the group (just over 6 g) demonstrates the degree of disturbance.

Wooden drain
A 19 m long wooden drain was unearthed in the Courtyard (Fig. 29). The drain was about 0.30 m in diameter and constructed of sections about 1.50 m in length. These were joined by iron collars, three of which were still *in situ* (SF 265, 341, 370 and 389). As the drain cut the masonry of the AB I Baths it probably belonged to the original construction of the bath-suite. At the south-east corner of the building the drain passed, after turning a sharp angle, under the Courtyard wall in a culvert composed of *tegulae* and *imbrices*. The drain continued in an east-northeasterly direction and was protected by a cover of re-used, and often fragmentary, roof tiles. The drain showed a slight but consistent fall to the east, indicating that the outfall was somewhere beyond the eastern gable wall of AB II. The junction between this drain and the main outflow drains was not identified.

Summary of the dating evidence
A coin (SF38 dated to AD 269–71) recovered from the floor of the hypocaust in Room 17a gives a rough date for the use of the bath-suite. The modifications to the cold plunge, the stoke hole and the construction of the T-shaped corn drier cannot be accurately dated. The decline and abandonment of the Bath-suite probably coincided with that of the building. Dating based on pottery suggests that this could have been as early as the mid-4th century AD, and no later than the third quarter.

Overview

No direct evidence for the date of the construction of AB I exists, but the presence of late 2nd century pottery and two late 2nd century coins in the demolition rubble indicates that the building was occupied by the end of the 2nd century at the latest. Similarly, there was no direct evidence for the demolition of AB I, but three coins dated AD 271–74 from a layer

Fig 34 View of the tiles used in the construction of the steps into the bath in Room 18 (photographed 1972)

Fig 35 View of the steps into the plunge bath in Room 18 (photographed 1972)

that sealed the foundations make it probable that the building was replaced by the end of the 3rd century.

A lack of evidence has made it difficult to reconstruct the form of AB I with any certainty. No postholes or stone pads were found, yet the overall dimensions of 30 m long by 12 m wide correspond to the proportions of aisled buildings generally (Smith 1997). On the basis of these measurements the nave would have been roughly 6 m wide and the aisles about 3 m. The presence of a bath-suite in the south-east corner is also typical of aisled buildings but is unique in not adopting the line of the aisle posts. Similarly, there was insufficient evidence to interpret the use of the hall area but such buildings have been designated as 'work halls', being extremely adaptable spaces (Hadman 1978, 187–95; Cunliffe 2008, 114–17).

In its original form AB II was 27 m long by 14 m wide, with a nave twice the width of its aisles. It was built as a direct replacement for AB I, albeit on a slightly different alignment, no earlier than AD 275. This date was supported by the recovery of a coin from the black soot on the floor of the hypocaust. The latest coin (SF 135 dated AD 353–57), recovered from the top fill of the Well, indicates that the building, if not already abandoned, was in serious decline by the mid-4th century AD.

Aisled buildings are relatively common in Hampshire, the Isle of Wight and West Sussex (Cunliffe 2008), but there is limited evidence concerning their architecture, particularly wall height and the style of the roof. Two roof forms are possible: a simple one in which the roof was of a single sweep from ridge to eaves (Smith 1964, 25–7) and the two-tier version with clerestory windows (Collingwood & Richmond 1969, 149). Limestone slates with nail or peg holes and ceramic *tegulae* and *imbrices* were abundant amongst the demolition debris and imply that AB II was indeed a basilica with a clerestory roof (King 1996, 61). The two types of roofing material could be associated with different roof pitches, the limestone nailed to the steeper roof over the nave, the *tegulae* and *imbrices* covering the gentler pitch over the aisles.

The flint walls were interspersed at regular intervals with horizontal lines of limestone slabs which were both structural and decorative, and would have given the building a distinctive appearance. Several alterations and modifications were made during the life of AB II, although close dating is not possible. It was constructed on a slightly different alignment to its predecessor, probably to alter the trapezoidal shape of the first Courtyard and make it more rectangular. It has been argued that this was designed to emphasise the importance of the Main House which faced the entrance (Smith 1997, 250).

The western gable end wall was demolished, the hall extended by 9m and two rooms created. The southern room (13) was later sub-divided to create an additional room (12). A mosaic pavement was then installed.

The cold plunge bath in the *frigidarium* was modified at least three times, while the *praefurnium* was adapted to accommodate a corn drier. There were signs of modifications and maintenance to the stoke hole and heating system, but no specific dates could be assigned to these changes.

The main hall contained two ovens, two hearths, and a corn drier as well as a large ceramic storage jar sunk into the floor. With domestic accommodation at the western end and a bath-suite in the south-east corner, the building provided both living and working quarters. The large barn-sized door in the east wall would have allowed easy access for both animals and vehicles thus keeping them outside the Courtyard. At some point a partition wall was constructed which enclosed a tile-built hearth and created a separate area (Room 23). Combining domestic accommodation and agrarian working space was not unusual in rural aisled buildings (Smith 1997, 36). The painted plaster and mosaic floor in Room 12 suggest that this was home for part of the owner's extended family or perhaps a bailiff, but certainly not the workers or slaves.

The building was abandoned in the late 4th century AD. No signs of disaster such as fire or evidence of systematic demolition was noted, but some of the useable building material was removed. Overall the structure was allowed to decay and collapse; this was seen very clearly in 1985 when excavation revealed that the southern wall had collapsed inwards.

Chapter 4

The Main House (Site D)

Introduction

The building later identified as the Main House was discovered during the 1965 trial excavations when a trench 2.75 m by 2.50 m was opened over Room 7 and a mosaic floor found at a depth of 0.84 m (Fig. 96). In 1966 a grid of 31 trenches of varying sizes, separated by baulks, revealed the plan of the building (Fig. 36). Subsequent excavations in 1967, 1969 and 1972 concentrated on specific areas to try to clarify the sequence of construction. All the trenches were dug by hand. Work in 1967 focused on Rooms 9, 9a, 10 and 11 (the latter containing a hypocaust), in 1969 Rooms 2, 3, 4, 5, 6, 7 and 8 were targeted and in 1972 the relationship of the Corridor to Rooms 2, 9, 9a and 10 was re-examined. It was confirmed that the original building consisted of a range of Rooms 4, 5, 6, 7, 8 and 9 fronted by a Corridor (Room 1). Rooms 2, 3, 9a and 10 were added later (Fig. 37).

Results of the excavation

Foundations

The foundations of the building were set in a trench 0.90 m wide and 0.46 m to 0.61 m deep, packed with small chalk blocks to the level of the natural. The first flint course was one or two flints wider than the wall above, producing an external offset, sealed by a layer of mortar.

Walls

Before excavation the location of the building was marked by a significant mound and the large quantity of flint and limestone rubble encountered suggested that masonry walls were originally employed to the full height of the House. On excavation it was found that the walls survived to the sixth course.

The initial building comprised seven rooms fronted by a Corridor. This was defined by Bembridge limestone quoins at each corner (Figs 36, 38 & 39). Although limestone blocks were used in the construction of the Courtyard Wall, the only use of this material in the Main House was for quoins and door jambs. At some point two rooms were added at each end of the house (Fig. 37) and additional limestone blocks were used at the corners. The extensions removed some of the original Courtyard Wall but it was subsequently rebuilt (p.80).

The external walls, varying in width from 0.68 m to 0.56 m, were carefully built of flint nodules, each of which interlocked with its neighbour. The interior flints were set with the pointed end embedded in mortar. Facing flints were laid lengthwise with the sharp edge embedded in mortar. The internal partition walls, 0.50 m in width, were constructed of mortared chalk blocks and included the occasional flint (Fig. 38).

In contrast to the walls of other buildings, there was no string-course of limestone slabs. At intervals the masonry was levelled with a mortar 'pad' on which the next course rested. At one point the mortar carried the single imprint of a hobnailed boot. There were signs that some of the flints had been roughly knapped, as waste flakes were found.

The exterior of the house was not obviously rendered, but had probably been generously pointed. The mortar was of poor quality however, (p.137–138) and any outer finish had disappeared. In one area of the southern wall there were long horizontal marks averaging 0.05 m in width. They extended below ground level and had been made before the foundation trench was backfilled.

Roof

Quantities of both hexagonal limestone slates and red ceramic *tegulae* and *imbrex* tiles were found. The main roof was evidently covered with limestone and tiles were found lying directly upon the floors. The Corridor and the end rooms (2, 3, 9a and 10) were probably tiled with *tegulae* and *imbrices*.

Individual rooms

Room 1: the Corridor

The Corridor ran along the front of the house: it was 21.65 m long by 2.75 m wide and gave access to several of the rooms. The outer wall, at 0.59 m wide was less substantial than the other exterior walls, and this suggests that the Corridor may have been fronted by a low wall. It also bore no trace of the yellow painted plaster evident on the inner wall. The 2.60 m wide entrance was not central, being nearer

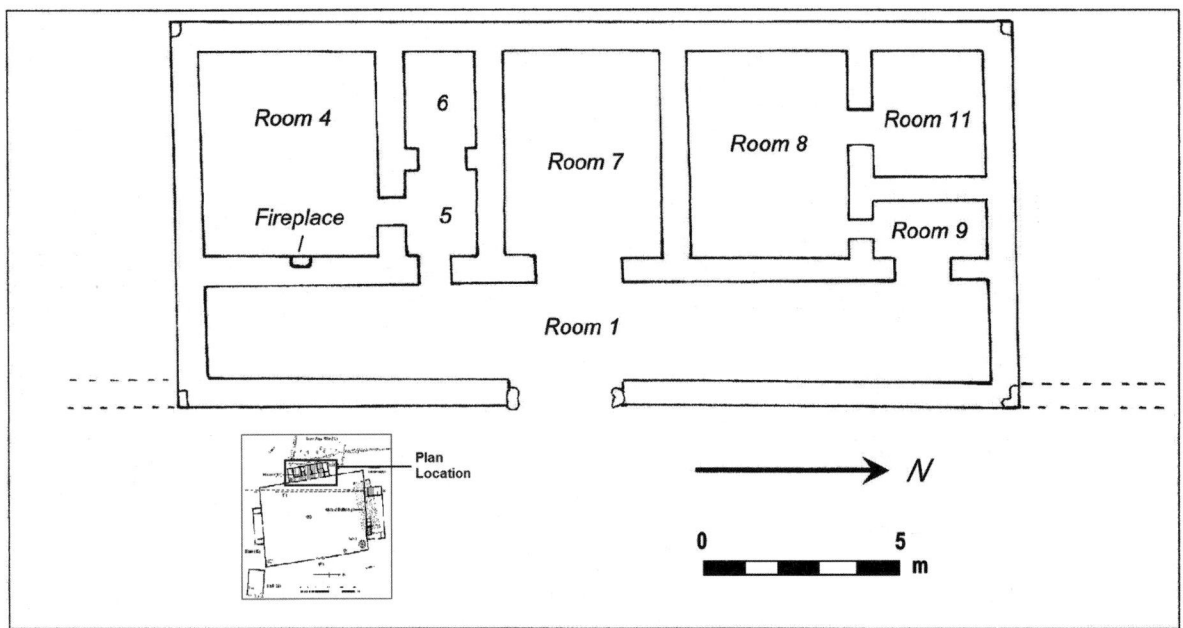

Fig 36 Outline plan of Phase 1 House (drawn by JD)

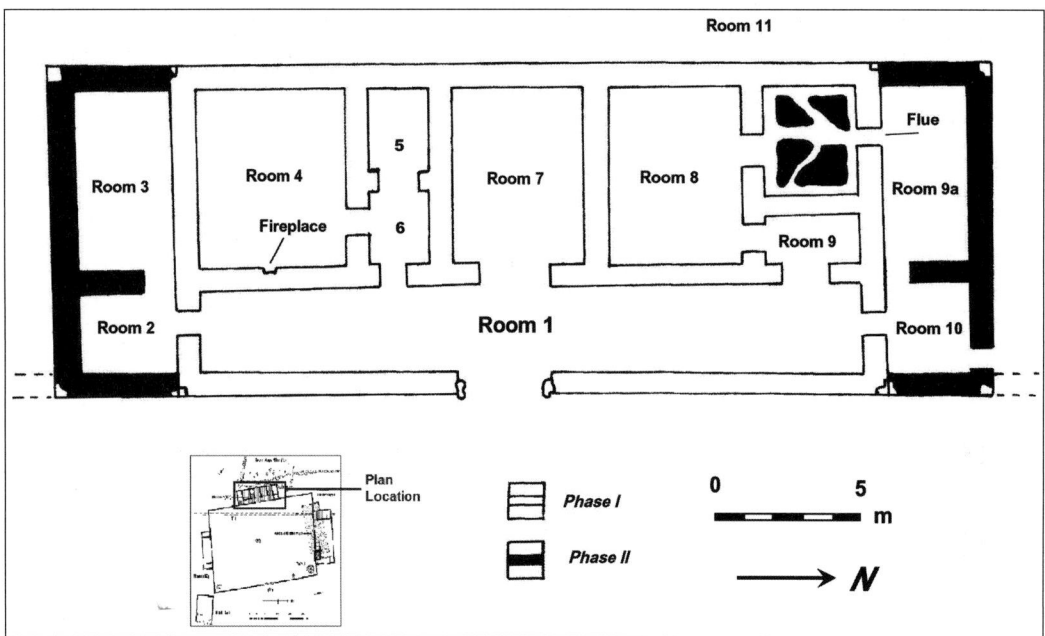

Fig 37 Outline plan of Phases I and II of the House (drawn by JD)

(by about 3 m) to the southern end of the building, nor was it directly opposite the principal room (7). It was defined by two limestone blocks, and the coarse red and pale grey *tesserae* of the Corridor floor, a tessellated pavement in a swastika-meander pattern, extended into the gap to create a threshold (Fig. 40) (Cosh & Neal 2005, 240)

The *tesserae* of this floor were set into a bed of mortar and chalk approximately 0.09 m thick over a levelling spread of brown clay (0.13 m thick) lying directly on the natural chalk (Fig. 41).

During the 1965 trial trenching a bronze *as* of Gordian III (AD 238–44) (SF 4) was discovered in the foundation material of the robbed inner wall. Although 191 sherds of pottery were recovered from the vicinity of the Corridor, none was in a stratified context, but all can be dated to the late 3rd to late 4th century.

Room 2

Room 2 was at the southern end of the House and was an addition to the building (see above). The

Fig 38   Example of an ashlar cornerstone (photographed 1972)

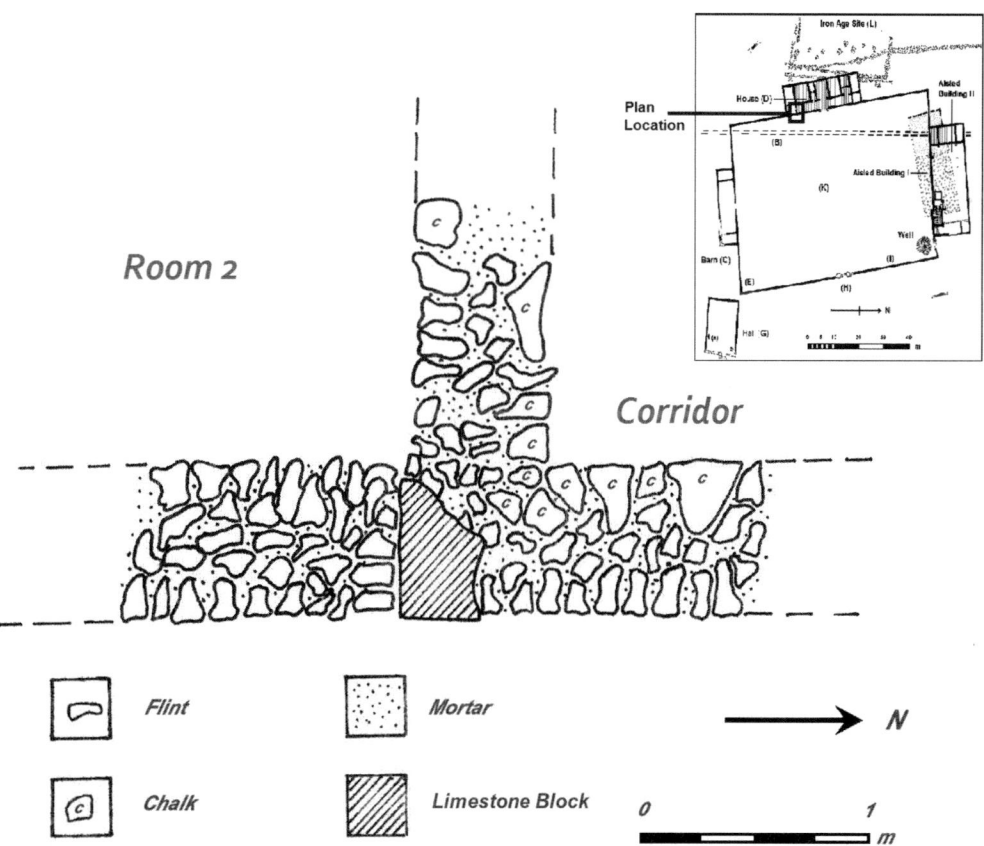

Fig 39   Plan of the south-east corner of the original building and Room 2 (drawn by JD, based on a sketch in a site note book)

Fig 40   View of the tessellated floor of the Corridor of the Main House (photograph by Jonathan Erskine)

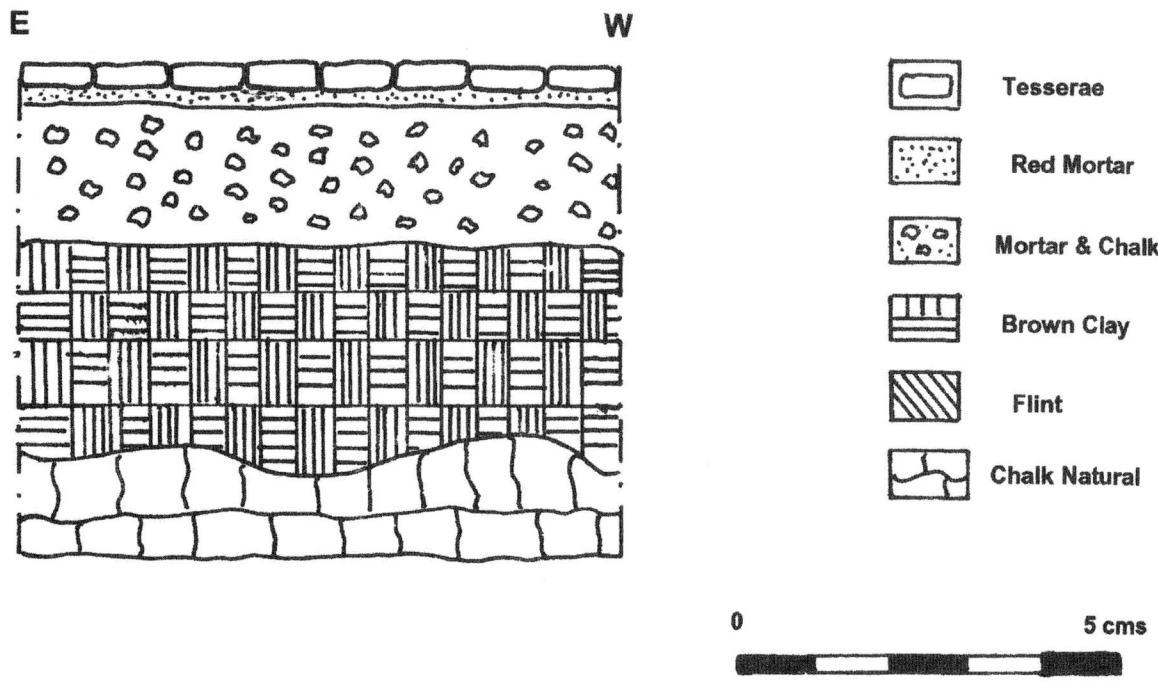

Fig 41   Section through floor of the Corridor (drawn by VH)

room was 3 m by 2.45 m and was entered from the Corridor through a door 0.85 m in width. The floor consisted of a red and grey chequered tessellated pavement set in a red border (Fig. 42) (Cosh & Neal 2005, 240). The pavement was set in a thin bed of red mortar above a layer 0.10 m thick of mortar, chalk, *tesserae* and animal bones. Beneath this was a spread of dark brown clay up to 0.18 m thick containing fragments of red tile (Fig. 43). In the north-east corner of the room the *tesserae* showed signs of intense burning, possibly caused by the heat from a brazier. Bright yellow wall plaster, with red splashes, survived in places to a height of 0.33 m above the floor.

Two sherds of pottery (south east Dorset BB1 and Hampshire late grog-tempered) were recovered from the north-south external wall of Room 2 (SPDLB and SPD LJ). Both can be dated to the very late 3rd to early 4th century, indicating that this part of the wall could not have been constructed before then.

Room 3

Room 3 (3.00 m by 5.80 m) was located to the rear of Room 2, through which it was accessed. The partition between the rooms was built of chalk blocks on a flint base. Room 3 had a floor of beaten chalk and crushed brick about 0.13 m lower than the pavement in Room 2. The plastered walls were covered in bright splashes of yellow, red, white and black paint. A *quinarius* of Allectus (AD 293–96) (SF 161) was found on the surface of the chalk floor. Pottery recovered from what may have been an occupation layer within the room (SPDEZ) dates from the late 3rd to at least the middle of the 4th century.

Room 4

This was the largest room in the House, measuring 5.80 m long by 5.50 m wide internally. A doorway 0.90 m wide between Rooms 4 and 6 appears to have been the only point of entry; there was no direct access from the Corridor. This room was part of the original building layout, but there was evidence of later modification.

The original floor, laid when it was built, was a simple surface of crushed red brick and mortar, 0.09 m thick, above the natural chalk. This was replaced by a simple red tessellated floor. Some of the *tesserae* had comb marks, showing that they were cut from box flue tiles.

The room contained the remains of a fireplace built directly onto the earliest floor and set into the eastern wall (Fig. 44). A splayed arrangement of three large *tegulae* survived in situ, forming the fireplace, but in the debris were other tiles, flints and chalk which had been part of its construction. The fireplace exhibited clear evidence of burning, with charring of the tiles and wall, and a sooty layer in the vicinity. The shattered remains of a large grog-tempered storage jar stood beside the fireplace on the tessellated floor and can be broadly dated to the 4th century AD. Apart from this jar, very little dating evidence was recovered.

Room 5

This was a small room, only 2.82 m by 2.28 m, accessed through a large (1.14 m wide) doorway from Room 6. The walls were undecorated. The floor was rough and uneven, consisting of beaten chalky mortar some 0.15 m below the level of the other rooms. Two small pits were cut into the floor (Figs 45 & 46). In the north-west corner an oval pit, 0.90 m x 0.45 m, had been covered by tiles. It was only 0.15 m deep and its loose mortar fill contained a coin (SF 144) of Claudius (imitation RIC 66) (AD 41–54). In the north-east corner was another oval pit measuring 0.76 m x 0.46 m x 0.30 m, covered by two limestone slabs. It contained the skeleton of an infant who died around 38–41 weeks (p.170–72). Radiocarbon dating produced a date from the mid-3rd century to the late 4th century AD.

A coin (SF 44) of Tetricus I (AD 271–74) was found on the chalk floor and 27 sherds of pottery came from the room; all date to the late 3rd to late 4th century.

Room 6

This room was entered from the Corridor by a narrow doorway 1.20m wide. As the room was only 1.75 m by 2.28 m, it probably acted as an anteroom for Rooms 4 and 5 (Figs 46 & 47). It had a coarse red and grey tessellated floor in conjunction with a strip of red *tesserae* running from the entrance to Room 5. It is conceivable that the red strip led to a staircase in Room 5, giving access to an upper storey, or the roof space. The sides of the tessellated pavement were either poorly laid or poorly repaired, and some of the *tesserae* had been replaced by chalk and flint and even a sherd from a beaded-rim mortarium (SF 182) in a brown-buff fabric. The form is comparable to the M17 mortaria produced by the Oxford potteries (Young 1977) but in a local fabric, probably from a Hampshire source dated c. AD 240–300 (Hartley 2012). The walls of the room were covered with red or pink-coloured plaster.

Room 7

This, the central room of the building, measured 5.80 by 4.30 m and contained an almost complete geometric mosaic (p.113–115, Fig. 96). There appears to have been only one entrance, a wide 2.40 m door from the Corridor. The doorway had been badly damaged, but was defined by an arrangement of several *tesserae* set on edge forming a shallow step up into the room. There was clear evidence that the room had been re-floored.

The original surface comprised a thin layer of red crushed brick on a mortar base and a flint nodule foundation. This lay above a thin coat of chalky mortar, covering the natural clay (Fig. 48). Five small

Fig 42 View of the tessellated floor in Room 2 of the Main House (photograph by Jonathan Erskine)

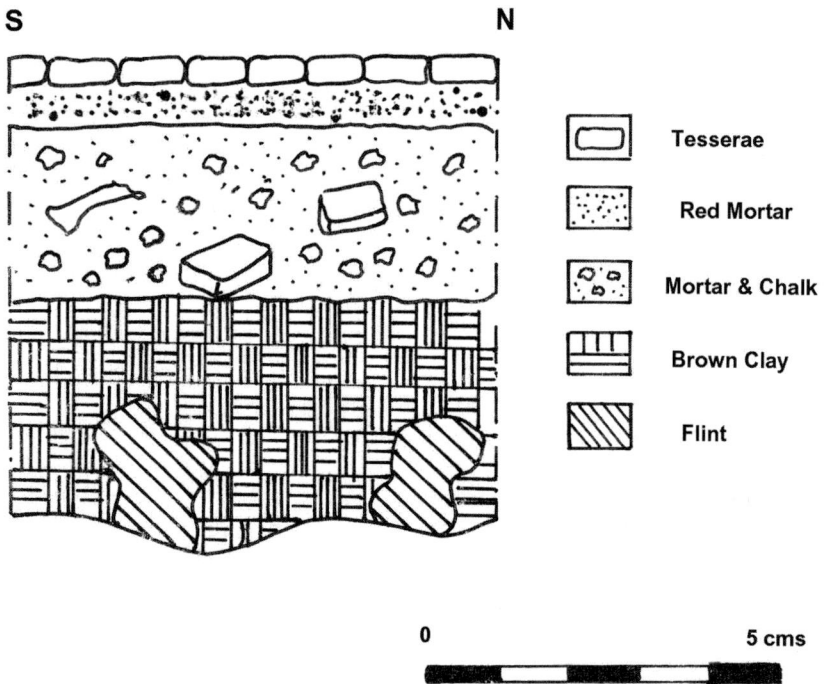

Fig 43 Section through floor layers of Room 2 (drawn by VH)

Fig 44   Fireplace built into the wall of Room 4 (photographed 1969)

grey ware sherds (SPDKN) were recovered from the make-up of the floor, but cannot provide a close date for its construction. A border of quadrant moulding, 60 mm wide, ran around the junction of the red floor and plastered walls; the latter were painted mauve with light green paint splashes, giving a marbled effect. A similar floor made from crushed brick was found in Rooms 12 and 13 in AB II. The floors could be contemporary but this cannot be proven.

At some point the red floor was replaced with the decorative mosaic (Cosh & Neal 2005, 241) and attendant border. A mortar quadrant moulding, painted red, edged the floor and the plastered walls were decorated with octagonal panels in deep red, outlined in white with green and white strips. The interior of the panels were painted light tan with oblique white strips. In the south-east corner of the room part of the mosaic was discoloured, probably the result of heat, perhaps from a brazier.

A silvered *antoninianus* (SF 39) of Gallienus (AD 253–68) was found in the north-east corner. Only 11 pieces of pottery were recovered from the room, all grey ware, dating from the mid 3rd to late 4th century.

Room 8

Room 8 measured 5.80 m by 4.50 m and was probably accessed through an anteroom (Room 9). The floor was made of coarse red *tesserae*, and saffron-coloured plaster was still *in situ* in the north-west corner. This room provided the only access to the hypocaust-heated Room 11. There was nothing in the room to help date its construction or determine its function.

Room 9

Room 9 was a vestibule or antechamber, providing the only access from the Corridor to Rooms 8 and 11. It was 3.30 m by 1.80 m with a simple patterned tessellated floor. Traces of saffron and white painted plaster survived *in situ* on the western and southern walls and reflected the colour scheme in Room 8.

The doorway from the Corridor was 1.52 m wide, with door jambs of flint and a threshold constructed from a neat double line of flints which would have been covered by the *tesserae*. The size of the aperture suggests it had double doors (as in Room 7); an iron bracket and nails might have derived from such features (SF 67, 68 and 72). The doorway to Room 8 was 0.91 m wide.

Rooms 9a and 10

Rooms 9a and 10 were part of the extension to the northern end of the building: the walls have straight joints with the original house and are 0.10 m wider. The vestigial remains of Ditches IV and I, which lie beneath the rooms, may have created structural problems, especially in the case of Ditch I which had been backfilled with flints. The floors of both rooms were of beaten chalk and the walls were not plastered. The rooms were separated by a party wall, the line of which was marked by the faint traces of a chalk-filled foundation trench.

Room 9a measured 5.50 m by 2.70 m and contained the stoke hole for the hypocaust system heating Room 11 (Fig. 49). It could be entered from Room 10, which provided access from the corridor. The

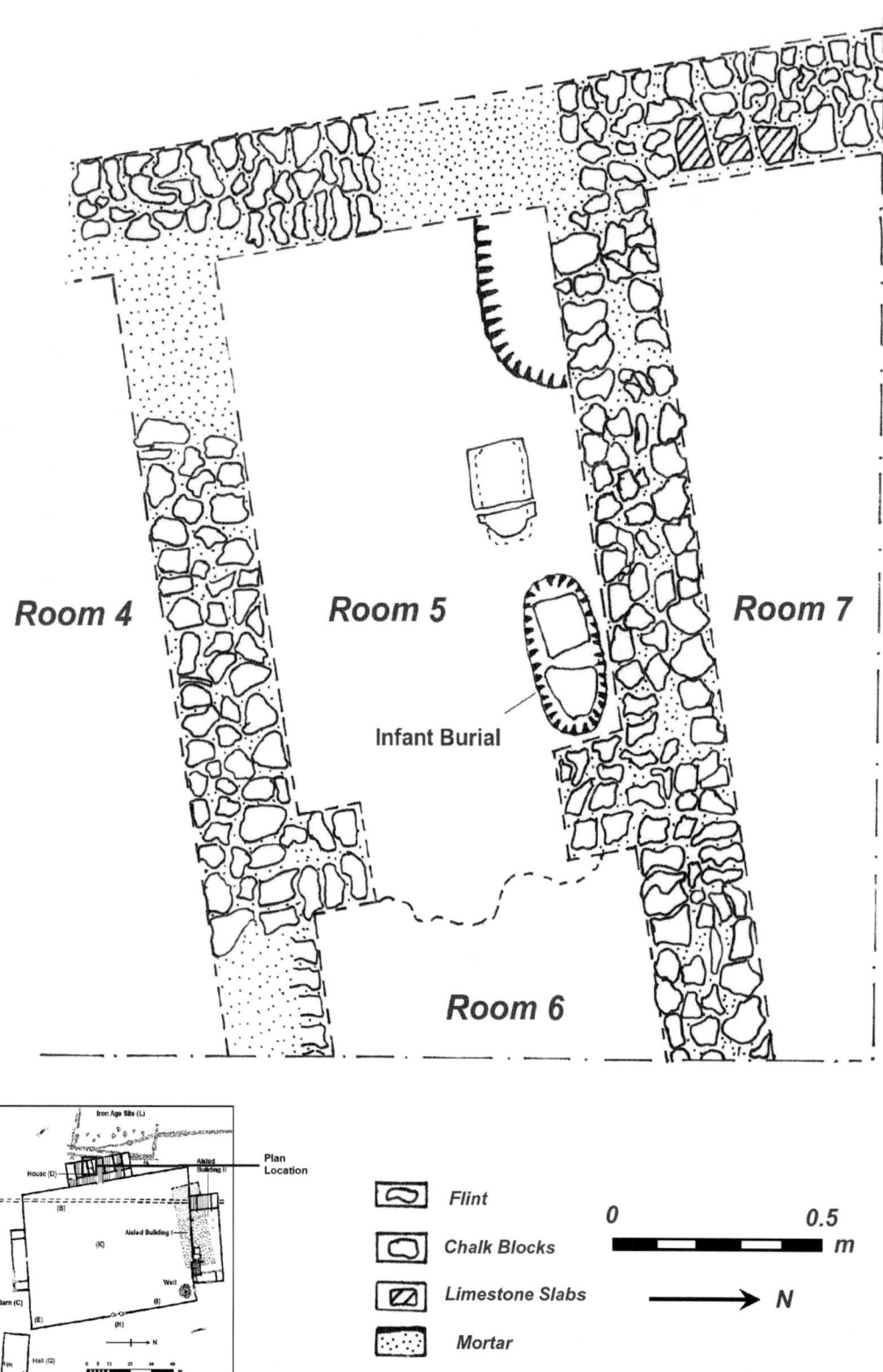

Fig 45   Plan of Room 5 (drawn by JD, based on original by CC)

Fig 46   Rooms 5 and 6 (photographed 1969)

chalk floor dipped towards the pit of the furnace. Ash from the last firings was still evident as a thick deposit. The stoke hole was offset some 45°, possibly to avoid the direct heat of the fire at the *praefurnium* arch. The arch had been thoroughly robbed out, with only the base, a brick with a limestone slab on it at the western cheek and three *tegulae*, lining the eastern side of the passage, surviving. A flat layer of hard buff mortar lay against the northern wall. It incorporated at least one limestone slab and was bordered by a brick set on edge. Associated with this spread was an *antoninianus* (SF 36) of Claudius II (AD 268–70). There were indications of a niche in the northern wall of the room, although this may have resulted from stone robbing activity.

Set in the floor was the base of a large grog-tempered pot about 0.35 m in diameter (SPDCO) cut off at floor level. It contained limescale and had probably been used as a water container. Some 159 sherds were recovered from Room 9a, the majority from the hypocaust stoke hole. All the fine wares were New Forest colour-coated vessels, dated to c. AD 270–400. There were two conjoining sherds from a New Forest parchment ware mortarium (Fulford Type 103), dated to c. AD 270–350.

Room 10 measured 2.70 m by 2.70m and was accessed by a doorway from the Corridor. The eastern wall of the room had a straight joint with the Corridor wall and part of the northern Corridor wall survived only as a foundation (Fig. 50), showing that the door was knocked through when Room 10 was added. An external door in the north wall gave access to the back of the House, presumably for bringing in fuel and for the disposal of rubbish; a midden was found in this locality.

The floor of Room 10 was beaten chalk, the walls were undecorated. The only feature was a simple structure of four large tiles and limestone slabs (Figs 51 & 52), the surface of which was heavily burnt. The burning extended deep into the surrounding chalk floor, showing that the structure served as a hearth.

Forty-seven sherds (SPDCE, SPDED) were found in the room, including New Forest grey ware jugs, jars and dishes all dating to c. AD 270–400. There was also a sherd from an Oxford colour-coated mortarium (Cool 2006). No other significant artefacts were recovered, but the disturbed skeletons of two infants were found beneath the floor (p.170–172).

Room 11

Room 11 measured 3.50 m by 3.40 m and was the only heated room (Fig. 49). The hypocaust was stoked from Room 9a (above). The only way in was from Room 8, to which it forms an inner chamber, while its mosaic floor indicates a room of similar status to Room 7. Most of the mosaic had been destroyed over the centuries and parts of it had collapsed into the hypocaust, but some large fragments survived (Fig. 53) (Cosh & Neal 2005, 242), as well as coarse red *tesserae*.

50 THE MAIN HOUSE (SITE D)

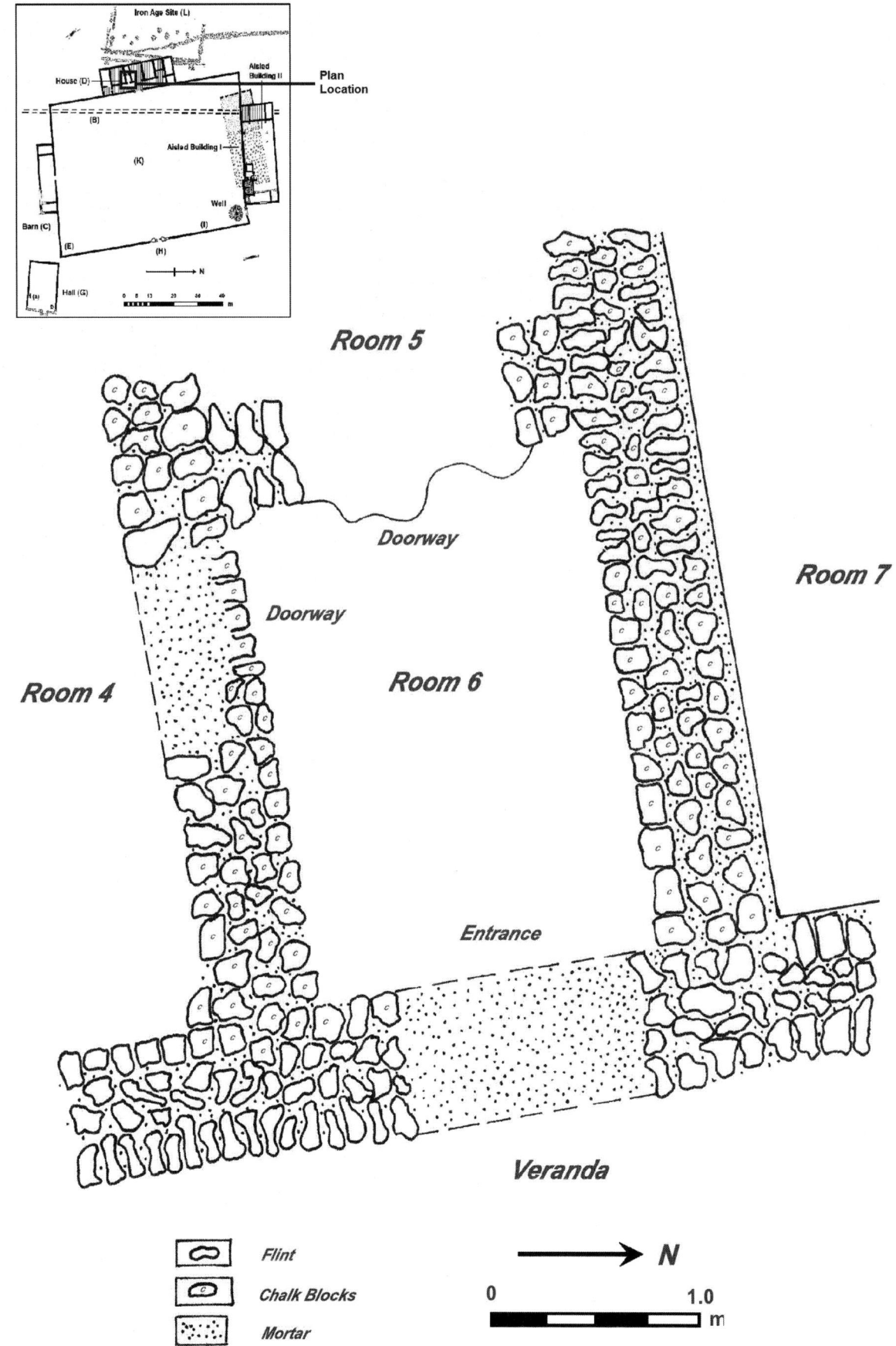

Fig 47 Plan of Room 6 (drawn by JD, based on original by CC)

Fig 48   Room 7 floor layers (photographed 1969)

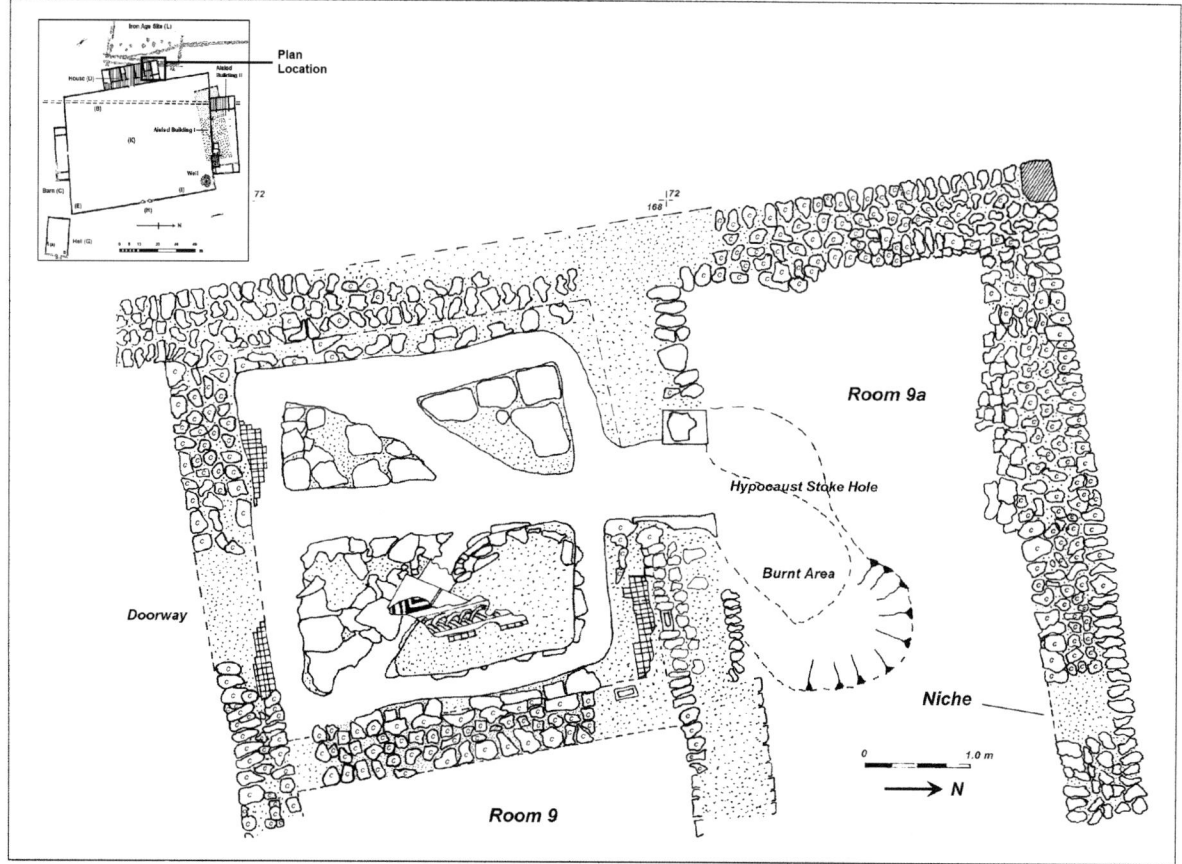

Fig 49   Plan of Room 9a and Room 11 (drawn by JD, based on original by CC)

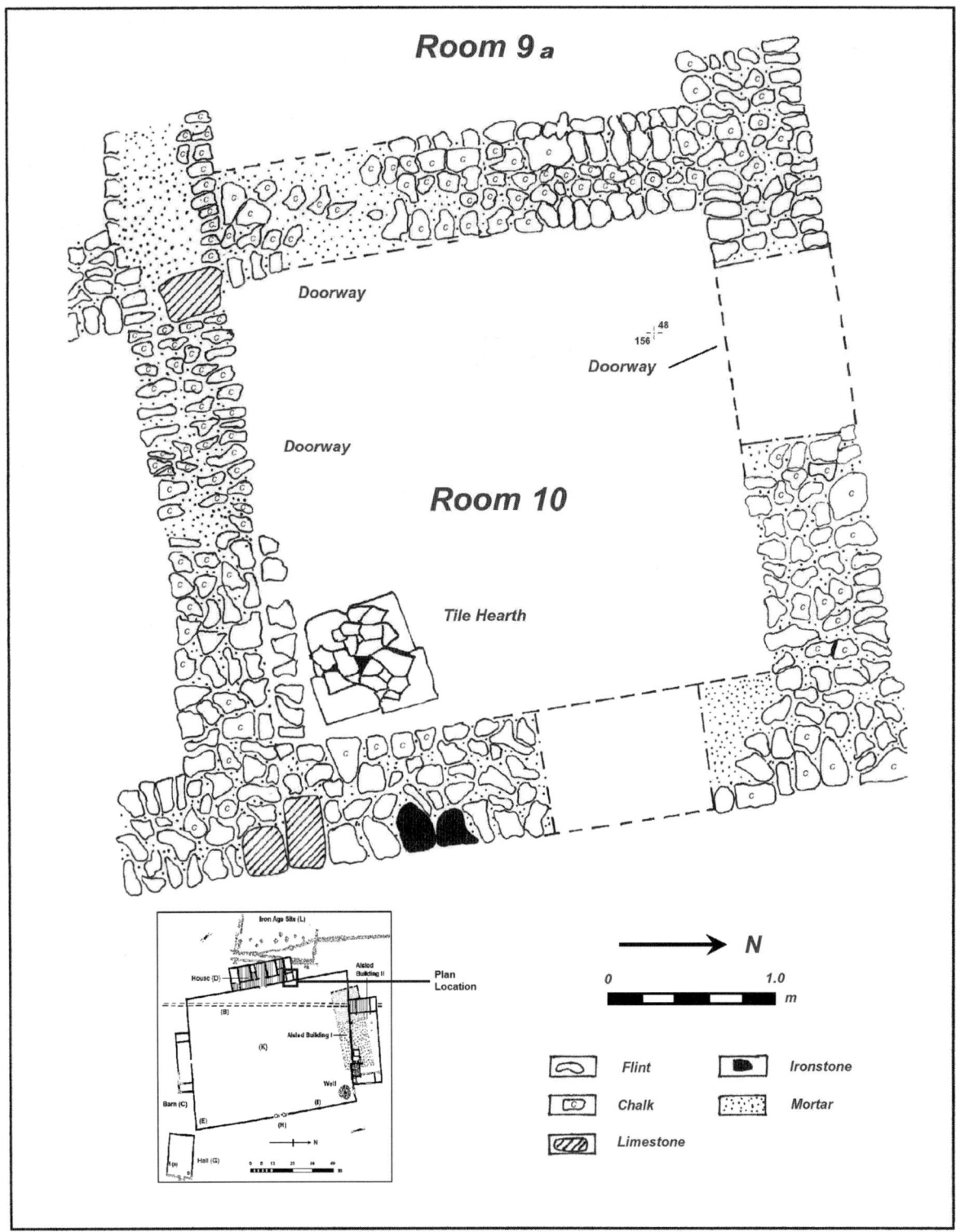

Fig 50   Plan of Room 10 (drawn by JD, based on original by CC)

Fig 51 Possible hearth in Room 10 (photographed 1966)

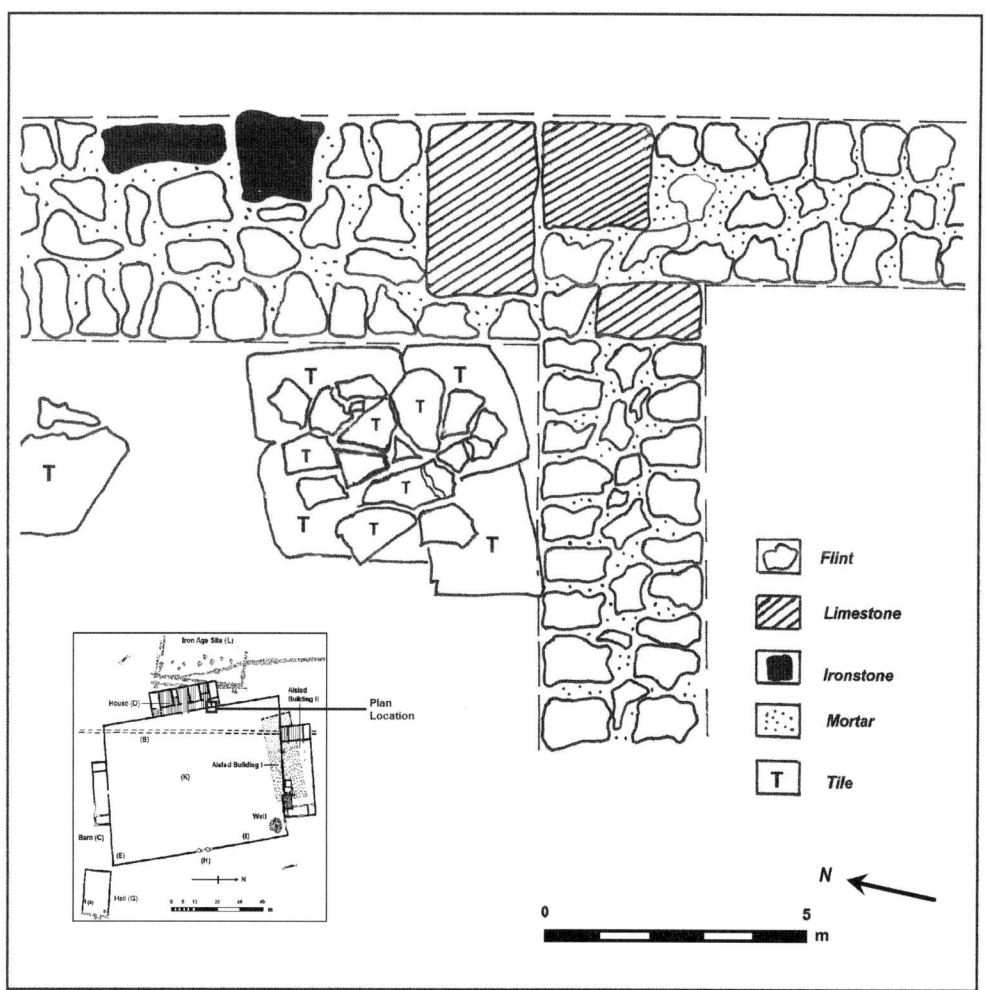

Fig 52 Hearth and butt joint of the corner of the north wing (drawn by JD, based on a sketch in a site note book)

Fig 53   Part of the border of the mosaic in Room 11 (photographed 1967)

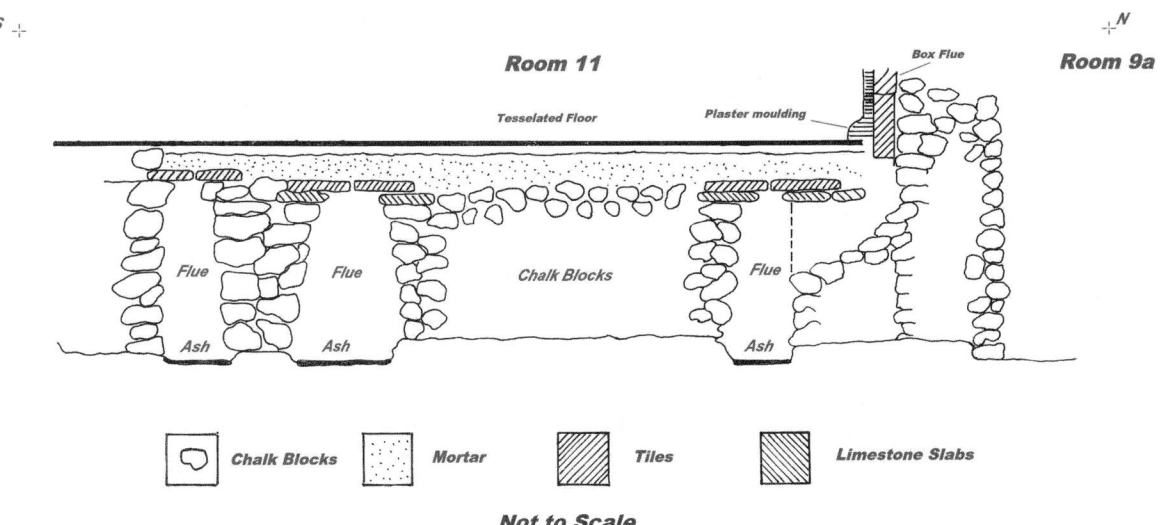

Fig 54   Section through hypocaust flues in Room 11 (drawn by JD, based on original by DEJ)

To install the hypocaust the entire room had been excavated to a depth of 0.60 m, destroying the evidence of earlier floors. The hypocaust supports were constructed from chalk capped with limestone slabs. Some of these were also built into the walls for additional stability. Bricks formed the final capping and the whole arrangement was capped with mortar (Fig. 54).

Vertically aligned box flue tiles survived set into the wall at the north-east corner of the room (Fig. 55) and presumably there were similar flues in the other corners. Fragments of flue tiles were discovered in the rubble and wall cavities below floor level.

A coin (SF 22) of Tetricus I (AD 271–74) was recovered from the ash layer in the hypocaust and the area also produced a large assemblage of pottery (691 sherds), the majority of which came from stratified contexts. Among the fine wares were indented beakers from the New Forest, and mortaria from both the New Forest and Oxfordshire. There were

Fig 55   View of Room 11 showing hypocaust box flues (photographed 1967)

several vessel forms that had ceased to be produced by the mid 4th century, such as Fulford Type 97 jars and Fulford Type 105 mortaria. The grey wares included bowls, dishes, jars and jugs, the majority from the New Forest and Dorset BB1 industries, and all were mid 3rd to late 4th century types. Other finds include fragments of window glass and painted wall plaster in saffron and red with splashes of black, red and white.

A disturbed area near the west wall of Room 11 may mark the location of the 1895 excavation (p.6).

Associated pits, ditches and middens

Pit V

Pit V, located to the north of the House (Fig. 56), was 2 m in diameter and 1.30 m deep; it cut the edge of Ditch IV. The contents of the pit were mainly pottery and animal bones. The uppermost fill contained two iron staples (SF 287 and 329) and the pit produced 118 sherds including a piece of New Forest red-slipped ware bowl (Fulford Type 61) dating to c. AD 340–70, which indicates that the pit was open in the mid-4th century AD.

Pit XIX

Pit XIX, which cut into Ditch II (Fig. 56), was 3.50 m from the north-west corner of the House. It was oval in shape measuring 3.50 m by 2.50 m, but was only 1m deep. The upper fill contained a glass object (SF 467), possibly the head of a large pin, but most of finds were of pottery. The assemblage was late Romano-British and comprised a uniform range of fabrics and forms. The high proportion of Late Roman grog-tempered ware (36%) might suggest a later 4th century date for this feature.

Pit XX

This was a deep rectangular pit, with near vertical sides measuring 2.35 m by 2.80 m, with a depth of 2.30 m (Figs 56 & 57). It was less than 2m from the south-west corner of the House and was cut by Ditch IV. The primary silt (10) was ashen in colour and contained pottery, bronze and iron objects, and a fine moulded glass bowl (SF 570) (p.156–157). Later layers (9, 8 and 7) represented a gradual accumulation of organic refuse, fine and slightly sandy in texture. A near complete skeleton of a fox (p.182) and a *barbarous radiate* coin (SF 502) dated c. AD 270–80 were found in layer 8. The upper fill of the pit consisted of building debris, including roof tiles, slates, flints, fragments of painted wall plaster and *tesserae*, and yielded three coins (SF 533, 586 and 594 – two *barbarous radiates* and one illegible) dated c. AD 270–80. Fragments of several bone pins were also recovered from this feature.

A wide range of animal bones were found in the pit, representing several species of which sheep/goats dominate, followed by cattle and pigs. The majority

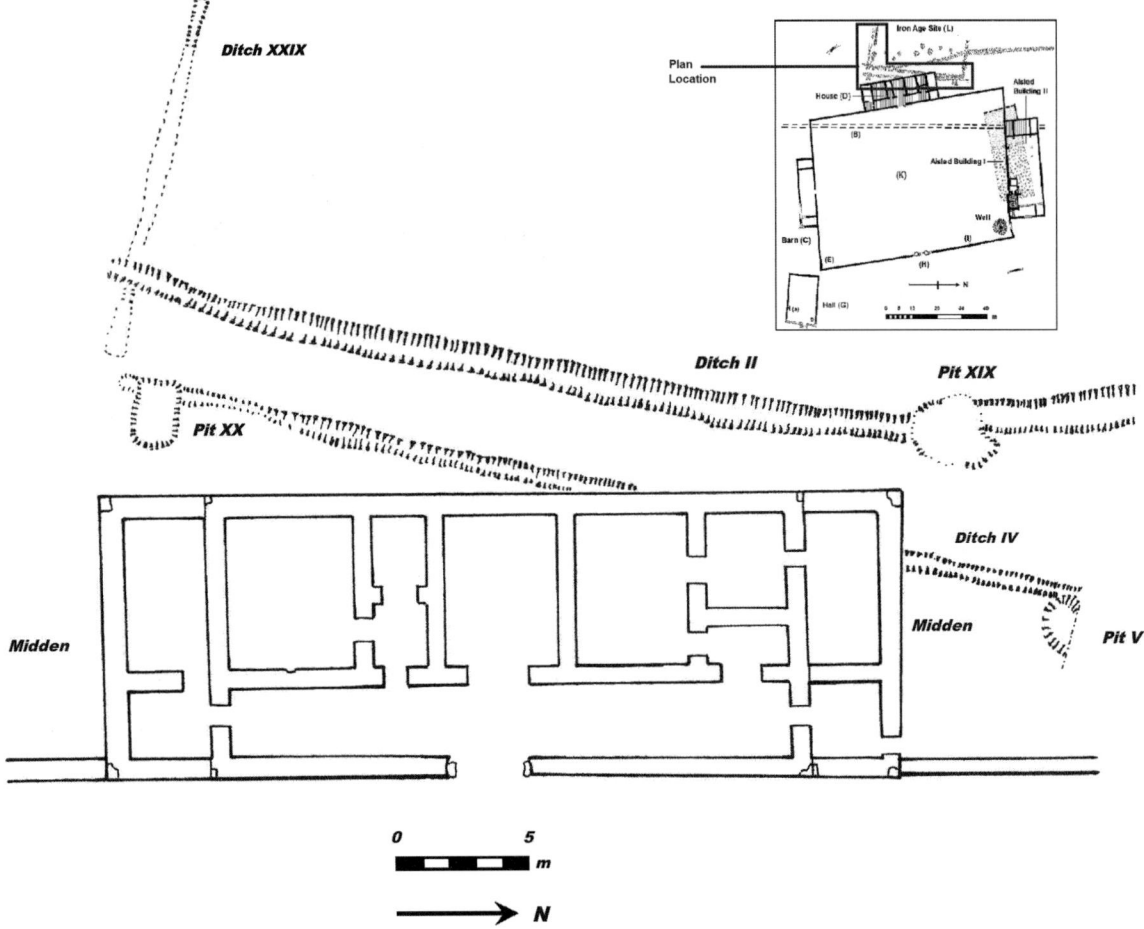

Fig 56 Plan of Roman ditches and pits in the vicinity of the Main House (drawn by JD)

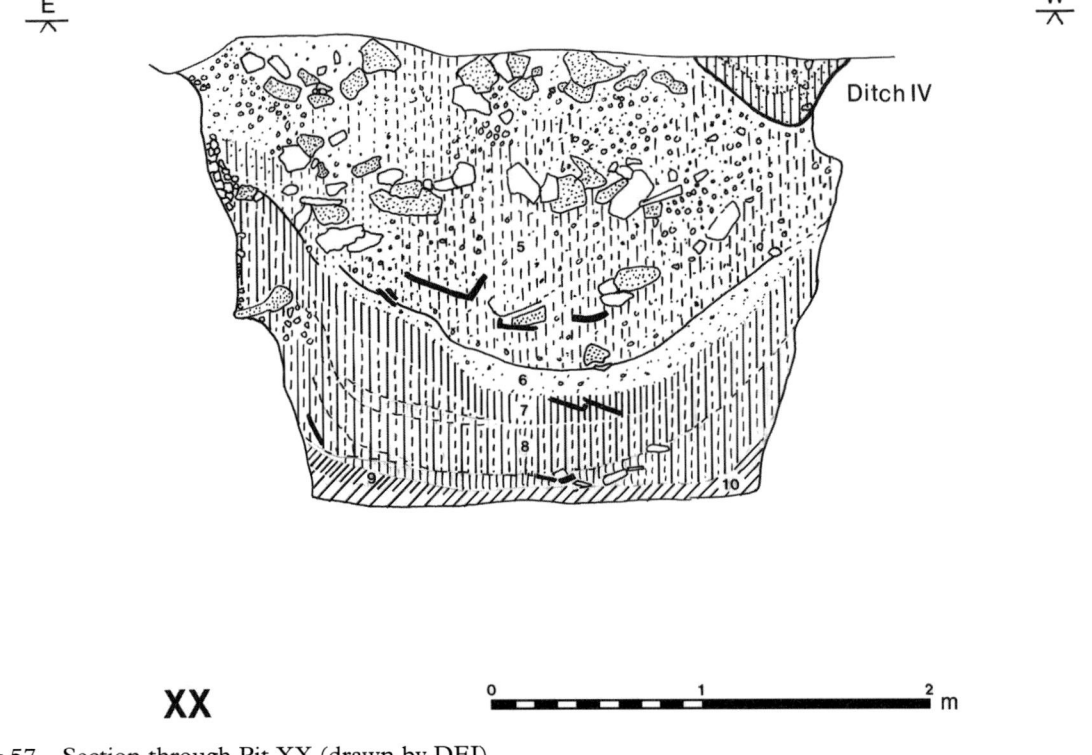

Fig 57 Section through Pit XX (drawn by DEJ)

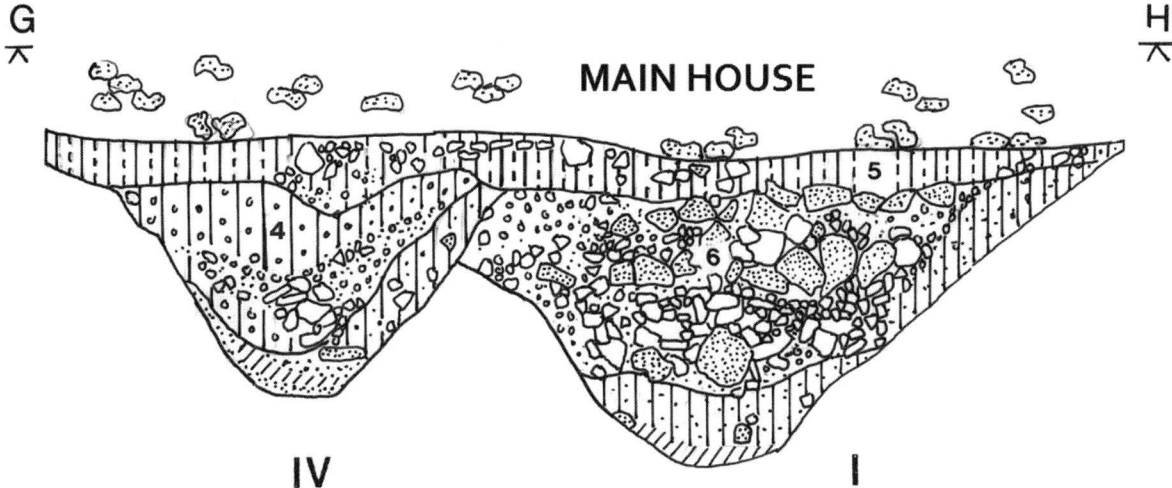

Fig 58 Section of Ditches I and IV at the junction with the north wall of House (drawn by DEJ)

of the sheep/goats and pig bones show cut marks suggesting that they could have been butchered on site (p.187).

The pit produced a large assemblage (2,499 sherds) of late Romano-British pottery. A single Central Gaulish black-slipped ware base and rims from three Central Gaulish samian (Dragendorff form 33) cups, all of late 2nd to 3rd century date, were residual finds. The British fine wares were dominated by New Forest colour-coated wares, predominately indented beakers, but also bag-shaped and globular-bodied beakers, flagons and red-slip ware bowls. Indented beakers were made throughout the life of the New Forest industry, but the other beakers belong to the 4th century.

Ditch I and Ditch IV

The House was built across the line of two ditches. Ditch I was part of the Iron Age enclosure (p.12). It must have been visible when the House was constructed, but that did not deter the builders although they (or their successors) had to underpin the north wall to prevent it subsiding into the feature (Fig. 58). The ditch produced quantities of Iron Age flint-tempered pottery. Late 3rd to late 4th century New Forest wares had accumulated in its uppermost levels, presumably as a result of subsidence.

Ditch IV was not part of the Iron Age occupation but had probable links with Ditch XXIX (see below). It had a V-shaped profile and was 0.60 m wide but only 0.50 m deep. It was shallower at the southern end where it reappeared from under the House. The only finds of note were a few sherds of grog-tempered ware of Late Roman date.

Ditch II

This ditch was to the west of the house (Fig. 56). It was fairly straight but gave the impression of having been dug in short sections of varying accuracy. It was also of variable width and only 0.45 m deep. The chalky fill suggested natural weathering. It produced a large assemblage of 491 sherds of late 3rd to late 4th century pottery including New Forest grey ware bowls (Fulford Type G6), jars (Fulford Type 30) and dishes (Fulford Type 19). Among the fine wares were flagons (Fulford Type 93) (Fig. 90, 19) and bowls (Fulford Type 89) in a parchment fabric dated to c. AD 320–40 (Fulford 1975, 72). A sherd recovered from the primary ditch fill (from a Type G6 bowl with part of a graffiti inscription) matched two conjoining sherds from the primary fill of Pit XX (Fig. 91, 42).

Ditch XXIX

Ditch XXIX was probably contemporary with Ditch IV, each forming one side of a rectangular enclosure. It was a precisely dug U-shaped feature, 0.45 m wide (Fig. 56). It produced quantities of animal bone and a few late 3rd to late 4th century sherds, including a fragment of New Forest colour-coated beaker.

Ditch 603

This ditch, which produced burnt flint and one Roman sherd, may have been part of the field system.

Ditch 604

This V-shaped ditch also contained a little Roman material.

Middens

On the north, west and south sides of the Main House were large quantities of domestic rubbish, including Romano-British pottery, coins and other occupation debris. The most substantial deposit was a midden to the south of the building, which contained a coin of Tetricus I (AD 270–80), pottery and other material. The pottery assemblage included jars, bowls and dishes from the New Forest kilns, all late 3rd to late 4th century, echoing the dating evidence from the House itself.

Overview

Nine coins were found during the excavation of the Main House. Three were unstratified, and a coin of Claudius (AD 41–54) found in a shallow pit in the corner of Room 5, may represent a foundation burial employing a family heirloom over two hundred years after it was issued. The other five coins, found on the floors of various rooms, reveal that the central core of the building was constructed in the mid to late 3rd century and the north and south wings were added a little later, a conclusion supported by the constructional evidence.

Among the improvements made to the House was the laying of the mosaic in Room 7. Stylistically, this pavement can be dated to the first quarter of the 4th century AD (Cosh & Neal 2005) and corroborative evidence comes from pottery found in the hypocaust, including a complete New Forest pedestal bowl (Fulford Type 17) dated AD 300–50, which may have been a deliberately placed deposit.

The changes to the building may indicate the increasing affluence of the owners and their desire to embrace the Roman way of doing things. The large central room with the decorative mosaic was only accessible from the Corridor and must represent an audience chamber. Room 11, on the other hand, which was heated and may have been either a dining room or bedroom, was only accessible through Room 8 an arrangement that controlled access and provided privacy. A similar arrangement can be seen at Bignor, West Sussex (Frere 1982).

Chapter 5

The Barn (Site C)

This building was situated on the southern side of the site, where the ground slopes gently to the east. It was visible as a mound comprising a dense layer of flints, limestone slates and slabs. It was first investigated during trial trenching (E1) in 1965 and was fully excavated in 1968 and 1969. The 'box excavation' involved 16 hand-dug 3m^2 trenches, but the baulks were later removed creating an open area. The rectangular building measuring approximately 26 m by 7.30 m (Figs 59 & 60) was defined as a barn on the basis of its simple layout and similarity to other known examples, such as Building 4 at Chilgrove 2, West Sussex (Down 1979, 92), and barns at Dunkirt Barn (Cunliffe & Poole 2008c) and Stroud (Moray-Williams 1909), both in Hampshire.

The north wall of the Barn formed part of the Courtyard Wall. The central room (Room 21) was approximately 16.90 m by 5.95 m, with two 3 m wide rooms (20 and 22) at either end (Fig. 59). Room 21 was entered through a cart-sized entrance, 1.8 m wide, in the north wall. The western room (22) was accessed from the Courtyard by a smaller door, approximately 1 m wide.

The foundations were not investigated but it seems reasonable to assume that in common with the other buildings trenches were used. The walls were solidly constructed of mortared flints and although much robbed in places they survived to a height of six courses (Fig. 61). The flints were laid laterally to the direction of the walls and in places appear to have been faced. In the interior there was evidence of mortar render, but no indication that the walls had been painted.

The outer walls of the building were approximately 0.60 m thick and had Bembridge limestone blocks, approximately 0.30 m^2, at the corners (Fig. 62). The partition walls were 0.50 m thick and had been keyed into the northern and southern walls indicating that the building was of a single construction. The Courtyard Wall abutted the Barn (Figs 62 & 63), demonstrating that the walling of the Courtyard post-dated the construction of the building.

The entrance to the Barn was marked by large limestone slabs, creating a threshold exactly halfway along the northern wall. Mortar had been laid directly onto this threshold and set into it were flints and broken limestone roof tiles – probable evidence that the entrance had been blocked (Fig. 64). If correct, it is difficult to understand how access was obtained. There was an entrance from the Courtyard into Room 22 but this would not have provided access to the main hall.

No evidence for a floor was identified in the central room (Room 21), although a layer, probably of beaten chalk and flints, may have sufficed. Nothing was cut into this layer and internally the room was bereft of features. The floor of the eastern room (Room 20) comprised a spread of mortar overlaid by a scatter of broken limestone roof slates; again there were no associated features. This flooring was over an earlier level of beaten chalk. In Room 22 a beaten chalk surface lay above the natural clay-with-flints and had been replaced by a surface comprising discarded Purbeck limestone tiles. This layer sealed a coin of Tetricus I (AD 271–74). A layer (8) of dark humic soil, which contained flecks of charcoal on top of the tiled surface, is interpreted as evidence of occupation. A large quantity of Purbeck limestone tiles in the demolition rubble denotes a tiled roof. There were, however, large quantities of ceramic *tegulae* and *imbrex* outside the north and south walls of Room 21 suggesting that this part may have been re-roofed with red tiles.

The majority of the pottery was recovered from unstratified contexts, either outside the Courtyard Wall or in the Courtyard, but a single sherd from an imported Trier black-slipped beaker, with the characteristic rouletted design (SPCJW), was discovered under the mortared floor in Room 20. This can be dated to c. AD 180-250 and indicates a date for the floor of the early to mid-3rd century AD.

Room 22 contained the largest amount of pottery (41 sherds). All can be assigned to the late 3rd to late 4th century AD; products of New Forest kilns, which were in use from c. AD 270 to 400, dominate the assemblage. A relatively high number of sherds were recovered from the probable occupational deposits, suggesting that Room 22 provided domestic accommodation.

A small amount of animal bone was recovered from an unknown location. The majority belonged to juvenile sheep/goats, in addition to the scattered remains of cattle and a large quantity of maxillary and mandibular teeth from adult sheep/goats. The juvenile sheep/goats were probably butchered for their meat. Overall, the small quantity of bone could

THE BARN (SITE C)

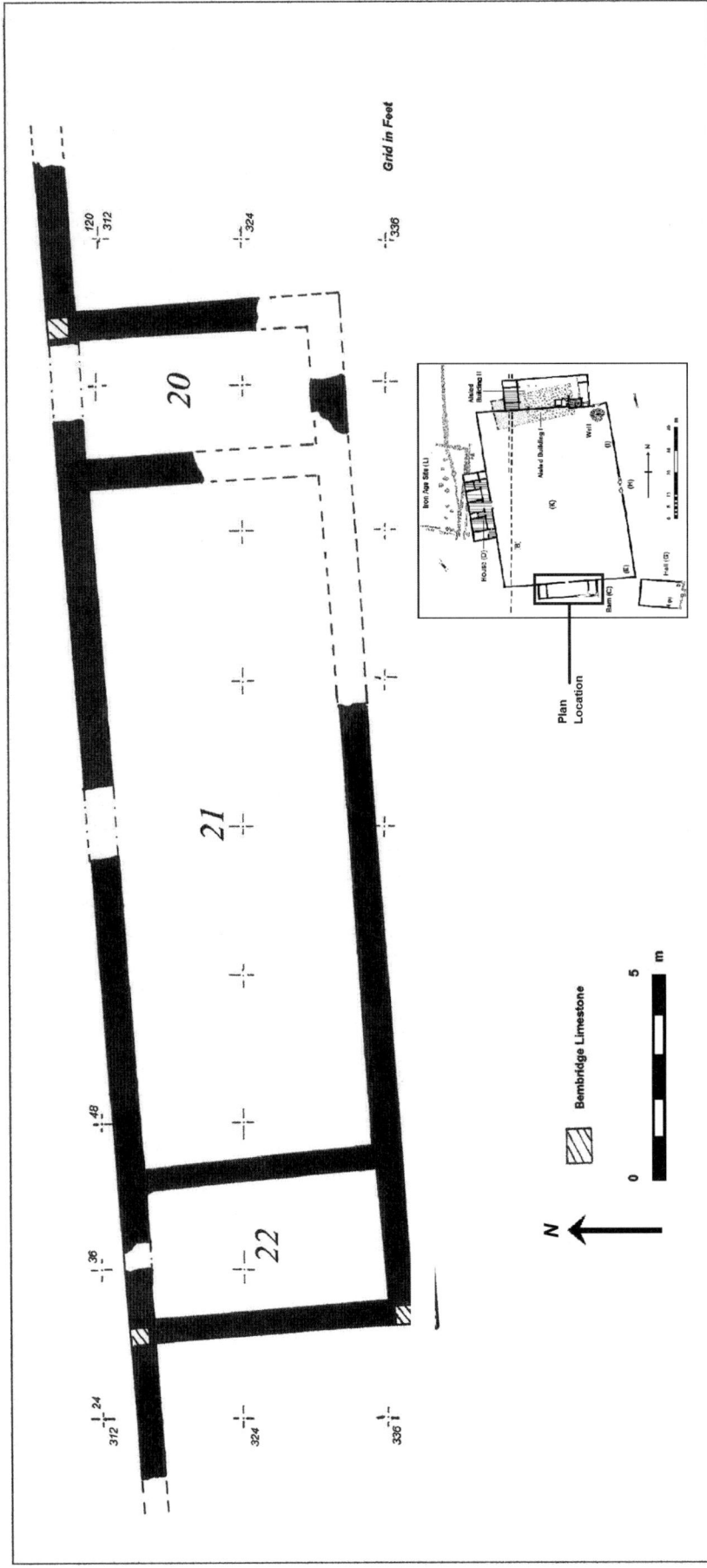

Fig 59   Outline plan of the Barn (drawn by JD)

Fig 60   General view of the Barn under excavation, looking west (photographed 1969)

Fig 61   North-east corner of Room 21 (photographed 1969)

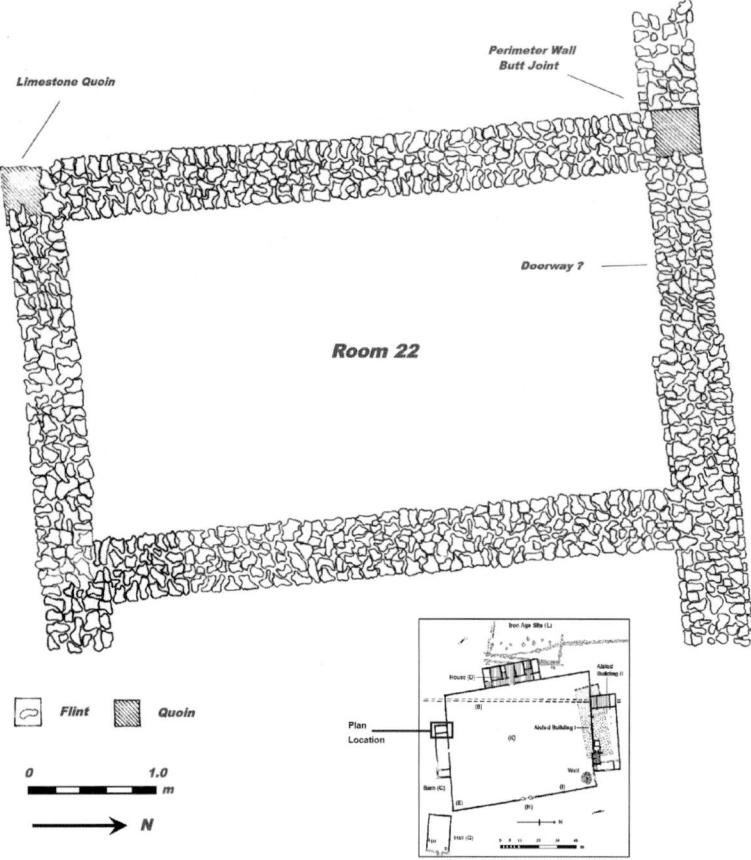

Fig 62　Junction of the wall of the Barn with the Courtyard wall (Drawn by JD)

Fig 63　The north-west corner of the Barn showing the abutted Courtyard wall (photographed 1969)

Fig 64   The blocked entrance to Room 21, looking south (photographed 1969)

have come from the sporadic dumping of material from other parts of the site and probably indicates that little, if any, processing took place in the building. The teeth, however, may have derived from ante-mortem tooth loss from sheep/goats stabled in the building.

Metalwork finds were restricted to four objects and cannot help identify the purpose of the building, although the general dearth of material suggests that it was systematically stripped of its fixtures and fittings.

Overview

The robustly constructed walls and tiled roof indicate a substantial masonry structure. Pottery, and the single stratified coin, suggests a period of usage during the mid-3rd to mid-4th century AD. A construction date around the mid-3rd century is likely and the structure was probably abandoned with the other buildings in the later 4th century.

The relationship of the Courtyard Wall to the Barn demonstrates that the Courtyard was walled after the construction of the Barn. This is supported by the fact that the walls of the Barn and Courtyard differed in their styles of construction. Moreover the walls of the Barn were built entirely of flints, in contrast to the other buildings that had been constructed from flints and chalk blocks. The difference may be chronological: it pre-dates the Courtyard Wall and is therefore earlier than Aisled Building II and probably the Main House. The small assemblage of 2nd-century AD samian pottery from unstratified layers by the Hall, which may have originally been associated with the Barn, is therefore potentially significant.

The Barn was probably associated with agriculture, but its precise function is unknown. The absence of corn-drying ovens and other internal features indicates that it may have housed stock, although the lack of drainage argues against this idea. Alternatively, it may have been used for the storage of equipment, a notion that is supported by the width of the entrance. The two entrances to the Barn were from the Courtyard, suggesting a strong association with this area and the activities conducted within it. The separate entrance to Room 22, in conjunction with the occupational-type deposits, suggests that it was used for domestic occupation, perhaps by farm workers.

There was no sign that the building had been destroyed or systematically demolished; rather it seems to have been abandoned and allowed to collapse. The fact that the main entrance was blocked suggests a transformation in how the building was utilised. It may indicate that at some point in the 4th century the central part of the building had deteriorated to such an extent that it was no longer safe to use.

Chapter 6

The Hall (Site G)

The Hall (Site G (Fig. 65)) was investigated through a series of eight hand-excavated trenches (G1–8) over three seasons (1968, 1970 and 1971). The building was located just outside the south-east corner of the Courtyard on the upper slopes of the dry valley and alongside the track that swung southwards to meet the main Winchester to Old Sarum road (p.2). Over the centuries the site had been badly affected by soil erosion but more recently the activities of the Forestry Commission posed a greater threat. Not only had the area been mechanically levelled but slots were cut in preparation for tree planting, which truncated the archaeology and made its interpretation problematic. A 1933 halfpenny (SF 109) found during the excavation probably belongs to this activity.

The stone foundations of a rectangular building, approximately 18 m by 12 m, were uncovered (Fig. 66), although much of the eastern wall had gradually eroded down the valley slope. The walls were 0.70 m thick and seem to have been laid directly onto the chalk bedrock; in places, however, broken limestone roof slates appear to have been used to create a level surface. The walls were constructed of two rows of flints with chalk packing between. The external wall flints were faced and produced a particularly fine edge, but no more than one course had survived.

Bembridge limestone blocks, measuring 0.38 m by 0.46 m and similar to those found at the corners of the Courtyard Wall, were discovered at both the north-west and the north-east corners of the building (Fig. 67). It is likely that similar blocks were originally built into the other corners.

The entrance to the building was in the eastern wall and was defined by two large flint-packed post-holes 0.70 m^2 and 0.90 m deep. Two steps had been cut into the hillside to facilitate access to this doorway.

Despite the damage to the building it was possible to identify the floor and some of the features that had been set into it. The surface was very variable and inconsistent and was composed of a cobbled layer of flints and ceramic tiles set in a thin layer of red clay. One of the few recognisable features was an arrangement of discoloured tiles/bricks (404) in the south-east corner, which is interpreted as a small hearth, roughly 0.30 m^2 (Fig. 68).

Cut into the floor in the opposing corner was an oven constructed from limestone blocks and tiles/bricks (Figs 69 & 70). It was roughly circular with a square end and measured 1.10 m by 0.95 m, but did not have a stoke hole. The reddish discolouration of the limestone blocks suggests that the temperatures reached in the hearth and the oven were not extreme, demonstrating that both were probably associated with domestic use, rather that industrial activities.

Near the foundation of the southern wall was a small shallow grave, essentially a scoop (Fig. 71), which contained the bones of possibly five neonates (p.170–172). There is evidence that the grave was disturbed and that the remains had possibly been reinterred from elsewhere possibly as part of a foundation ritual. Radiocarbon dates produced a relatively broad date range of the mid-3rd to late 4th century AD. Although it is not unusual to find infants and foetuses buried below Roman buildings it is relatively rare to encounter multiple interments in a single grave (Cocks 1920–21; Moore 2009, 33–54).

The insubstantial foundations and the limited amount of flint rubble suggest that the Hall was probably timber-framed and rested on low mortared walls. It appears, however, that much of the masonry had been reclaimed from the other villa buildings. Also amongst the demolition rubble was a large quantity of Purbeck limestone slates suggesting a tiled roof.

No securely stratified evidence was available to date the construction of the building. Five coins were recovered from the demolition rubble. The earliest was a *denarius* of Elagabalus (AD 218–22) and the latest was an imitation of a coin of Claudius II (AD 270–80). The majority of the pottery was of the late 3rd to late 4th century and came from unstratified layers, probably domestic refuse from the main villa. There was, however, a very small amount of earlier material, mainly 2nd-century samian, which could have been residual from the occupation of either AB I or the Barn.

The animal bones demonstrate that sheep/goat and cattle were the most abundant species, followed by horse, but there were very few bones from any other animal. Some fallow and red deer are present, however, including a number of red deer antlers: two appear to have been collected, while the third is a probable sawn-off tine point. The evidence is typical

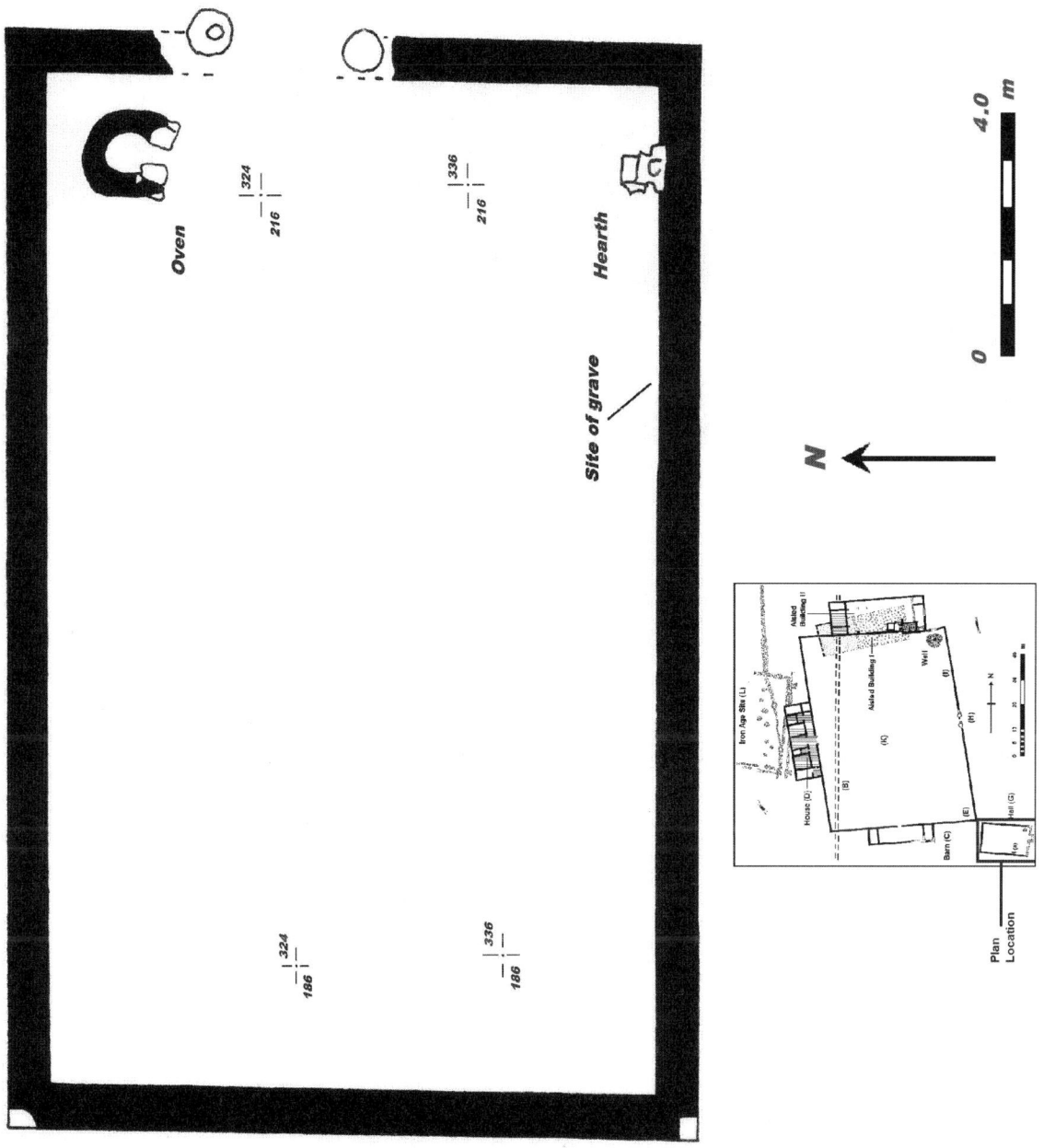

Fig 65 Outline plan of the Hall (drawn by JD)

THE HALL (SITE G)

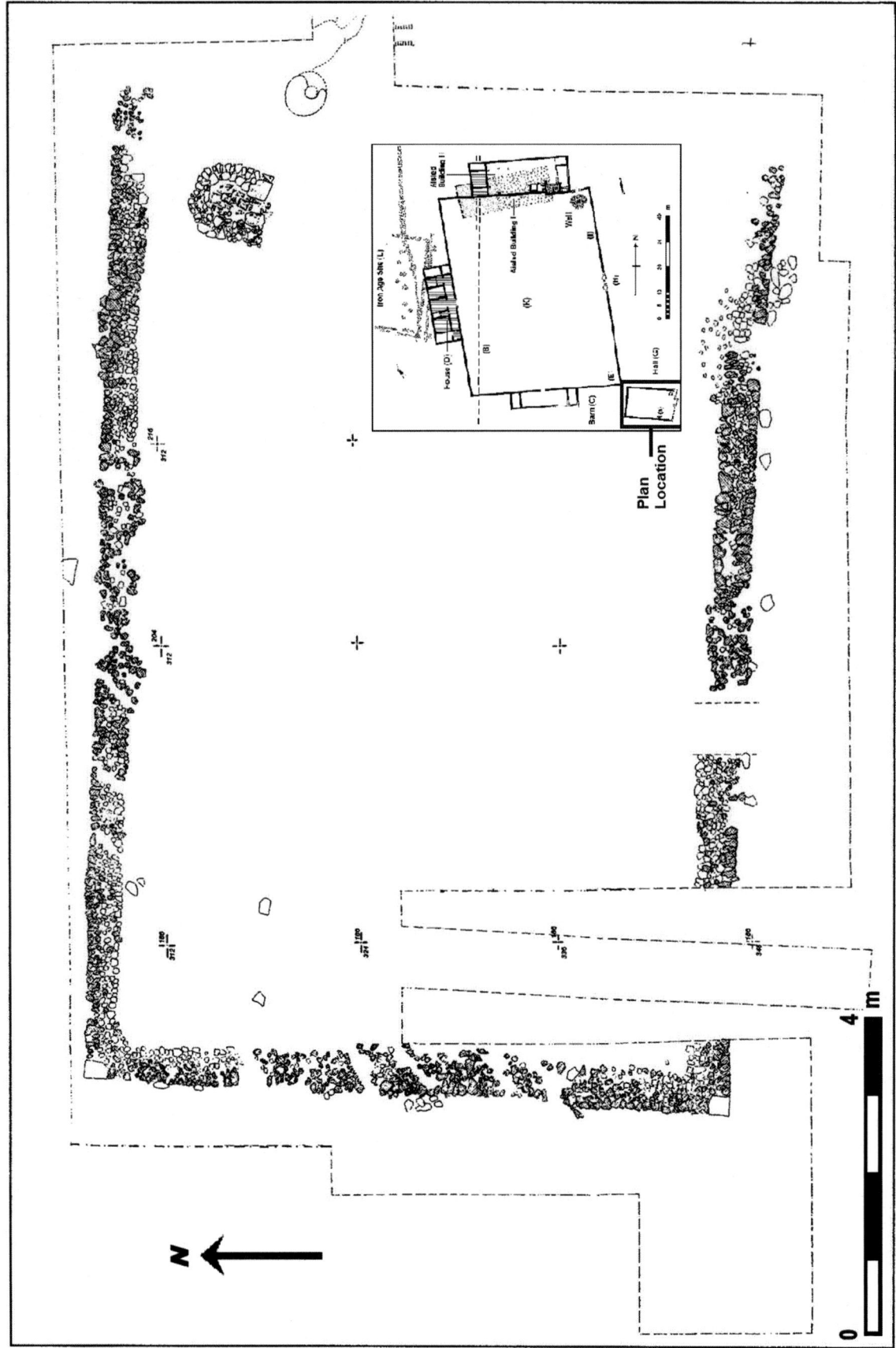

Fig 66   Detailed plan of the Hall (drawn by CC)

Fig 67   North-west corner of the Hall (photographed 1970)

Fig 68   Tiled hearth against the wall of the Hall (photographed 1970)

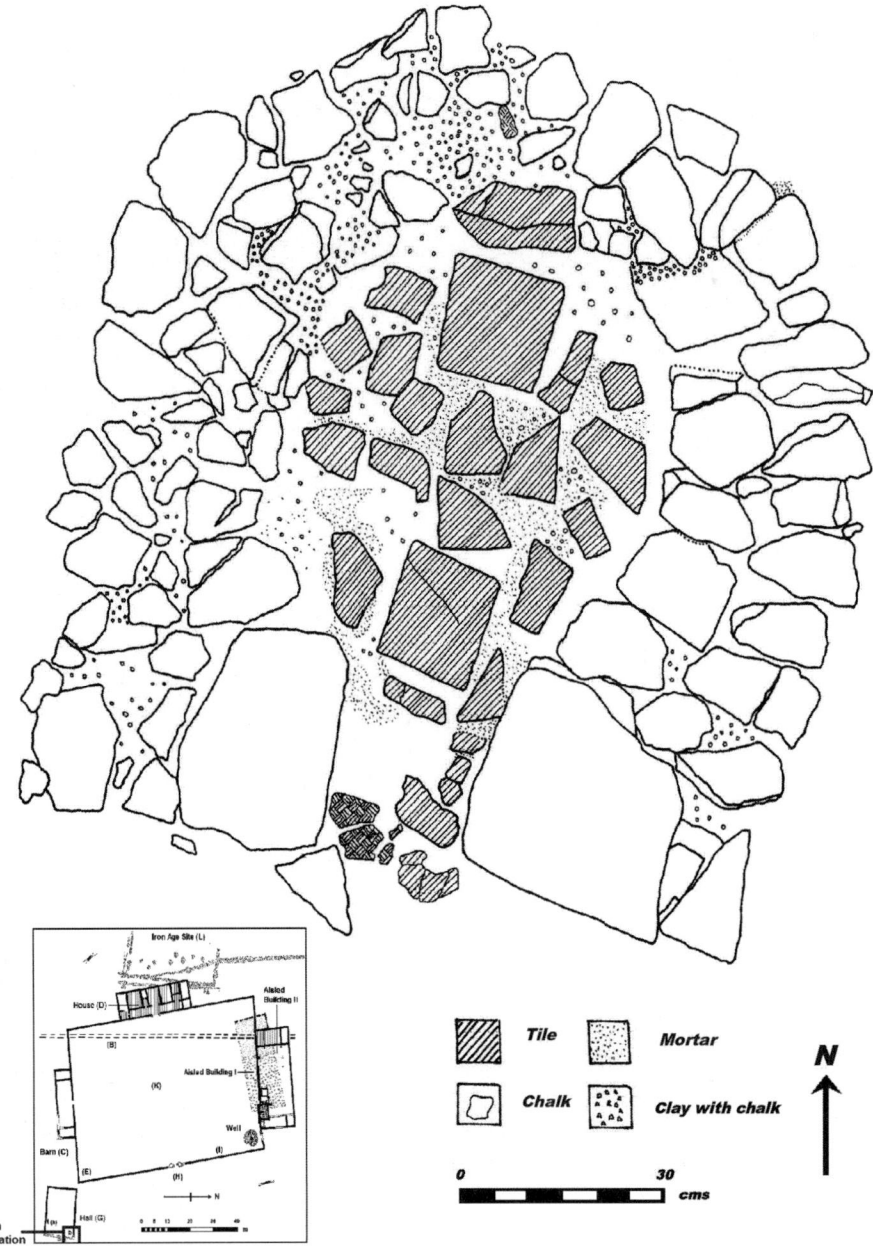

Fig 69   Plan of the oven in the Hall (drawn by VH & DJ)

of domestic refuse – a mixture of non-meat bones and bones discarded after the consumption of meat.

The majority of the metalwork from the villa comes from the Hall, but unfortunately the largest group comprises miscellaneous pieces that cannot be readily identified or could have served a range of purposes, such as iron rings and plates. The site, however, produced the greatest number of nails and structural pieces, suggesting that it was not as thoroughly stripped of its fittings as the other buildings.

Overview

The paucity of the archaeology has limited what can be said about the building. Nevertheless, the lack of foundation trenches is in contrast to the situation elsewhere on the site. Overall, the building appears to have been a simple hall-type structure with few, if any, divisions within it. The provision of both an oven and a hearth suggests that it was a domestic building, but the nature of the floor and the lack of wall plaster would have made for a very simple dwelling. There is no evidence to suggest why it was situated outside the Courtyard Wall, although at the courtyard villa at Brading, Isle of Wight, a similar building has been interpreted as a detached kitchen (Tomalin & Hanworth 1998, 17). That the entrance to the Hall probably opened onto the track which connected the villa with the Winchester to Old Sarum road suggests that it may have been sited here for convenience.

Fig 70   Post-excavation view of the oven (photographed 1970)

Fig 71   'Grave' of infant burials (photographed 1970)

No stratified dating evidence was found, but the evidence from the coins and pottery indicates that the building might have been inhabited in the late 3rd to the 4th century AD. The insignificant nature of its construction, in conjunction with its location outside the Courtyard, may indicate that the structure was occupied after the main villa had been abandoned, a date that could be as late as the late 4th century AD. The re-use of building material would support this theory, although there is no evidence to demonstrate where the masonry was actually salvaged from. The structure remains an enigma.

Chapter 7

The Courtyard

The walled Courtyard was rhomboidal in shape. The northern side incorporated the Aisled Building, the southern wall the Barn, and the western wall the Main House. In the midway point of the eastern wall, and directly opposite the Main House, was the entrance to the Courtyard (Fig. 72). The only major feature to be identified in the interior of the Courtyard was the Well.

The Courtyard wall

Introduction

The wall that enclosed the Courtyard connected the otherwise separate buildings. The northern and southern walls were approximately 55 m long; the eastern and western walls approximately 78 m long. The main entrance to the Courtyard was in the middle of the eastern wall and there was a smaller one at the east end of the northern wall.

The eastern wall was sampled in 1965 (Trenches E4–E9) and its extent was established. In 1966 a series of 1.80 m wide trenches were dug over its full length (Fig. 73) and the main entrance to the villa (see below) was revealed.

The southern wall was sampled in 1965 (Trenches E1–4 and C2–3) and again in 1968 as part of the investigation of the Barn (C). Four trenches were dug over the wall and close attention was paid to where it joined the Barn.

The western wall was first investigated in 1966. Four trenches (T18, 23, 30 and 31) were dug which examined the relationship between the wall and the Main House. In 1972, Trench 23 was re-excavated to try to establish the relationship between the southern wing and the Corridor of the House. Additionally, as part of an excavation to the west of the House, a trench was dug to establish the relationship between the Courtyard Wall and the north-east corner of the House.

In 1965 the northern wall was first sampled and an area at the western end of AB II was targeted. In the following year both ends of AB II were excavated (Trenches F1, F2 and F9) and this showed that the Courtyard Wall formed the southern wall of the building. In 1967 the north-east corner of the wall was located (Trench F18), while in 1970 an extension to Trenches 9 and 27 revealed the southern wall of an earlier building (AB I). The area was reinvestigated in 1985 (Trench F38) and this building was found to be integral with an earlier Courtyard Wall. A minor entrance into the Courtyard was also discovered.

Results of the excavation

Each side of the Courtyard Wall demonstrated similar methods of construction: mortared flint nodules set in a chalk-packed foundation trench. Some subtle variations were observed: the flint nodules of the eastern wall were set longitudinal to the line of the wall, while large roughly rectangular flints formed the foundation layer of the southern wall and were followed by smaller flint nodules. The eastern wall was approximately 0.60 m wide, and both this wall and the southern wall were in trenches 0.90 m wide (Fig. 74). By contrast the foundation trench for the western wall was slightly wider at just over 1.00 m.

The preservation of the walls was variable. Parts of the eastern wall had been completely robbed out, but in places up to two strings of flints survived; sections of the southern wall survived to six courses high. At the south-west corner of the southern wall (Trench C2) a large corner stone of Bembridge limestone was discovered which was probably both structural and decorative (Fig. 75). Investigations at the three other corners uncovered large Bembridge ashlar blocks, suggesting that there had also been limestone quoins at each of these too. Demolition rubble along the line of the eastern wall consisted of limestone slabs, ceramic roofing tiles and mortar which suggests that the wall may have been faced with mortar and topped with either limestone or ceramic tiles, or possibly both. There was no evidence that the other walls were similarly treated.

The relationship between the Courtyard Wall and individual buildings was examined, producing important evidence for the development of the villa. The relationship between the Courtyard Wall and the Barn (Site C) was investigated in 1968 and revealed that the northern wall of the building abutted the Courtyard Wall. Limestone foundations had been inserted into the Courtyard Wall to bond it with the Barn. This shows that the Courtyard was enclosed after the construction of this building (p.63).

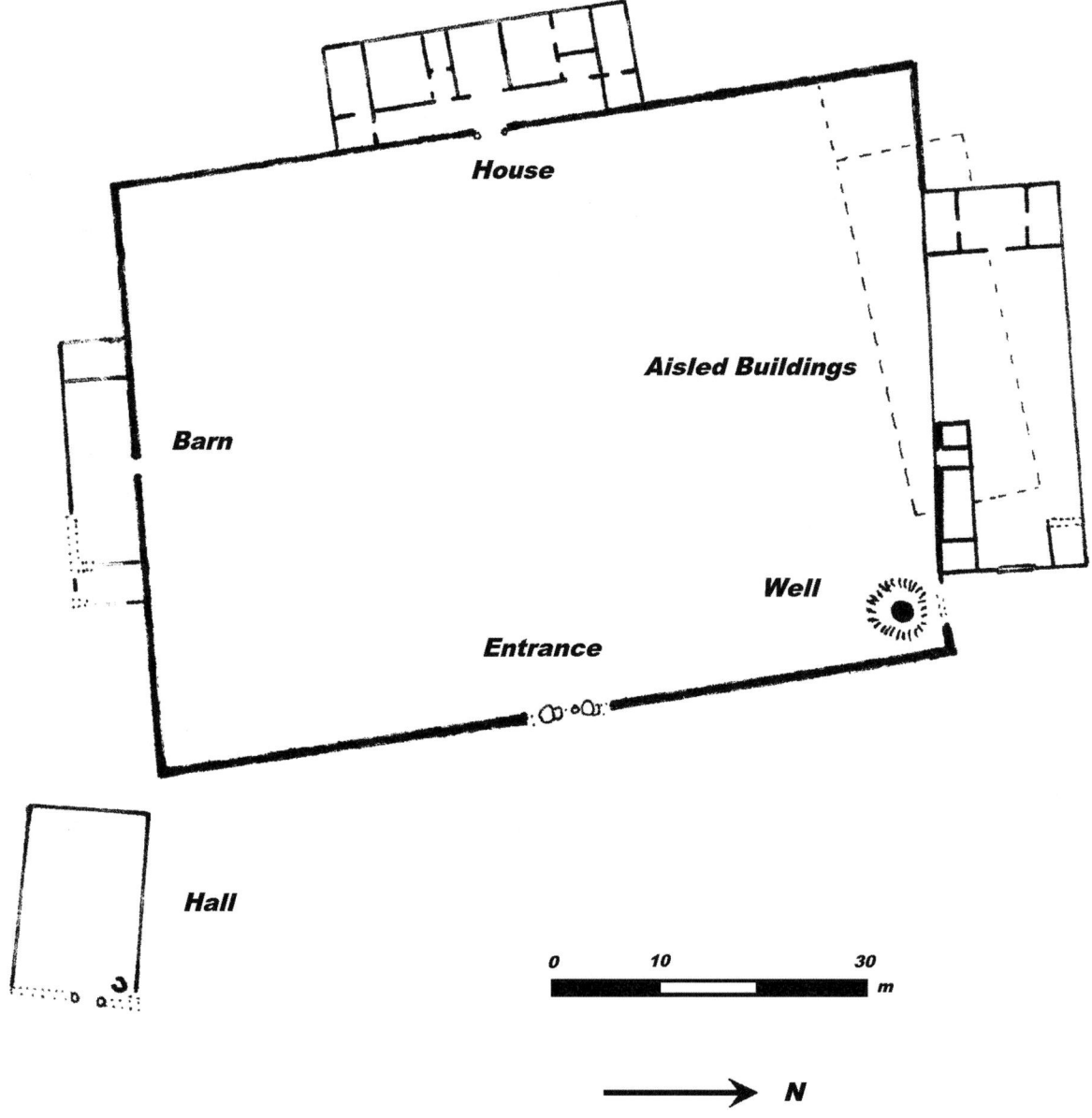

Fig 72   Site plan showing area enclosed by the Courtyard Wall (drawn by JD)

Work on the western wall revealed the association between it and the Main House. Large limestone ashlar blocks had been placed at the corner junctions where the House joined the Courtyard Wall thus delineating the two. The flints of the Courtyard Wall had been aligned longitudinally at right angles to the direction of the wall and carefully laid in mortar, while the trench for the Main House was much deeper (Fig. 76). In particular, the walls for Room 2 and the Corridor were far more substantial than those of the Courtyard Wall.

A complicated sequence of features was investigated during work on the northern Wall. An extension to Trench F9 and Trenches F29, 31 and 32 identified two walls on the southern side of AB II: a flint and chalk wall constructed as part of AB II and to its south an earlier wall which was on a different alignment. Only a few flints and the packed chalk foundation trench of the latter survived. The earlier wall was integral to AB I and was of a similar size and style to the other stretches of the Courtyard Wall, demonstrating that the villa was fully enclosed by at least the mid-3rd century AD. The southern wall of AB II was far more substantial than its predecessor and was constructed of mortared flint nodules with an infilling of chalk blocks. Red tiles and bricks had also been incorporated into its construction. The alignment of AB II resulted in an alteration to the angle of the northern wall and made the Courtyard more rectangular in shape.

Trench F38 located the substantial footings of the northern wall and also identified a large post-hole probably from a gate post (Fig. 77). This gate gave access to the Courtyard and the Well.

Summary

The original area enclosed by the Courtyard Wall was trapezoidal in shape and measured approximately 70 m x 50 m, but the replacement of AB I resulted in the enlargement of the area and a concomitant change to its shape. The northern wall was now at a different angle to the eastern and western walls, resulting in a more rectangular Courtyard. Two entrances afforded access to the Courtyard: through the main gate in the eastern wall (see below), and via a smaller side entrance in the northern wall.

That each stretch of the Courtyard Wall was built in a similar way demonstrates that the villa was walled in one episode over a very short period of time. In fact, re-excavation of the south-east corner in 1966 (Trench E4) indicated that that the eastern and southern walls were constructed at the same time. Very little dating evidence was recovered, however, so it is difficult to ascertain when the Courtyard was enclosed. A coin (SF 89) of Antoninus Pius (AD 138–61) was recovered from unstratified rubble, possibly from an earlier bank/ditch associated with AB I. There is no direct evidence for such an earthwork, however; if there had been one it is assumed that the construction of the masonry wall destroyed all evidence of it.

The walls may have been rendered and capped with either ceramic tiles or limestone slabs and whilst their height is unknown they were certainly substantial and would have made an imposing feature. The walling of the villa complex would have been a significant event in the development of the villa estate and was a clear statement of the wealth and status of the owners.

Walled courtyards villas were not uncommon in southern England. Examples at Bignor (Aldsworth 1983), Binsted (Cole 1988), Chilgrove 2 (Down 1979) and Stroud (Moray-Williams 1909) are all comparable to Sparsholt. These villas comprised a series of separate buildings arranged around a courtyard; the wall brought order and structure to a hitherto unenclosed space and probably acted as a status symbol.

The entrance to the Courtyard

Introduction

In 1966 seven trenches (E3–E9) were dug to establish the eastern limit of the Courtyard Wall. In trenches E7 to E9 no trace of it was found, but the presence of pits filled with disturbed soil was assumed to be evidence of robbing. In 1969 the area was reinvestigated and an 8.4 m by 3.5 m trench revealed a series of intersecting pits that have been interpreted as the remains of at least three separate phases of gates that formed the entrance to the Courtyard (Site H).

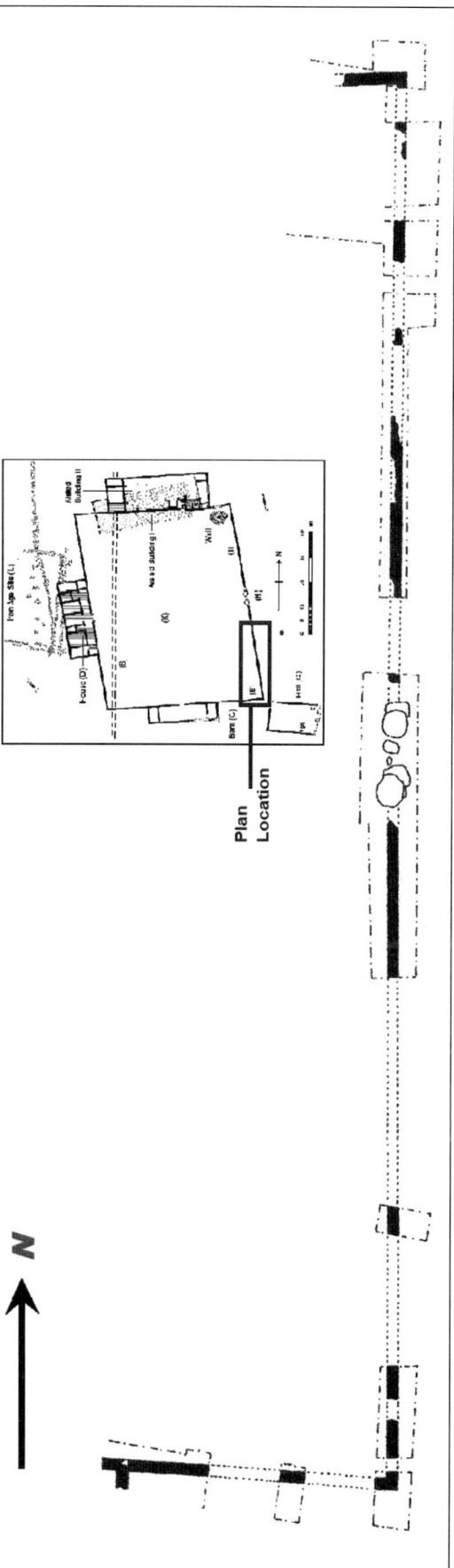

Fig 73 Outline plan of the eastern Courtyard Wall (drawn by JD, based on original by DEJ)

THE COURTYARD

Fig 74 Eastern wall under excavation (photographed 1968)

Results of the excavation

The entrance was in the middle of the eastern stretch of wall and on either side of it were three sets of differently sized post-holes indicating at least three phases (Fig. 78). Phase one was represented by a pair of roughly rectangular post-holes (H1 and H2, contexts 14 and 29, 1.20 m²) approximately 3 m apart and dug into the chalk to a depth 0.91 m (Figs 79 & 80). The holes, which were packed with chalk and flints, would probably have supported a wooden double-leaved gate about 3 m wide; H9, a shallow depression 0.20 m deep, probably represents a gate-post stop.

The post-holes did not produce dating evidence but it seems likely that the gateway was constructed at the same time as the Courtyard was walled. The post-holes had been disturbed by later activity which removed evidence of the post voids. Pottery recovered from the foundation trench of the Courtyard Wall would seem to indicate a 3rd-century date for its construction, with some sherds dating to around the middle of the century.

This first gateway was replaced by a far more substantial structure. In the next phase two large rectangular pits (H3 and H4, contexts 19–23 and 33) cut the earlier post-holes. H3 and H4 were approximately 1.65 m deep and would have supported a very substantial structure with an entrance about 3.0 m wide (Fig. 79). Both post-pits were packed with layers of flints and mortar. No sign of post voids was identified which suggests that it was a masonry gateway, or that massive timber posts rested on stone pads. The construction of large monumental gates would clearly signal the wealth of the owners and, although conjectural, this phase may be contemporary with the construction of the Main House.

Gateways of this size are known from Bignor, West Sussex (Aldsworth 1983), and Stroud, Hampshire (Moray-Williams 1909). David Johnston suggested that the Sparsholt example may have comprised a large arched gateway, but there is no substantive evidence to support this idea except for the size of the pits and the nature of their fills.

This entrance was demolished and replaced by a much simpler double-leaved gate (Phase 3). Two post-holes (H5 and H6, contexts 16 and 19) were set into backfilled post-holes (H3 and H4); both were circular, about 0.70 m in diameter, and were again filled with flints that probably served as packing. The posts were approximately 4 m apart and a smaller post-hole (H8) may have acted as a gate-post stop.

A final modification (Phase 4) was represented by H7 (contexts 16, 17 and 18), a probable replacement for H6 that reduced the width of the gateway to less than 3 m. The only dating evidence comprised three sherds of pottery from a New Forest coloured-coated beaker, which has a long date range extending from c. AD 270 to 400, demonstrating that the entrance continued in use well into the 4th century.

Summary

The entrance to the villa Courtyard has a complex history and could reflect the changing fortunes of the villa owners and more generally the Romano-British economy: a simple wooden gateway was replaced by what was possibly an impressive masonry structure, only to revert once again to a more modest wooden gateway.

Fig 75 South-west corner of the Courtyard Wall (photographed 1965)

While dating evidence was limited, the first gateway was probably constructed along with the Courtyard Wall, in the mid- to late 3rd century AD, and the last would have gone out of use with the villa in the later 4th century AD.

The interior of the Courtyard

Introduction

In 1965, 12 hand-excavated trenches, about 1 m wide and of varying length, were dug across the middle of the Courtyard (Site B). Another ten machine-cut trenches, using a toothed bucket, 0.60 m wide and of various lengths, were dug in 1970 (Site K). Despite the extensive sampling of the Courtyard the only major feature found was a well.

The existence of a well was known and is referenced in *Hampshire Notes and Queries* which states 'a somewhat extensive hollow appears to mark the site of the well' (Godwin 1924, 75). Over the centuries much of the outer rim of the Well had collapsed into the shaft creating a large 'crater' (Fig. 81). The Well was situated in the north-east corner of the Courtyard and was sampled in 1966 (Trench F4) and re-examined in 1968 (Site I). Hampshire River Authority suggested that the Well might be as deep as 61 m (200 ft), an estimate that was based on the depths of the three wells nearest to the villa site (Headworth 1970) and the costs and difficulties associated with an excavation to that depth precluded a full investigation.

Results of the excavation

The crater was excavated in quadrants down to the top of the Well shaft at which point, for safety reasons, the excavation was stopped. The crater was funnel shaped and angular in profile, while the top of the Well shaft was approximately 5.5 m below the surface with a diameter of 1.22 m. Over 70% of the pottery from the crater was from the topsoil, or a layer of rubble immediately below it. All the pottery from the lower layers can be dated to the 4th century AD; in addition there was a coin (SF 135) of the Emperor Constantine II (AD 353–57), which was the only example from the site of common 4th-century coinage minted after AD 330.

The quantity of artefacts recovered from the Courtyard, all of which came from the topsoil, was minimal. One coin (SF 3), an imitation of a coin of the Emperor Claudius II (AD 270–80), was recovered from Trench B8. In addition, there were only 11 sherds of Roman pottery, which had a date range extending from the early 2nd century (Central Gaulish samian) through to the mid-4th century (New Forest colour-coated cup). All this material was unstratified and only indicates that the Courtyard was in use during this period.

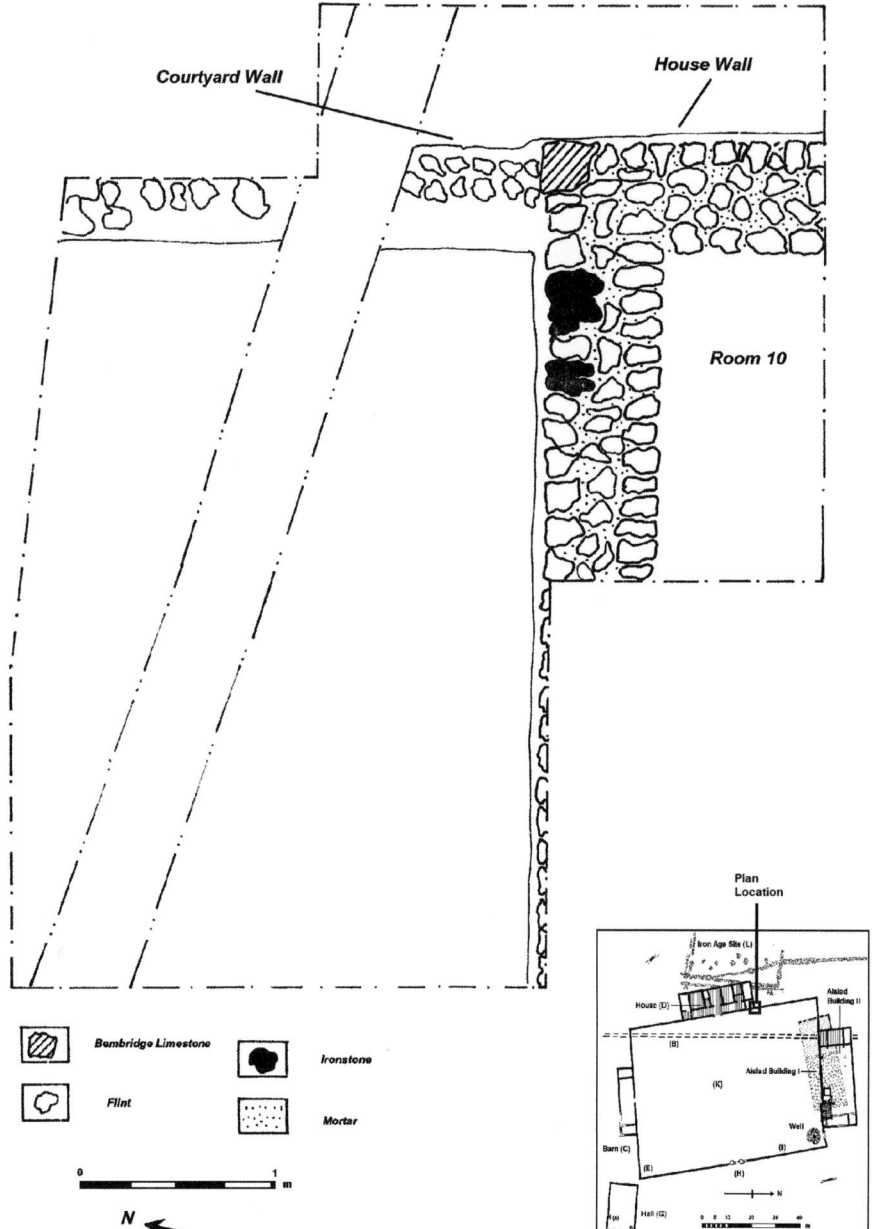

Fig 76 Plan of the junction of the Courtyard Wall and the Main House (drawn by JD, based on a sketch in a site note book)

The surface of the Courtyard appears to have consisted of the natural clay-with-flints and had the appearance of a farmyard rather than a cobbled area or cultivated garden. An amorphous, roughly semi-circular feature (600), which had been partly destroyed by a mechanical digger, was identified. It had the appearance of a natural hole that had started to silt up but which had been topped up with a layer of re-deposited chalk; although it is undated, it may represent a levelling-up of the Courtyard in Roman times.

Summary

As a result of incomplete excavation the date of the Well is unknown, but it is reasonable to assume that it would have been dug to supply the occupants of AB I with water. All the material excavated from the crater of the well head probably derived from the natural erosion that followed the site's abandonment in the mid- to late 4th century AD.

Overview

The term 'courtyard villa' denotes one with domestic rooms on three sides (Smith 1997, 163) as evidenced by the villa at Frocester, Gloucestershire (Price 2000,

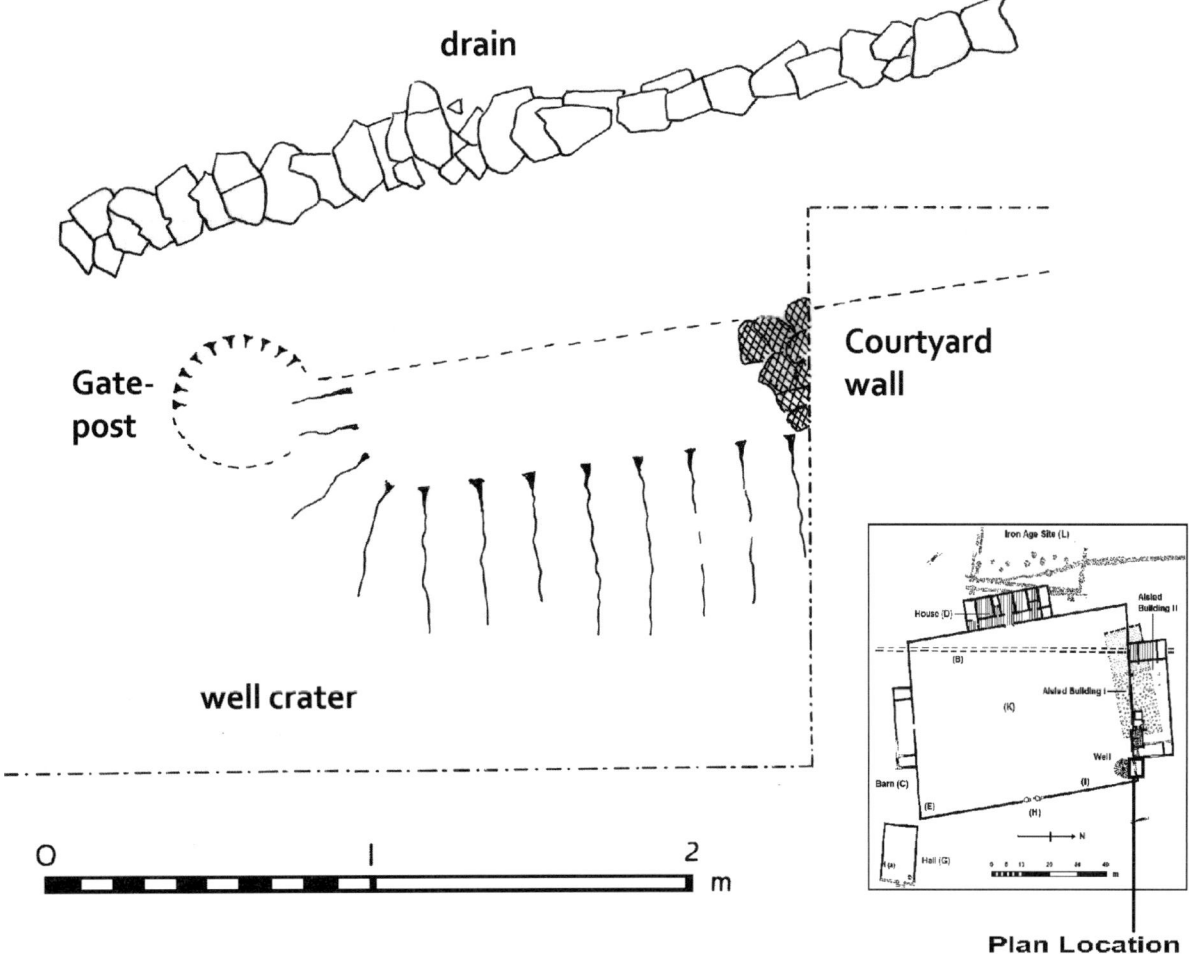

Fig 77 Plan of the eastern end of the north wall of the Courtyard (drawn by JD)

105–9). Sparsholt had domestic buildings on two sides, of which the Aisled Building was used for both domestic and agricultural purposes, in addition to an agricultural building (the Barn) on the third side. The Courtyard Wall was an integral part of the site, linking the otherwise separate buildings, while the arrangement of the buildings around the Courtyard may have had social and economic significance (Smith 1997, 171).

Apart from the Well, the lack of any recognisable evidence, such as cobbling or garden features, suggests that the Courtyard was a farmyard. There are similarities to Chilgrove 1 and 2 (Down 1979), which were both courtyard villas with 'stockyards'. Moreover, these villas were on similar chalk downlands to Sparsholt and probably had the same agricultural regimes. The skeletons of two foxes were discovered at Sparsholt (Pit XX and Site F) indicating the threat of predators. The wall was probably dual purpose: to keep stock in and predators out.

An understanding of the relationship of the Courtyard Wall to the individual buildings is essential if the overall development of the villa complex is to be understood and a chronology for the site established. This is very difficult to achieve because stratigraphic relationships were limited and only a small amount of stratified dating evidence was recovered. In particular there is a lack of evidence for the relationship between the Courtyard Wall and both the Main House and the Aisled Buildings. So although it is fairly certain that AB I was the first building in the Romano-British period, and that the end of the villa is characterised by the demolition of the main buildings and possibly the construction of the Hall, it is the sequence of activity between these events which is unclear. Below is the preferred sequence: it describes the growth, decline and eventual abandonment of the villa complex, but at certain points the lack of evidence allows for alternative models.

Phase I (mid to late 2nd century AD)

Unenclosed. This phase consisted of the construction and occupation of AB I. The presence of both 2nd-century AD pottery and blue-green bottle glass in demolition layers associated with this structure indicate that it was occupied by at least the late 2nd century AD. There may well have been a simple bank

Fig 78   Excavated entrance looking south (photographed 1969)

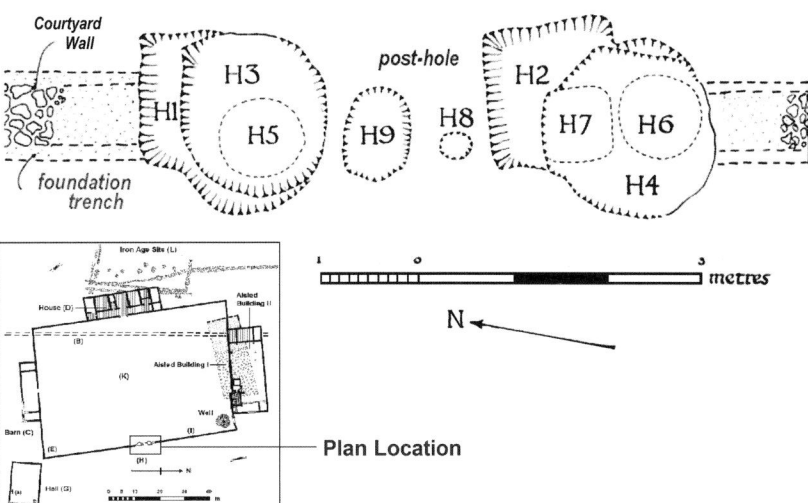

Fig 79 Plan of the entrance to the Courtyard (drawn by DEJ)

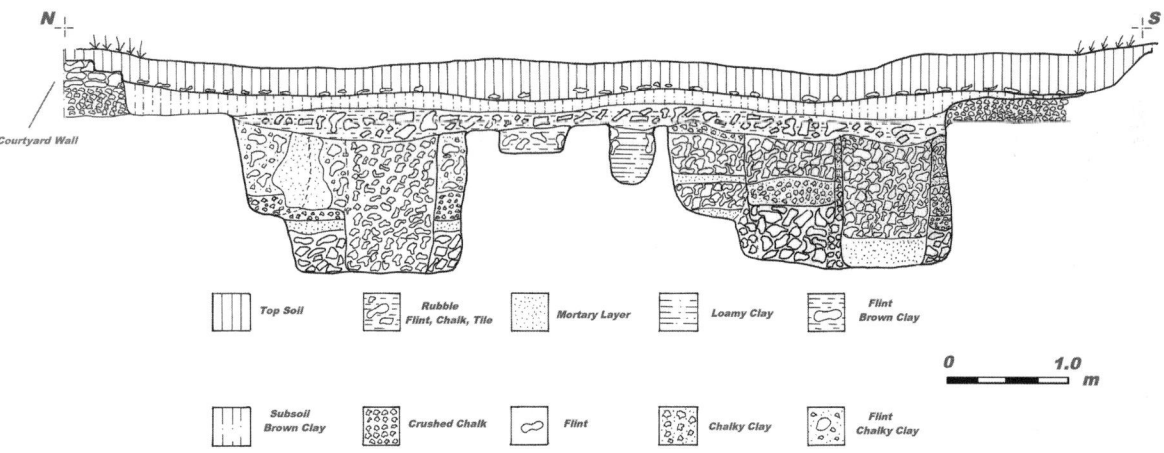

Fig 80 Section through the entrance (drawn by JD, based on original by CC)

and ditch enclosing the Courtyard but all evidence of this would probably have been destroyed by the construction of the Courtyard walls. The Well was probably dug during this phase, but because it was not fully excavated this remains conjectural.

Phase II (mid- to late 3rd century)

Enclosure. This phase saw the construction of the Barn and Main House in addition to the enclosure of the Courtyard (Fig. 82). The exact sequence of events is unclear but it is known that the Courtyard Wall abutted the Barn, indicating that it post-dated the construction of the building. Evidence of the junction between the Courtyard Wall and the south wall of AB I had been destroyed when the structure was demolished to make way for AB II. Yet the dimensions of the foundation trench for the Courtyard Wall indicate that it was similar in style to the southern stretch of walling and is therefore likely to be contemporary. The other stretches of the wall were also similar in size and style demonstrating that the Courtyard was enclosed as a single act after the Barn was constructed. Coin and pottery evidence from the Barn suggests that it was in use by the mid- to late 3rd century AD.

The junction between the Main House and the Courtyard Wall was destroyed when the wings were added in Phase III so the relationship between them is unknown. The dating evidence demonstrates that the Main House was built around the mid-3rd century, so it seems likely that it also pre-dates the enclosing of the Courtyard. Thus the principal buildings originally faced each other across an unenclosed Courtyard, the Barn was added and then the complex enclosed. A possible problem with this model is that it places the enclosure of the Courtyard close to the demolition of AB I and the construction of the new stretch of wall that accompanied AB II (Phase III).

The villa was entered via a 3 m wide double-leaved door, which was probably contemporary to the walling of the Courtyard in this phase.

Fig 81   View of the crater and the top of the well shaft (photographed 1969)

Phase III (end of the 3rd century–early 4th century)

Rebuilding and refurbishment. Towards the end of the 3rd century, AB I was demolished and replaced by AB II, which was on a slightly different alignment (Fig. 83), probably to make the Courtyard more rectangular. The northern wall was also demolished and replaced with a more substantial one. A small part of the original wall was retained at its eastern end and a gap between this and AB II is evidence for a small gate that provided access into the Courtyard. Robbing and modern disturbance have meant that the junctions between the Courtyard Wall and AB II were not properly investigated, but it seems probable that the new wall was integral to AB II in order to maintain the security of the Courtyard.

During this phase the Main House was significantly upgraded with the installation of a hypocaust, the laying of two mosaics and the construction of extensions at both ends of the building. This activity is dated to the early 4th century. The original Courtyard Wall was demolished and rebuilt up to the new extensions. At both ends of the building the junction where the extensions and the walls abutted were delineated by large limestone ashlar blocks. At the northern end of the Main House the Courtyard Wall was narrower and set in shallower foundations than the outer wall of Room 10, indicating that the two walls were constructed at different times. In addition, at this junction the limestone chippings that had lined the foundation trench of the Courtyard Wall had been re-laid above the foundations of the House extension, also indicating different periods of construction but demonstrating that the Courtyard Wall had been in place prior to the addition of rooms at either end of the building.

At this stage it is probable that the entrance to the Courtyard was enlarged, an act that witnessed the addition of a far more substantial structure, probably of stone. This phase seems to represent the pinnacle of the villa owner's affluence.

Phase IV (late 4th century)

Decline. The final phase of the site saw the abandonment of the principal buildings. The construction of the Hall outside the Courtyard to its south-east is also placed in this phase, although the evidence is at best tenuous. The coin sequence from the site comes to an end: there are no coins that date after AD 357 (SF 135 is the latest); in fact there are only four coins that were minted during the 4th century. Although in a state of ruin, the main buildings were probably substantially intact. There was, however, evidence of robbing, with material being used in the construction of the Hall, including *pilae* from the hypocausts and limestone roof tiles. The insubstantial nature of the hall and the re-use of salvaged building material suggest a late 4th-century AD date for this phase.

THE COURTYARD

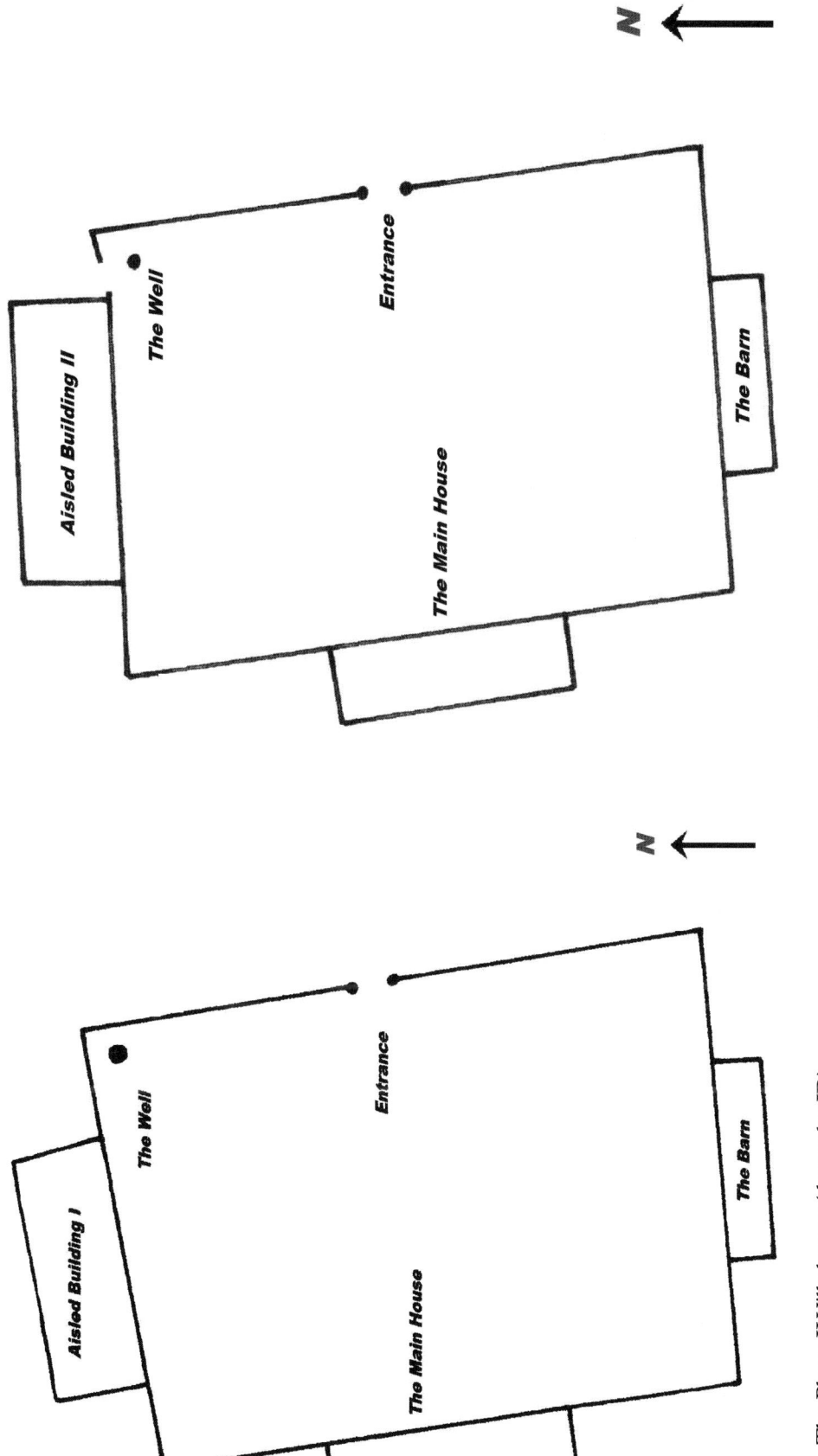

Fig 82 The Phase II Villa layout (drawn by JD)

Fig 83 The Phase III Villa layout (drawn by JD)

Chapter 8

Discussion

The site of Sparsholt villa is located in ancient woodland and it was the tree cover that largely protected the ruins from agricultural wear and tear. Although tree-root damage had taken its toll, trial excavations revealed that the level of archaeological preservation was excellent. This, along with the threat posed by the proposal to bulldoze a new woodland ride through the area, led to the programme of excavation from 1965 onwards.

At the time, relatively few British villas had been investigated on such a scale, and even today the extent of the undertaking, in conjunction with the recovery of the complete plan of this courtyard villa, marks Sparsholt out as noteworthy. Despite the size of the investigation, however, the evidence does suffer from a number of limitations. The excavation did not benefit from a systematic approach, with trenching, open-area excavation and a box-grid system being used variously. The latter was mainly employed during the first few seasons with the consequence that the initial emphasis was placed on defining stratigraphical relationships, rather than revealing the layout of the buildings.

A number of reasons can be identified for the siting of the villa. Topography was clearly important; the small spur overlooking a shallow valley afforded views of the surrounding countryside, and although today the valley is dry, in the past it could have supplied water. The occupants were also able to sink a well. The chalky soils provided good drainage and the slopes to the west would have been ideal pasture. The more level ground to the south and east could have been used for arable. Access to a major routeway would also have been significant, with the Roman road from *Venta Belgarum* to *Sorviodunum* lying only 650 m to the south. Johnston estimated that it would have taken only twenty minutes to travel by carriage to *Venta* and about two hours to drive livestock to market there. A further factor may well have been that the site had been occupied previously, in the not-too-distant past.

The Iron Age period (Fig. 84)

The spur first saw significant use during the Iron Age. Although sealed partly beneath the villa, the major part of the prehistoric settlement lies to the west (Fig. 3). The full extent of the site was not explored but three sides of an enclosure were examined as well as an entrance on the south side. The complex is estimated to cover about 0.25 ha but it is quite possible that Iron Age Sparsholt consisted of more than one enclosure. Earthworks evident in the adjacent woodland may represent more substantial features than just an extensive field system.

The site is dated by its pottery, which places it firmly in the Middle and Late Iron Age periods (400 – 50 BC). A radiocarbon date of the 1st century BC from the female skeleton buried in the upper fills of the enclosure ditch shows that by the Late Iron Age the features had silted up and it appears to be around this time that the site was abandoned.

Sub-rectangular enclosures up to a hectare in extent occurred widely throughout Wessex in the Middle Iron Age (Cunliffe 1993, 180). It is common for them to have contained roundhouses, storage pits, post-built granaries and other features and they functioned as farmsteads, occupied by an extended family or small community (Cunliffe 2005, 43). Sparsholt produced a number of pits but no structural evidence, and the relevant features may well lie in the unexcavated areas.

Pits also occur widely on Iron Age sites throughout Wessex (Cunliffe 1993, 186) and have been associated with the storage of grain such as emmer and spelt wheat (van der Veen 1989, 302–19). These two crops would have been quite suitable for cultivation on the local soils. Pollen evidence indicates that by the end of the Iron Age much of southern England was being exploited for agricultural purposes (Dark & Dark 1997, 94) and the Sparsholt area was no exception.

The pits and ditches also produced animal bones, indicating that the economy included pastoral farming. The three main species were cattle, sheep and pig and the local conditions would have suited the rearing of sheep in particular (Dark & Dark 1997, 112). There was also evidence of 'special deposits', the deliberate burial of parts of animals, in this case the leg of a cow, as propitiatory offerings to the gods (p.184).

The Danebury Environs project, with its detailed study of 450 square km of chalk landscape (Cunliffe 2000) and to a lesser extent the excavations along the M3 corridor (Fasham 1985), allow the ebb and flow of later prehistoric settlement in central Hampshire

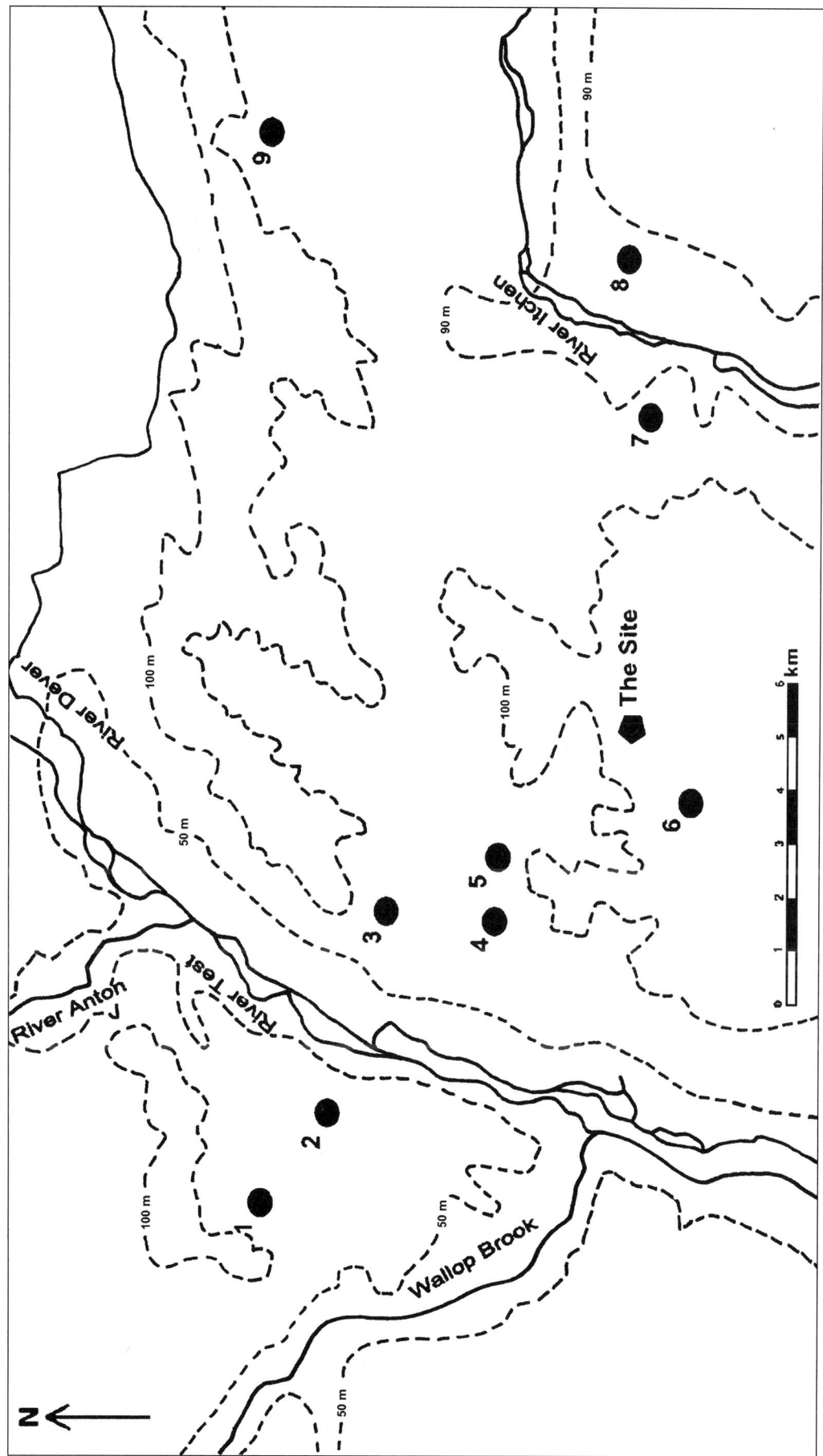

Fig 84 Comparative Iron Age sites (drawn by MB & NS). 1) Danebury 2) Houghton Down 3) Woolbury 4) Somborne Park Farm 5) Little Somborne 6) Farley Mount 7) Oram's Arbour 8) Winnall Down 9) Micheldever Wood

to be appreciated. The comparatively isolated nature of the Sparsholt evidence means that there no known neighbouring sites to consider as possible precursors, but the presence of pieces of Dressel 1A amphora in one of the pits is evidence of late trading contact with areas outside the region. This type of pottery was imported from the Mediterranean region into southern England between 100 and 50 BC through a number of ports including Hengistbury Head (Peacock 1971, 161–88, Cunliffe 1987).

By this period the Roman annexation of Gaul (52 BC) may have precipitated the movement of Belgic immigrants into southern England. Indeed, the Roman name for Winchester was *Venta Belgarum* (the market town of the *Belgae*). It is possible that this influx to the native forerunner of the Roman town (Oram's Arbour) caused disruption to the local farming population (Cunliffe 2005, 127) and may have been a factor in the abandonment of the settlement at Sparsholt.

The Romano-British period (Fig. 85)

Mid-2nd century to mid-3rd century AD

The Iron Age enclosure was abandoned during the 1st century BC and it appears to have been at least 150 years before the site was re-occupied. The period immediately following the Roman conquest (AD 43) was a relatively peaceful one for southern England and some Hampshire villa sites were developed, e.g. Twyford in the Itchen Valley (Johnston 1981, 50) and Rockbourne near the River Avon (RCHME 1980) but not, it would seem, Sparsholt.

The first building in the new settlement appears to have been Aisled Building I (AB I). Coins, imported *terra sigillata* pottery and glass, all recovered from demolition layers indicate a date of construction in the mid-2nd century. As the first structure on site it would have been the principal building, but few details are known because much of it was erased when Aisled Building II was constructed. As the main building, it could have provided shelter and accommodation for both humans and animals and may have contained a suite of rooms. It certainly housed a bath-suite in the south-east corner although it is not clear whether this was part of the original layout.

The plan and dimensions of AB I are consistent with examples of aisled buildings from southern England (Cunliffe 2008, 114–20) and although the excavation did not reveal clear architectural features because of the later activity, it was replaced by an indisputable aisled structure (AB II). Aisled buildings were often the earliest structures on villa sites in the region, as at Thruxton, Clanville and Houghton Down, for example, while at Grateley South and Dunkirt Barn it is believed that the aisled buildings preceded the corridor houses (*ibid*, 125).

From the mid-2nd century, Sparsholt consisted of a single building fronting onto a yard, an arrangement similar to the villa at Clanville, near Andover (Percival 1976, 100). It is not known if the yard at Sparsholt had been enclosed by a wall at this stage and it is possible that the area was demarcated by a bank, ditch or hedge.

The Barn was located on the opposite side of the yard to AB I. It was probably constructed in the early to mid-3rd century and signals renewed development of the site and the yard was formally enclosed with the Courtyard Wall. At Brading, on the Isle of Wight, a farm building and aisled building were on opposing sides of a walled courtyard (Smith 1978, 126).

The Barn was divided into three rooms, a main hall with a room at either end and although structures of comparable size are known, e.g. from Grateley South and Dunkirt Barn, no direct parallels for Sparsholt have been identified. Grateley South and Balksbury come closest, each having a single small room at the west end of the building (Cunliffe & Poole 2008b, 121, fig. 3.23). The Barn was probably a multi-purpose building used for the storage of agricultural equipment and produce. It was entered via a doorway in the north wall, which although relatively wide at 1.8 m, is smaller than the entrances recorded at Pitney, Somerset (2.6 m), Great Casterton, Rutland (2.44 m), and Langton, Yorkshire (2.47 m) (Morris 1979, 67). At some point the main entrance was blocked, thus preventing access to the central room, which perhaps signals a change in the economic practices of the villa. No other modifications, or evidence of deliberate destruction, were recorded and it appears that the Barn was abandoned along with the other buildings in the mid-4th century.

The entrance to the villa was located in the middle of the eastern boundary of the yard and in the early 3rd century probably comprised a timber gateway. Also taking its place in the yard was the Well. Although undated, it is likely to have been an early feature, Mid to late 3rd century.

Significant changes occurred in the mid to late 3rd century when a new building – the Main House – was constructed along the west side of the courtyard. Architecturally it can be viewed as marking a clear departure from the styles previously employed on the site. The building was a 'row', or Corridor, house, consisting of a set of five rooms, two of which were sub-divided. The entrance to the Corridor was located directly opposite the main villa gateway. Corridor houses appear in Hampshire from the 2nd century onwards, e.g. Rockbourne (RCHME) and particularly in the 3rd century, e.g. Grateley South (Cunliffe & Poole 2008b, 125). Similar row houses have also been discovered at Chilgrove (Down 1979), Dunkirt Barn (Cunliffe & Poole 2008c) and Warblington (Dicks 2010).

The Main House was built to a typical plan, with an entrance giving access to a Corridor that fronted a standard range of rooms (Perring 2002, 73). The large middle room (7) was almost in line with the entrance an arrangement designed to place the emphasis on the middle room. Room 7 was clearly an audience chamber, or reception room, in which guests were received and estate business was con-

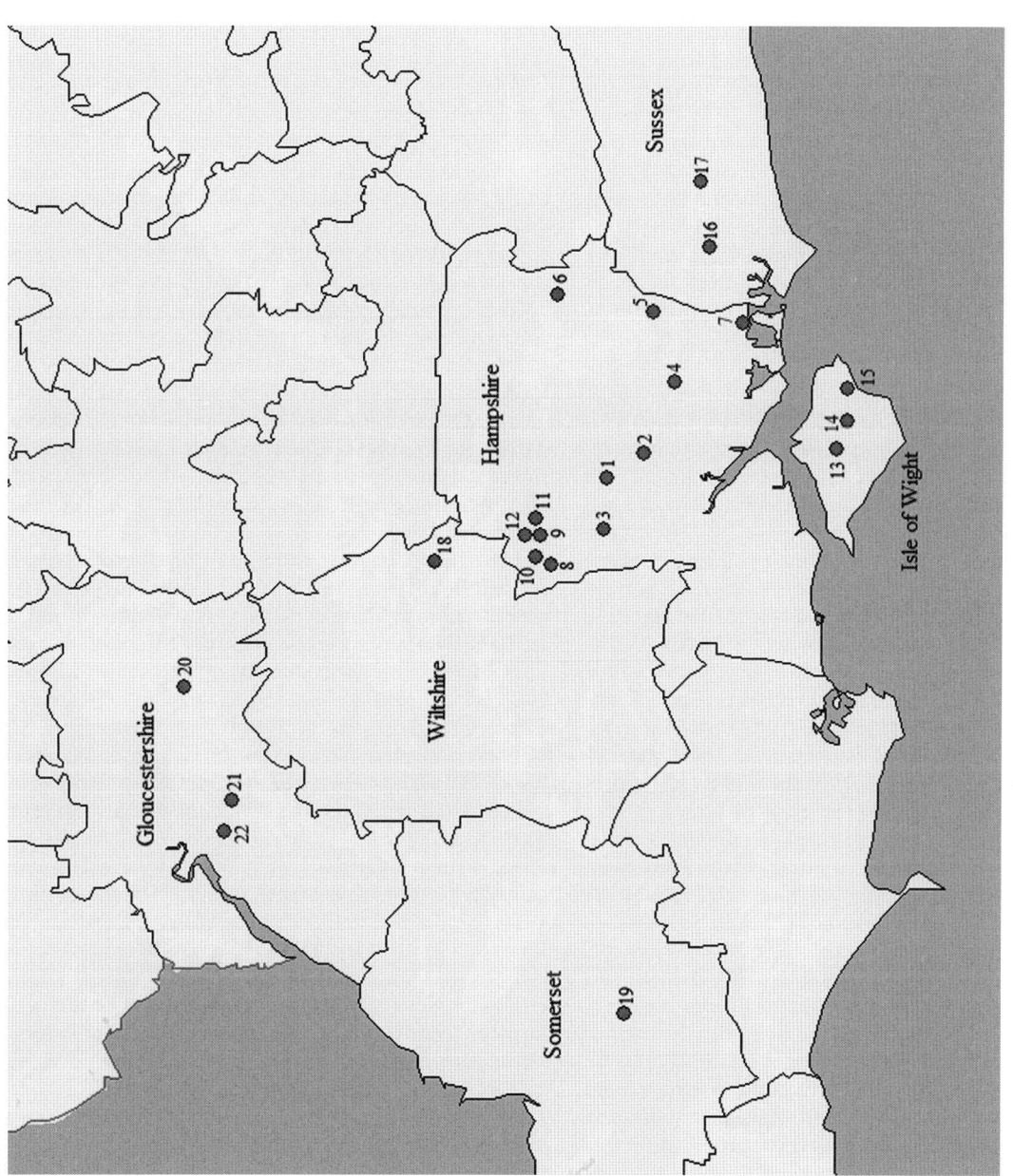

Fig 85 Comparative Romano-British sites. 1) Sparsholt 2) Twyford 3) Houghton Down 4) Meonstoke 5) Stroud 6) Binsted 7) Warblington 8) Grateley South 9) Dunkirt Barn 10) Thruxton 11) Balksbury 12) Clanville 13) Newport 14) Combley 15) Brading 16) Chilgrove 17) Bignor 18) Great Bedwyn 19) Pitney 20) Chedworth 21) Woodchester 22) Frocester (drawn by NS)

ducted. Rooms lay to either side of Room 7; each was accessed from an antechamber that led to a main room, while there was a smaller room to the rear (*ibid*, 187–8). The suite to the right (north) contained a room with a mosaic floor (Room 11), heated by a hypocaust. According to Perring (*ibid*, 191) the main bedroom would have been a heated and well-furnished space, a description consistent with the character and location of Room 11. Two other large rooms (4 and 8) could have functioned as informal dining rooms or additional bedrooms. Each suite may have belonged to a different family group (Smith 1997, 46–8), served as private quarters, or been used seasonally (Perring 2002, 203). A similar arrangement of rooms is found at Newport (Isle of Wight), while good examples of central reception rooms can be cited from both Chilgrove 1 (Room 6) and Chilgrove 2 (Building I, Room 2) (Down 1979), and Dunkirt Barn (Buildings 2 and 4) (Cunliffe & Poole 2008c). The discovery of an infant burial, in addition to the separate burial of a coin of Claudius, in Room 5 at Sparsholt may indicate that the room contained a shrine.

It was the construction of the Main House at right angles to AB I that resulted in the creation of a 'courtyard villa'. Sparsholt belongs to the 'entrance-court' type of villa, with the yard acting as the approach to the Main House (Morris 1979, 53–4). A similar development took place at Houghton Down, where a modest central hall house and workshop were added to an aisled building, while at both Grateley South and Dunkirt Barn an aisled building preceded a corridor house (Cunliffe 2008, 125). Sparsholt is closest in form, however, to the walled courtyard villas at Brading (Isle of Wight) and Clanville (Hampshire) where an aisled building and house faced each other across a rectangular walled enclosure (Johnston 1978, 78, Smith 1978, 78, Scott 1993, 86).

The corridor house provided a suite of private spaces and is evidence for the movement away from communal and vernacular architecture to a style more closely allied with Rome (Cunliffe 2008, 121). The allocation of space in such a way probably represents a change in the social status of the owners and a desire to articulate it symbolically by creating separate public and private spaces.

A further major development occurred shortly after the completion of the corridor house. Aisled Building I was demolished and replaced by a larger structure (AB II). The roof structure of this large aisled barn stood on square stone post-pads, with two pairs of supports set in the gable ends. The high central nave was probably illuminated by clerestory windows and the building would have dominated the site and the surrounding landscape. It seems to have been a direct replacement for the earlier structure and, based on pottery and coin evidence it was constructed in the last quarter of the 3rd century. In its earliest phase it was, like its predecessor, open plan and contained a bath suite in the south-east corner. It was not uncommon for baths to be housed in aisled buildings, e.g. Combley (Isle of Wight) Houghton Down (Cunliffe 2008, 117) and Dunkirt Barn (Cunliffe & Poole, 2008c). Baths generally comprised a compact group of rooms with a combined *apodyterium* and *frigidarium* with a cold plunge bath, a *tepidarium* and a *caldarium* (Johnston 1978, 78–82) and Sparsholt conformed to this pattern.

Aisled buildings are particularly common in Hampshire and occupied a key place in the layout of villas (*ibid*, 80). Where they were part of a complex within a walled courtyard, they were usually located at right angles to a main house (Perring 2002, 53), as at Sparsholt. In its original form AB II was probably subsidiary to the Main House and its chief purpose was probably agricultural (Morris 1979, 55–65), coupled with some domestic provision. The aisles could have been divided into stalls to accommodate cattle (Hadman 1978, 192) but the lack of drainage suggests otherwise and it is more likely that some of the large open space was used for storage (Perring 2002, 53). Crop processing is indicated by the corn drier in Room 15 and the hearths suggest workshop-type activities, while the ovens could have provided food for the entire establishment. The open space, or at least part of it, could have provided accommodation for members of the extended family or farm workers, while the Baths would have been utilised by all the occupants of the villa. Evidence for dividing up an aisled barn comes from Thruxton, where the southern end of the building may have been reserved for living and sleeping, while the north-west corner was used for cooking (Cunliffe & Poole 2008e, 107) and Dunkirt Barn, where separate rooms and corn driers were under the same roof (Cunliffe & Poole 2008c.).

Access to AB II was at the east end via a large 3.85 m wide doorway, approached by the track that followed the edge of the Courtyard Wall and also led to the small entrance by the Well. The main door was considerably wider than entrances of 'cart width' found in some barns, e.g. at Meonstoke where the centrally positioned entrance was 2.85 m wide (King 1996, 61), while the average from Great Casterton, Langton and Pitney is 2.5 m. This suggests that vehicles were expected to enter the building before offloading. It is significant, however, that the door is located outside the courtyard, potentially excluding some agricultural activities from the heart of the villa complex. The courtyard may have been left as a formal empty space to create a buffer between the private areas and the outside world (Scott 1990) and could explain why the buildings are located on the periphery of the walled area, an unusual situation, though mirrored at Clanville.

That AB I was replaced by a structure of the same type demonstrates the continuing importance of the aisled building. At Sparsholt the new structure was constructed on a slightly different alignment to its predecessor and this was also the case at Dunkirt Barn (Cunliffe & Poole 2008c), while at Castle Copse, Great Bedwyn, the replacement building followed the same orientation as the earlier one, but moved to the south-east (Hostetter & Howe 1997, 79). The greater capacity of AB II probably reflects the increase in output that the estate was now enjoying. The historical context for these developments may be sought in the political and economic changes to the Empire in the 3rd century. Barbarian incursions led to the loss of major grain-producing regions on the Continent (Watson 1999) and Britain became increasingly important as a source of food, particularly for the Roman army on the Rhine. The investment in new buildings at this time could signify greater confidence, or opportunism, by the existing proprietors, or a change of ownership.

Early 4th century AD

This economic upturn may have been responsible for the next phase of development when both the Main House and Aisled Building II were extensively modified. The House was enlarged with the addition of a pair of rooms at either end (Fig. 37). Dating evidence indicates that this work took place no earlier than the late 3rd century and possibly in the 4th century. The building was further enhanced with the laying of a fine mosaic floor in Room 7, dated on stylistic grounds to the first quarter of the 4th century (p.113–115 and Fig. 96).

In winged-corridor villas the small end rooms created corner pavilions that projected outwards and were given architectural emphasis, e.g. Fullerton (Cunliffe & Poole 2008d). At Sparsholt they did not extend beyond the line of the Corridor and are best termed pseudo-wings (Perring 2002, 73–4, Smith 1978, 126). Nevertheless, the Main House was directly opposite the entrance to the villa and visitors entering through this gate would have been presented with an impressive view.

The House now provided 230 m^2 of accommodation, divided into public or social and private or domestic areas. Room 7 continued to be the main reception room and the rich decoration of the mosaic floor and painted walls were clearly intended to impress on the visitor the wealth of the villa owners.

The modifications to AB II involved the demolition of the west wall and addition of a suite of rooms which extended the length of the building. This partitioning may reflect a need for more private space and is a common development (Perring 2002, 169). There was no dating evidence for the changes at Sparsholt but at Houghton Down such a development took place in the mid-3rd to mid-4th century (Cunliffe & Poole 2008a, 59) while at Thruxton it was the second half of the 4th century (Cunliffe & Poole 2008e, 108). The aisled building at Clanville was extended and saw a subdivision of space that included the addition of baths (Cunliffe 2008, 117).

The result of the changes at Sparsholt was that AB II was now divided into at least three functional areas and in its final guise belongs to Perring's 'Developed Type' (2002, 53) which has a set of rooms at one end, but still contained a large open communal area. Such structures are interpreted as typical farm buildings that coupled domestic accommodation with agricultural storage (King 2006, 357). At Sparsholt the bath-suite continued to serve the needs of the whole villa, while a new hearth, for the preparation of food, was built in the south-west corner of the hall. The presence of a mosaic in Room 12 suggests that this may have been a dining room, the mosaic perhaps intended to demonstrate a level of opulence comparable to that in the Main House, and implies that it was not used by farm labourers. Alternatively the new rooms, including Room 12, may have been created to provide a formal location where estate business was conducted. The iron plough coulter discovered in Room 12, which from its position was either leaning against or hanging on the wall, may support this idea. In contrast, Smith (1997, 45) has suggested that the presence of different suites of rooms may indicate separate family groups, although this has been challenged by Perring (2002, 202–6). Either way it seems clear that the non-agricultural function of AB II increased over time.

Although undated, it seems likely that the refurbishment of the entrance to the courtyard coincided with the other early 4th-century developments at Sparsholt. The entrance was widened and the gateway replaced with a more substantial structure, possibly in stone. A consequence of constructing AB II on a slightly different alignment to its predecessor was to make the Courtyard more rectangular. It has been suggested that this was meant to emphasise the importance of the Main House by drawing attention to the building (Smith 1997, 250).

The interregnum and disruption caused by the two usurper-emperors, Carausius and Allectus (AD 286–96), does not seem to have had a long-lasting effect on the agricultural economy of southern England. Consolidation of the Empire under Constantine and the restoration of peace seem to have ushered in a new affluent phase. Rural villa owners invested in lavish bath houses and mosaic pavements as at Bignor (Frere 1982, 135–95), Woodchester (Mann 1963) and Chedworth (Esmonde Cleary 2012). It is intriguing, therefore, that at Sparsholt the Main House was not enlarged even further and this presumably indicates that the owner could not afford to rebuild on such a scale.

By the 4th century the elite were investing in villas, using this as a way to improve security and express their status and many were now predominantly based in the countryside (Esmonde Cleary 2012, 109–10). There appear to be relatively few villas in the vicinity of Sparsholt, however, in an area defined to the north and south by the Roman roads and to the west by the River Test. There is the possible site at Up Somborne, but larger groups of villas exist to the north and east of Winchester and in the Andover area. It is always possible that Sparsholt was the centre of an agricultural estate containing a number of secondary settlements. *Venta Belgarum* would have been its principal market where produce was sold and taxes paid. The development of the site in the late 3rd century may have come from wealthy citizens (*decurions*) of *Venta* perhaps wishing to invest in the countryside after Diocletian's tax reforms, as may have happened at *Noviomagus* (Chichester) (Percival 1976, 145–65).

Decline and abandonment

The Hall was constructed outside the Courtyard Wall in the south-east part of the site. The absence of foundation trenches, at odds with the other structures and the re-use of building material, show it was of comparatively rudimentary construction. There was an oven and hearth, however, suggesting that it provided accommodation of sorts. There was no dating evidence for the Hall's construction but the relatively large quantity of 4th-century grog-tempered pottery shows that it was in use during that century. What is not clear is whether it was an additional asset to the villa layout or represents a decline in fortunes and was used in place of the earlier structures.

Sparsholt was abandoned during the 4th century. There are only four 4th century coins from a total of 43 found and the sequence ends with a coin of Constantius II dated 353–57 from the upper fill of the Well and three worn late 4th century copies. A similar pattern was detected at Houghton Down (Cunliffe & Poole 2008a), Dunkirt Barn (Cunliffe & Poole 2008c) and Chilgrove 1 (Down 1979). This is not the normal coin loss picture for villas in the south of England, however, with most showing an abundance of coins from 330 to 378 (Reece 1991, Fig. 86). *Venta* also records a profusion of coinage during these years (Reece 1991, Fig. 87). While commercial activities continued in Winchester, at Sparsholt the coinage suggests a marked decline. Although it is difficult to draw conclusions from such limited evidence, there appears to have been a significant deterioration in the fortunes of the villa owners, perhaps as early as the second quarter of the 4th century.

There is no evidence at Sparsholt for a traumatic event that may have caused this desertion, such as the fire at Grateley South which resulted in the destruction of a crop-processing building (Cunliffe & Poole 2008b, 178). Nor is there evidence for a decline in the upkeep of the villa buildings, or a reduction in the number of rooms in use. There was, however, some evidence that building material had been salvaged from the site, although it is impossible to know when this occurred and whether it was part of a gradual process of demolition and decay.

While environmental or economic factors may have caused Sparsholt's demise a historical explanation may be sought in the political and military events of the mid 4th century. After the death of Constantine I (AD 337) there was a period of civil unrest as two of his sons fought for control of the Western Empire. The winner was himself killed in a coup in 350 by the followers of Magnentius, who then took the purple. It has been claimed that Magnentius was of British origin and that on his defeat, by Constantius II (353), a campaign was launched against his British supporters (Moorhead & Stuttard 2012, 202–4). While some villas in southern England continued to flourish until the end of the century, others were deserted because of these reprisals. Whatever the reason, the second half of the 4th century witnessed the abandonment of Sparsholt Roman villa.

DISCUSSION

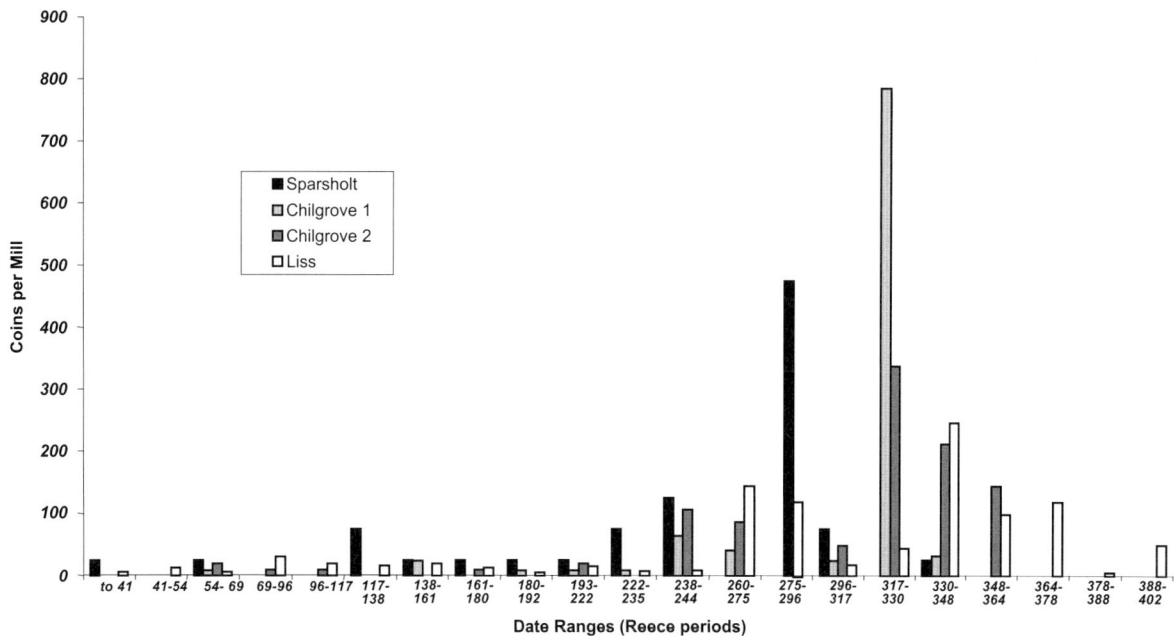

Fig 86 Coin loss pattern comparisons with rural villas

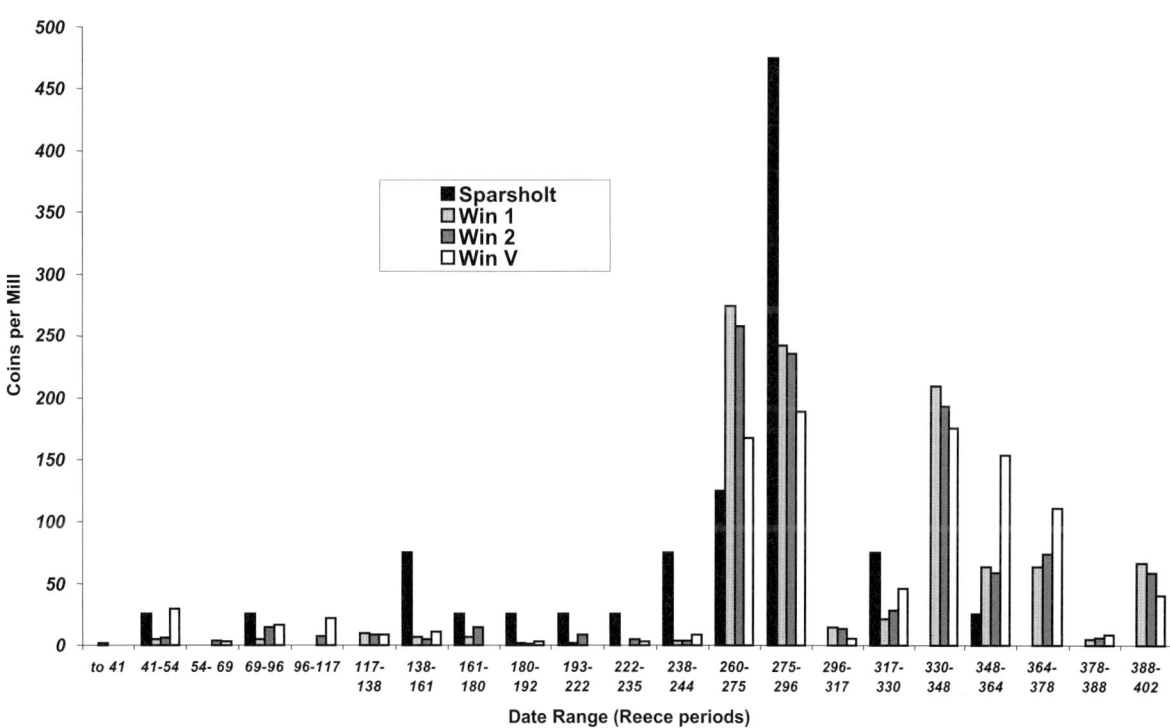

Fig 87 Coin loss pattern comparison with Winchester

Chapter 9

Pottery

The Iron Age pottery

David E Johnston

Introduction

The Iron Age features below the Aisled Building (p.20) cannot be phased precisely; they produced very little pottery and are not considered here. This analysis therefore comprises the pottery from the enclosure ditch of the settlement and the pits inside it (all Phase 2). After the removal of 29 Roman sherds (contamination from the re-cutting of the ditch) and the amphora, some 578 sherds were examined, all of which are of Middle Iron Age date. This is a small sample, and sophisticated statistical analysis was thought to be inappropriate. Method and presentation are based on those of J W Hawkes in the reports of comparable sites in Micheldever Wood (Fasham 1987), at Easton Lane (Fasham *et al.* 1989) and at Winnall Down, Winchester (Fasham 1985) and of S M Davies at Old Down Farm (Davies 1981). The analysis of potttery from Danebury (Cunliffe 1984) has also been used. The respective distances from Sparsholt to these sites are (in miles): Micheldever Wood 13½, Easton Lane 8½, Winnall Down 8½, Danebury 12 and Old Down Farm 18½.

The reliability of this analysis is affected by the small size of the sample; statistical distortion is caused by the fact that some pots were represented by a single sherd, others by 50 or more, and one almost complete saucepan in two pieces is counted as two sherds. There were, however, few matching or contiguous rim sherds, and the figure of 75 rim sherds gives a reasonably accurate minimum number of about 65 vessels. At a rough estimate, the whole assemblage comprises the remains of about 150 vessels. It should be remembered that the material comes from the excavation of approximately half of site L, which was itself one element in a larger complex (p.12).

Variations within the material were not sufficient to augment or refine the phasing of the site from the evidence of excavation. Ditch and pits display a unity that is reflected in the pottery; the material remains must represent occupation from the Middle Iron Age to the 1st century BC.

Methodology

The pottery is stored in bags, as received from the site. Within each bag the material was sorted visually according to fabric, surface finish, rim form and vessel form, and quantities recorded and tabulated. Form-fabric correlation was not attempted. Similar information was drawn from reports on the Middle Iron Age phases of the four sites mentioned above and compared. Statistical comparison with Danebury has not been attempted. Individual specimens were then selected for drawing and description. These are now boxed and stored separately; the detailed record sheets, pottery catalogues and drawings form part of the Level III archive. Only a summary of conclusions is presented here.

Fabrics

Three fabric types were identified on visual examination: those with fine sand in the paste, those with crushed flint (of varying particle sizes and concentrations) and those with organic temper. With the exception of 14 and 15, no predominantly grog- or shell-tempered fabrics were recognised (see Fig. 88). The quantities (in sherds) were: sand (106), flint (445), organic (10), undetermined (6) and non-local (11) (nos 14, 15, 16). Table 3 compares Sparsholt with contemporary phases of four local sites.

The high ratio of flint to sand temper at Sparsholt might indicate a relatively late date in the Middle Iron Age, on the evidence of Easton Lane where a transition from sand to flint fabrics was suggested in phases 7 and 8 (Fasham *et al.* 1989, 94); on the other hand, the exceptionally high incidence of sand

Fabric	SP	WD	MW	EL	ODF
Sand	18.6	5.2	17.6	30.3	69.5
Flint	78.0	89.0	70.7	60.6	24.0
Organic	1.7	1.0	3.9	9.1	3.7

Table 3: Sparsholt fabric types compared to local sites (SP=Sparsholt, WD=Worthy Down, MW=Micheldever Wood, EL=Easton Lane, ODF=Old Down Farm)

temper at Old Down Farm probably merely reflects the character of the nearest available clay source. Fabric variations between sites therefore indicate that most of the pottery was made in or near the settlement, as was the case at Danebury (Cunliffe 1984, 244–5). The Sparsholt ratios are in fact most closely matched at Micheldever Wood.

Forms

Six general forms were used for identification, to which 162 sherds could be assigned; 405 sherds were of indeterminate form. Forms were:

1. Simple bowl (20 sherds)
2. Bipartite saucepan/narrow-mouthed jar (4)
3. Straight-sided saucepan (5)
4. Incurving saucepan (31)
5. Outward-flaring saucepan (40)
6. Round-shouldered jar (62)

Inter-site comparison was difficult, owing to differences of presentation and classification (especially jars). For example, at Old Down Farm the saucepans were undifferentiated. At Winnall Down the pot count was used, at the others the sherd count. The Easton Lane data (Fasham *et al.* 1989, table 12) covered the entire Iron Age; since, however, the Middle Iron Age pots were only in fabrics A1, A2, B1 and B3 only these parts of the table were used for percentages of fabric (above) and form. All the sherd counts suffer from two disadvantages: first, certain pot forms were more robust than others, and produced fewer sherds when broken; second, an assessment by weight would have produced different figures (markedly so at Old Down where both were used in Davies 1981, fig. 27). Nevertheless, accepting these variables, the comparative percentages are presented in Table 4.

The range of forms is typical of sites in the saucepan-type tradition. The percentages of different fabrics suggest that all or most of the pots were made locally; the analysis of the forms points to the same conclusion. At Sparsholt there are high percentages of bowls, outward-flaring saucepans and incurving saucepans and a particularly low percentage of straight-sided ones. This is presumably a local preference, and of no functional significance. However, the small size of the sample should be stressed. The figures for jars, too, should be treated with caution, since they are hard to classify with confidence and some cannot easily be distinguished, without a full profile, from incurving saucepans (e.g. 8 and 11).

The potter (or potters) may have been experimenting cautiously with rim forms, occasionally (e.g. 1) producing a true bead rim and in one case (11) forming the bead *inside* the pot. One possible idiosyncrasy should be noted: some jars (e.g. 4 and 8) exhibit a carefully tooled facet inside the rim. When this occurs on Roman jars (and especially when it forms an internal ledge) it is taken to be a lid-seating. Ceramic lids, however, are not found with pottery of

Form	SP	WD	MW	EL	ODF
1	12.3	16.0	2.9	?	6.9
2	2.4	?	4.0	?	3.0
3	3.0	29.6	29.6	24.2	?
4	19.1	37.5	6.1	23.2	?
5	24.6	7.8	0.6	11.1	?
6	38.2	?	1.7	?	?

Table 4: Sparsholt form types compared to local sites

the saucepan tradition, and these facets are too steep to be effective. They are best regarded as a stylistic peculiarity.

Decoration

The decoration, with lightly burnished lines and impressed dots, is unremarkable and generally rather faint. In common with all pottery in this tradition, there is little interest in a tidy regularity. Those who handled and used this pottery must have been aware of the contrasting confidence and surface relief of the imported Glastonbury ware, a good example of which was recovered (16). This latter find, as Dr Williams points out below, may be at the most easterly limits of its range. Its rarity would have drawn attention to its decoration, and it is at least possible that the apparently elliptical elements in the decoration of no.5 were inspired by their deeply grooved counterparts in the imported piece.

Manufacture and use

It is seldom acknowledged that handmade pots bear in themselves the evidence for their manufacture and use – evidence that can be verified by a few hours' practical pot making. It is generally assumed that pottery of this period was either coil- or ring-built, and made without the use of a fast-turning wheel. In fact, a skilled potter can produce an exactly circular pot that looks wheel-thrown. This, however, takes a long time and the use of a turntable or tournette can produce a similar effect more quickly. There are signs that some of the pots in this study might have been made on such a simple turntable, though variations of density and thickness remain. Some of these irregularities were the result of adding plates of clay to thicken the walls and carefully smoothing them down to match the profile. On the other hand, no signs of rings or coils were detectable in the section, as they sometimes are in experimental replicas; this fact, with the occasionally faceted surface and variations of density and thickness, could be explained by the practice of *beating* – a technique that has not been advanced in any of the specialist reports consulted in this study, although there is plenty of ethnographic evidence for its use in more modern times.

Beating can produce the hard, shiny areas that are conventionally ascribed to burnishing. In fact, the surface finish of these pots could not be characterised simply as burnished or unburnished. At times, the surface, inside and out, resembled the matt coating which on Roman pots is described as slip. This effect can actually be produced by working very wet, the hands dripping with liquid slurry, and it is suggested that this was the case with some of the Sparsholt pots (one or two, by contrast, using clay that was too dry, or 'short', resulting on firing in a crackled surface of fine hairlines). Sometimes this wet slurry was then evidently wiped, either with a coarse textile or a handful of grass. As the pot dried, it was often smoothed with a polished tool (a bone or pebble), eventually producing a true burnish. This tool was also a finishing tool, used with bold vertical or oblique strokes to remove the final surface irregularities and also to shape the rim. On no.11 the latter operation left an irregular lip of excess clay still visible just inside the top of the rim. At its broadest, the finishing tool left a mark nearly 4 mm wide; generally it left a faint groove some 1.5 mm wide. On no.1 the marks of a scraping tool, intentionally or unintentionally serrated, were noted. In most cases the true decoration of lines and dots, probably done with the blunted point of the finishing tool, was as faint as the random burnishing, and recognisable only by its regularity.

Within each pot the density of the added temper varied, often quite considerably. This, and the ever-changing thickness of walls and bases, will have made these pots vulnerable to thermal shock. Presumably only those that survived the potter's bonfire reached the site, the casualties being crushed for grog temper. Many, of course, were not then used for open-fire cooking, and most breakages are therefore to be ascribed to rough or careless handling, or to throwing away pots that had gone foul.

Some sherds, however, exhibited deposits of coarse carbonised organic matter inside the pot, and occasionally even on the broken edges, which might represent food residues and suggest that the pots actually disintegrated into the fire while being used for cooking.

It is understood that pots travelled long distances either as objects of value in their own right or as containers for valuable substances. The first category might explain the arrival of no.16 from distant south-west Britain. Nos 14 and 15, too, appear not to be of local manufacture (see below); the fact that no.15 was also undecorated suggests that it was a container for something unusual.

The role of the amphorae is quite ambiguous; Dressel 1 and 2-4 (there is uncertainty over the form of the latter, see below) were containers for wine (Dressel 1 for Falernian); whatever their primary function, these vessels would have been valuable even when empty, and they might have been used in the settlement for water storage.

Conclusion

A relatively small assemblage of Middle Iron Age pottery was recovered from the enclosure ditch and pits. Too much emphasis should not be placed on the results, especially when it is remembered that the site was only partially excavated. However, comparisons with other Hampshire sites confirm that most pots were made locally, although the 'Glastonbury ware bowl' testifies to links with south-western England, while the Roman amphora is probably indicative of external contacts over a much wider area.

Unusual pieces

Four specimens from Iron Age levels at the site, including an amphora sherd (not illustrated) were examined by David Williams, who reports as follows:

1. (Fig. 88, 16). Part of the shoulder and neck of a 'Glastonbury ware' bowl, displaying tooled curvilinear decoration. The fabric is hard, smooth on the outer surface but rough on the inner, and darkish-grey in colour throughout. Thin-sectioning and study under the petrological microscope shows a clay matrix containing frequent rounded fragments of sandstone, shale, siltstone and mudstone, together with some igneous material, flecks of muscovite mica and quartzite. However, the most prominent inclusions are discrete grains of alkali feldspar, in particular sanidine. The fabric of the sherd from Sparsholt very closely matches Peacock's (1969) Group 5 (Sanidine) fabric division of Glastonbury ware. It was suggested by Peacock that the inclusions in this group were probably derived from the Permian of south-western England, in particular the area north of Watcombe to Exeter and along the Crediton Valley as far as Colebrook (*ibid*). This particular fabric of the Glastonbury ware series has a wide but thin distribution, even reaching across the Channel to France (Williams 2005, 100–1). Close dating is difficult for the various divisions of Glastonbury ware, but the vessel probably reached the site during the later Iron Age (Cunliffe & Brown 1987).

2. (Fig. 88, 9). Three small adjoining sherds with cordoned decoration, in a fairly hard, smoothish, sandy fabric containing visible inclusions of angular flint and some argillaceous material. As Sparsholt lies on the Upper Chalk, this flinty fabric may well have its origin fairly close by (1 in Geological Survey Map of England, sheet 299).

3. (Fig. 88, 15). Plain rim with large straight-sided undecorated body sherd from a middle Iron Age saucepan pot. It is in a hard, rough sandy fabric with large pieces of shell clearly visible in the hand-specimen, greyish-buff in colour. Thin-sectioning reveals some re-crystallisation of the shell suggesting that it is fossiliferous. The lack of any sign of chalk or flint in the sherd, which might point to a more local origin, suggests instead that the fossil shell most likely comes

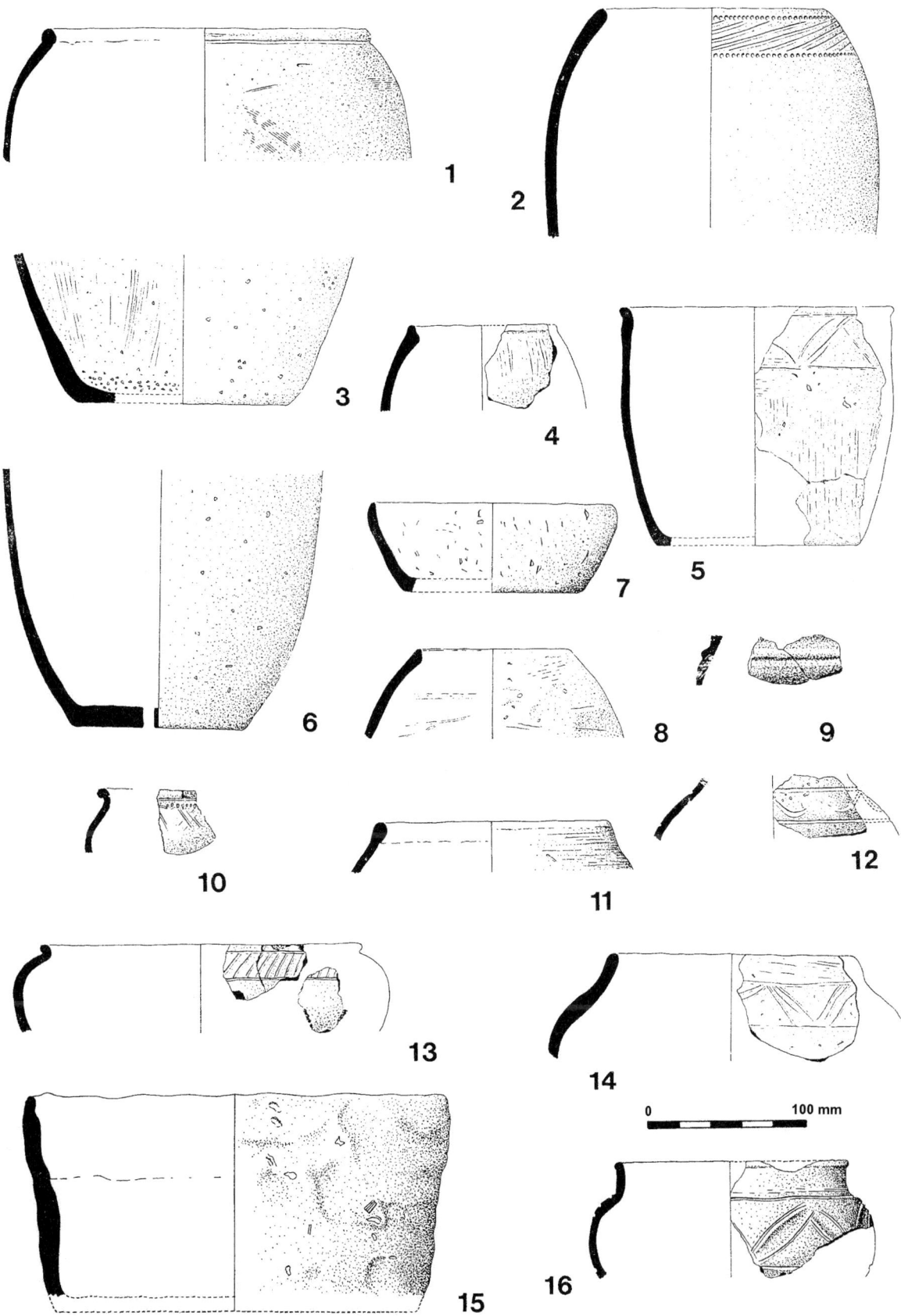

Fig 88 Iron Age pottery (drawn by DEJ)

from a shelly limestone region. It is difficult to be certain without the identification of diagnostic fossils, which seem to be lacking in this sherd, but it is possible that the shell in this fabric is derived from the Jurassic, the nearest formations of which lie some 30 miles to the south-west of Sparsholt (1 in Geological Survey Map of England, sheet 298).

4. (not illustrated). Large plain body sherd of a Roman amphora in a hard, smooth, sandy fabric, light buff outside surface and red inner surface and core. Thin-sectioning shows a clay matrix containing grains of green augite and quartz, together with a little limestone and some volcanic material, and is texturally similar to Italian amphorae previously analysed by the writer. Unfortunately, the Sparsholt sherd exhibits no typological features, but it seems likely that it belongs to either the form Dressel 1 or Dressel 2-4, both of which were made in Italy, normally carried wine and were widely distributed (Peacock & Williams 1986, Classes 3, 4 and 10; Williams & Keay, 2006). The earliest form of Dressel 1 amphora, the A variety, was produced from about 140/130 BC, while the main Italian production of Dressel 2-4 did not outlast the first century AD (*ibid*). Theoretically, the Sparsholt sherd could lie anywhere within that date range. However, the thickness of the wall of the sherd indicates that it comes from the Dressel 1 form rather than the thinner-walled Dressel 2-4, and therefore probably dates from between c. 140/130 BC and the end of the first century BC, when the Dressel 1B variety ceased to be made.

Catalogue of illustrated Iron Age pottery (Fig. 88)

1. *Ditch 1*. Jar in hard grey fabric fired black inside and out with fine flint temper, burnished inside and out. The bead rim has been thickened internally with additional material. The surface has been scraped externally with a rough or serrated tool, the marks being largely obliterated by burnishing.

2. *Pit XV, Layers 6, 10, 11*. Jar in smooth grey fabric with sand temper, burnished externally. The decoration is stabbed and grooved.

3. *Pit XII, Layer 5*. Jar in hard grey fabric with coarse flint temper, scraped internally.

4. *Pit XII, Layer 5*. Jar with a weak bead rim in hard grey fabric with flint temper. The exterior is lightly burnished with vertical striations. Note the internal rim facet.

5. *Pit XV, Layers 10, 11 and passim*. Vertical-sided saucepan in grey-brown fabric with fine sand-gritted temper. The exterior is heavily burnished, vertically and horizontally. The decoration is lightly tooled.

6. *Ditch XXI*. Jar (18 sherds) in soft, grey-brown fabric of uneven thickness with sand and flint temper. The exterior is lightly burnished. At least two neat, circular and vertical perforations in the base were made before firing.

7. *Pit VII, Layers 7, 10*. Shallow saucepan in hard grey fabric with organic temper.

8. *Pit XII, Layer 5*. Round-shouldered rimless jar in hard grey fabric with flint temper, smoothed and lightly burnished outside. The interior has been wiped and shows occasional broad burnished areas.

9. *Pit XIII, Layer 4*. See report by Dr D F Williams, p.92.

10. *Pit XVII, Layer 2*. Jar in hard grey fabric with flint temper, smoothed and lightly burnished inside and out. The rim shows a slight external facet caused by folding over and tooling. The decoration is stabbed and very faintly burnished.

11. *Ditch I*. Incurving saucepan (?) in hard grey fabric with flint temper, carefully smoothed with horizontal strokes. The rim has been folded for internal thickening.

12. *Pit XVII, Layer 6*. Jar in hard grey fabric of uneven thickness, with flint temper. The interior has been smoothed and the exterior lightly burnished and decorated with two horizontal lines and 'swag' decoration.

13. *Pit XIII, Layer 4*. Bowl in hard grey fabric with coarse flint temper, smoothed inside and out. The exterior is lightly burnished with tooled decoration.

14. *Pit 15, Layer 6*. Jar in grey-brown fabric with sparse temper of crushed shell and grog. Lightly burnished exterior with tooled decoration.

15. *Pit XII layer 5*. See report by Dr D F Williams, p.92–4.

16. *Pit XVII layer 6*. See report by Dr D F Williams, p.92.

The Romano-British pottery

Rachael Seager Smith and Kayt Marter Brown

Introduction

In total, 14,221 sherds (202,960 g) of Romano-British pottery were recovered and retained. Recognisably early Romano-British material was scarce and mainly restricted to imported finewares; the majority of sherds were assigned a post- to mid/late 3rd-century AD date. Overall, the material survived in moderate condition, with an average sherd weight of about 14 g (averages of between c 10 g and 20 g are generally expected for Romano-British assemblages from sites across southern England), although there was some variability (c 12–25g) between the different buildings/areas investigated during these excavations. The majority of sherds showed the surface abrasion and edge damage characteristic of repeatedly re-deposited material.

Limitations of the assemblage

In common with many other sites excavated during the late 1960s and early 1970s, the Sparsholt villa buildings were investigated by means of a series of regular trenches separated by baulks. One of the main disadvantages of this method is that a trench could examine more than one room or feature, while different trenches could also examine the same feature or deposit, thus complicating the description of stratigraphic relationships and making it difficult to assign artefacts to the correct contexts. Furthermore, the artefacts were collected in bags assigned a single letter code (A–L), indicating site sub-division and a double-letter 'bag' code (e.g. AB, CG) which links to features and deposits described in the site note books. If more than one individual excavated a single deposit, they were each assigned different bag codes; if they worked on the same deposit for several days, more and different bag codes were used. Although the well-maintained *bag lists* and the *site note books* have been used as far as possible to assign artefacts to their correct contexts, the limitations of the grid system of excavation and the finds collection procedure, while standard techniques of the time, have, in many instances, made it very difficult to assign the finds to specific contexts with any degree of certainty. Securely stratified groups are therefore rare and a considerable proportion of the assemblage is effectively unstratified, deriving from topsoil, subsoil and/or other insecurely identified deposits.

The fragmentary nature and abraded condition of the sherds has also limited the level of analysis possible or appropriate for this assemblage. Many of the sherds have lost their surfaces, limiting the potential to assign them to specific ware groups with any degree of certainty. Similarly, with the exception of material from Site L, there were few complete or re-constructible profiles. Rims represented some 13% of the total assemblage by sherd count, but the majority were broken at or above the neck/shoulder junction, hampering the precise identification of vessel forms.

Methodology

As a consequence of the limitations discussed above, the assemblage was subjected to a detailed scan rather than fully quantified fabric and form analysis. It was recorded using the site sub-division and double letter code bag numbers described above. The contents of the individual bags were examined and assigned to broad fabric groups (e.g. oxidised wares, flint-tempered wares) or, where appropriate, to specific fabric types from known sources (e.g. New Forest parchment ware). Given the condition of the assemblage and well-known difficulties in distinguishing between the products of various major greyware industries (e.g. New Forest, Rowlands Castle and Alice Holt) as well as other, unsourced local centres, the greywares were recorded as a single group. The oxidised wares, too, represent a catch-all group encompassing all the unsourced pale-firing (white, buff, orange) wares containing variable quantities of sand and/or mica. In order to provide a basic archive conforming to nationally recommended guidelines for Roman pottery (Darling 1994, 3–5), the sherds in each bag were quantified by sherd count and weight within these fabric groups; this information is summarised in Table 5. Standard type series (such as Fulford 1975, Young 1977) were used to describe the range of vessel forms present. These were quantified by rim count (Tables 6 and 7), while other details such as the presence of unusual surface treatments, decoration and evidence of use or repair were noted in a free-text field. These data has been entered into an Excel spreadsheet which forms part of the project archive. Vessels have been selected for illustration, based primarily, though not exclusively, on intrinsic ceramic interest rather than stratigraphic grounds.

Results
Fabrics and forms

The Romano-British assemblage conforms to that expected of a late Roman villa in the south of England; coarse, fine and specialist wares from all the principal pottery manufacturing industries in the region are represented, whilst the range of forms is consistent with domestic activity. Detailed inter-site comparisons are, however, hampered by the lack of quantified assemblages from other sites in the area, particularly the late Roman groups from Winchester, which, as cantonal capital, is likely to have played a major role in the marketing and redistribution of ceramics and other commodities produced and used in its hinterland.

Following the definitions proposed by Booth (1991, 5) and shown to be effective in distinguishing site status in Roman Oxfordshire (Henig & Booth 2000), the assemblage was divided into two main groups: fine- and specialist wares and coarsewares. The fine- and specialist wares here comprise samian and other imported finewares, amphorae, mortaria, Oxfordshire and New Forest products as well as a small number of unsourced colour-coated wares, including one piece probably from the Nene Valley. The coarseware group encompasses all the remaining fabrics, focusing on the more utilitarian vessels used predominantly in a variety of food preparation and storage roles, although it is recognised that some of these, especially the finer greywares and oxidised wares, could also have been used as serving vessels, providing a range of medium-quality vessels within the assemblage.

Fine- and specialist wares
Overall, these wares represented 13% of the Romano-British assemblage. Imports were limited to samian, Central Gaulish black-slipped ware, Moselkeramik and a single body sherd from a Dressel 20 amphora in a Baetican fabric, the production of which commenced in the late 2nd century AD (BAT AM 2; Tomber & Dore 1998, 85). These vessels were used to transport olive oil from southern Spain, but were subsequently extensively traded in their own right as empty containers. The samian included undecorated cup and bowl/dish forms (forms 18/31, 27, 31, 33, 36 and 79) from southern, central and eastern Gaulish sources spanning the period from the late 1st to the early 3rd century AD, but all the sherds were residual in the contexts in which they occurred. One Central Gaulish form 31 bowl base preserved part of a stamp (Fig. 92, 54), unfortunately too incomplete and worn to be legible; a small (c 2–3mm in diameter) post-firing perforation drilled through the centre of the base of this vessel suggests that it had been repaired using metal staples in antiquity.

Most of the Central Gaulish black-slipped ware and Moselkeramik beaker sherds were found asso-

Fabrics	No.	Wt (g)	Rim count
Fine and specialist wares:			
Samian: South Gaulish	5	15	1
Samian: Central Gaulish	51	566	15
Samian: East Gaulish	3	18	1
Central Gaulish black-slipped ware	58	169	1
Moselkeramik	28	49	2
Dressel 20 amphora	1	302	–
Mortaria: New Forest colour-coated ware	2	37	–
Mortaria: New Forest whiteware	35	3211	19
Mortaria: Oxon red colour-coated ware	22	285	8
Mortaria: Oxon white colour-coated ware	4	64	2
Mortaria: Oxon whiteware	12	485	2
New Forest colour-coated ware	1076	11928	137
New Forest parchment ware	261	4901	51
New Forest red-slipped ware	117	1480	28
Oxon red colour-coated ware	153	2460	21
Oxon parchment ware	7	132	4
Oxon whiteware	1	46	–
Misc colour-coated ware	3	26	–
subtotal:	1839	26174	292
Coarsewares:			
Greyware	7954	88544	1038
Grog-tempered ware	3607	75269	351
South-east Dorset BB1	674	11844	170
Oxidised ware	143	1104	20
Overwey/Tilford type	4	25	0
subtotal:	12382	176786	1579
Overall total	14221	202960	1871

Table 5: Fabric totals

ciated with the Baths (Site F, particularly Trenches 25–28). The Central Gaulish sherds were derived from at least two fairly globular beakers (Symonds 1992, 21–4, fig. 9, 173–93), one indented and one dimpled form (*ibid*, 26, fig. 12, 241–54) with rouletted decoration. The Moselkeramik sherds were from similar beakers (*ibid*, 49–53, figs 24 and 25), including one funnel-necked, fluted or indented form (Fig. 89, 10) and at least one other globular-bodied vessel. The Central Gaulish black-slipped wares were imported from *c* AD 150/160–200/250, while the Moselkeramik vessels are slightly later, mostly arriving during the 3rd century AD. The overall paucity of imported wares is entirely consistent with the late Roman date of the assemblage as a whole, which falls outside the main period of ceramic importation.

Early Roman imported mortaria were absent, again reflecting the later Roman chronology of this assemblage, rather than deliberate consumer choice (with the exception of samian mortaria, these vessels were not imported much after *c* AD 150). Rims from two Central Gaulish samian mortaria (form 45) of late 2nd- to early 3rd-century AD date were identified, one (Fig. 91, 45) unstratified from Site L, the other preserving the lion-headed spout (Fig. 92, 59). Central and Eastern Gaulish samian mortaria body sherds were also found in Pit XX on Site L, as well as in Layer 6 in the well located close to the Baths, in a rubble layer over chalk in Trench 26 and in Layer 6e in an unknown trench, all on Site F. With the exception of these vessels, all the mortaria present derived from the New Forest and Oxfordshire industries, represented by almost equal numbers of sherds (Table 5). Pale-coloured mortaria were almost twice as common as their colour-coated counterparts, with New Forest parchment ware vessels (Fulford 1975, types 102 (Fig. 89, 2), 103 (Fig. 91, 43), 105 and 106) being the single most numerous group, 19 vessels being represented by rim count. However, among the colour-coated vessels, Oxfordshire products (Young 1977, types C97 and C100), both typically of 4th-century AD date, were more common than those from the New Forest, perhaps reflecting a longer production period for Oxfordshire vessels or their better quality.

Vessel type	Form		No. sherds	Rim count
beaker	Ful 27		141	79
	Ful 30		11	7
	Ful 33		1	1
	Ful 35		3	1
	Ful 38		4	2
	Ful 42.2		3	1
	Ful 44		5	5
	Ful 49		1	1
	Ful 52		1	1
	Ful G1		10	6
	WA 10		1	1
	Young C22		3	3
	Young C38		1	1
	bead rim beaker		4	1
	funnel-necked beaker		3	1
		beaker total	*192*	*111*
bowl	form 18/31 series		3	2
	form 31		3	3
	form 36		1	1
	Ful 59		5	4
	Ful 60		4	3
	Ful 61		1	1
	Ful 63		21	9
	Ful 67		3	3
	Ful 70		2	2
	Ful 71		1	1
	Ful 86		11	7
	Ful 88		3	3
	Ful 89		18	15
	Ful 101		5	3
	Ful G3		2	1
	Ful G6		215	145
	Ful G7		3	3
	Ful G8		5	3
	Ful G9		3	3
	Ful G10		2	2
	Ful G15		2	1
	WA 22		1	1
	WA 24		1	1
	WA 25		165	68
	Young C45		23	7
	Young C51		10	6
	Young P24		4	3
	dropped flange bowl		103	47
	flat flanged bowl		3	1
	grooved rim bowl		6	4
	imitation form 38		1	1
	incipient flanged bowl		5	4
		bowl total	*635*	*358*
cup	form 33		15	7
	Ful 53		1	1
		cup total	*16*	*8*
dish	form 79		1	1
	Ful 99		4	3
	Ful G5		5	4
	Ful G19		127	102
	WA 20		93	58
	WA 21		1	1
	dog-dish		77	34
		dish total	*308*	*203*
flagon	Ful 11		3	3
	Ful 93		41	1
	Young C8		2	2
		flagon total	*46*	*6*

Table 6: Vessel forms assigned to specific types (*continued overleaf*)
Ful = Fulford 1975; WA = Seager Smith and Davies 1993; Young = Young 1977; form = Dragendorff; L&J = Lyne and Jefferies 1979; D = Dicks 2009

Vessel type	Form		No. sherds	Rim count
flask	Ful 1		2	2
	Ful 7		1	1
	Ful 8		4	2
		flask total	*7*	*5*
jar	Ful 97		17	13
	Ful 98		1	1
	Ful G24		1	1
	Ful G25		12	11
	Ful G26		4	1
	Ful G27		7	4
	Ful G28		1	1
	Ful G30		584	458
	Ful G30.4		13	8
	Ful G30.11		1	1
	Ful G31		37	41
	Ful G32		10	7
	Ful G33		5	5
	Ful G33.2		1	1
	Ful G35		111	17
	L&J early class 1		4	3
	L&J late class 1		12	10
	L&J late class 4		2	1
	WA 2		4	2
	WA 2/3		18	15
	WA 3		47	20
	WA 9		6	1
	Young C16		1	1
	D181		5	1
	everted rim jar		306	189
	necked, cordoned jar		1	1
	upright-necked jar		1	1
		jar total	*1212*	*815*
jug	Ful 23		2	1
	Ful G20		119	38
	Ful G20		1	1
		jug total	*122*	*40*
lid	Ful 87		4	2
	Ful G23		10	10
	lid		1	1
		lid total	*15*	*13*
mortarium	form 45		2	2
	Ful 102		2	2
	Ful 103		8	7
	Ful 104		1	1
	Ful 105		3	3
	Ful 106		6	3
	Young C100		8	5
	Young C97		4	3
	Young M17		1	1
	Young M18		1	1
	Young M22		6	1
	Young WC7		2	2
		mortarium total	*44*	*31*
storage jar	Ful G40		13	9
	large, high-shouldered forms		141	3
	everted rim forms		37	25
	rope rimmed forms		23	17
		storage jar total	*214*	*54*
strainer	Ful G37		5	4
	bases		12	11
		strainer total	*17*	*15*
Overall total			**2828**	**1659**

Table 6: (*continued*)

Vessel type:

Fabric	beaker	bowl	cup	dish	flagon	flask	jar	jug	lid	mortarium	storage jar	strainer	Total
Site A													
Greyware	3	11					22	4				1	41
Grog-tempered ware		8		6			20				3		37
New Forest colour-coated ware	4												4
New Forest parchment ware		3							1				4
New Forest red-slipped ware		4											4
Oxidised ware		1											1
South-east Dorset BB1	1	7		3			4						15
A Total	8	34		9			46	4	1		3	1	106
Site C													
Greyware	2	14		6			15						37
Grog-tempered ware		6		1			8						15
Mortaria: Oxon red colour-coat ware										1			1
New Forest colour-coated ware	1												1
New Forest parchment ware		4											4
New Forest red-slipped ware		1											1
Oxon red colour-coated ware	2		1										3
Samian: Central Gaulish		1											2
South-east Dorset BB1		6		1			1						8
C Total	5	33	1	8			24		1				72
Site D													
Greyware	1	35		28			117	4	3	1	1		189
Grog-tempered ware		11		7			39		1		2		60
Mortaria: New Forest parchment ware										7			7
Mortaria: Oxon white colour-coated ware										2			2
New Forest colour-coated ware	15					1							16
New Forest parchment ware		3		3			4		1				11
Oxidised ware							1						1
Oxon red colour-coated ware	1	4			2		1						8
Samian: Central Gaulish		1											1
South-east Dorset BB1		19		11			11						41
D Total	17	73		49	2	1	173	4	5	9	3		336
Site E													
Greyware							1						1
South-east Dorset BB1				1									1
E Total				1			1						2
Site F													
Central Gaulish black-slipped ware	1												1
Greyware	3	29		25			194	7	2	3	3		266
Grog-tempered ware		14	1	9			64			16	1		104
Mortaria: New Forest parchment ware										4			4
Mortaria: Oxon red colour-coated ware										4			4
Mortaria: Oxon whiteware										2			2
Moselkeramik	2												2
New Forest colour-coated ware	40	3				1							45
New Forest parchment ware		6					4						10
New Forest red-slipped ware		6											6
Oxidised ware		5					1						6
Oxon parchment ware		4											4

Table 7: Vessel types from each site correlated with fabric (rim count shown) *(continued overleaf)*

Fabric	beaker	bowl	cup	dish	flagon	flask	jar	jug	lid	mortarium	storage jar	strainer	Total
Oxon red colour-coated ware		2											2
Samian: Central Gaulish		1											1
South-east Dorset BB1		16		19			13						48
F total	**46**	**86**	**1**	**53**		**1**	**276**	**7**	**2**	**10**	**19**	**4**	**505**
Site G													
Greyware		26		21		6	86	6					145
Grog-tempered ware		3					20				8		31
Mortaria: New Forest parchment ware										2			2
Mortaria: Oxon red colour-coated ware										1			1
Mortaria: Oxon whiteware										1			1
New Forest colour-coated ware	24				2								26
New Forest parchment ware		3					2						5
New Forest red-slipped ware		3											3
Oxidised ware		2					2						4
Oxon red colour-coated ware	1	3											4
Samian: Central Gaulish			1										1
South-east Dorset BB1		5		2									7
G total	**25**	**45**	**1**	**23**	**2**	**6**	**110**	**6**		**4**	**8**		**230**
Site H													
Greyware		1		1			7		1				10
Grog-tempered ware				1			2				2		5
Mortaria: New Forest parchment ware										1			1
New Forest colour-coated ware	2					1							3
Samian: South Gaulish		1											1
H Total	**2**	**2**		**2**		**1**	**9**		**1**	**1**	**2**		**20**
Site I													
Greyware		5		1		1	23						30
Grog-tempered ware		1		1			2						4
New Forest colour-coated ware	3	1					1						5
South-east Dorset BB1		5								1			6
I Total	**3**	**12**		**2**		**1**	**26**			**1**			**45**
Site J													
Greyware		7					10	2	1				20
Grog-tempered ware							1						1
Mortaria: New Forest parchment ware										1			1
New Forest colour-coated ware	1												1
Samian: Central Gaulish					1								1
South-east Dorset BB1					1						1		2
J Total	**1**	**7**			**2**		**11**	**2**	**1**	**1**	**1**		**26**
Site L													
Greyware		25		20			141	17	3	1			207
Grog-tempered ware		7		6			44				13		70
Mortaria: Oxon red colour-coat ware										1			1
New Forest colour-coated ware	26	1					2						29
New Forest parchment ware		9					4					1	14
New Forest red-slipped ware	1	11											12
Oxidised ware	2						2						4
Samian: Central Gaulish			5							1			6
Samian: East Gaulish				1									1
South-east Dorset BB1		7		18			7						32
L Total	**29**	**60**	**5**	**45**			**198**	**17**	**3**	**3**	**13**	**1**	**377**

Table 7: *(continued)*

The British finewares were dominated by New Forest products, principally the colour-coated wares and, to a lesser extent, the red-slipped and parchment wares (Fulford 1975, 24–6, fabrics 1a, 2a–b). Despite the prevalence of these wares, which together represented almost 80% of all the fine- and specialist wares by sherd count, the range of forms was somewhat limited (Table 6). Among the colour-coated wares (Fulford fabric 1a), indented beakers (type 27; Fig. 90, 34) were by far the most common type, accounting for 79 (74%) of the 107 vessels by rim count in this ware group, with small numbers of plain (type 44; Fig. 90, 35; five examples) and decorated (types 49 and 52; one each) bag-shaped beakers, globular beakers (types 30–38; Fig. 92, 56, 11 examples), cups (type 53; Fig. 90, 24), flasks (types 1, 7 and 8; four examples) and flagons (type 11; Fig. 90, 28). The red-slipped ware forms were restricted to the most common types produced in this fabric (types 59–61, 63, 67, 70, 71; Fig. 90, 33 and Fig. 92, 53) – all bowls imitating earlier samian forms. Although heavily abraded and thus only tentatively assigned to this fabric, a small fragment from a flat base with pre-firing perforations, found in the topsoil of Site L (SF no. 437; not illustrated), indicates the at least occasional production of strainer vessels in these wares. The parchment wares included pieces from at least three lids (type 87) as well as bowls (types 86 (Fig. 89, 1), 88 (Fig. 90, 21), 89, 90 and 101 (Fig. 90, 31)), jars (type 97; Fig. 90, 27), dishes (type 99) and a flagon (type 93; Fig. 90, 19). The majority of the New Forest forms were made throughout the period of production from the third quarter of the 3rd century AD through to the late 4th century AD, although types 1, 7, 8, 35, 44, 52, 61, 69–71 and 90 have more restricted, specifically 4th-century dates. None of the red-slipped wares exhibited the rosette stamped decoration characteristic of second half of the 4th century AD, but this may be due in part to the poor condition of the sherds themselves, rather than any scarcity of later 4th-century AD vessels in this particular fabric type.

Products of the Oxfordshire industry occurred in far smaller quantities, representing approximately 9% of this group by sherd count. Only the red/brown colour-coated wares occurred in any quantity and all the vessel forms are paralleled within the repertoire of forms made by this industry (Young 1977, types 8, 16, 22, 23, 45 and 51). Three small dimples worn into interior surface of a small, flanged bowl (Fig. 89, 6) found on Site F (1966, Trench 18, Layer 2) are comparable with marks recorded on samian (Taylor 2007, 242; Seager Smith *et al*. 2011, 119, pl. 1) and occasionally other tablewares (Seager Smith in prep) from Kent, but these are generally of later 1st- to 2nd-century AD date. It is possible that these dimples derive from attempts to reduce small quantities of the fabric to a powder for use elsewhere, as a 'jeweller's paste', for use in the preparation of foodstuffs, cosmetics or medicinal substances, for example, although the reasons why this should be desirable remain unclear. The single piece of Oxfordshire whiteware (an abraded base fragment) and all seven sherds of parchment ware from this region were from Site F. The parchment wares included sherds from two wall-sided bowls (Young 1977, type P24; one with traces of painted decoration surviving (Trench 29, Layer 2), the other more abraded and from an unlisted context) as well as a fragment from a bead rimmed bowl form (Room 15, Layer 2).

In contrast to the mortaria, where deliberate choices appear to have been made between the products of the New Forest and Oxfordshire industries, the frequency of the tablewares from these regions appears to reflect the relative distances of the industries from villa itself, the New Forest kilns being located some 25 miles to the south of the site while the Oxfordshire pottery kilns were twice that distance, 54 miles to the north-west. The miscellaneous colour-coated wares comprised two unsourced beaker body sherds both from the rubble in Room 23 of AB II, as well as a single piece of Nene Valley colour-coated ware, derived from a beaker with rouletted decoration. This was found in the subsoil (G3) of Site G, the Hall; its presence may reflect informal, hand-to-hand exchange or the movement of individuals within the late Roman villa community rather than any deliberate trade between these two very distant areas.

Coarsewares

The coarseware group formed the bulk of the assemblage, 87% by sherd count. The sandy greywares were the single largest fabric, representing 64% of the coarseware sherds and 56% of the whole Romano-British assemblage. These wares are likely to include products from a variety of different centres, perhaps spanning a wide date range. Some may derive from as-yet unlocated, local kilns, but the proximity of the New Forest pottery industry suggests that the majority are likely to be from this source. A few sherds were, however, attributable to the Rowlands Castle and Alice Holt production centres, highlighting the possibility of greater quantities from these sources amongst the less diagnostic pieces. Definite Rowlands Castle products included, for example, an everted rim jar (Dicks 2009, 60–1, class D1) (SF 162; Site D, baulk 28/31/33, topsoil) and part of a necked jar from Pit XX (Layer 5) on Site L. The Alice Holt greyware vessels of later Roman date included rims from ten cordoned jars with flat-topped rims (Lyne & Jefferies 1979, 37, fig. 22, late class 1A) and two sherds from a single bead rimmed jar (*ibid*, 28, fig. 15, class 4) found in Layer 6e in Trench 28, Site F. The handful of Overwey/Tilford-type wares made from *c* AD 330 into the 5th century AD (*ibid*, 35–7) were all found on Site F (Layers 2 (rubble) and 3 in Trench 29 and the backfill of Trench 31). Sherds from three necked cordoned jars akin to vessels produced in the Alice Holt district between AD 50 and 150 (*ibid*, 20–2, fig. 6, class 1), from Trench 10/15, Room 11 on Site D and Trench 5/8 to the east of the Baths on Site F, may hint at earlier Roman activity in these areas, although none are definite Alice Holt products.

Jars dominated the greyware assemblage, primarily the everted rim forms made throughout the later 3rd and 4th centuries AD, in the New Forest (Fulford 1975, 100, type 30), at Alice Holt (Lyne & Jefferies 1979, 42, late class 3B) and the more minor production centres. The rim of a small everted rim jar found in a rubble layer in baulk 1/2/3 in Room 16 in Site F, carried a post-firing graffito (Fig. 89, 11) scratched onto the inner part of its rim while a miniature vessel (Fig. 92, 60) survived complete. Other jars included narrow-mouthed ovoid forms (Fulford 1975, type 24), as well as bead rimmed types (*ibid*, type 25), some handled (Fig. 89, 3; type 26) of post-AD 350 date, or lid-seated (type 27), and a range of narrow-necked, globular-bodied types (e.g. types 31–6; Fig. 92, 52). Rims from nine large storage jars (type 40; Fig. 92, 46) and numerous thick-walled body sherds were also present, although these large vessels were far more common in grog-tempered fabrics. One of the rope-rimmed jars (unlisted context, Site G3) was pierced around its neck before firing, while three thick-walled greyware storage jar sherds, all from Site F (Trenches 25, 26 and 28, Layer 9b), had both pre-firing perforations and finger-smeared exterior surfaces. Similar vessels are known from excavations at High Post (Jones 2011, 62, fig. 27, 30) and at Durrington (Wessex Archaeology 2011), both to the north of Salisbury, while these features also occur on a distinctive type of oxidised Black Burnished ware vessel dated to the very late 4th or early 5th century AD (SEDOWW; Gerrard 2010; Seager Smith & Davies 1993, type 12). The function of these vessels remains a matter for conjecture (Gerrard 2010, 15). A small number of greyware beakers, dated to *c* AD 300–50 (Fulford 1975, 89, type 1) were also found on Site A (unlisted context), Site C (unlisted context and in an occupation layer in Room 22), in Trench 17 north of the house on Site D and in baulk 17/19 and the topsoil of Trench 21 on Site F. A simple bag-shaped form (Fig. 90, 20) in an unsourced, non-New Forest sandy greyware fabric was found in Ditch II, Site L.

The greyware bowls were likewise comparable to Fulford's type series (types 3, 6–10, 15, 37) with the bead-and-flanged type (type 6) by far the predominant form (145 vessels by rim count). One of these vessels (Trench 17, north of the house, Site D) was noticeably small, with a rim diameter of 100 mm and just 40 mm high. Evidence of possible re-use was noted on two vessels (Trench 31, Room 2 on Site D and an unlisted 1969 context on Site J) where the rim appears to have been trimmed, possibly as a means of prolonging the life-span of the vessel. One of the two reed-rimmed bowls (type 10) identified has a much thinner and flatter rim than the example illustrated by Fulford but is a close enough parallel; this form dates to the first half of the 4th century AD, while the wide-mouth bowl with an out bent rim (type 15) belongs within the second half of the century (Fulford 1975, 94). With the exception of four shallow dishes with flanged rims (type 5), the remaining greware dishes (120 by rim count) all comprised simple, shallow, plain rimmed forms (type 19; Fig. 90, 30), a common type made in a wide range of other fabrics. Other more minor vessel types included jugs (Fulford 1975, type 20; Fig. 91, 38) and a single ring-necked flagon not easily paralleled among the New Forest types. Rims from four greyware strainers (Fulford 1975, type 37) were also identified (Sites D and G2 and two unlisted contexts, 1965 and SF 139), while nine base sherds with small, pre-firing perforations (Sites A, C and F) can be attributed to similar vessels. Nine lid fragments (Fulford 1975, type 23), one with a bifurcated rim (Fig. 89, 9), and a single lid handle are also likely to be New Forest greywares whereas an additional lid, from Trench 21 in Room 9A on Site D, occurring in a fine-grained sandy fabric is quite different to the other sherds in this vessel class and may have been made at another centre.

Graffiti was noted on ten sherds or groups of joining greyware sherds (three from Site F, one each from G2 and G8, and five from Site L). Six comprised various arrangements of grooves or notches cut into the inner part of the rim of jars (e.g. Fig. 89, 11 and Fig. 91, 41) and, in one instance, the flange of a dropped flange bowl, while a group of joining body sherds probably from a beaker (e.g. Fulford 1975, 89, type 1) had similar deeply incised vertical grooves on the middle part of the body. A flat jar-type base found in Ditch II on Site L had an X scratched into its underside, while sherds from a dropped flanged bowl found in various contexts in Ditch II and Pit XX carried literate graffito consisting of at least six letters (Fig. 91, 42) but now incomplete, written on the exterior wall while the vessel was in an inverted position. A small, thin-walled, rather battered rim sherd from another dropped flanged bowl also found in Ditch II (SF 588) carried an incomplete scratched graffito, the letters AX or V surviving on the exterior wall, just beneath the rim. Such graffiti generally represent names, initials or illiterate marks of ownership (Evans 1987; Biddulph 2006) although alternatives may include numbers, indications of capacity, weight or intended contents, or apotropaic marks intended to charm the pot or to protect its contents (Going 1987, 108).

Late Roman grog-tempered wares, also known as Hampshire grog-tempered ware (Tyers 1996, 191; HAM GT Tomber & Dore 1998) accounted for 29% of the coarseware group by sherd count and 25% of the whole assemblage. The fabric of these handmade vessels is quite distinct – coarse and sometimes oxidised, with finger-tip impressions or finger smears on the interior surfaces which also occasionally display a limescale-type residue. Thick-walled storage jar sherds were common in these wares, with rims from at least 43 different vessels being recognised. Three basic forms were identified: rope-rimmed jars (17 examples), often with incised herringbone decoration on the inner part of the rim (e.g. Fig. 89, 13); large, everted rim jars (25 examples), one measuring at least 340 mm diameter; and 179 sherds (5372 g) from a single high-shouldered vessel with an inturned rim with a flat, scored surface, almost as if a rolled or everted rim was not added to the last coil of the shoulder, were derived from a variety of contexts (Layers 5, 9b, 12 and 12/6c) in Trench 28, Site F.

Although no production sites are currently known for the late Roman grog-tempered wares, the non-storage jar forms (most commonly everted rim jars, shallow, plain-rimmed dishes and dropped flanged bowl/dishes) are heavily influenced by the south-east Dorset Black Burnished wares, and were probably copied from this industry, albeit with considerable variation in detail. The assemblage also includes a few vessels with grooved rims, some with a curved profile (e.g. Fig. 90, 29) and others with straighter walls (e.g. Fig. 90, 32), probably based on the variant dropped flange bowls with high, short, almost residual flanges dated to the last quarter of the 4th century AD at Exeter (Holbrook & Bidwell 1991, 109, type 47) and other sites within the heartland of the south-east Dorset Black Burnished ware industry. A single lid fragment and a base sherd with pre-firing holes, presumably from a strainer (Site F, Trench 25, Layer 8), were also identified, while a post-firing incised X graffito was also noted on the underside of a jar base (Fig. 89, 15).

South-east Dorset Black Burnished wares were the only other coarseware to occur in any significant quantity (5% of the coarseware sherds). Vessel forms were dominated by the standard range of late Roman types: everted rim jars, shallow, plain-rimmed dishes and dropped flanged bowls/dishes (Seager Smith & Davies 1993, 231, types WA 2, 3, 20 and 25; Fig. 89, 7, Fig. 90, 17, 25, Fig. 91, 39, 40, 44). In addition, single examples of a handled, bead rim jar (WA 9), an oval 'fish-dish' (WA 21; Fig. 90, 26), a flat-rimmed bowl/dish (WA 22), a grooved-rimmed dish (WA 24) and a miniature bead rim beaker (WA 10) were also identified, all of 2nd- to 4th-century AD date. Many sherds with the characteristically late 'wiped' surface treatments and decorative styles (e.g. obtuse-angled lattice beneath grooves, the Redcliffe motif) emphasise the late Roman nature of this assemblage. At least seven instances of graffito were noted on sherds of this fabric. All consisted of single letters (e.g. Fig. 91, 36 and Fig. 92, 55) or abstract marks (e.g. Fig. 89, 5 and Fig. 91, 40).

The oxidised wares (Table 5) represented only a minor component of the assemblage. All these probably derived from fairly local sources, and are likely to be of late Roman date. Rims from four jars, two shallow, plain-rimmed dishes (one with straight, one with convex sides) and eight bowls were identified, with many body and base sherds likely to be derived from flagons and a few beaker forms. One of the bowls copied samian form 38 and may be a very badly abraded colour-coated ware vessel; this may be true for a number of the plain body sherds in this category.

Intra-site comparisons
Introduction

With the exception of Site L, which is discussed in more detail below, the pottery assemblages from each of the different excavation areas are largely homogeneous in terms of fabrics and vessel form composition, the quantity present being the primary distinction. The combination of relatively small amounts of pottery and their poor stratigraphic associations masks any overt functional differences between the buildings, at least in ceramic terms, except at the broadest of levels. However, the material from the five main areas is briefly considered below.

Sites A and F: the Aisled Building

The main part of this structure was examined as Site A, while Site F investigated a bath suite at the eastern end of the building. Traces of an earlier building were located beneath the main structure (AB I), but the limited stratigraphic information available does not permit the identification of, or differentiation between, the features and deposits belonging to these phases.

The assemblage from AB II (Site A) totalled 1033 sherds weighing 12,843 g. Although of later 3rd- to 4th-century AD date, very few diagnostic pieces derived from contexts which could provide any reliable indication of date for the construction and use of this building. The relatively low average sherd weight (12 g) for this group reflects the insecurely stratified nature of the deposits (approximately half could not be reliably assigned even to a particular room). Overall, the fine- and specialist wares (60 sherds, 647 g) represented just 6% of the assemblage by sherd count. New Forest products, especially the colour-coated wares, predominated, with a handful of bowls in red-slipped and parchment ware (e.g. Fig. 89, 1) fabrics. Earlier, imported fineware sherds (Central Gaulish samian and black-slipped ware and Moselkeramik), dating from *c* AD 150 into the early 3rd century AD, probably derive from the earlier structure in this area. The coarsewares mainly comprised sandy greywares (49% by sherd count), grog-tempered wares (37%) and south-east Dorset Black Burnished wares (6%). Vessel forms in all fabrics comprised the standard range described above.

Undiagnostic body and jar base sherds (7 sherds, 128 g; greyware and grog-tempered fabrics) were found in the backfill of Room 12. The 61 sherds (1196 g) from Room 13 included two pieces of greyware from a 'red layer' (second floor layer) and 38 grog-tempered and one greyware body sherd from a 'mortary layer' (first floor layer); all the others were undiagnostic, grog-tempered and derived from backfill or demolition/tumble deposits. The much larger group (236 sherds, 3435 g) from Room 23 at the eastern end of this building mostly derived from rubble deposits; the pieces from a 'chalk layer' (17 sherds, 46 g), 'slate scatter' (28 sherds, 285 g) or the 'first burnt area' (7 sherds, 31 g) could only be assigned a late 3rd- to 4th-century AD date. Similarly, none of the sherds (a greyware jar base and five bodies, two grog-tempered bodies and a scrap of Moselkeramik beaker) from a 'natural floor layer' in this room could be assigned anything more than a generalised late Roman date.

Greater quantities of pottery were associated with the main aisled room of this building (Room 19; 203 sherds, 2044 g). Many were derived from backfill, demolition or rubble deposits and the majority of those from layers to which stratigraphic relationships could potentially be assigned, while spanning the period from the mid-2nd to 4th century AD, were again too small, abraded and otherwise undiagnostic to provide anything more specific than a generalised late Roman date. However, factors such as the relatively high proportion of Late Roman grog-tempered wares (62 sherds; 30% of the total) and the presence of a New Forest parchment ware lid dated to *c* AD 320–400 (Fulford 1975, 70, fig. 23) found in a floor layer (Trench 2) and a greyware bead rim jar (*ibid*, 98, type 25; unlisted context, bag eBF2) dated to *c* AD 270–350, indicate that activity in this room continued well into the 4th century AD.

The greatest quantity of material (5305 sherds, 69,716 g) was found in the area of the bath suite (Site F), at the eastern end of the building. The average sherd weight, however, is just 13 g, and the fine- and specialist wares (548 sherds, 5650 g) comprised a surprisingly low component of this assemblage, at just 10% by sherd count. This is comparable with the figure from the Main House (Site D), but lower than that from the Barn (Site C) and Hall (Site G). Within the fine- and specialist ware group, the New Forest products were again dominant, with beakers the most prevalent and wide-ranging form (Fulford 1975, types 27, 30 and 44). A small, internally worn flanged bowl (Fig. 89, 6), colour-coated ware beaker sherds from the Oxfordshire region (Young 1977, types C51 and C22) and fragments from two Moselkeramik beakers (Fig. 89, 10) were also present although these latter sherds may well be residual finds contemporary with the earlier structure in this area. In total, beakers comprised 9% of the vessel forms, compared with 5% at the Main House (Site D). Amongst the coarsewares, greywares remained predominant, representing 55% (by sherd count) of the whole assemblage from this area. The grog-tempered wares accounted for 30% and the south-east Dorset Black Burnished wares 4% of the sherds. At least 12 grog-tempered storage jars were represented by rims, including the high-shouldered vessel with an inturned, poorly formed rim (Layers 5, 9b, 12 and 12/6c, Trench 28) described above. Fragments from a large 4th-century AD rope-rim grog-tempered storage jar which may have been set into the ground were found in Trench 30. Internally finger-smeared pieces from a greyware storage jar were perhaps contained within it, while sherds from the layer surrounding this deposit included further fragments from both these vessels as well as plain body sherds of New Forest parchment ware and Black Burnished ware. The relatively high incidence of beakers and storage jars in this area may be linked to activities within the bath house, such as drinking and the storage of liquids, either for consumption or bodily applications.

Some 198 sherds (2094 g) were found in the Well (Trench 4). Greywares and New Forest colour-coated wares were the dominant fabric groups and indicate a late 3rd- to late 4th-century AD date, although a residual samian mortariium (form 45) body sherd was found in Layer 4. The fine- and specialist ware element of this assemblage, at 13%, was slightly higher than on the rest of Site F, although only three vessels (all New Forest indented beakers) were recognised from rims. Sherds from at least seven south-east Dorset plain-rimmed dishes and two everted rim jars were found amongst the coarsewares, although all were relatively small fragments. The other coarsewares included pieces from dropped flange and moulded-rim bowls and everted rim jars in both greyware (Fulford 1975, types 6, 8, 24 and 30) and the grog-tempered fabrics. No complete or even reconstructible vessels (ie dropped into the Well during use) were recovered from this feature.

Site C: the Barn

Only 267 sherds (4639 g) were found in this area and, of these, 94 pieces (37%) were effectively unstratified, being from unlisted or topsoil contexts. Only 58 sherds (1217 g) occurred within the building, the remainder being found outside, in the adjacent Courtyard. The majority of pieces showed signs of heavy abrasion normally associated with re-deposited material, although, at 17 g, the average sherd weight was comparatively high.

The fine- and specialist wares (59 sherds, 1124 g) represented 18% of the sherds from this area, mostly derived from the New Forest, while the grog-tempered and sandy greywares dominated the coarseware group. The majority were of late 3rd- or 4th-century AD date, although few provided more specific dating evidence for the construction/use of this building. Part of a shallow, plain-rimmed dish was found in a context associated with the construction of the wall of Room 22 but it cannot be dated with any certainty within this late Roman period. Of the 26 sherds (457 g) recovered from the probable occupation deposits inside Room 22, 20 were grog-tempered; other fabrics included sherds from a greyware beaker and New Forest red-slipped and parchment ware bowls (Fulford 1975, types 1, 59 and 88), providing further evidence for continued activity into the 4th century AD. Seven sherds of Central Gaulish samian, comprising four from a form 33 cup, a rim scrap from a form 18/31 series dish and two plain bodies, were found in rubble layers outside Rooms 21 and 22 and in two unlisted contexts, while a scrap from an East Gaulish form 27 cup came from a demolition layer outside Room 20. These pieces, together with a single piece of Central Gaulish black-slipped ware (unlisted context), were all of late 2nd- to 3rd-century AD date and were probably residual here. A small undiagnostic body sherd in an Iron Age sandy fabric found above the natural outside Room 22 also hints at earlier activity in this area.

Site D: the Main House

A total of 2178 sherds (38,921 g) were recovered from a combination of trial trenches and excavation in this area, although just over a quarter of the assemblage (by sherd count) was recovered from topsoil or deposits located outside the building. Sherds were in a relatively good condition, with an average weight of 18 g, although the proportion of fine- and specialist wares was lower than that recorded in other areas, comprising 12% by sherd count. New Forest colour-coated vessels were the dominant fineware fabric (156 sherds; 61% by sherd count) but the range of vessels, represented by rim count, was restricted to a single flask (Fulford type 1), 14 indented beakers (Fulford type 27) and a parchment ware mortarium (Fig. 89, 2). Sherds from single central Gaulish black-slipped ware and Moselkeramik beakers occurred as residual finds within Trench 17, to the north of the house. As within the overall assemblage, greywares were the principal coarseware (60% by sherd count), followed by later Roman grog-tempered ware (23%) and Black Burnished ware (7%). Oxidised wares were present as plain body sherds only.

With the exception of Room 11 where sherds were located within a collapsed hypocaust, the quantities of pottery deriving from individual rooms are low. Consequently detailed analysis, in terms of functional or spatial patterning, has not been possible across the building. The overall Site D assemblage has a broad date range encompassing the late 3rd to late 4th centuries AD. However, the material from Room 11 (693 sherds, 13,082 g) contains at least three forms consistent with a mid-4th century AD or later date. Two of these vessels are greywares: a New Forest round-bodied bowl with down-turned rim (Fulford type 15) and a two-handled, bead-rim jar (Fulford type 26; Fig. 89, 3). In addition, sherds from a Black Burnished ware jar decorated with obtuse lattice are unlikely to date any earlier than the mid-4th century AD. It is unclear whether a complete New Forest two-handled, pedestal bowl (Fulford type 26; currently held at Winchester Museum and not quantified here), found in the hypocaust, is a fortuitous survival or a deliberately placed deposit. This form has been dated by Fulford to the first half of the 4th century and if it is contemporary with the rest of the assemblage it may represent a form of 'closure' deposit some time around the mid-4th century AD, presumably as the villa structure was abandoned. This would tally with the date assigned to the large pit (XX) on Site L, which appears to have been deliberately filled at the same time.

Sherds recovered from a midden located in the Courtyard, to the south of the Main House, reflect the main assemblage and although three layers were identified it was not possible, with the surviving sherds, to distinguish between them or to assign a more closely refined date other than the late 3rd to 4th century AD.

Site G: the Hall

A total of 1021 sherds (13,694 g) were found in this vicinity. The fine- and specialist wares represented 22% of this total. The bulk of the sherds were from unlisted or poorly stratified contexts and most exhibited the heavy surface abrasion and edge damage characteristic of re-deposited material. The average sherd weight was 13 g. The majority of the vessels came from the New Forest kilns (grey- and colour-coated wares; 55% and 16% of the sherds respectively), with the late Roman grog-tempered wares, assigned to the 4th century AD, representing 20% of the sherds overall. Jar forms were the dominant vessel class (48% by rim count), with bowls the only other significant class (19% by rim count), proportions broadly similar to those from the Main House (Site D) (51% and 22% respectively).

Site L: pits and enclosures to the west of the Main House (Site D)

The pottery from this area warrants further discussion given the peculiarity of the deposits (discrete pits and ditches) and chronological range of material present. The complete assemblage from this area amounted to 4428 sherds weighing 60,161 g, of which 765 sherds (10,624 g) were of Iron Age date. Five features contained only Iron Age material (Ditch XXI and Pits VII, IX, XII and XVII; see above, Johnston, p.12–15), while Pits XIII and XV, probably of Iron Age date, also contained minor quantities of intrusive Romano-British sherds. Pits XX, XIX and V, however, contained only Romano-British material. Overall, 3663 sherds, 49,537 g, of Romano-British pottery were recovered.

Over half of the Romano-British assemblage was found in Pit XX (2518 sherds, 30521 g), which was probably filled during the mid–late 4th century AD. A single Central Gaulish black-slipped ware beaker base and rim sherds from three Central Gaulish samian form 33 cups, all of late 2nd- to 3rd-century AD date, were probably residual in this feature. The British finewares were again dominated by the New Forest colour-coated wares, predominantly from indented beakers (e.g. Fig. 90, 34) although bag-shaped (Fig. 90, 35) and globular-bodied beakers, flagons (Fig. 90, 28) and red-slipped ware bowls including bead rimmed forms and vessels imitating samian forms 31 and 38 were also noted. One New Forest colour-coated ware cup or small bowl had white-painted decoration (Fig. 90, 24). The indented beakers were made throughout the life of the New Forest industry, but the others were all of more specific 4th-century AD date. The New Forest parchment wares were also predominantly of 4th-century date (Fulford 1975, types 88, 89, 97 and 101; Fig.

90, 21, 27 and 31). Other fine- and specialist wares included body and base sherds of Oxfordshire colour-coated ware, including pieces from mortaria and a flanged bowl (Young 1977, type C51) and a single New Forest parchment ware mortarium base. The coarsewares were also dominated by greywares and grog-tempered wares, and included the standard range of vessel forms. One of the grog-tempered everted rim jars was more or less complete (Fig. 91, 37). Other less common forms included two grog-tempered bowls with grooved rims (Fig. 90, 29 and 32) and a plain-rimmed bowl with pronounced curved wall (Fig. 90, 30). The south-east Dorset Black Burnished ware vessels comprised the three standard late Roman forms, along with a fish-dish (Fig. 90, 26), probably of 4th-century AD date. One of the everted rim jars from this region survived intact (Fig. 91, 39).

The proportion of fine- and specialist wares within Pit XX (408 sherds; 16% by sherd count) mirrors that for the whole assemblage from Site L (579 sherds; 16% by sherd count) and it is therefore unlikely that these wares were specially selected for disposal in this feature. It is probable, though, that this pit was filled relatively quickly, as numerous cross-context joins were noted amongst the material. While there are no overt signs of the selective discard of ceramics within this feature, it is interesting to note the presence of a dog skeleton in Layer 8. This may of course be completely fortuitous, being simply an obvious way to dispose of a carcass, but dogs are known to have been associated with a number of Celtic deities, in particular the mallet god Sucellos (Black 2008, 2), who is also represented by a jar (olla) and hammer. Evidence from the Lydney shrine also suggests associations with Nodons, the god of hunting and healing (Ross 1968, 275), while in Gaul the dog was associated with healing and the underworld (Green 1976, 13 and 33). Black lists numerous examples from domestic contexts in south-east England, particularly Kent, including at Springhead (Seager Smith *et al.* 2011, 133, fig. 47), where incomplete pots have been found with dog skeletons and other artefacts in large pits or shafts. To the west, examples are known from Butterfield Down (Rawlings & Fitzpatrick 1996, 13, fig. 9, feature 310) and on the adjacent land south-east of Amesbury sites (Cooke *et al.* in prep, shaft 3092).

The assemblages from Pits V (121 sherds, 1765 g) and XIX (85 sherds, 639 g) comprised a similar range of fabrics and forms, but relatively few were more precisely datable within the late 3rd- to 4th-century AD period. However, part of a New Forest red-slipped ware bowl (Fulford 1975, 64, type 61), dated to *c* AD 340–70, was found in Pit V, while the high proportion of late Roman grog-tempered wares (55% by sherd count; 67 sherds, 1338 g) could suggest a later 4th-century AD+ date for this feature.

Two of the ditches, I and IV, extended underneath the House (Site D), and the material contained within them therefore offers some assistance in dating the construction of this building. Only six sherds (76 g) could be assigned to Ditch IV: an unstratified base, a plain body sherd from Layer 7 (both sandy greyware) and four grog-tempered body sherds from Layer 4, assigned a 4th-century AD date on fabric grounds alone. Ditch I contained a more substantial assemblage consisting of 182 sherds, 3323 g. The single largest fabric group, however, comprised Iron Age flint-tempered wares (79 sherds, 1229 g). These included part of an ovoid jar with an internally thickened rim (see Fig. 88, 11), possibly part of the Middle/Late Iron Age 'saucepan-pot' tradition of central southern England, and a single undiagnostic body sherd from a different vessel came from the primary silts. These sherds were associated with another late Roman grog-tempered ware sherd although, at just 5 g, the possibility that this piece is intrusive cannot be excluded. However, the lower average sherd weight of the Iron Age material (15 g, compared with 20 g for the Roman material) may provide a further indication of the residual nature of the prehistoric pieces. The rest of the assemblage was of late 3rd- to 4th-century AD date, but sadly not more closely datable within this period. Greywares accounted for a further 24% (44 sherds, 555 g) of the sherds from this feature and the grog-tempered wares 15% (28 sherds, 880 g). Forms included a dropped flanged bowl/dish, a bowl with an inturned rim, everted rim jars, jugs, and plain rimmed dishes (Fulford 1975, types 6, 7, 19, 20 and 30). The New Forest colour-coated vessels were restricted to body sherds from indented beakers (*ibid*, type 27). None of these forms are particularly closely datable. The only other identifiable form present was from a south-east Dorset Black Burnished ware dish (Seager Smith & Davies 1993, WA 20), a form widely traded from the later 2nd century AD onwards.

Conclusion

Although predominantly of late 3rd- to 4th-century AD date, the ceramics suggest that Romano-British activity commenced during the later 2nd century AD, with the main focus of this earliest activity concentrated in the area of the Baths (Site F) and to the rear of the Main House (Site L). Overall, the assemblage was dominated by New Forest products, reflecting the proximity of this industry, while other coarsewares were obtained from the Surrey/Hampshire borders and as yet unidentified, local sources. Hampshire grog-tempered wares, Black Burnished wares from the Wareham/Poole Harbour region of Dorset and a variety of Oxfordshire products also formed significant components of the assemblage. The paucity of imports, here limited to a single Dressel 20 amphora sherd, small quantities of samian and dark colour-coated ware beakers from Central Gaul and the Mosel regions, is entirely consistent with a later Roman date and known distribution patterns across southern Britain as a whole, while a small number of sherds in a variety of handmade, mostly grog-tempered, fabrics may extend the date range of this assemblage into the early 5th century AD. The vessel forms were predominantly utilitarian, encompassing the standard range of types characteristic of the period in this region – jars of all sizes, straight-sided bowls/dishes, together with a small range of less common types (flagons, lids, beakers, strainers etc). Only limited evidence for re-use or repair was encountered, perhaps indicating easy access to the wider market economy and a ready supply of replacement vessels. In broadest of brush terms, then, the Sparsholt assemblage conforms with all the expected features of other assemblages, both urban and rural, from the area.

Catalogue of illustrated sherds

Site A

1. New Forest parchment ware bowl with an external flange, Fulford type 86. Trench 16, 2 (bag SPAβ$_4$K)

Site D

2. New Forest parchment ware mortarium, Fulford type 102. Unlisted context (bag KG1)
3. Greyware handled, pulled-bead rim jar, Fulford type G26. Room 11 (bags HB and HE)
4. Greyware dropped flange bowl/dish, Fulford type 6. Unlisted context (bags HK1 and GY3)
5. South-east Dorset Black Burnished ware body sherd with neatly incised, post-firing, abstract graffito on interior surface. Trench 33, rubble layer 2 (bag JX)

Site F

6. Oxfordshire colour-coated ware flanged bowl with worn, internal dimples, Young type C51. Trench 18, Layer 2 (bag FB)
7. South-east Dorset Black Burnished ware dropped flange bowl/dish, WA type 25. Trench 25, under plaster (bag PD2)
8. Greyware upright-necked jar, Fulford G30. Trench 25, under plaster (bag PH1)
9. Greyware lid, Fulford G23. Trench 25, under plaster (bag PH2)
10. Moselkeramik funnel-necked beaker, fluted or indented form. Baulk 26/27 (bag OY)
11. Greyware everted rim jar with a post-firing, scratched graffito on the inner part of the rim, Fulford type G30. Room 15/16, baulk 1/2/3, rubble (bag CM)

Site G

12. Greyware bowl with an out bent, reeded rim, Fulford type G9. Unlisted context, Site G2 (bag K)
13. Grog-tempered ware rope rim storage jar with herringbone decoration on the inner part of the rim. Trench 4, Layer 6, flint cobbling. SF 340 (bag G)
14. Greyware everted rim jar with a post-firing, scratched graffito on the inner part of the rim, Fulford type G30. Unlisted context, Site G2 (bag BG)
15. Grog-tempered jar base with a post-firing, scratched graffito on the underside. Unlisted context, Site G5 (bag C)

Site L

Ditch II

16. Grog-tempered grooved flange bowl/dish. Layer 3 (bag AR)
17. South-east Dorset Black Burnished ware dropped flange bowl/dish, WA type 25. Unstratified Ditch II (bag H)
18. Greyware bowl with an out bent, reeded rim, Fulford type G9. Unlisted context (bags B and Q2)
19. New Forest parchment ware flagon with dark brown painted decoration, Fulford type 93. Unlisted context (bag JJ)
20. Greyware bag-shaped beaker with a beaded rim, burnished decoration. Unlisted context (bag JP)

Pit XX

21. New Forest parchment ware bowl with a thickened rim and painted decoration, type 88. Layer 5 (bag IB)
22. New Forest colour-coated ware beaker/flagon shoulder sherd with incised decoration. Layer 5 (bag JY)
23. Greyware bowl with a rolled out rim, Fulford type G30.4 or G37. Layer 5 (bag IW)
24. New Forest colour-coated ware cup/small bowl with white painted decoration, Fulford type 53. Layers 5 (bag IW) and 8 (bag JD)
25. South-east Dorset Black Burnished ware everted rim jar, WA type 3. Layer 5 (bag IW)
26. South-east Dorset Black Burnished ware shallow, straight-sided, plain-rimmed dish, oval in plan ('fish-dish'), WA type 21. Layer 6 (bag KG)
27. New Forest parchment ware jar Fulford type 97. Layer 6 (bag KG)
28. New Forest colour-coated ware flagon, Fulford type 11. Layer 7 (bag KE)
29. Grog-tempered grooved rim bowl with curved walls, Layer 7 (bags KI and KL)
30. Grog-tempered shallow, plain-rimmed dish with curved walls. Layer 7 (bags KE, KI and KL)
31. New Forest parchment ware bowl/dish with short, external flange, Fulford type 101. Layer 7 (bag KE)
32. Grog-tempered grooved rim bowl/dish. Layer 7 (bag KE)
33. New Forest red-slipped ware flanged bowl, Fulford type 63. Layer 7 (bag KL)
34. New Forest colour-coated ware indented beaker, Fulford type 27. Layer 7 (bag KL)
35. New Forest colour-coated ware bag-shaped beaker, Fulford type 44. Layer 7 (bag KL)
36. South-east Dorset Black Burnished ware jar base with a post-firing scratched T graffito on underside. Layer 8 (bag KS)
37. Grog-tempered everted rim jar. Layer 8 (bag KH)
38. Greyware single-handled jug with burnished-line decoration, Fulford type G20. Layer 8 (bag KR)
39. South-east Dorset Black Burnished ware jar with burnished line decoration, WA type 3. Unlisted context, SF 607
40. South-east Dorset Black Burnished ware shallow, groove-rimmed dish with a post-firing scratched graffito on the underside of the base, WA type 20. Layer 7 (bag HC), SF 537
41. Greyware everted rim jar with a post-firing scratched graffito on the inner part of rim, Fulford type G30. Layer 5 (bag KB), SF 622

Ditch II and Pit XX

42. Greyware dropped flanged bowl with post-firing scratched graffito consisting of at least six letters (now incomplete) written on exterior wall while the vessel was inverted. Unlisted contexts (bags HE, HJ and HM), SF 525

Other vessels from Site L

43. New Forest parchment ware mortarium, Fulford type 103. Unlisted context (bag FA3)
44. South-east Dorset Black Burnished ware shallow, plain-rimmed dish, WA type 20. Unlisted context (Bag FC2)
45. Central Gaulish samian form 45 mortarium. Unstratified (bag FD)

1965

46. Greyware rope-rimmed storage jar, Fulford type G40. C, trial trench 265S 21W (bag 37)
47. Greyware jar with burnished line decoration, Fulford type G30. C, trial trench 265S 21W (bag 37)
48. Greyware dropped flanged bowl/dish, Fulford type G6. C, trial trench 265S 21W (bag 37)
49. Greyware dropped flanged bowl/dish, Fulford type G6. C, trial trench 265S 21W (bag 37)
50. Oxfordshire colour-coated ware flanged bowl, Young form C51. C, trial trench 265S 21W (bag 37)

51. Grog-tempered jar body sherd with an incomplete post-firing, scratched graffito on its exterior surface. C, trial trench 235S (bag 43)
52. Greyware narrow-mouthed lid-seated jar, Fulford type G35. C, trench 238S, topsoil (bag 67)
53. New Forest red-slipped ware cup/bowl, Fulford type 67. A1, trench 50S 50E (bag 76)

Other vessels

54. Central Gaulish samian form 31 bowl base with faint (very abraded) stamp and traces of a small, post-firing perforation through the centre of the base, indicative of repair with a metal staple. Unlisted context, SF 187
55. South-east Dorset Black Burnished ware dish base, decorated with burnished line random scribbling on the exterior and a 'Redcliffe' motif on the interior as well as a post-firing scratched X graffito in the centre. Site J, SE quadrant level 3 over natural (bag D)
56. New Forest colour-coated ware indented globular beaker, rim slightly misshapen and dunting cracks in foot and neck; dull matt brown firing, Fulford type 33. 1967, unlisted context, SF 69
57. Grog-tempered ware everted rim jar. 1969 (Site C?), Trench 1–2, demolition, SF 185 (Room 22, Layer 7)
58. Oxfordshire red colour-coated ware bowl, Young C45, 1969 (Site C?), Trench 1–2, demolition, SF 186
59. Central Gaulish samian form 45 with surviving lion-headed spout. 1972, unlisted context, SF 518
60. Greyware miniature everted rim jar, black slip on rim and shoulder, Fulford type G30.11. Unlisted context, SF 360

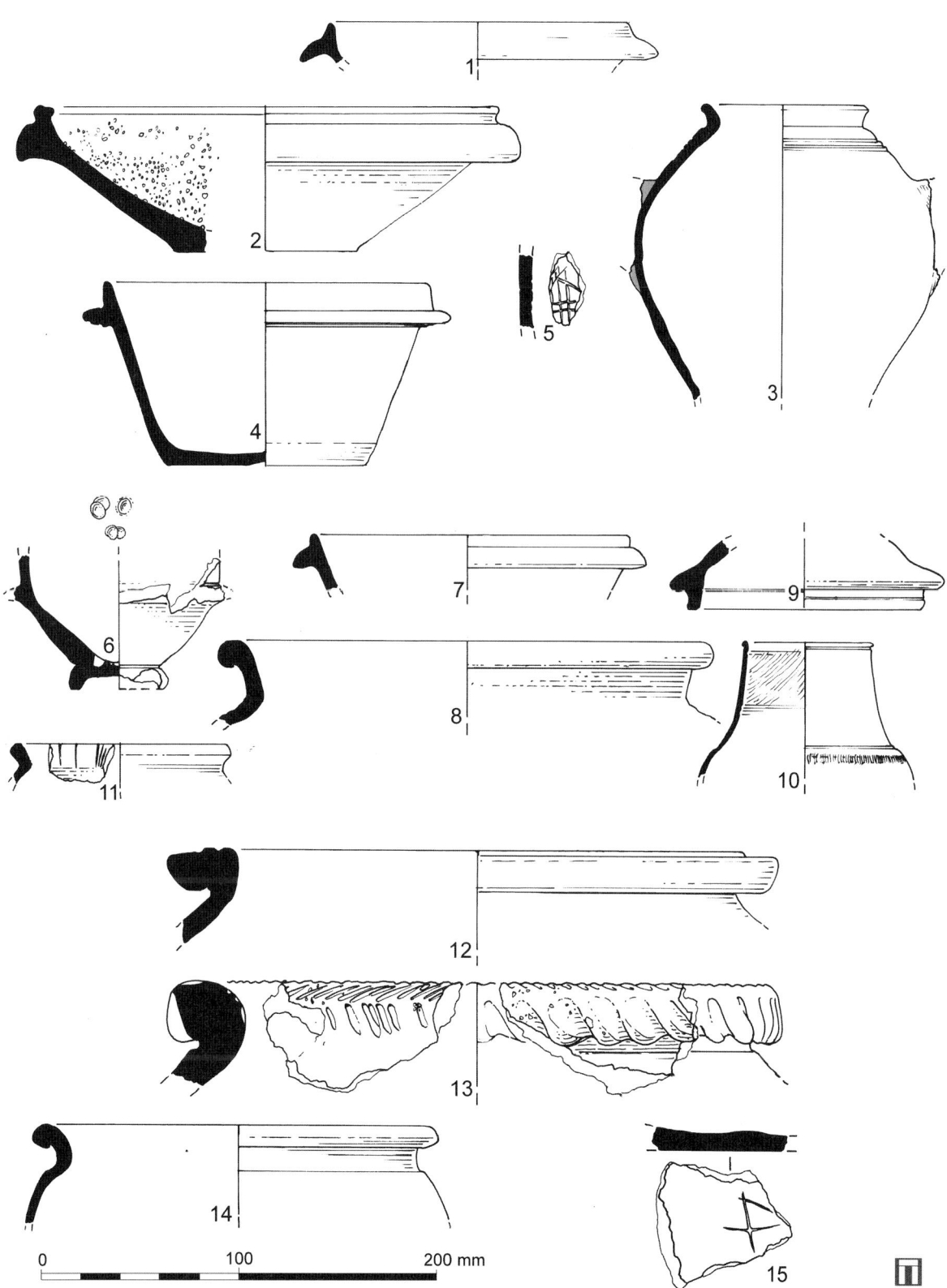

Fig 89   Romano-British pots 1–15 (drawings by S E James)

110   POTTERY

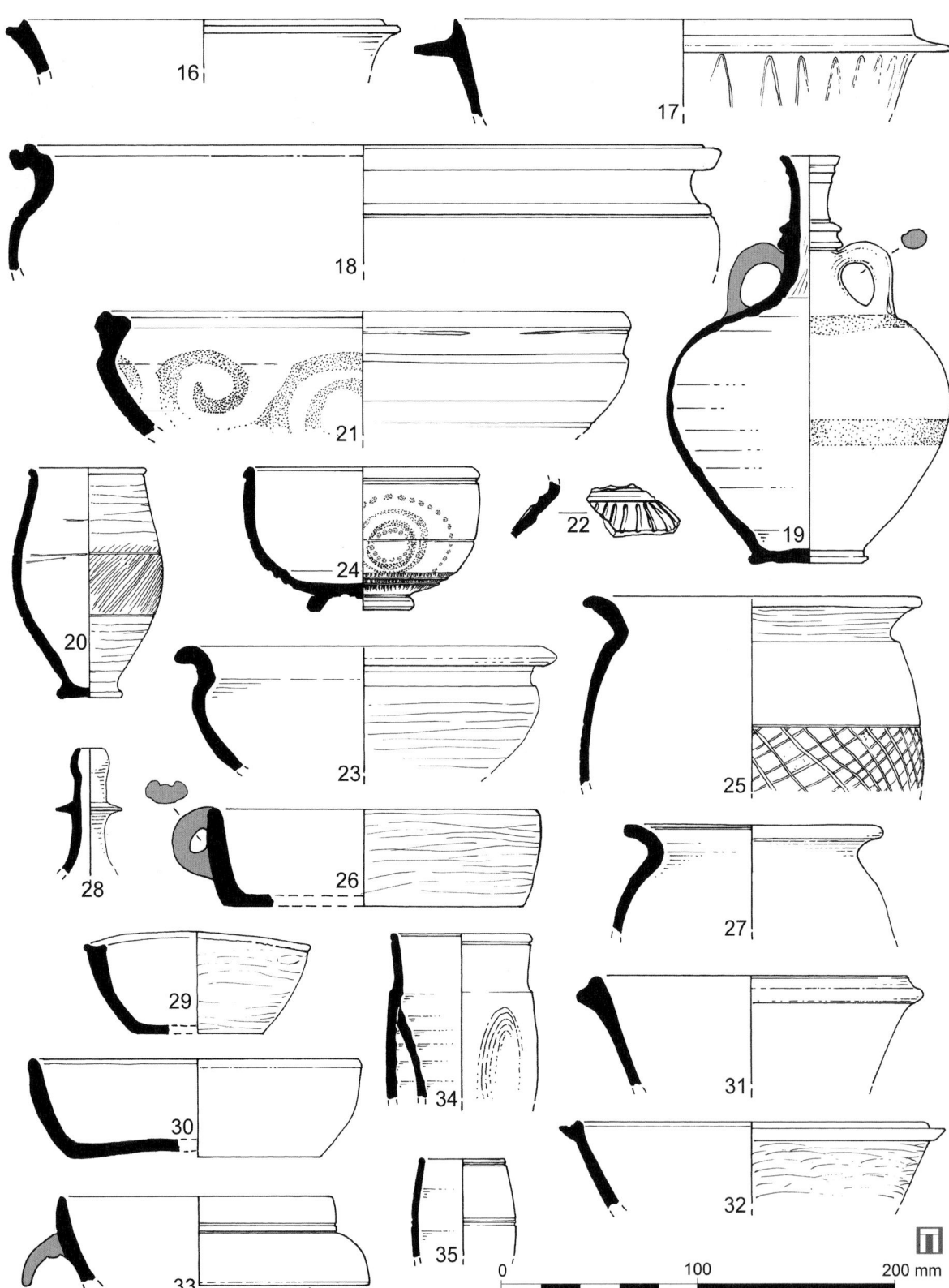

Fig 90   Romano-British pots 16-35 (drawings by S E James)

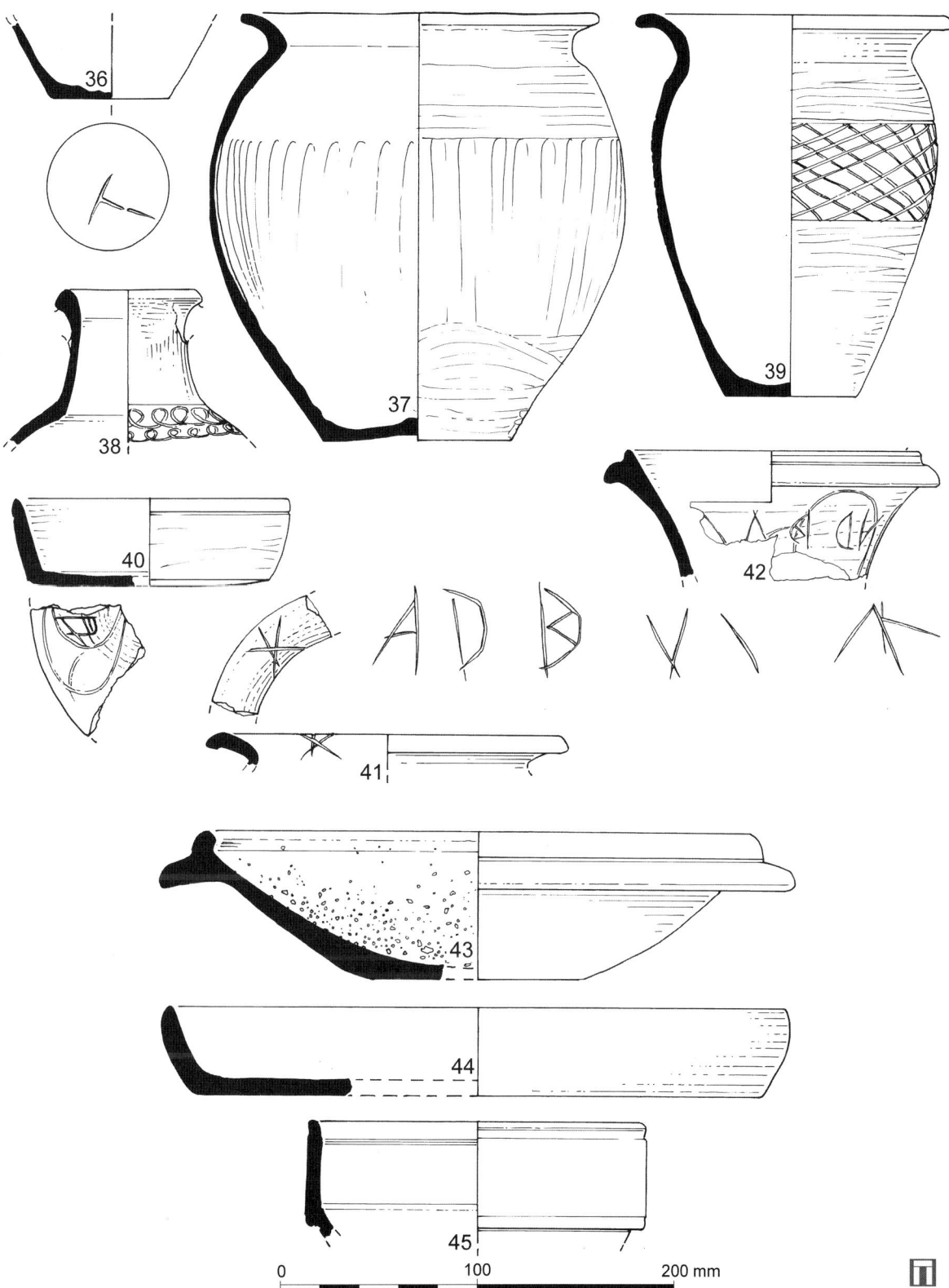

Fig 91   Romano-British pots 36–45 (drawings by S E James)

112 POTTERY

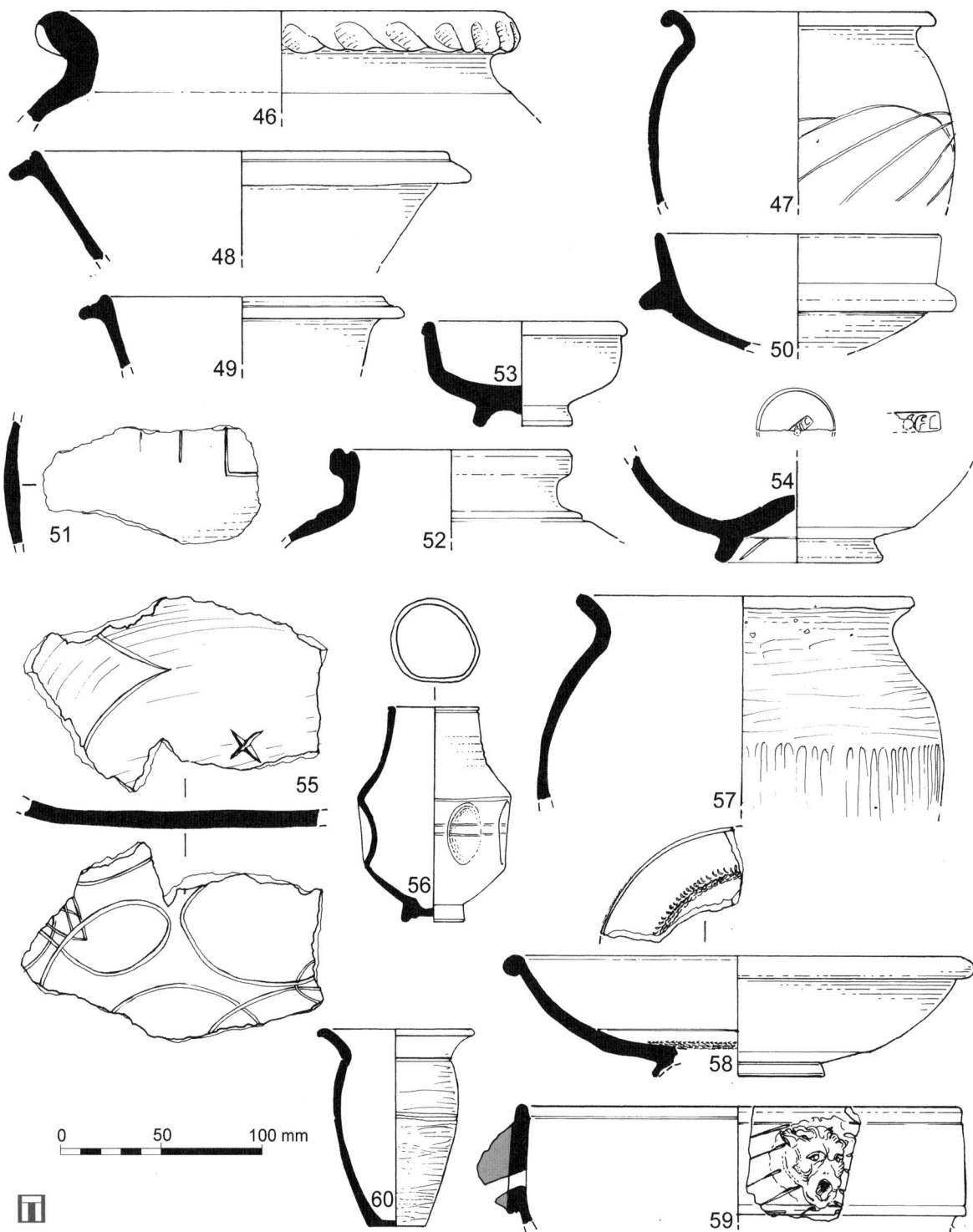

Fig 92　Romano-British pots 46-60 (drawings by S E James)

Chapter 10

The Mosaics

by Steve Cosh

Note: The numbers following a mosaic refer to the volume, site and mosaic number in Roman Mosaics of Britain *by Cosh & Neal 2005 (Mosaic II) or Neal & Cosh 2009 (Mosaic III), where full references are given. The Sparsholt mosaics are given the site prefix 322.*

Two rooms of the Main House had fine mosaics (Fig. 93); by far the most complete one came from Room 7, the central room, and the other, a fragmentary mosaic, paved a channelled hypocaust in Room 11. The Corridor (*porticus*) also had a mosaic with a repetitive geometrical design, accurately executed in larger tesserae. Five other floors were coarse tessellated pavements, either with simple patterns in grey and red, or plain red. Room 2 had a chequered panel in grey and red (Fig. 94; Mosaic III, 322.2), while two anterooms (Rooms 6 and 9) had bands predominantly of red and grey, although there is a fair degree of intermixture of the colours, conceivably resulting from the re-use of badly sorted tesserae. These simple and commonplace 'mosaics' are adequately described above. The other large rooms (4 and 8) had plain red tessellated pavements.

AB II (built over an earlier masonry structure, AB I) was developed to incorporate a bath suite in the south-east corner and a cross-range of three rooms at the western end. The central room of the cross-range, Room 13, had a coarse red tessellated floor with a grey band (Mosaic III, 322.8) and the southern one, Room 12, was paved with a fine mosaic (Mosaic III, 322.7). The bath suite yielded fine wall plaster, including a representation of a mosaic showing bands of guilloche (Davey & Ling 1981, 158–9, pl. LXXII, fig. 36); other examples of painted tessellation occur, for example from Bignor, West Sussex, and it is doubtless meant to portray what would be expensive wall mosaics in the same way as marble veneer is imitated on wall-plaster.

The Main House dates to the late 3rd century but, except in the *porticus*, the mosaics covered earlier floors and belong to a period of refurbishment during the first half of the 4th century, probably in the first quarter, if damage near the entrance on the principal mosaic was the result of wear. Within the floors themselves a *terminus post quem* is provided by a tessera from the tessellated pavement in Room 6 made from a sherd of a mortarium belonging to the late 3rd or early 4th century. The mosaic from Room 7 and the largest fragment from Room 11 were lifted; the former is displayed in the Winchester City Museum. The other mosaics were reburied.

MAIN HOUSE

Porticus 1 (Fig. 95)

MOSAIC 322.1. *Dimensions: room 21.65 m by 2.75 m. Tesserae: red and grey, 25 mm.*

The *porticus* pavement (Fig. 40) survived almost complete except at the southern end. Unlike the other mosaics from the building, it appears to be a primary feature, with no underlying floor. It comprised a neat swastika-meander with triple returns in coarse red tesserae on a grey ground. This is flanked by bands of pale grey (11–12 rows) and red beside the walls. There are several examples of swastika-meander design decorating the length of corridors, but these are with double returns or, less frequently, single returns – no other has the third return. No comparable pavement is close geographically. However, a red and 'white' *porticus* pavement from Winchester (Building VIII, 1; Mosaic III, 328.5) has a related design of spaced latchkey meander and is dated to the late 3rd/early 4th century. Three rows of red and three of white are used in the design as opposed to the two rows of each colour at Sparsholt, so the similarities are not close enough to speculate that the same craftsmen were responsible for both pavements.

References: Wilson 1966, 214; Johnston 1965, 46; Johnston 1972, 5; Knowles 1981, 117; Neal & Cosh 2009, 240, figs 215–216a and b.

Room 7 (Fig. 96)

MOSAIC 322.4. *Dimensions: room 5.80 m by 4.30 m; panel: 3.20 m square. Tesserae: black (dark grey), white, red, grey-blue and buff, 13 mm; border: red, 25 mm.*

This near-complete mosaic paved the central room, with a broad doorway on the east side opposite the corresponding gap in the *porticus*, and thus may be identified as the main reception room or summer dining room. The scheme is a series of concentric circular bands within square borders. Working from the outside of the panel the square framing bands comprise: triple fillets of buff and white; a band of L-blocks (alternately orientated) outlined black and shaded red, buff and white; four-strand guilloche (shaded as the L-blocks); and a dark grey double fillet. Tangent to the last is a linear circle enclosing circular bands of simple guilloche; swastika-meander; dark grey wave pattern; and double fillets of red and dark grey. At the centre is an eight-petalled flower with white, yellow and red petals overlapping to create an inner ring of smaller petals around the corolla; this is segmented and infilled red and white 'millefiori' style, with a small circular centre quartered and shaded red and white. The spandrels contain two motifs, those diagonally opposite being the same: one is a bold calyx urn shaded in bands of colour with a 'jewelled band' midway, and flanked by volutes springing from the tips; and the other a fan motif (with concave instead of the normal convex tops), the elements shaded concentrically, all with white centres, the outermost red, the inner ones buff and the pointed central one buff and grey-blue. The mosaic has a coarse red outer border, the panel being set centrally in the room, and not set forward in the room as is often the case in such rooms.

The panel was lifted 1969 with funds raised by the Hampshire Field Club and Archaeological Society, along with a grant from the then Ministry of Public Buildings and Works, and is displayed in Winchester City Museum.

The workmanship is quite good and the geometry fairly accurate. The scheme is very similar to the near-circular Mosaic III, 321.98 from Room 18, Building XXVII, 1, at Silchester. The L-blocks are identical to those on Mosaic III, 316.3 from nearby Itchen Abbas and Mosaic II, 238.1 from Castle Copse, Wiltshire, the latter belonging to the late 3rd-/early 4th-century phase, while they are similar to a row bordering Mosaic III, 308.2 from Bramdean. The calyx urn is very closely matched on Mosaic III, 399.1 from Chilgrove, West Sussex, possibly by the same craftsmen (see below); an early 4th-century date was ascribed to the latter.

References: Wilson 1967, 196, 198, pl XV, 1; Wilson 1970, 301; Johnston 1972, 6, frontispiece; Johnston 1977, 206, pl. 7.IV a; Knowles 1981, 117; Neal 1981, no. 71; Neal & Cosh 2009, 240–1, figs 215 and 219.

Room 11 (Fig. 97)

MOSAIC 322.6. *Dimensions: room 3.50 m by 3.40 m; panel about 2.20 m square; fragment 1.12 m by 0.43 m (max). Tesserae: dark grey, white, red and grey, 12 mm; border: red, 25 mm.*

Only the fragment illustrated (Fig. 53) remains of the mosaic paving a channelled hypocaust, apart from small areas of coarse red tessellation beside the north and south walls, which extends into the recess of the elaborate doorway. The fragment largely comprises a band of three-strand guilloche outlined dark grey with strands of red, grey and white, presumably originally framing a square panel; this is separated from the coarse red border by a triple fillet of white. Only traces of the internal design survive, including dark grey double fillets which are probably part of a swastika element in the corner of the panel, but whether this is part of a band of spaced swastika-meander or an all-over scheme is not certain. All that survives of the motif in the space in the swastika-meander are a single fillet of red, forming a right angle, and white infill with one yellow ochre tessera. The style and workmanship of the mosaic is similar to those in Room 7 and the Aisled Building (Room 12); it is therefore probably contemporary with them. The fragment was lifted and retained by David Johnston.

References: Johnston 1972, 6; Knowles 1981, 118; Neal & Cosh 2009, 242, figs 215 and 220a–b.

Aisled Building

Room 12 (Figs 98 & 99)

MOSAIC 322.7. *Dimensions: room 5.04 m by 2.76 m; panel 2.18 m by 1.92 m. Tesserae: dark grey, white, red and grey, 13 mm; border: grey and red, 25mm.*

Only fragmentary remains of this mosaic survived at the margins (Fig. 23). It appears that the lost central square compartment is surrounded by a spaced swastika-meander with single returns (the swastika elements being in the corners) and a band of simple guilloche outlined dark grey with strands of red, grey and white. At the eastern end was a band of four-strand guilloche (shaded as before) and framing the whole is an inward-facing dark grey dentillated line. The outer border is of coarse grey tesserae, with a red band against the east wall. Johnston (1977, 207) noted that this mosaic is similar to Mosaic III, 316.2 from Itchen Abbas, only 12 km away, and attributed it to his Central Southern Group (see below).

References: Wilson 1967, 198; Johnston 1972, 5; Johnston 1977, 207, pl. 7.II b; Neal & Cosh 2009, 242–3, fig 221.

Discussion

With the possible exception the *porticus* pavement, the mosaics are of the same style and were almost certainly contemporaneous. They provide important information about the living arrangements and can be compared with other mosaics in relation to building plans from central-southern Britain. The best-preserved mosaic paves the central Room 7 opposite the entrance into the *porticus*, and was probably the reception room and dining room for summer use. A fragmentary mosaic of high quality originally paved the heated room, which perhaps functioned, at least on occasions, as a winter dining room. Thus there

THE MOSAICS

Fig 93 Sparsholt plan of main building showing mosaics (artwork by S R Cosh)

116 THE MOSAICS

Fig 95   Sparsholt Room 1 (detail) (painting by S R Cosh)

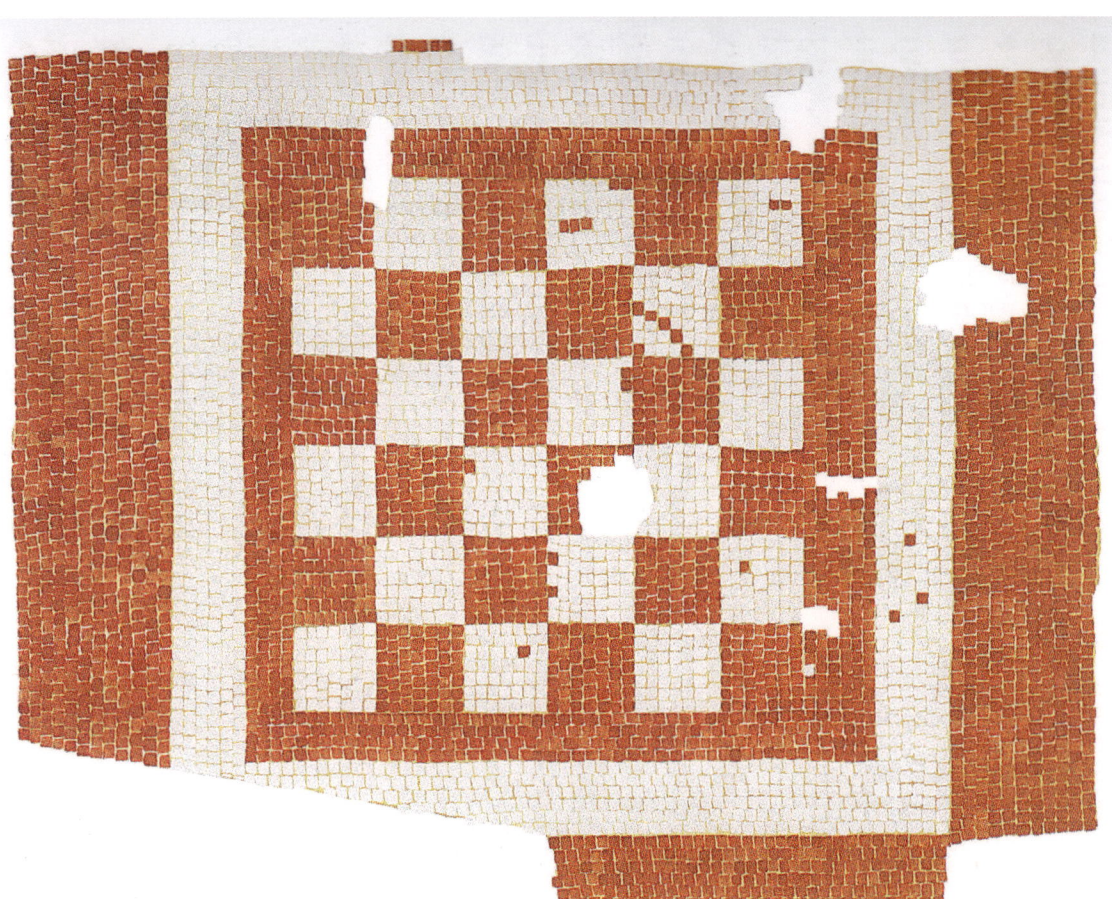

Fig 94   Sparsholt Room 2 (painting by S R Cosh)

is a clear distinction between rooms used by guests (*porticus* and dining rooms) and those for private and family use with inferior floors. The same arrangement occurs east of Winchester at Bramdean, a villa more or less contemporary with Sparsholt and having mosaics possibly laid by the same contractor (see below), although at Bramdean the hypocaust is in a wing-room. The same can be said of Chilgrove, West Sussex, and the very similar villa at Downton, Wiltshire (Mosaic II, 241.1) which also has comparable mosaics and dating. The *porticus* and anterooms at Sparsholt, as well as the living quarters, have coarse, simply patterned or plain tessellated floors. This same arrangement, including the position of the fireplace, is most closely paralleled at Newport villa, Isle of Wight, but there late industrial activities resulted in the mosaics of the central and wing-room hypocaust being stripped out – assuming these lost mosaics originally existed.

Fine mosaics are not infrequent in aisled buildings, many having the same arrangement of rooms as at Sparsholt. West Meon (Lippen Wood) and Thruxton, in Hampshire, and Carisbrooke and Combley on the Isle of Wight all have a fine mosaic in a room at the end of one aisle, equivalent to Room 12, rather than a central room. The arrangement of rooms at the partially excavated villa at Itchen Abbas suggests that the mosaics are also from an aisled building. The square central room at Sparsholt has coarse tessellation in line with simple tessellated pavements in equivalent rooms in other aisled buildings: red and grey chequers at West Dean on the Hampshire-Wiltshire border, Castle Copse in Wiltshire and Carisbrooke, Isle of Wight.

The Central Southern Group

The scheme and motifs of Room 7's mosaic led David Johnston to recognise similar features on other mosaics in the area and identify them as possibly by the same contractor. He termed this the Central Southern Group (Johnston 1977). The craftsmen were probably operating in the early 4th century, mainly in Hampshire and just beyond its borders. Similar schemes and motifs are found on mosaics at Itchen Abbas and the later phase additions, Rooms 17 and 18, Building XXVII, 1 at Silchester. He recognised similar and distinctive motifs on other pavements in the area, notably the unusual calyx urn and the L-block border. His analysis led to the following list of sites:

Basildon, Berkshire (Mosaic III, 272.1)
Bignor, West Sussex (Mosaic III, 396.1–6)
Bramdean, Hampshire (Mosaic III, 308.1–2)
Chichester – David Greig site (Mosaic III, 398.5)
Chilgrove, West Sussex (Mosaic III, 399.1)
Itchen Abbas, Hampshire (Mosaic III, 316.1–3)
Silchester, Ins XXVII (Mosaic III, 321.98)
Sparsholt, Hampshire (Mosaic III, 322.4, 322.6–7)

The mosaics from Bignor, however, can be considered too superior in quality for inclusion in the Group: the schemes are not closely related and the form of the L-block bands, on which the attribution is largely based, is very different. Recently a mosaic from Dinnington in Somerset has provided a much better parallel for the Bignor mosaics, hinting that skilled craftsmen from the West Country were commissioned to lay them. Also, Mosaic III, 398.5 from Chichester has many 2nd-century characteristics and should certainly be excluded from the listing; the Basildon mosaic is also suspect, its identification based on the presence of 'spiked knots', a motif Johnston considered exclusive to the Group, but which is now known not to be so. Since Johnston defined the Group the fragment of Mosaic II, 238.1 has been discovered at Castle Copse, Wiltshire, which features the same distinctive band of L-blocks. The similarity between the Chilgrove mosaic and Mosaic II, 240.1 from Downton, Wiltshire, suggests that the latter may also be attributable to Johnston's Group. It should be noted too that a mosaic from West Meon has the same scheme, technique and position as the three-panelled mosaic from Itchen Abbas, and has an anteroom in parti-coloured red and grey reminiscent of Sparsholt's Room 9.

The amended list might read as follows:

? Basildon, Berkshire (Mosaic III, 272.1)
Bramdean, Hampshire (Mosaic III, 308.1–2)
Castle Copse (Mosaic II, 238.1)
Chilgrove, Sussex (Mosaic III, 399.1–2)
Itchen Abbas, Hampshire (Mosaic III, 316.1–3)
Silchester, Ins XXVII (Mosaic III 321.97–8)
Sparsholt, Hampshire (III, 322.4, 322.6–7)

Ignoring Bignor, the mosaics from the Group are largely geometric and the similar figures of Flora from Itchen Abbas and the Season from Silchester are quite crudely executed, but the lost pavements from Bramdean had a fine series of figured compartments; these were perhaps the work of separate, possibly itinerant, craftsmen who worked with the Group on this commission. The Group, based on the amended list, seems to be centred on Winchester, although no example of the work of the craftsmen has been found in the town, and Johnston was wise to term it the 'Central Southern Group' without speculating on a base or workshop (*officina*). It is notable that this group's *floruit* was earlier than the other 4th-century groups.

David Johnston's Central Southern Group still stands up to scrutiny, despite the inevitable minor revisions as a result of new discoveries and research (see Cosh 2012), as has happened to all postulated groups. (For a summary of the other mosaic groups identified at the time of David Johnston's work, see Smith 1969). Clearly the mosaics at Sparsholt, Itchen Abbas and Silchester (Insula XXVII) are by the same hand, while other attributable mosaics show fewer affinities. The same can be said of Durnovarian Group mosaics, mainly in Dorset: Hinton St Mary and Frampton are very similar to each other, as are Fifehead Neville and Hemsworth, but one pair has few features in common with the other. Unlike the other groups (except the Durnovarian), the Central Southern does not rely on a limited range of schemes, although they are normally concentric in nature. The guilloche is generally red, 'grey' and white throughout – as is the case with the Durnovarian mosaics further west; some motifs are common to both groups, such as the distinctive black-edged red band and form of Z-pattern. The Durnovarian group also shows an adaptable approach to schemes, and is clearly not such a discrete group as was formerly envisaged. Perhaps we are seeing in the Durnovarian Group and the Central Southern Group a regional style practised by various itinerant craftsmen, and not a single *officina*. This may indicate that the Central Southern Group is another loosely formed ensemble, and conceivably the groups are connected. Like the Durnovarian Group, if they were a single band of craftsmen, they were innovative in their designs, freely adapting standard repertoire, thus making their work difficult to identify, in contrast to most other groups which seem to have a more limited range and rigid use of schemes and motifs. Given that at least some of the Durnovarian mosaics are generally considered later than the Central Southern Group, the notion that craftsmen moved west with their style and idiosyncrasies is a real possibility.

Fig 96   Sparsholt Room 7 (painting by D S Neal)

THE MOSAICS 119

Fig 97 Sparsholt Room 11 (painting and reconstruction drawing by S R Cosh)

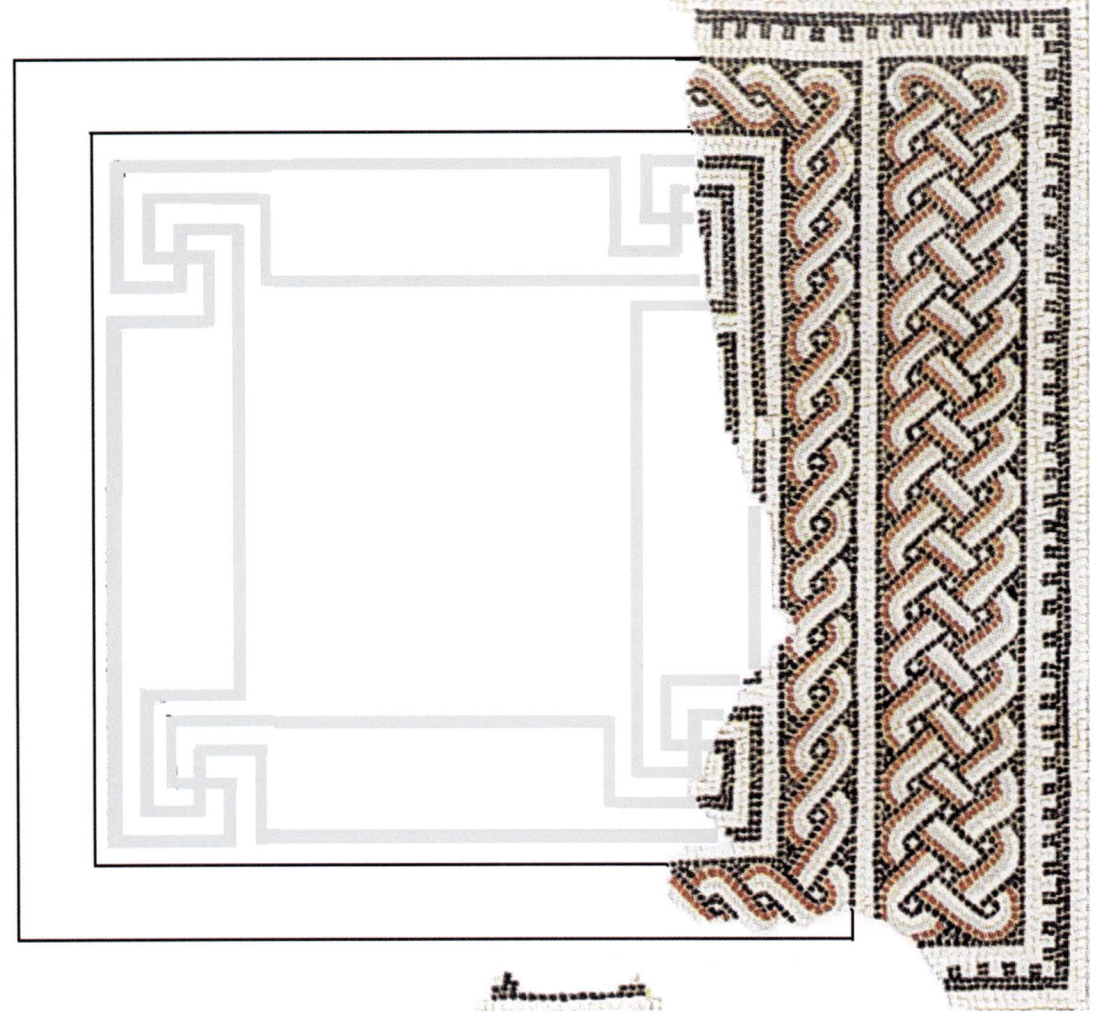

Fig 99 Sparsholt Room 12, probable reconstruction (artwork by S R Cosh)

Fig 98 Sparsholt Room 12 (painting by S R Cosh)

Chapter 11

Ceramic Building Material

Rachael Seager Smith and Kayt Marter Brown

Introduction

A total of 394 pieces (294,725 g) of ceramic building material (CBM) was retained from the investigations in the 1960s and 1970s, including a number of complete tiles and bricks. Unfortunately the provenance of some of the retained material has subsequently been lost, primarily due to the deterioration of labels over the subsequent 30 or more years. Where feasible all context information and any additional details have been recorded, but, as this was not possible for a significant proportion of the assemblage, detailed consideration of key context groups and/or spatial patterning could not be undertaken. This report therefore describes and characterises the retained assemblage, and highlights the most salient pieces.

Methodology

Individual pieces, or groups of joining fragments, were identified by type and quantified by fragment count and weight; they were assigned an individual record number (RN) as a means of identification. There was considerable homogeneity within the fabrics observed and although no detailed analysis of these has been undertaken, samples have been collected to show the range present. The bulk of the assemblage comprises a fine, oxidised, slightly sandy fabric with varying proportions of ferruginous inclusions and streaks of cream-coloured clay, although a small number of light buff-coloured pieces were also present.

Different types of keying present on the box flue and voussoir tiles has been noted, and a selection of complete and more unusual tiles have been photographed. Tile thickness has also been recorded and, in the case of plain flat fragments, has been used to distinguish between flat tiles (probably *tegula* fragments) and bricks. The range of tile types present comprise *tegula*, *imbrex*, ridge tiles, *bessales*, *lydion*, plain flat tiles, box flue and voussoir, and have been quantified below by fragment count (Table 8).

Type	No. Fragments
Tegula	132
Imbrex	52
Brick	72
Plain flat fragments	42
Box flue	25
Voussior	21
Box flue/voussior fragments	39
Semi-circular	11
Total	394

Table 8: CBM types by fragment count

Results

Roof tiles

The roof tiles, primarily *tegula* and *imbrex*, formed the largest category and included several complete pieces (Table 9). Twenty-one cut-aways were recorded within the retained assemblage, all simple vertical forms, comparable to Warry's type C4 (Warry 2006, 44), a type assigned to the mid-2nd to mid-3rd century (*ibid*, 97).

A range of signature marks were also present: simple finger-smeared concentric circles (one, two or three lines), finger-smeared Xs, combed intersecting arcs, and incised Xs were all recorded on the open end of tiles. Signature marks may be indicators of different tile makers, but few are chronologically distinctive. The exceptions are the combed signatures, which are a late 3rd-century phenomenon, as is combed decoration on *imbrices* (Warry 2006, 91). Four of the *tegula* from Sparsholt display these signatures (RNs 25, 129, 130 and 166), which comprise two combed intersecting arcs, made with either a 6-, 7- or 9-toothed comb. Similar examples are known from The Brooks, Winchester, Portchester (Cunliffe 1975) and the Isle of Wight (Foot, in archive).

Twelve *imbrices* had lines of combing, between 5- and 15-toothed combs occurring parallel with the widest end of the tile. A single *imbrex* (1972, SF 633) had combed decoration on the ridge and crossing the width of the tile, in addition to three incised wavy

Type	Context/RN	Weight (g)	Length (mm)	Width (mm)	Thickness (mm)
Tegula	SPF/RN52	4,469	380	280	25
Tegula	RN96	5,000	375	280–305	23
Tegula	SPAAG/RN100	4,342	400	305	18
Tegula	RN136	5,476	420	300	24
Tegula	RN156	6,555	440	305	30
Tegula	RN158	4,822	385	285–310	25
Imbrex	RN46	2,536	375	120–175	18–20
Imbrex	RN95	2,598	372	120–170	20
Imbrex	RN202	6,400	420	255–310	–
Bessale	RN56	2,227	210	200	40
Bessale	RN57	2,583	205	200	35
Bessale	RN58	2,320	193	193	35
Bessale	RN77	2,079	190	185	38
Bessale	RN78	2,345	195	195	38
Bessale	RN162	2,519	190	200	38
Bessale	RN163	1,990	177	175	40
Lydion	RN175	5,000	416	275	44

Table 9: Dimensions of complete pieces

lines along the lower edge, possibly a highly stylised 'leaf' motif, in its upper surface (Fig. 100).

Three complete *imbrices* were recorded (Table 9), including one very large example (6.4 kg) with dimensions approximately twice the size of the more standard *imbrex*.

A further 10 fragments of similarly large tiles were recorded, all in the same fine, slightly sandy oxidised fabric, and frequently with combed decoration on the upper surface. Brodribb (1987, 27) refers to these as ridge tiles, designed to cover the gap where the *tegula* met at the apex of the roof, and lists similar examples from Littlecote, Alchester and Newport (Isle of Wight). More locally, fragments from similar tiles have been recorded from The Brooks, Winchester (Foot in archive).

Bricks

In the absence of complete dimensions, brick fragments were identified by being more than 30 mm thick, which is greater than the thickness recorded for any of the *tegula*. Complete examples of the smaller brick types, bessalis, were identified, as was a single *lydion* (Table 9), although it is likely that more of these types, and possibly also *pedalis*, are present within the amorphous brick fragments.

Five examples of the complete *bessalis* display a combed X on the upper surface. Three of these occur in an iron-rich clay (RNs 56, 57, 68), and two in the more common fine, slightly sandy oxidised fabric (RNs 78, 79). Combing was also recorded on brick fragments, presumed to be *bessalis*, mostly X designs but also one combed 3-line cross pattern (RN 1111, site D). Evidence of manufacture using a wooden former was noted on several of the brick fragments.

Cavity walling

Both box flue tiles and hollow voussoirs had been retained, in addition to a number of pieces too small

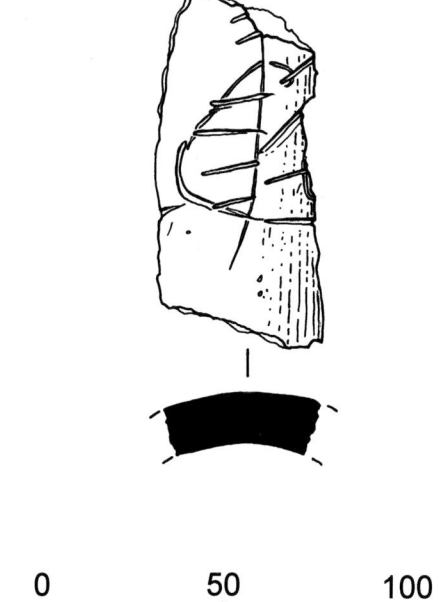

Fig 100 *Imbrex* fragment with a pre-firing incised graffito (drawing by S E James)

or fragmentary to be clearly assigned to either type. Some sizable fragments had been retained, from which dimensions could be taken, though no complete examples were present.

The combed faces on the box flue tiles measure *c* 190–200 mm wide, displaying a combed cross surrounded by combed edges or, less commonly, three vertical lines or a 'union-jack'-type design, the combs used being 7-, 8- or 12-tooth varieties. The most complete measurements of a voussoir are 150 mm widening to 180 mm and 230 mm long (18–25 mm thick), with similar combed faces. All fragments occurred in a fine slightly sandy oxidised fabric.

The ceramic roofing material

Peter Warry

The ceramic building material assemblage comprises a full suite of floor, wall, hypocaust and roofing tiles. In addition to *tegulae* and *imbrices*, the roofing tiles include ceramic ridge tiles which are not present on many sites. The ridge tiles were patterned with a toothed comb. The one example with a complete section measured 270 mm wide by 90 mm high: these dimensions would have suited a roof with a pitch of just over 30°. The *imbrices* varied in length from 317 mm to 375 mm compared to an average length of *imbrices* across the country of 400 mm. The longest-length Sparsholt *imbrices* could have matched the lengths of some of the shorter *tegulae* (after allowing for overlaps) but there was no match for the shorter ones which means that they must have been out of step with the *tegulae* when placed on the roof.

Tegulae may be distinguished by the forms of their lower cut-aways which were used to assist the overlapping of the tiles on a roof (Warry 2006). Only two forms were present in the Sparsholt assemblage (Types 5 and 7). The Type 5 forms part of the Group C cut-away family and typically dates to the mid-2nd to mid-3rd centuries, although it can be found in earlier contexts in major urban locations. Type 7 is a regional form which only appears in Hampshire in the later 3rd and 4th centuries. It is a derivative of the Type 1, Group D form found in the rest of the country with which it either runs in parallel or, more probably, follows on from. The sizes of the Sparsholt *tegulae* are shown in Table 10. The Type 5 *tegula* is compared to the national average but there is only one other recorded complete Type 7 *tegula* (from Crookhorn) whose size falls between the largest and smallest from Sparsholt.

Unfortunately very little contextual information on the *tegulae* has survived the passage of time. Table 11 summarises all the data that can be reconstructed but even then not all the entries are completely certain. Fortunately these limited records point in the same direction, indicating that the Type 5 *tegulae* were incorporated into a hearth integral with the wall of AB II and thus contemporary with its construction, whilst the Type 7 *tegulae* (and the residual Type 5 tile 156) were primarily part of another hearth feature placed against an outside wall of this building but with no excavation evidence to show whether the feature was contemporary with the building or not.

It seems probable that the Type 5 *tegulae* came from the demolition of AB I which was below AB II and were incorporated into this second building. This fits very well with dating of this *tegula* form. Type 7 *tegulae* were presumably used on the roof of the new building which would suggest construction in the first half of the 4th century. However, stone tiles were also recovered in the excavation and these would typically be 3rd- or 4th-century in date. It is therefore possible that stone tiles were used on the roof of the latest building with the ceramic tiles placed on a portico (or vice versa). Brading villa on the Isle of Wight similarly has two main phases of ceramic tiles and one of stone tiles and at that site the best inter-

	Length (mm)	Upper Breadth (mm)	Lower Breadth (mm)
Type 5			
Sparsholt	440?	315?	300
National average	416	317	306
Type 7			
Sparsholt largest	398	308	306
Sparsholt smallest	375	295	284

Table 10: Sparsholt *tegulae* dimensions

Sparsholt No.	Warry No.	Cut-away Type	Context information
100	1901	7	SPAAG Aisled Building II/mortary layer
101	1902	(7)	
130	1911?	7	SPFPD Aisled Building II/demolition rubble by bath house
135	1918	7	Tegula 1, Trench 28, hearth tile feature
140	1921	5	SPLKE Pit XX, Layer 7
156	1923	5	Trench 28, hearth tile feature
157	1924	7	Trench 28, hearth tile feature
158	1925	7	Tegula 2, Trench 28, hearth tile feature
–	3503	5	Trench B4, tile incorporated into perimeter/Aisled Building wall
–	3504	5	Trench B4, tile incorporated into perimeter/Aisled Building wall

Table 11: Contextual data

pretation is that the stone tiles were employed in a 3rd-century building phase that lay between the 2nd century (Type 6 *tegulae*) and the 4th century (Type 7 *tegulae*) (Warry 2013). Thus consideration should also be given to the possibility that the stone tiles derived from a different building (or that the ceramic tiles came from a different building).

Type 5 tegulae

The Type 5 *tegulae* were unusual in having an intrusion into their flanges and smooth undersides. These *tegulae* would have been produced in upright four-sided moulds. The wettish clay would have been placed into the mould and literally punched into the corners and against the sides to ensure the mould was fully filled. This process does not tend to produce smooth undersides to the resulting *tegulae* unless some further finishing is undertaken after the tile has been removed from the mould. The flanges were formed by cutting out the centre of the tile with a wire, using the ends of the mould as a former, and the resulting flanges were then smoothed by running hands down their length (Warry 2006, 28–34). However, the Sparsholt tiles then appear to have had some sort of frame inserted between the flanges after they had been formed. The frame was probably inserted from the upper (wider) end of the tile and pushed down to a point just short of the lower cutaway (Fig. 101). This has resulted in a small bulge in the flange of surplus clay beyond the point where the frame finishes which would not have occurred if the frame had been placed vertically down onto the tile.

In total seven Type 5 *tegulae* were recovered of which four had complete lower breadths and each of these measured 300 mm across. In fact the dimensions of all the Type 5 *tegulae* are so similar that it seems likely that they came from a single mould (which would suggest just a single phase of supply to Sparsholt of this *tegula* type). The positioning of the frame was also consistent, with all but one tile having the frame positioned 80 mm from the bottom of the tile and, again with one exception, the frame was neatly centred between the flanges. Evidence for such a frame has not been encountered on any other site and there can be no certainty about its use; the most likely explanation is that it was to allow the tiles to be stacked on top of each other during the drying process. The majority of tile producers of this period left their tiles outside to dry for roughly a week before they were hard enough to be turned as evidenced by the frequent animal footprints found on tiles. There are no footprints on the Sparsholt tiles (albeit only seven tiles have survived) which indicates that these tiles could have been dried in a workshop where space would have been at a premium, resulting in the need for the tiles to be stacked on top of each other. This occurred at Liss (on the eastern edge of Hampshire) but here the tiles were stacked directly on top of each other without an intervening frame and as a result a number of the tiles were distorted (Warry 2008).

The smooth undersides also require explanation as these would not have been easily achieved with the conventional manufacturing method where the underside is never accessible until the tile is dry. One possibility is that the stacking frame was used to invert the tile thereby exposing the underside and allowing it to be smoothed. Indeed it is possible that the frame was designed so that it sat between the flanges of pairs of stacked tiles, the lower one being the correct way up and the upper inverted. This would be consistent with all of the tiles showing evidence of the frame between the flanges whereas only half would have had this evidence if the upper tiles had not been inverted. As all the *tegulae* had smooth undersides one has to assume that all of them were inverted and then half returned to the upright position before the second tile was placed on top. However, whilst this provides an explanation for how the flange marks and smooth undersides might have been produced it does not provide a rationalisation for why smooth undersides were considered necessary in the first place.

Type 7 tegulae

In the later 3rd century some tile makers switched from upright four-sided moulds to inverted moulds which were a more efficient method of forming tiles, albeit the moulds would have taken more time to make (Warry 2006, 28–34). The Type 1 *tegulae* from Group D can be made in either upright or inverted moulds but the Type 7 which derives from the Type 1 has only ever been observed with inverted mould manufacture (as at Sparsholt). Normally the lower cut-away of a *tegula* was formed by removing part of the corner of the tile but leaving the inside of the flange unaffected, thereby maintaining the integrity of the barrier preventing rain water getting beneath the tiles as it ran down the roof. In inverted box manufacture the lower cut-away is formed by inserting a wooden block into the corner of the mould, thus creating the gap in the clay that becomes the cut-away. Through time, the thickness of the block used for Type 1 manufacture was gradually increased, thereby reducing the remaining thickness of the flange until ultimately the block replaced the flange entirely to create the Type 7 cut-away. Figure 102 shows the process: the left-hand tile still has a residual element of the flange adjacent to the cut-away present but in the right-hand tile that part of the flange is completely absent.

Several sites have examples of *tegulae* showing the stages of this evolution but it is particularly stark at Brading villa on the Isle of Wight. Here tiles with different degrees of flange thickness adjacent to the cut-away appear at discrete locations on the site thereby demonstrating phases of development at different times, almost certainly following the evolutionary path described above (Warry 2013). All but one of the Type 7 *tegulae* at Sparsholt are in the final form which could suggest that there may be a hundred

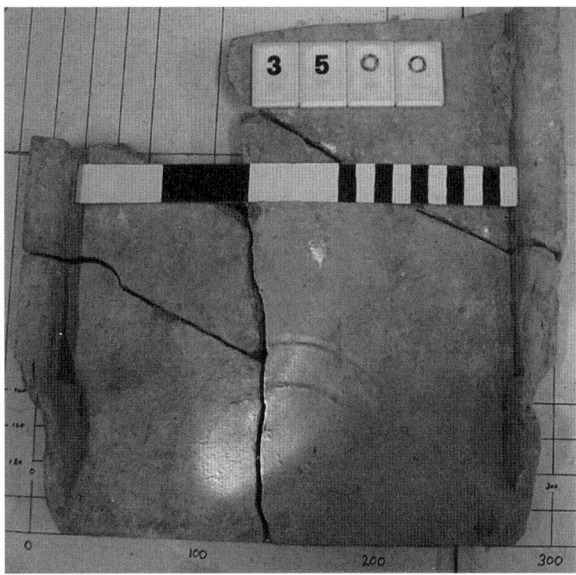

Fig 101 Type 5 *tegula* showing inserts into flange (Photograph P Warry)

Fig 102 Left, cut-away with residual flange remaining; right, flange absent (Photograph P Warry)

years separation between the original supply of the Type 5 *tegulae* and the subsequent Type 7 *tegulae*.

Detailed measurement of *tegulae* can be used to differentiate the moulds from which they were produced. Such an exercise will be affected both by differential shrinkage in firing caused by slightly different consistencies in the clay and different temperatures in the kiln. It will also be affected by measurement error, no doubt some of it human error, but mainly due to the difficulty of giving a precise quantity to an object where the edges may be rounded and non-uniform. As a result one should expect a tolerance band of at least ± 2 mm on every measurement. Despite this difficulty, when the measurements of individual tiles are plotted on a scatter-diagram a surprising amount of differentiation is possible. The validity of this approach has been demonstrated on a number of sites where different groupings on the scatter-diagram have tallied neatly with different characteristics of the tiles or physical locations on site (for example, see Warry 2010; Warry 2013).

Figure 103 plots the flange height against the flange width for all the Type 7 *tegulae* at Sparsholt and these have then been grouped by cut-away length. It can be seen, with the odd exception, that the flange dimensions for different cut-away lengths group reasonably well together. As the cut-away length was determined by the size of the blocks inserted into the mould one would expect little variability in this other than the unavoidable measurement inaccuracy and differential shrinkage in firing, so the fact that different cut-away lengths appear to be associated with different flange sizes would tend to suggest that they were made in different moulds. This conclusion is reinforced by the observations of the few *tegulae* for which we have complete measurements of the overall tile size that these sizes are also associated with the cut-away lengths (Table 12).

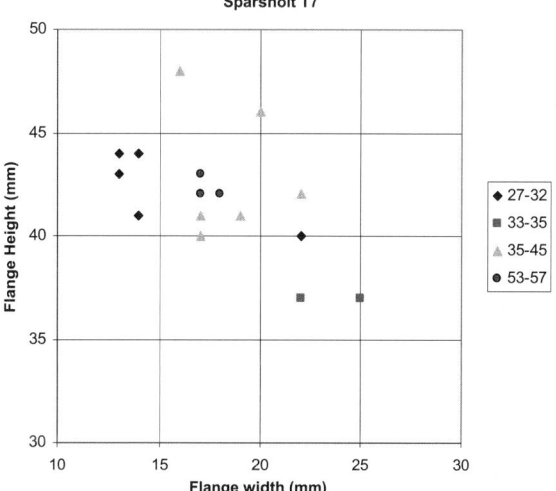

Fig 103 Flange dimensions grouped by cut-away lengths

Many *tegulae* carry signatures which in most civilian tile works are normally semi-circular markings made at the bottom of the tile when wet using one or more fingers. These signatures are best interpreted as the tile maker identifying his work. As can be seen from Table 12, the signatures are strongly correlated with the hypothecated mould sizes; thus the 35–45 mm cut-away group have either distinctive intersecting semi-circle combed signatures (RC) or a cross (X) made with a finger, neither of which are found on other tiles. The large cut-away group (53–57 mm) have no signatures and the other two cut-away groups have similar signatures, primarily comprising a cross within a sub-circular form (BX). The signatures reinforce the view that these *tegulae* were produced in at least four different moulds and as there are at least three different signatures present the inference is that there were at least three different tile makers. A typical Romano-British tile works

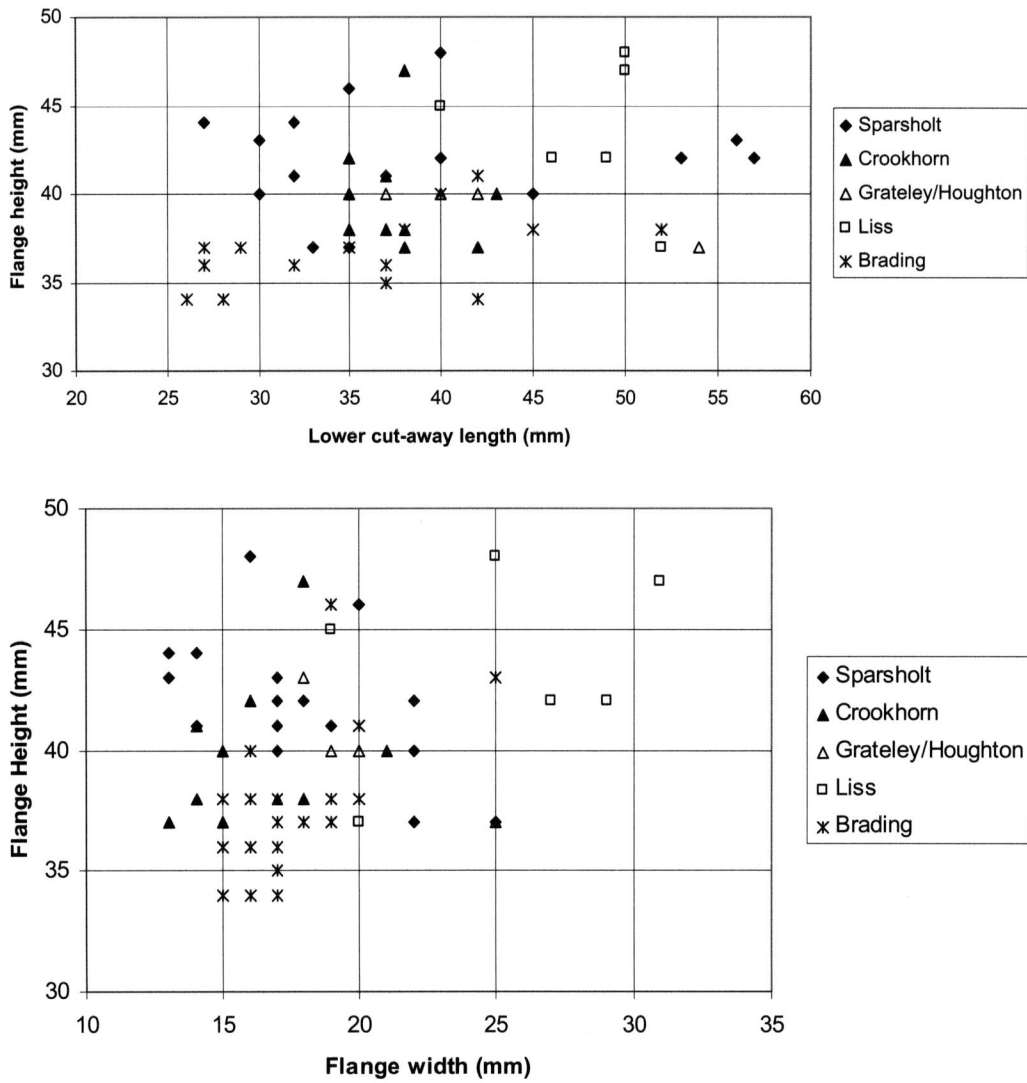

Fig 104 and 105   Size distributions of Type 7 *tegulae* from all recorded sites

seems to have employed around half a dozen people, only one of whom was involved in the tile making with the rest gathering wood and preparing clay (Warry 2012, 52–6). So are the distinct signatures on the Sparsholt tiles the product of an unusually large tile works supporting at least three tile makers or were they produced by several generations of successive tile makers at a standard-sized kiln?

To explore this further we need to consider the supply of Type 7 *tegulae* more widely. Figures 104 and 105 plot all the recorded Type 7 *tegulae* from sites in Hampshire, first with flange height against cut-away length and then flange height against flange width. Both charts show that the Brading size distribution is distinct from the others but none of the other sites is a perfect match for Sparsholt, with perhaps Crookhorn coming closest. Crookhorn lies just outside Portsmouth and is the site of an early 4th-century kiln which could potentially have supplied Sparsholt by road or possibly by sea. There are only two near-complete Type 7 *tegulae* from Crookhorn, one of which has the unusual combed intersecting semi-circle signature (RC) similar to the ones at Sparsholt but which has not been observed on any other site. The dimensions of this *tegula* are a close match to the 35–45 mm cut-away length group at Sparsholt with the combed signatures. However, none of Sparsholt signatures were made with the same 6-toothed comb used at Crookhorn and all of the Sparsholt Type 7 *tegulae* are bright orange-red whereas the Crookhorn *tegulae* are drab orange-cream. Moreover, the second near complete *tegula* from Crookhorn which is dimensionally similar has no signature, a feature which only occurs at Sparsholt on *tegulae* with the longest cut-away lengths. Thus it appears that although similar production methods and signatures were employed, the two sites were not otherwise linked. Fabric analysis would provide further verification, but this has not been undertaken.

Flange height	Flange width	Cut-away type	Cut-away length	Upper cut-away length	Signature	Overall length	Overall breadth
44	13	7	27	40	BX	379	300
43	13	7	30	40		368	
40	22	7	30		BX		
44	14	7	32	46	B	375	295
41	14	7	32				
37	22	7	33	50	BX	398	308
37	25	7	35		BX		
46	20	7	35		RC		
41	19	7	37		RC		
41	17	7	37		RC		
42	22	7	40	36	X	386	
	15	7	40		RC		
48	16	7	40	45	X	387	302
40	17	7	45		RC		
42	18	7	53		0		
43	17	7	56				
42	17	7	57		0		

Table 12: Size analysis of all Sparsholt Type 7 *tegulae*

This suggests that Sparsholt was supplied from another, as yet unidentified, tile works which, judging by the number of moulds and signatures in contemporary use, was a much larger operation than normal. The complete absence of impressions of animal feet on these tiles shows that the *tegulae* must have been dried in an enclosed building rather than laid outside, very probably in an integrated workshop with drying space and stoke hole which appears to have become a common arrangement in the 3rd and 4th centuries AD and is closely correlated with the adoption of inverted box mould manufacture. The combed signatures at Sparsholt and Crookhorn and others at Brading which are similar but not identical to ones at Sparsholt suggests that, alongside the use of the Type 7 cut-away, local tile makers also created new signature forms. It would be interesting to know whether this was simply fashion or whether it reflects tile makers moving between sites or possibly even common ownership.

Chapter 12

The Wall Plaster

Introduction *by Nick Stoodley*

The wall plaster has been examined on several different occasions. The most comprehensive study was by Susan Scott (completed in November 1971), which resulted in a provisional report containing general information about the material, in addition to details about the types of plaster from individual rooms. It does not include the plaster recovered in 1972 or 1985. The author also intended to update her report after checking the provenance of certain pieces, but the archive does not contain a revised report and there is no mention of work commencing on it. Despite these omissions, the information is considered valuable and it has been decided to reproduce the general section and the descriptions of rooms where the provenance of the material is secure. The absence of attribution of plaster to a particular room does not mean that room did not produce wall plaster; Scott may have had doubts over the provenance of the plaster and consequently omitted it.

A number of pieces of wall plaster were restored from fragments by Dr Norman Davey and are accompanied by photographs and drawings in Davey and Ling's (1982) monograph on wall painting in Roman Britain. The pieces are:

AB I, painted imitation of a mosaic border (Davey & Ling catalogue No. 35)

Main House, Room 7, two pieces belonging to an upper part of a fawn-coloured dado (Davey & Ling catalogue No. 36)

AB II (Baths), (a) arch with part of the supporting wall or jamb from doorway leading into Baths; (b) part of the jamb of a doorway between Rooms 17 and 18 depicting the bust of a female (Davey & Ling catalogue No. 37).

Four samples of wall plaster were submitted to RSK Environment Ltd (Hemel Hempstead) (batch number 12587) for scientific analysis. Petrography using optical microscopy, augmented by scanning electron microscopy (SEM) with in-built microanalysis, was performed.

Wall plaster (provisional report) *by Susan Scott*

General points

Most of the painted design is in good condition and can be divided into two types: grey plaster recovered chiefly from the Main House and the west end of AB II and a pink plaster found at the east end of AB II. The latter may be a layer applied to the top of the grey, usually 1.3 cm thick, or may be entirely pink.

The grey plaster contains flint grit and chalk, usually in small fragments, but in some cases larger lumps. The plaster is hard, does not crumble easily and usually has a good smooth surface to which the paint was applied. Many pieces of grey plaster have a very thin white layer beneath the paint, which may have been intended as a primer on the bare wall. It does not appear that the paint on these pieces was more durable, nor that the finished surface was any better.

The pink plaster contains flint grit, chalk and crushed brick. The surface is not usually as smooth as the grey plaster and sometimes a thin (approximately 1 mm) layer of fine white plaster is applied on top. This does not last so well and easily flakes off when the plaster is handled. Most plaster from Rooms 17a–b (AB II) is of this type, although plaster from Room 18 (AB II) has the design painted straight onto the base plaster and the design is thus better preserved. Some pieces have two layers of pink plaster, a lighter-coloured layer on top of a darker one. One layer does not appear finer than the other.

In addition to these main types, a few pieces were found which do not fit into either category. For example, pieces of bright salmon-pink plaster with large pieces of brick in the fabric. On one piece, grey plaster covers the broken edges; it is possibly from the earlier bath house but was re-used in the later structure. Very few pieces were found and they are crumbly. In Rooms 17a–b evidence was found of plaster being re-used as building material. Also in Room 17b a light plaster with an aerated appearance was found as well as a curved piece of light whitish plaster, thickness 3.01–3.66 cm.

The thickness of the plaster varies considerably; some pieces as thick as 6.99 cm were found with no brick impressions on the back, but most pieces are between 1.27 and 2.54 cm. In the case of any mouldings, these may be entirely of grey plaster, entirely of pink or a layer of pink over an already moulded piece of grey. On the back of a probable fillet moulding there are cross hatchings. Is it possible that the fillet was moulded independently and then cemented into place on the wall? Many different kinds of mouldings were found, both angles and curves, painted and unpainted. Some mouldings of rough heavy plaster with uneven surface – some painted, some not – pose an interesting problem as it seems unlikely that they would have been used in conjunction with the smooth well-finished plaster from the walls.

The surface of most of the pieces is very smooth, but some have uneven grooves on them, possibly trowel marks. Some pieces from Room 18, mainly pictorial, have a definite ridged appearance as if finished by a shallow comb.

The paint used on most of the pieces seems to be the same, giving a very dense flat colour, similar to a child's powder colour. The surface is always matt. Colours are predominantly 'earth' colours: red and yellow ochres of various shades and a dull bluish-green. Plenty of white was used frequently as either a wash line or a thick line over a join of two colours. Very little black is used and then as only an occasional motif, or line in a border, or in a picture. Sepia is more often used when a dark colour is required. Blue is used infrequently, but was found in the Main House: a little in Room 7, and two or three pieces from Room 4, while Room 18 (AB II) produced some pictorial pieces.

Most of the colours can be mixed from a very restricted palette, using red and yellow ochre, white, ultramarine and medium green. The blue paint is unusual: in some instances it has a thick curdled appearance, where there is a base of thick white paint with powdered blue mixed in but not dissolved, or else it has a gritty texture. There are also some plain matt pieces, so the two variations would appear to be deliberate designs. In some pieces the pink also has a gritty appearance.

Some of the colours are generally less worn than others, white was particularly durable, followed by the various pinks and reds. Greens are the most worn.

The majority of the designs are painted rather roughly, the joins are inexact often overlapping, or not matching in places. In one place a drip had been roughly brushed away. Most lines seem to have been done with one stroke of the brush. There are, however, some exceptions where the lines are carefully painted.

There is little redecoration in any of the rooms. Paint of a different colour does appear beneath some pieces, but this is usually where a base colour is applied first with the design following later. Exceptions are: two pieces where yellow shows beneath green, one piece where yellow shows beneath red, and three pieces with pink beneath green. All these examples derive from Room 7 (Main House) where many pieces with no trace of redecoration were found. Some pieces, all from Room 18, also have signs of different colours or designs beneath the paint, but these are the exceptions. Two pieces from Room 11 (Main House) also show signs of redecoration and may represent a change of plan on the artist's part or were designs which were replaced because they were worn.

Individual rooms
Main House

Room 2: Relatively little plaster, but it is of a distinct type. The colours white, red ochre, dark green, saffron marbled red and white are found. There was probably a dado of saffron marbled red and white and trowel marks show on these pieces; it may have been carelessly done as it was in a difficult to reach place or not easily seen. Bands of red ochre and dark green with white lines cover the joins. There are some panel pieces in shades of pinkish-buff linked to a pale green.

Room 4: The colours are mauve, marbled green, white and red, white, saffron, red ochre and dark green. The marbled plaster probably formed a dado, although this colour dado was also found in Room 7, so these pieces may have come from there. Most of the pieces are ordinary grey plaster with a fine white limey layer beneath the paint. There are few patterned pieces, but they display a precise design and are of a very good plaster. Border patterns of red ochre, pink, saffron and white and cream buff and white. Also found was a dark red moulding of 150°, but this matches the mouldings found in Room 7, so it may have derived from there.

Room 5: There was very little plaster and the colours are red ochre, dark pink, white and saffron. Mauve marbled red and white were also found.

Room 7: All the plaster from this room is in fairly good condition (see also Davey & Ling 1982, 46). The paint is well preserved: white is usually in the best condition, red ochres and yellows generally good, while green is in a poorer state. Very little blue is found. The scheme is mainly earth colours, and red ochres in various tones predominate. Decoration seems to be mainly pattern and border. Angles of 140°, 90°, 80°, 45° and 40° were found. Angles measured at 140° make a nine-sided figure, which may have formed a ceiling panel, but it is difficult to measure these angles accurately because the design in all cases is roughly painted. Pieces of moulding (150°) were also found. Panels seem to have only lines and crossed lines as decoration. Only a few pieces with circles and curves were found. There was a marbled dado, in some places mauve, in some pink, and a pink moulded fillet joined the mosaic floor. There are some pieces where another colour shows beneath the top coat, but not enough to suggest complete redecoration.

Room 8: This room was predominantly saffron and red ochre. A dado of saffron marbled red and white, then bands of red ochre and saffron joined by a white line. The panel above this may have consisted of thick lines of red on saffron. Also some pieces of greyish-pink and mauve.

Room 9: Very little plaster, but there was probably a dado of saffron marbled white and red. Other colours found are white and red ochre with red ochre mouldings, also pink fillet similar to those found in Room 7. These pieces have cross hatchings on the back, which seems unusual.

Room 11: Good-quality grey plaster. Dado of yellow marbled red, white and sepia. Other colours are predominantly red ochre and white. Red ochre comes above dado joined by white wash line. Patterned pieces are present; some have a coloured line on white, on others, generally worn pieces, the design is imprecise, but may be shading on a picture. One large piece of border with red ochre, white and two shades of green is similar to pieces from Room 18. It also has a layer of pink plaster over the grey plaster which is not found anywhere else in this building, so it probably originated from AB II.

Aisled Building II (west end)

Room 12: Very little plaster was recovered and no patterned pieces were found. The main colours were white, red ochre, turquoise, and also unpainted pieces.

Room 13: Small quantity of hard grey plaster. Colours are predominantly white, red ochre and marbled saffron. It probably had a dado of saffron, which has an uneven surface and a coarse fabric containing large lumps of chalk. Above this are bands of white and then red ochre. Two pieces display parts of a circle in red ochre on a white ground.

Room 14: The colours are as Room 13. Once again a dado is present, probably saffron, marbled red and white with bands of red ochre, white and saffron above it. Red ochre mouldings are also found at an angle of 150°. One piece of bright pink plaster was found unlike any other type identified: it had traces of mortar on the broken edges so it could possibly have been used in rebuilding.

Aisled Building II (east end)

Room 15: Plaster was found that shows some green and white paint with an interesting small wheel-type pattern, plus some pieces of rough moulding, painted white with red ochre lines.

Room 17a (Baths): A lot of plaster was recovered from this room and all of it exhibits a layer of pink plaster. On the whole the paint is in poor condition. The colours are predominantly pink and red ochre. Many concave pieces were found, curved in one or two directions, suggesting that the domed ceiling and apse were painted pink. Other colours present are white, saffron, dark green and white with saffron lines. Many pieces of moulding were also found, both painted and unpainted and including angles and curves. Some pieces of very crumbly pink plaster were recovered, quite different in fabric to the usual plaster. This room may have had a marble veneer in addition to the painted plaster.

Room 17b (Baths): The plaster is as Room 17a, except that it has a thin 'limey' layer of plaster beneath the paint. This is very loose and much of the design has disappeared. There were enormous quantities of white plaster from this room, some with a double curve, so presumably the ceiling in this room was white. Other colours are mainly shades of yellow and red ochre. The design appears to be stripes and bands of yellow, in places on white crossing. The joins are sometimes decorated with circles of another colour and there are many curved and angled pieces.

Room 18 (Baths): All the plaster from this room has a layer of *opus signinum*, which varies in thickness: on one moulded piece it is almost 2.54 cm thick behind the flat surface. At one point the plaster is 6.35 cm thick and very heavy. A tile imprint appears on the back of one unpainted piece.

Petrographic examination of wall plaster samples *by Ian Sims*

Four Roman wall plaster samples were received by RSK Environment Ltd, at its Hemel Hempstead office (Table 13). A summary of the procedures and results are presented below; the full laboratory report is held in the Sparsholt site archive.

Visual and optical microscopy

Each plaster sample was examined, variously using the unaided eye and optical microscopy, including the inspection of thin-sections under a high-power petrological microscope, following the methods given for concrete in ASTM C856-11 (standard practice for the petrographic examination of hardened concrete, American Society for Testing and Materials, West Conshohocken, Pennsylvania, USA). Thin-section specimens were prepared to include the full thickness of each sample, including the painted outer surface.

Scanning electron microscopy and microanalysis

A portion from each plaster sample, including the full thickness and its painted surface, was subjected to further examination at higher magnification using scanning electron microscopy, with an attached EDX microanalysis facility. This work was undertaken by specialist consultant, Nick Winter, of WHD Microanalysis Consultants Ltd.

Results

The methods and findings of the visual and optical microscopical examinations are detailed in the RSK certificates (archive report). The methods and findings of the scanning electron microscopical examinations and microanalyses are given in the WHD report (archive report).

Sample reference			Advised details		Approx. size as received (mm)
RSK	Client	Building	Room	Notes	
12587/A1	A	AB I	26	Earliest structure on site	70 × 50 × 8
12587/A2	B	AB II	17/18	Replaced AB I	82 × 65 × 10
12587/A3	C	Main House	7	Room with main mosaic	83 × 65 × 35
12587/A4	D	Main House	3	Later addition to House	90 × 55 × 30

Table 13: Sample received

Sample 12587 RSK/ Client	Building/Room	Main Binder	Aggregate/Filler	Details	Paint
A1 / A	AB I 26	carbonated lime (2 coats)	flint & quartz sand + minor brick & limestone (incl. chalk)	trace of ?hydrated silicate & repaired pre-painting surface defect	limewash, overlain by iron-pigmented red limewash
A2 / B	AB II 17/18	carbonated lime (1 coat)	crushed brick + minor limestone & quartz	trace of hydrated silicate: possible limebrick pozzolanic reaction	one coat of deteriorated limewash
A3 / C	Main House 7	carbonated lime (2 coats)	flint & quartz sand + minor brick	hair reinforcement & time lapse between coats?	two coats of limewash
A4 / D	Main House 3	carbonated lime (2 coats)	flint & quartz sand + minor brick & limestone	trace of hydrated silicate: possible limebrick pozzolanic reaction & repaired pre-painting surface defect	two coats of limewash

Table 14: Summary of results

Summary of findings (Table 14)

The four wall plaster samples each comprised carbonated lime binder, with an outer surface coated or painted with limewash.

Sample A (Room 26, AB I) was 8 mm thick, comprising two coats of lime:sand plaster, with a minor crushed brick content. The plaster surface had been repaired prior to painting with two coats of limewash, the first being white and the second of which was iron-pigmented and red in colour.

Sample B (Room 17/18, AB II) was 10 mm thick, comprising a single coat of pinkish lime plaster with a largely crushed brick aggregate and some evidence of a possible pozzolanic lime-brick reaction. The plaster surface exhibited a deteriorated single coat of white limewash.

Sample C (Room 7, Main House) was 35 mm thick, comprising two coats of lime:sand plaster, with a minor brick content and some hair reinforcement; there was evidence of a time lapse between the two coat applications. The plaster surface had two coats of white limewash.

Sample D (Room 3, Main House, later addition) was 30 mm thick, comprising two coats of lime:sand plaster, with a minor brick content and some evidence of a possible pozzolanic lime-brick reaction. The plaster surface had been repaired prior to painting with two coats of white limewash.

Further compositional detail could possibly be obtained by chemical analysis for soluble silica and more exhaustive scanning electron microscopy.

Chapter 13

Analysis of Concrete and Mortar Samples

by Ian Sims (written in 1975)

Summary

Various samples from Sparsholt Roman Villa were examined, seven of them in detail, in order to establish the composition in terms of aggregate content and cement type. The concretes were found to be made with non-hydraulic lime cement, mixed systematically with both sand and coarser gradings. Cream-coloured concretes contain only chalk and flint as coarse aggregate, whereas the pink-coloured concretes also contain brick as both a fine-grained additive and as coarser particles. Variations in these general types are described below. No evidence was found of a pozzolanic reaction between crushed brick particles and the lime matrix.

Introduction

Analysis of the concrete samples from Sparsholt Roman Villa was undertaken in order to establish the composition in terms of aggregate content and cement type. Since the type of relative dating pioneered by Van Deman (1912) was not required, no widespread and systematic collection of concrete samples was carried out. Instead, 19 samples were collected during the final season of excavation (1972), representing the variety of types and occurrences that could be observed in exposed parts of the site. These were the Aisled Building and bath house areas (Site F), and samples were taken from both AB I and AB II, the Main House (Site D), and the pit and ditch complex west of the Main House (Site L).

The samples are listed in Table 15, their numbers being prefixed by the site location code. Broadly speaking, the samples fell into two categories based on their overall colours: a) pale cream-coloured concrete used as mortar and flooring; and b) pale pink-coloured concrete (*opus signinum*) used as flooring and wall rendering in the bath buildings. One exception, F11, was orange-pink in colour. The aggregates appeared to be mostly chalk and flint, with brick fragments mainly associated with the pale pink-coloured concretes. The obvious content of abundant chalk particles led to an earlier assumption that the concrete had been made from puddled chalks rather than the more conventional slaked lime. All the concrete samples were soft and porous and most were also extremely friable, whilst four samples were too disaggregated and contaminated to be of use in this analysis. Two further samples of gastropod shells that appeared to be in situ in the wall mortar were collected.

Methods of treatment

Thirteen of the samples were impregnated with blue-stained araldite and then prepared into both a plane surface and a thin-section for macroscopic and microscopic examination respectively. The presence of abundant chalk in the samples made the simple acid-dissolution technique, as used by Davey on samples from the Park Street Villa (Davey 1945), inoperable. However, the difficulty of obtaining a representative thin-section of concrete containing aggregate particles occasionally exceeding 11 mm in diameter and the extremely fine particle size of much of the sand made point-counting under the microscope unreliable. Consequently, a more complicated chemical technique, combining a total acid-dissolution of the concrete with the dissolution of separated matrix, was devised and carried out on seven specially selected samples (see Table 15).

This chemical technique required two different specimen preparations from each sample. Firstly, a representative piece of the concrete was set aside (up to 130 g) and, secondly, another piece of concrete was gently broken down by hand and then sieved through a boulting cloth. Preliminary microscopic examination had shown that the particles of sand, or of the sand and brick mixture, rarely exceed 600 μm, whilst the chalk particles are generally larger. Consequently, the fraction passing a 600 μm boulting cloth would represent the lime:sand/sand and brick ratio in the matrix and, since disaggregation was carried out gently by hand, contamination by the chalk would be

Sample No.	Weight (g)	Building phase	Locality	Colour	Condition
F1**	320	II	Mortar from chalk wall, Room 15 ?	Pale cream	Soft, friable, porous
F2	425	II	Concrete from floor of W. apse	Pale cream	Disaggregated, poss. contaminated
F3*	381	II	Concrete from plunge bath, phase 1	Pale cream	Soft, friable, porous
F4*	1327	II	Mortar from S. Wall, building W. of apses	Pale cream	As F1
F5*	378	II	Concrete from foundation trench	Pale cream	As F1, chalk aggregate
F6**	717	II	Concrete, floor of Room 18	Pale pink	As F3
F7*	460	II	Concrete from plunge bath, phase 2	Very pale pink	As F3. Layers of pink and cream, former used
F8**	228	I	Infill of stoke hole, Layer 6c.	Pale pink	Soft, friable, porous
F9	960	I	As F8	Pale cream	Completely disaggregated. Contains charcoal and shells
F10*	1431	?	Concrete from N. side of cistern	Pale cream	Single lump of soft friable material
F11**	425	II?	Concrete oven-surround, Trench 29	Orange-pink	Soft, friable, porous
D12**	107		Mortar, ext. N–S Corridor wall, Trench 1.	Pale cream	Soft, friable, porous; little sample
D13	147		Concrete from beneath floor, Trench 1.	Pale cream	Completely disaggregated. Contaminated. Soil & bone
D14	78		Concrete in which tesserae were set	Pale pinkish-cream	Sample small & contaminated
D15**	111		Mortar from E–W wall of Room 2 – Corridor	Pale cream	As D12, only chalk aggregate
D16*	449		Mortar from ext. N–S wall, Room 2	Pale cream	Soft, friable, porous
D17			Shells from D15		
F12		II	Shells, AB II wall		
L1**	943		Concrete flooring from Pit XX	Pale cream	Soft & porous but compact lumps

Table 15: List of the samples collected. * = plane surface & thin section. ** = detailed analysis. F = Aisled Building; D = Main House; L = Iron Age/Roman site.

minimal. Tests showed that this method of specimen preparation was repeatable.

Both the concrete lump and the matrix separation were then treated with dilute HCl (10%) to remove the soluble material. The filtered insoluble residue from the former was then sieved, while the residue from the latter was retained in a gooch crucible. Weighing of the sieved fractions allowed for an accurate proportional analysis of the insoluble aggregates but yielded only a single figure for total soluble material, while weighing of the gooch crucible residue yielded a figure for the lime:sand ratio (less than 600 μm). Since the sand (less than 600 μm) figure was also obtained in the total dissolution, it was possible to derive relative proportions for carbonated lime and chalk. The point-counting method was used to determine the percentage of visible voids and the proportions of sand and brick in the fine aggregate from the microscope thin-sections.

The nature of the cement was examined by X-Ray Diffractometry on powdered samples extracted from the matrix. The residues of sand or brick dust (less than 600 μm) were also examined by X-Ray Diffraction for traces of insoluble cement hydrates. In several cases, aggregate particles were identified by Infra-Red Spectrophotometry.

A brief series of experiments was carried out to test the effect of heat on the matrix colour of Roman concrete. Eight samples of cream-coloured concrete from F4 were each subjected to heat for one hour, at temperatures ranging from 100°C to 800°C, in a muffle furnace, the resultant colour change on cooling being recorded.

The gastropod shells were identified, and ecological information supplied, by Mr J N Carreck of Queen Mary College, London.

Results

Hand specimen and plane surface examination

Table 16 summarises the visual observations. The concrete samples may be divided into two categories: a) pale cream-coloured paste with chalk and flint coarse aggregates; and b) pale pink-coloured paste with chalk, flint and brick fragments as coarse aggregate. The cream concrete occasionally contains brick fragments or rounded lumps of re-used pink concrete, but their rarity suggests accidental inclusion. Two samples of the cream-coloured concrete contain mostly chalk aggregate with little or no observed flint or brick. The rounded brown-coloured lumps up to about 2 mm in diameter, observed in three samples, were found by infra-red analysis to be aggregations of finer quartz grains cemented together by smaller amounts of clay mineral. Finally, charcoal fragments, in some cases up to 10 mm in length, were observed in four of the concrete samples.

Two samples, F10 and L1, were clearly fragmental slabs of flooring 50 mm and 40 mm thick, respectively. On the other hand, samples F3 and F7 were clearly wall renderings, the latter consisting of a layer of cream-coloured mortar 20 mm thick over a layer of very pale pink-coloured mortar (18 mm thick).

Thin-section examination

Table 17 summarises the observations and determinations made in thin-section. All the concrete samples were found to consist of micro-crystalline calcite, of a brownish-buff colouration, together with various aggregates. The calcite paste varied greatly in porosity from being relatively dense and filled with sand particles to being extremely porous, occasionally honeycombed, and often devoid of aggregate particles. This variation probably reflects the difficulties of obtaining a thorough mixing using only crude techniques. The overall porosity (i.e. percentage of visible voids) of each sample is given in Table 17, but may only reflect the weathering and leaching effects of age.

Secondary calcite of a coarser grain size (5–10 μm) was observed infilling circular-section air cavities (500–800 μm in diameter) and the peripheral shrinkage cracks that surround many of the pottery fragments (see below). The larger (up to 1 mm), more irregularly-shaped areas of this coarser calcite may result from the slower crystallization of lime particles or trapped patches of slaked lime.

Although, as mentioned earlier, most of the chalk particles exceeded 600 μm in size, there was a small proportion of finer chalk dust and chalk microfossils scattered throughout the matrix of most samples. It is possible, of course, that some of this fine chalk is residual material from imperfect calcination (producing the lime). The chalk forms rounded particles of a mostly relatively dense, light grey variety (i.e. in thin-section) but, in five samples there is a small additional amount of extremely porous chalk. The chalk particles are distinctly more fine-grained than the calcite matrix.

Quartz is the predominant constituent of the fine aggregate in all of the samples, forming angular to sub-angular grains ranging in size from 10 to 400 μm in diameter. Seven of the samples have subordinate amounts of sub-rounded feldspar grains, up to 600 μm across, and nine of the samples have subordinate amounts of sub-angular to very angular flint particles, often ranging in size into the coarse aggregate gradings. Eight of the samples contain very small amounts of pottery and/or hydrated iron minerals. The cream-coloured concretes from Main House seem to contain a more quartz-rich sand than those from the Aisled Building (Site F) or that from Pit XX.

The pink-coloured concrete samples contain irregularly shaped crushed brick particles in the fine aggregate, ranging from tiny particles of reddish-brown or opaque interstitial material (up to *c* 100 μm) to larger pieces containing angular quartz tempering. As shown in Table 17, the point-count analysis indicates that the sand to brick ratio in the fine aggregate is usually about 1:2. There appeared to be no evidence of a pozzolanic reaction between these brick particles and the surrounding matrix, nor was any mineral apart from calcite observed in the paste.

Sample F11, which has an overall orange-pink colouration in hand specimen, differs from all the other samples in thin-section. The calcite matrix, whilst still being micro-crystalline, is distinctly coarser than the other samples (the crystallites are 1–2 μm in diameter) and gives the appearance of being equi-granular. Also, there is no discernible difference in grain size between the calcite paste and the chalk particles. Finally, despite the orange-pink colouration, there is no brick content in the fine aggregate.

An additional thin-section was cut through an inclusion of pink concrete in sample L1. The petrography of both the lime matrix and the fine aggregate was found to be very similar to the orange-pink-coloured sample F11.

Analysis of seven samples by an acid-dissolution technique

The constituent proportions obtained by the acid-dissolution technique are tabulated in Table 18, whilst Table 19 lists the size distributions of the insoluble aggregate materials.

The data in Table 19 seem to indicate the validity of dividing the aggregates into fine (less than 600 μm) and coarse gradings, with the possible exception

Sample No.	Paste colour	Coarse Aggregates			Charcoal fragments	Re-used pink concrete	Brown Agg.	Comments
		Flint	Chalk	Brick				
F1	Pale cream	P	P					
F2	Pale cream cream	P	P	Ps		Ps		
F3	Pale pink	P	P	P	Ps			Painted surface
F4	Pale cream	P	P		Ps	Ps		
F5	Pale cream	Ps	P					
F6	Pale pink	P	P	P				
F7	V. pale pink & pale cream	P P	P P	P				Layered – 20 mm cream uppermost on 18 mm very pale pink
F8	Pale pink	Ps	P	P				
F9	Pale cream	P	P		Ps			Includes large shells
F10	Pale cream	P	P		Ps			Slab 50–55 mm thick on sand base
F11	Orange-pink	P	P					
D12	Pale cream	P	P					
D13	Pale cream	P	P					
D14	Pale pinkish-cream	P	P	Ps				
D15	Pale cream		P	Ps			Ps	
D16	Pale cream	P	P	Ps			Ps	
L1	Pale cream	P	P		Ps	Ps	Ps	Includes a large piece of re-used pink concrete, 30 mm

Table 16: Observations from plane surface and hand specimen examination. P = present. Ps = Present in small amount. F = Aisled Building; D = Main House; L = Iron Age/Roman site

Sample No.	Features of calcite matrix	Aggregate							Point Count Analysis		
		Dense chalk	Porous chalk	Quartz	Feld.	Flint	Brick	Other	Voids %	Fine Agg. Sand %	Brick %
F1	–	P	Ps	P		Ps			15		
F3	Infilled cavity	P	Ps	P	Ps	Ps	P		12	31.7	68.3
F4	Secondary calcite	P	Ps	P	Ps	Ps		Pvs	20		
F5	Secondary calcite	P	Ps	P	Ps	Ps		Pvs	6		
F6	–	P		P	Ps	Ps	P		13	26.9	73.1
F7	Infilled cavity	P	Ps	P	Ps	Ps	P		7	35.6	64.4
F8	Carbonated patches of unslaked lime and trapped slaked lime	P		P	Ps	Ps	P		8	36.1	63.9
F10	Secondary calcite	P		P		Ps		Pvs	10		
F11	Secondary calcite	P		P				Pvs	11		
D12	–	P		P				Pvs	7		
D15	–	P		P				Pvs	5		
D16	Secondary calcite	P		P		Ps		Pvs	12		
L1	–	P		P	Ps	Ps		Pvs	13		

Table 17: Observations and determinations from thin section examination. P = present. Ps = present in small amount. Pvs = present in very small amount

Sample No.	Paste colour	Coarse aggregates %			Fines %	Paste %	Fines/paste ratio	Total agg./ paste ratio
		Flint	Brick	Chalk				
F1	Cream	20.76	–	22.77	19.11	36.52	0.52	1.71
F6	Pink	–	44.72	31.07	9.18	15.04	0.61	5.65
F8	Pink	–	32.42	0.66	26.60	39.84	0.67	1.50
F11	Orange	26.28	–	16.14	21.39	36.10	0.59	1.77
D12	Cream	5.56	–	35.65	22.25	36.31	0.61	1.75
D15	Cream	2.84	–	37.21	14.85	44.79	0.33	1.22
L1	Cream	19.50	–	4.41	36.82	39.10	0.94	1.55

Table 18: Composition of seven selected concrete samples as determined by the acid-dissolution technique

Sample No.	F1	F6	F8	F11	D12	D15	L1
Wt. sample (g)	17.55	~8.65	45.66	155.02	38.32	26.42	129.57
Wt. residue (g)	7.14	20.83	27.16	74.04	10.74	4.75	73.19
% Residue	40.71	53.89	59.50	47.76	28.04	17.99	56.48
Retained by sieve size:	Percentage by weight						
11.2 mm	44.22	–	–	48.08	–	–	–
9.5 mm	–	–	–	–	–	–	–
4.75 mm	5.57	60.06	10.22	5.80	17.40	12.10	0.54
1.18 mm	1.67	0.12	37.23	0.91	1.90	3.21	16.72
600 μm	1.19	2.78	7.48	0.34	0.69	0.75	17.37
150 μm	5.22	5.99	16.54	9.10	2.84	6.43	47.40
75 μm	7.37	5.69	13.30	10.75	4.49	10.42	8.19
Less than 75 μm	34.75	5.36	15.22	25.02	72.69	67.09	9.78
Total	99.99	100.00	99.99	100.00	100.00	100.00	100.00

Table 19: Size distributions of the insoluble aggregates

of sample L1. The cream- and orange-coloured concretes from the Aisled Building (Site F) and the Main House display a distinct bimodal distribution into fine (less than 75 μm across) and coarse (exceeding 4.75 mm) particles. They differ in that D12 and D15 contain predominantly the fine grading, whereas F1 and F11 have more coarse aggregate, mostly present as particles greater than 11.2 mm in diameter.

The pink-coloured concretes, on the other hand, have a more uniform distribution of the finer gradings and coarse aggregate predominates, not exceeding 9.5 mm in size. In fact, the pink samples F6 and F8 are quite dissimilar, the latter having more fine aggregate and most of the coarse particles between 600 μm and 4.75 mm in size, whilst the former has coarse particles mostly exceeding 4.75 mm in diameter.

The cream-coloured sample, L1, has a bimodal distribution with a dominant fine grading of particles mostly between 600 μm and 75 μm in diameter and coarse particles not exceeding 9.5 mm.

Table 18 shows that similar patterns are reflected in the constituent proportions for the whole concrete. Samples F1 and F11, cream- and orange-coloured respectively, are clearly similar in composition. D12 and D15, on the other hand, are broadly similar in their coarse aggregate content but the latter is a richer mixture of lower fines:paste ratio. The pink concretes F6 and F8 are similar in containing brick as coarse aggregate, but differ significantly in that the former also contains chalk and an altogether higher total aggregate:paste ratio. The apparent lack of flint particles in these samples of pink concrete, which were observed to contain flint in plane section, emphasises the difficulty of obtaining truly representative fragments for analysis. Finally, the different nature of L1 is again highlighted, since the total aggregate:paste ratio is comparable to the other samples whilst the fines:paste ratio is much higher.

Analysis of the paste by X-Ray Diffraction

X-Ray Diffraction analysis of the cement and fine aggregate matrix confirms the presence of both calcite and quartz, with small quantities of additional aggregate materials such as feldspar (both plagioclase and K-Feldspar) and clay minerals. No calcium silicates, calcium aluminates or their hydrated forms were detected. There was no significant difference between diffractograms for the pink concretes and those for the cream-coloured concretes. Diffractometry on brick particles extracted from samples F6 and F8 revealed mostly quartz from the tempering, suggesting that the interstitial material is probably amorphous and explaining the observed similarity of the diffractograms for pink and cream concretes.

Analysis of the acid-washed residues identified only the insoluble aggregate materials and again no cementitious hydrates were detected in either the pink or the cream concrete samples.

Experiment to study the effect of heat upon the matrix colour of Roman concrete

The absence of brick dust from the orange-pink-coloured concrete F11, its distinctive texture in thin-section and its origin from an oven-surround led to the suspicion that its colouration may be due to the effect of heat. Experiments, using a muffle furnace and cream-coloured concrete samples, showed that no colour change took place at 100°C or 200°C, but that a pale pink colouration occurred at 300°C and 700°C. Between 400°C and 600°C, however, the resultant colouration was an orange-pink, very similar to that observed in Sample F11. At 800°C, the colour changed to a greenish-grey and calcination started to take place (Table 20). The orange-pink colouration is probably due to crystal lattice distortion (Wells 1962) which may accompany a partial or complete recrystallization.

Furnace temperature for 1h (°C)	Overall colour after cooling
100	Pale cream
200	Pale cream
300	Pale pink
400	Orange-pink
500	Orange-pink
600	Orange-pink
700	Pale pink
800	Greenish-grey

Table 20: The colour changes observed after heating for one hour at temperatures in the range 100–800°C. All samples started pale cream in colour

Identification of the gastropod shells

Different species were recognised, all of which are terrestrial and typically inhabit wooded areas, whilst several have a particular affinity for calcareous soils. It therefore seems unlikely that these shells were an original constituent of the concretes or mortars.

Discussion

Both thin-section and X-Ray Diffraction analysis has shown the cement paste to consist in all cases of only micro-crystalline calcite with no detectable insoluble hydrate phases. It is therefore concluded that the original 'quicklime' was of the non-hydraulic variety, probably produced from the calcination of local white Upper Chalk (Davey 1961). The presence of charcoal fragments, and the distinct difference in both colour and grain size between the paste and chalk particles, confirms this use of a lime cement rather than the 'puddling' of crushed chalk.

The concretes appear to have been mixed deliberately using both a fine sand grading and a coarser grading for bulking. The acid-dissolution analysis on seven samples suggests that the proportions of lime paste, fine sand and coarser aggregates are systematic, although the original mix design would have been volumetric. With the exception of L1, the paste to fine sand ratio is about 1:½, whilst the paste to total aggregate ratio is, with the exception of F6, about 1:1½. This suggests that, except for F6, the Sparsholt samples are more cement-rich than is normally expected of Roman concretes (Davey 1945, 1961; Vitruvius) (see Table 18).

With the exception of L1, the fine sand is composed of mostly sub-angular to angular grains of quartz, the majority of which are less than 75 μm in diameter with subordinate quantities of feldspar, flint, clay minerals and iron compounds. The angularity of the particles suggests a fluviatile origin, whilst the fineness may result from either deliberate grading or natural sorting of the type that can occur during river transportation (Hatch et al. 1965). L1 has a noticeably coarser sand (mostly greater than 150 μm) that is less well sorted and probably of a different origin.

The pink-coloured concretes have crushed brick dust added to the fine sand in the sand to brick ratio of about 1:2. Brick and tile dust was added to lime concrete in Britain as a substitute for the pozzolanic volcanic earths found in Italy (Davey 1961), which react with lime and water at normal temperatures to form insoluble hydrated calcium silicates and calcium aluminates (Lea 1970). Any reaction would be at the surface interface of the brick particle with the lime matrix, but no such reaction was observed in thin-section and nor were any such hydraulic compounds identified by X-Ray Diffraction. This would seem to indicate that reaction has not in fact taken place. Malinowski et al. (1962), however, in their work on concrete from Caesarea and Tiberias, found some evidence of reaction along particle boundaries but no reaction products, and have suggested that, 'age seems to favour the formation of calcite as the stablest mineral'. Idorn (1959), on the other hand, working on concrete from Roman aqueducts in Provence, has successfully identified micro-crystalline hydrated calcium silicate in the paste.

Experiments have shown that cream-coloured Roman mortar changes to an orange-pink colour when subjected to temperatures between 250°C and 750°C. The distinctive colouration of both Sample F11 and the inclusion of pink concrete in L1, together with the lack of brick dust and evidence of recrystallization, suggests that these samples were originally of the cream-coloured variety but have been subjected to such a temperature regime.

Thin-section analysis has revealed an inadequate mixing of the slaked lime paste and fine sand, leading to inhomogeneity, trapped slaked lime (which has since slowly carbonated) and aggregations of sand particles. The spherical voids are probably the result of poor compaction, since there are too few to suggest the sort of deliberate entrainment described by Idorn (1959), whilst the severe honeycombing or disaggregation of many samples is the result of leaching due to weathering processes.

Conclusions

The concretes have been made using a non-hydraulic lime cement probably manufactured using local Upper Chalk.

Systematic volumetric mix designs appear to have been employed, mostly using both a fine-grained angular sand of probable fluviatile origin and a coarser grading. Mixing and compaction appear to have been inadequate for the production of a high-quality Roman concrete.

The cream-coloured concretes from the Aisled Building (Site F) contain both chalk and flint as coarse aggregate, with the amount of flint slightly exceeding the amount of fine sand. One sample of this concrete was found to be discoloured by subjection to temperatures between 250° and 750°C.

The cream-coloured concretes from the Main House were made with a more quartz-rich fine sand that exceeds the amount of flint present, but the aggregate balance is maintained by the presence of larger quantities of chalk.

The cream-coloured concrete from Pit XX is distinctly different from the other samples and is therefore of unknown origin, although it does contain pieces of heat-affected concrete very similar to that found at the Aisled Building (Site F).

The pink-coloured concretes from the Aisled Building (Site F) contain crushed brick dust added to the fine sand and brick fragments in the coarse aggregate. No evidence of a pozzolanic reaction, between the brick particles and the lime matrix, was observed.

The pink concrete from Aisled Building I is made with mainly brick as the coarse aggregate material, whilst that from Aisled Building II has flint, chalk and brick of a larger grain size, as well as a very high aggregate:paste ratio.

Chapter 14

The Coins

by Hugh Williams

Forty-three coins from the Roman period, together with two 20th-century coppers, were reported from the excavations. A further coin, found in the area in the late 19th century was also reported. This was said to be a Republican denarius of L. Marcus Philippus (104 BC). Such an early coin is not surprising, and other Republican denarii, probably brought to Britain during or shortly after the invasion, are sometimes found in the South of England. The coin may well have no direct connection with the villa itself.

Such a small sample of coins makes the drawing of any firm conclusions a problem. Just two or three coins from any period, missed during excavation, would change the Reece bar-chart radically. Nevertheless, the conclusions outlined below provide a picture that is worthy of some consideration.

With the exception of three silver denarii, all the coins found were of base metal, and most were probably of little monetary value when lost. There were four sestertii from the Antonine period, and a British imitation of a Claudian as. This in no way indicates probability of 2nd-century occupation. The coins show evidence of much circulation, and it is widely accepted that many such worn sestertii remained in circulation in the province until the 260s.

Bearing this fact in mind, the earliest coins that indicate possible financial action in the villa would appear to be the three denarii, two of which were struck about 220. There is then a large gap until the 260s before a continuous coin series is recorded. It is possible that the denarii were not lost until this period.

The largest group of coins from the villa date from the time of the Gallic Empire (258–73) and the period immediately after. There were four regular antoniniani, and more significantly 19 radiate copies which date to the late 270s or 280s. The number of copies is extremely high, indicative of the shortage of supply of regular coinage at this time.

The British Empire of Carausius and Allectus is represented by only one coin, a 'quinarius' of Allectus struck at the London Mint. There is then a complete gap in the coinage until the appearance group of three small bronzes struck in about 321.

The rest of the numismatic evidence is most surprising. Most villa sites produce an abundance of Constantinian coinage from the 330s and 340s. At Sparsholt there is none. There is also no representation of the Magnentian revolt (350–53). It seems probable that this complete lack of coinage indicates that the villa may have been abandoned, for whatever reason, shortly after 321.

There are three much later finds. All are very worn and crude late 4th-century copies. This could indicate a token reoccupation, or the coins may have been losses from random visitors to the derelict villa.

Once again, caution should be exercised, as such a small sample cannot be assumed to be totally representative of the financial history of the villa.

COIN CATALOGUE

1. Claudius, bronze, imitation of RIC 66, AD 41-54. Site D, Room 2 rubble, s.f. 144
2. Domitian, As, rev. Monita, AD 81-96. 53. Site F, unstrat rubble, s.f. 53
3. Antoninus Pius, Sestertius, rev. Pax, as BMC pl. 48.8, AD 138-161. Site C a, top soil (SPCA), s.f. 77
4. Antoninus Pius, Sestertius, rev. Annona, AD 138-161. Site H, H1 (SPHB), s.f. 89
5. Antoninus Pius Sestertius, uncertain rev., AD 138-161. Site F, Trench 31, top soil, Layer 1, s.f. 485
6. L. Verus, Sestertius, rev. Victory, as BMC pl. 79.6, AD 161-169. Site F, unstrat. Rubble (SPFPZ), s.f. 430
7. Commodus, Denarius, BMC 249, AD 180-192. Site A, Room 19, rubble on chalk floor, s.f. 24
8. Elagabalus, Denarius, BMC 167, AD 218-222. Site G3, Layer 4 rubbish (SPGO), s.f. 93
9. Severus Alexander, Denarius, BMC 232, AD 222-235. Site A, courtyard rubble, s.f. 1
10. Gordian III, As, obv. IMP GORDIANVS PIVS FEL AVG, laureate, draped and cuirassed bust right, seen from behind, rev. VIRTVTI AVGVSTI SC, Hercules standing naked right, resting right hand on hip and left hand on club, RIC 309, AD 238-244. Site D, Trench 5, Corridor floor, s.f. 4
11. Gallienus, Sestertius, obv. IMP C P LIC GALLIENVS AVG, laureate, cuirassed bust right, rev. CONCORDIAE AVGG, Concordia standing left, holding patera and double cornucopia, Rome mint, RIC 207, AD 253-268. Site G, Trench 8, s.f. 391
12. Gallienus, silvered Antoninianus, obv. GALLIENVS AVG, radiate head right, rev. FORTVNA REDVX, Fortuna standing left, holding a rudder on a globe and cornucopia, Rome mint, RIC 193, AD 253-268. D1/3/5, Room 7, on floor (SPDEP), s.f. 39
13. Postumus, Denarius, Elmer 129/85, AD 260-269. Site D, Trench 28, possible midden outside building, s.f. 33
14. Claudius II, Antoninianus, obv. IMP C CLAVDIVS AVG, radiate, draped and cuirassed bust right, rev. FIDES AVG, Mercury

standing left with purse and caduceus, Antioch mint, RIC 207, AD 268-270. D21, Room 9a, deep in rubble (SPDEA), s.f. 36

15. Victorinus, Bronze, rev. Pax Aug, Elmer 682, AD 269-271. F3, Room 17a, between pilae (SPFBK), s.f. 38
16. Victorinus, rev. Pax Aug, Elmer 682, AD 269-271. Site G, wall rubble on floor, s.f. 233
17. Victorinus, rev. Pax Aug, Elmer 682, AD 269-271. Site L, top soil, s.f. 498
18. Claudius II, imitation, AD 270-280. Courtyard, s.f. 3
19. Imitation radiate, AD 270-280. Site F, Trench 3, rubble, s.f. 64
20. Tetricus I, imitation, rev. Hilaritas Augg, AD 270-280. Site D, top soil over midden, s.f. 159
21. Claudius II, imitation, AD 270-280. Site G, Outside Layer 6, s.f. 195
22. Imitation radiate, AD 270-280. Site F, Trench 29, outside building, s.f. 446
23. Imitation radiate, AD 270-280. Site F, Trench 29, top soil, s.f. 450
24. Imitation radiate, AD 270-280. Site F, Trench 28, Layer 5, s.f. 458
25. Tetricus I, imitation, AD 270-280. Site F, Trench 31, top soil, s.f. 475
26. Imitation radiate, AD 270-280. Site L, Pit XX, Layer 8, s.f. 502
27. Imitation radiate, AD 270-280. Site L, Pit XX, Layer 12, s.f. 533
28. Imitation radiate, AD 270-280. Site L, Pit XX, Layer 5, s.f. 594
29. Tetricus I, rev. Pax Aug, Elmer 771/5, AD 271-274. D10/15, in hypocaust ash (SPDCR), s.f. 22
30. Tetricus I, rev. Pax Aug, Elmer 771/5, AD 271-274. Site D, top soil, s.f. 32
31. Tetricus I, rev. Comes Aug, Elmer 770/4, AD 271-274. D1/3/6, Room 5, on floor, s.f. 44
32. Tetricus I, rev. Pax Aug, Elmer 771/5, AD 271-274. Site C, Room 22, on floor, s.f. 122
33. Tetricus I, rev. Pax Aug, Elmer 771/5, AD 271-274. Site F, Trench 28, Layer 5 (SPFTJ), s.f. 454
34. Tetricus I, rev. Hilaritas Augg, Elmer 789, AD 271-274. Site L, Pit XX, Layer 4, s.f. 563
35. Tetricus II, rev. Spec Publica, Elmer 769, AD 272-274. Site F, Trench 29, top soil, s.f. 440
36. Allectus, Quinarius, obv. IMP C ALLECTVS P F AVG, radiate, cuirassed bust right, rev. VIRTVS AVG, galley rowing left, London mint, RIC 55, AD 293-296. Site D, Room 3, chalk floor, s.f. 161
37. Crispus, Follis, obv. CRISPVS NOBIL C, laureate cuirassed bust left with shield and spear, rev. BEATA TRANQLITAS, globe on altar inscribed VO/TIS/XX, 3 stars above, London mint, RIC 279, AD 317-326. Site A, Room 14, unstrat., s.f. 343
38. Constantine II Caesar, obv. CONSTANTINVS IVN NOB C, laureate, draped and cuirassed bust right, rev. BEATA TRAN-QVILLITAS around globe on altar inscribed VO-TIS-XX, Lyon mint, RIC 148, AD 317-337. Site A1, Room 13, on tessellated floor, s.f. 16
39. Constantine II Caesar, London mint, RIC 216, AD 317-337. Site A, east of entrance? (AB II), s.f. 428
40. Constantine II, rev. Fel Temp Reparatio, AD 353-357. Site I, Layer 16, Crater?, 6 feet down, s.f. 135
41. Illegible, Late Roman. Site G, Layer 3, on floor, s.f. 200
42. Illegible, Late Roman. Site F, Trench 26, rubble in courtyard, s.f. 247
43. Illegible, Late Roman. Site L, Pit XX, Layer 5, s.f. 586

Chapter 15

The Finds

THE METALWORK

by Nick Stoodley

Introduction

In total there are 266 metal artefacts, of which the great majority are iron (232/87%), followed by copper alloy (23/8.6%) and lead (11/4%). In addition, there are seven objects (five unidentified iron pieces, a buckle of unknown material and a piece of lead) that have not been seen and are not included in the report. The metalwork was deposited with Winchester Museums Service (WINCM: ARCH 2923) in 2006. The archive also includes a set of small finds notebooks that contain preliminary identifications made when the objects were first discovered, along with contextual information and measured sketches. A selection of ironwork was radiographed, and the x-rays are stored with the archive. Most of the ironwork is in a very poor condition, and it has been impossible to identify securely a large proportion of it. In addition, just prior to the publication of this report a box containing a large quantity of nails, plus a small number of hobnails, many unprovenanced, was discovered in the museums stores in Winchester. The total weight of these artefacts is 11.07kg and they have not been included in the analysis.

All the examined metalwork is included in this report, but only selected finds are illustrated. The majority of the artefacts are Romano-British, although a very small number came from Iron Age contexts. In addition, there are several medieval and modern objects, which are included for the sake of completeness.

Each object has retained the unique small finds number that it was assigned on its discovery. The majority of the metalwork was recovered from the villa buildings. Where known, contextual information is provided, but most artefacts are only recorded as deriving from a certain trench and/or layer.

The catalogue is organised by material. Measurements are given; unless otherwise stated, these are maximum dimensions. Where possible, each object has been classified by type and, where appropriate, sub-type. The artefacts have been classified into functional categories based on Manning (1985) and the type series used are, in most cases, those devised by Manning. Comparisons are cited, but for multiple artefacts of the same type they are provided only for the first example. Most of the pieces are chronologically undiagnostic and cannot assist in dating.

Overall patterns and comparisons (Table 21)

The report begins by considering the different categories of artefact starting with the ironwork. Not surprisingly, given the poor preservation of the bulk of the ironwork, the majority falls within the miscellaneous category. Following this, structural pieces record the highest total, the majority of this group being simple staples, lugs and strips of various forms. Nails are also numerous and should probably be considered along with structural evidence. Where the head has survived most are circular in form, although SF 35 has a probable diamond-shaped head, while SF 43 exhibits a domed head capped with copper alloy. The remainder of the ironwork is fairly evenly distributed in small quantities amongst the other categories.

The copper alloy assemblage is not spectacular, boasting only four pieces of jewellery (personal): two brooches (SF 100, a Fowler Type A2 penannular brooch and SF 417, a simple fibula brooch), a bracelet (SF 601) and a loop-headed pin (SF 521).

Category	Ironwork n/%	Copper alloy n/%	Lead n/%
Agricultural	5/2	0	0
Footwear (cleats & hobnails)	16/7	0	0
Household	4/2	1/4	0
Knives	14/6	0	0
Nails	36/16	0	0
Miscellaneous	69/30	18/78	8/73
Personal	9/4	4/17	0
Structural	66/28	0	0
Tools/industrial	9/4	0	3/27
Transport	3/1	0	0
Weapons	1/1	0	0

Table 21: Metalwork divided by category (%= of that particular metal)

Site	Copper alloy	Iron	Iron nails (min. #)	Lead
Grateley South	41/3	91/7	1200/89	10/1
Fullerton	26/2	121/10	1000/86	13/1
Thruxton	23/4	133/24	400/61	5/1

Table 22: Quantities of metalwork at villas investigated by the Danebury Environs Roman Project (no./%)

Category	Chilgrove 1 n/%	Chilgrove 2 n/%
Agricultural	3/7	7/15
Household	4/10	7/15
Knives	5/12	4/11
Nails	0	1/2
Misc.	7*/17	5/11
Personal	7/17	1/2
Structural	8/19	8/17
Tools	8/19	13/28

Table 23: Chilgrove 1 & 2, types of ironwork. *= there were 'many more' strips not listed in the catalogue

The other notable pieces include a (locking) key (SF 163), currently on display in Winchester Museum, in addition to several fittings, such as SF 547, which appears to be a plate mount with a rectangular perforation in the centre. Otherwise, the majority of the copper alloy is made up of unidentified fragments. Finally, a small group of lead was collected, but this comprises mainly undiagnostic fragments, although it does include a perforated disc (SF 202) and several pieces of slag.

The assemblage from Sparsholt can be put into context by comparing it to metalwork from other Roman sites, especially in Hampshire. The county has produced a range of Roman period sites with large assemblages of metalwork produced by the excavations at Silchester (Richards 2000) and Winchester (Rees et al. 2008) (towns), Neatham (Redknap 1986) (small town) and Portchester (Webster 1975a; 1975b) (military site), for example, but because these are non-rural settlements they are not directly comparable. It is, however, interesting that at Neatham the proportion of copper alloy to ironwork is roughly equal (47/49%), while at Portchester copper alloy finds clearly outnumber iron (63/36%).

It is more accurate to compare Sparsholt with other villas, a number of which have recently been investigated in Hampshire. At Monk Sherborne a winged corridor house, part of an aisled building and traces of another stone structure, occupied from the middle of the 3rd century until the end of the 4th, were investigated (Teague 2005). The site has produced 240 metal artefacts and in common with Sparsholt ironwork predominates: in fact 99% of the corpus is ironwork, the two copper alloy objects being a finger ring and a length of chain. The ironwork is dominated by nails (n=158/66%), with footwear, mainly hobnails, making up the next largest category (n=74/31%). The remaining objects are structural and household pieces, plus several miscellaneous artefacts. The Danebury Environs Roman Project has investigated several Roman villas on the Hampshire downland and all but Rowbury Farm and Flint Farm have yielded large metalwork assemblages. At Grateley South, Fullerton and Thruxton iron objects easily outnumber those of copper alloy and lead (Table 22), and the majority of the identified ironwork is again made up of nails. At Fullerton the next most numerous objects are cleats, structural items and tools, while at Grateley South it is structural pieces, tools and cleats in that order. The proportion of nails at Thruxton, however, is lower than at the other sites and the majority of the other identified artefacts are cleats 20/16%, structural fittings 13/10%, tools 7/9% and personal items 4/3%. At Sparsholt and the other Hampshire villas, structural pieces and cleats were frequent finds; tools were also common.

Overall, the metalwork from Sparsholt and the other Hampshire villas is dominated by ironwork and this pattern is also observed outside the county. Relatively small quantities of metalwork were recovered from the villas at Chilgrove 1 and 2 (West Sussex) (Down 1979). At Chilgrove 1, 54 pieces were found of which 42 (78%) were iron, while at Chilgrove 2, of the 63 pieces 46 were iron (73%). The non-ferrous group from Chilgrove 1 contains mainly personal items (n=10), of which five are brooches, while at Chilgrove 2 the sample is also dominated by personal items (n=13). At both villas the ironwork is dominated by structural pieces and tools, while at Chilgrove 1 personal items are relatively numerous, but at Chilgrove 2 agricultural and household items are the next most frequent (Table 23).

Spatial distribution

General

Iron is the most common material from Sparsholt and also accounts for over three-quarters of the metalwork from each individual site. There are particularly large concentrations from the Hall and the west end of AB II, with relatively large quantities from the Main House and the Iron Age settlement (Table 24). It has been possible to identify the room in which some artefacts were found, while in some cases the feature/deposit from which they were recovered is also known, although by this stage the samples are often too small to be meaningful. A quantification and distribution of the ironwork by area is attempted, but each one is broadly comparable in terms of the types of ironwork. Overall, structural objects and nails figured prominently in all the major areas. In each of the areas the miscellaneous category is well represented, a result of the poor preservation of many of the finds. The assemblage of copper alloy is small, and probably unrepresentative, and it is not possible to provide an accurate understanding of either the distribution of the finds or the use to which they were put.

By building/site (Table 25)

The provenance of most of the finds is known, although eight artefacts are unstratified or ascribed simply to 'Site L' (Iron Age settlement), and include several hobnails (SFs 527, 529 and 531) and various strips and unidentified objects. Site L produced the largest group of copper alloy objects (21%); several were retrieved from Iron Age Pit XV (SF 521, loop-headed pin and SF 641, ring, top layer), while a fragmentary rod (SF 431), possibly part of a bracelet, and a fragment (SF 429), came from Iron Age Pit VIII or IX. It is interesting that apparently no ironwork was found in the two Iron Age pits that produced copper alloy artefacts. A decorated copper alloy ring (SF 480) was found in Roman Ditch II, but the majority of the stratified material (n=13) came from Roman Pit XX (Table 26), which also produced over half of the pottery for this site and a wide range of faunal remains. One copper alloy artefact (SF 547) was recovered: a perforated fitting from Layer 12. Two iron pieces were recovered from a layer (8) that also produced the skeleton of a fox. A range of finds were found in other layers, for example a reaping hook (SF 595 from Layer 7), a chisel or punch (SF 597), plus structural pieces, such as staples (SFs 559, 616, 632) and a double-spiked loop (SF 546). In fact, the majority of the structural fittings from this area came from this pit, which suggests the deliberate deposition of this material.

Aisled Building II overlay an earlier structure (AB I), but it was only possible to assign two artefacts to its predecessor: SFs 619 and 624, lead slag from the rubble fill of the hypocaust stoke hole. The finds from AB II can be divided between the east and west ends. The former contained a bath suite and several rooms and has produced the second largest group of metalwork from the villa, although the majority of finds could not be assigned to a room or context. The notable exceptions are a tie/holdfast (SF 9) from a rubble context in Room 15 and a composite iron and wood object (SF 532) from a plaster infill in Room 17. A collection of objects, mainly nails, was discovered from the stoke hole (Room 16) and hypocaust channel (Room 15). In addition, an unstratified tripod-shaped object (SF 560) is one of the more interesting items, possibly the head of a cauldron chain. At this end of the building the area associated with the southern wall produced a number of finds. A goad (SF 472) was stratified above the floor cobbling but below a tile feature and this area also produced a copper alloy ring (SF 434) in Layer 2 'tumble' and a cleat (SF 539) from the tile feature. A group of 32½ (SF 457) hobnails was found in a layer (1) of backfill to the south of the south wall of Room 17b, and another two were unstratfied (SFs 455, 458). Three iron pipe collars were found *in situ* in a drain to the south of the south wall; this facilitated the draining of water from the bath into a possible sump in the courtyard. The east end also produced evidence for an oven and associated burnt area and produced a nail (SF 468) and an unidentified object, possibly a fragment of spiked loop or a figure-of-eight loop (SF 582) in a mortar layer (5). The east end is also notable for having produced the largest sample of lead, with three pieces (SFs 519, 543 and 462) coming from burnt layers connected with the hypocaust channel and fill associated with the stoke hole. Most of the lead is fragmentary and probably derived from the demolition of this structure.

Site	*Fe*	*Cu*	*Pb*	Totals	*Fe*	*Cu*	*Pb*
		Number				Percentage	
IA/RB	26	7	1	34	76.47	20.59	2.94
ABII (W)	17	2	0	19	89.47	10.53	0.00
ABII (E)	71	2	8	81	87.65	2.47	9.88
Main H	27	6	1	34	79.41	17.65	2.94
Barn	3	1	0	4	75.00	25.00	0.00
Hall	81	4	1	86	94.19	4.65	1.16
Totals	225	22	11	258			

Table 24: Material by building/area

AB II (west end)	#	%	Main House	#	%
Footwear	0	0.00	Agricultural	0	0.00
Household	0	0.00	Footwear	0	0.00
Metalworking	0	0.00	Metalworking	0	0.00
Transport	0	0.00	Weapons	0	0.00
Unknown	0	0.00	Unknown	0	0.00
Personal	1	5.88	Personal	1	3.70
Tools	1	5.88	Tools	1	3.70
Weapons	1	5.88	Transport	1	3.70
Agricultural	2	11.76	Household	2	7.41
Knives	2	11.76	Nails	4	14.81
Nails	3	17.65	Knives	5	18.52
Structural	3	17.65	Misc.	6	22.22
Misc.	4	23.53	Structural	7	25.93
AB II (east end)	#	%	Hall	#	%
Household	0	0.00	Agricultural	0	0.00
Weapons	0	0.00	Weapons	0	0.00
Knives	1	1.41	Unknown	0	0.00
Metalworking	1	1.41	Footwear	1	1.23
Transport	1	1.41	Household	1	1.23
Unknown	1	1.41	Metalworking	1	1.23
Agricultural	2	2.82	Transport	1	1.23
Tools	2	2.82	Tools	2	2.47
Personal	3	4.23	Personal	4	4.94
Footwear	11	15.49	Knives	5	6.17
Nails	11	15.49	Nails	11	13.58
Misc.	17	23.94	Structural	23	28.40
Structural	21	29.58	Misc.	32	39.51
Site L (IA/RB re-use)	#	%			
Household	0	0.00			
Knives	0	0.00			
Metalworking	0	0.00			
Personal	0	0.00			
Transport	0	0.00			
Weapons	0	0.00			
Unknown	0	0.00			
Agricultural	1	3.85			
Tools	1	3.85			
Nails	2	7.69			
Footwear	4	15.38			
Misc.	8	30.77			
Structural	10	38.46			

Table 25: Ironwork by category and by building/area

The west end of AB II produced a small quantity of metalwork, although the majority could be assigned to specific rooms. The animal remains indicate this was probably a domestic area involved in the production of food. Room 12, part of a suite of rooms that was a later addition to the building, produced the greatest number of stratified metal finds. In particular, an iron plough coulter (SF 12) was found in chalk rubble and on the basis of its position seems to have been either leaning against, or hanging on, the wall. The object is evidence for arable cultivation – an assertion that is supported by the parched grain recovered from the villa (Johnston 1978, 72). Another agricultural implement was a goad (SF 609), although this was unstratified. Along with the pair of agricultural tools from the east end, it suggests that certain areas of the building were used to store agricultural equipment. Three other artefacts possibly come from Room 12: a knife (SF 17) from a rubble context above the floor of either Room 12 or 19, and two rings (SFs 401, 582) which may also have come from Room 19. On the floor of Room 13 were a nail (SF 381) and a rod (SF 380), while in Room 14 an unstratified copper alloy fitting (SF 21) was recovered, along with a plate from a rubble deposit. The main room (19) yielded only a copper alloy strip (SF 5), while a chisel or punch (SF 357) came from a rubble layer north of the room. A stylus

SF number	Object type	Context
546	double-spiked loop	11
559	staple	section 4
616	staple	?
632	staple	7
605	strip with nail	5
67	slag	19
595	reaping hook	7
626	nail	5
597	chisel/punch	5
574	plate	section 4
569	strip	18
634	strip	8
500	bind	8

Table 26: Ironwork from Pit XX. Context = layer unless stated otherwise

(SF 536) came from above a wall at the west end of the building.

Only 25% of the metalwork from the Main House came from recorded contexts. Of this total the majority (n=5) came from Room 1 (the Corridor): three pieces, two nails (SFs 68, 72) and a staple (SF 67), were found in the doorway to Room 9. A knife/razor (SF 37) was recovered from outside the wall of Room 3 in a context that is dated by coins and pottery to the late 3rd to mid-4th century. Room 11 produced a copper alloy binding (SF 73) from the floor of the hypocaust flue (completed by the final third of the 3rd century). The rest of the artefacts were recovered from the topsoil or were apparently unstratified and include copper alloy (bracelet SF 601, disc SF 173 and ring SF 155) and iron (?modelling tool SF 152 and pin/stylus SF 610) objects. The midden in the courtyard to the south of the building yielded a possible binding from a vessel (SF 157) and a possible scraper (SF 158) from the topsoil layer overlying it. Overall, this is a very modest group which provides little insight into the either the functions associated with this building and its individual rooms or the economic and social importance of the occupants, although the small group of copper alloy finds is generally typical of the debris from a villa.

The Barn produced just four objects. A copper alloy penannular brooch (SF 100) of Fowler Type A2 was found in the baulk of Room 21; a composite iron and copper alloy bracket or binding, for furniture or a box, was retrieved from an unknown location (Trench E2) in Room 22; while an iron staple (SF 120) came from the entrance. There is also an unstratified nail (SF 133). The metalwork does not help identify the function of the building. The single find from Site E (trial trenching to the south-east of the Barn) is a possible bolt from a barb-spring padlock.

The majority of the metalwork comes from the Hall, but the largest group comprises miscellaneous pieces that cannot be readily identified or could have served a range of purposes, such as iron rings and plates. The building was not sub-divided into separate rooms and the majority of the finds came from unrecorded or poorly stratified contexts within individual trenches. The group contains four copper alloy objects of which an Iron Age fibula brooch (SF 417, possible Nauheim derivative) found outside the structure and below a pile of slates is the most notable, the other artefacts being fragments. Compared to the other buildings, there are a slightly higher number of tools and knives, but this does not necessarily indicate that the structure was used primarily for industrial activities and there is only one piece of slag (SF 334). A small group of hobnails (SF 408) was found below rubble on the floor, while a buckle (SF 405) was discovered below rubble in the entrance to the building. Interestingly, the site has produced the greatest number of nails and structural pieces, which may suggest that it was not as thoroughly stripped of its fittings as the other buildings. Most of these are unstratified, except for several nails found in layers of black humus, a hook or loop (SF 339) from the flint and clay cobbling, a staple (SF 353) from debris west of the building's wall, and a composite iron and copper alloy nail/rivet head (SF 352) from chalk packing in the corner of the building. Overall, the finds provide no clues as to why the structure was located outside the north-east corner of the villa complex.

The catalogues

Copper alloy

Introduction

This assemblage consists of four items of personal adornment (all from separate sites), several fittings, and a disparate collection of fragmentary artefacts that lack firm identification. The latter contains a group of six rings, which could have been used for suspension, although it is possible that several may have been finger rings, especially the examples with simple ornament. In addition, there is a lever-lock key, which is very similar in appearance and function to a modern key. Three artefacts (SFs 431, 521 and 641) were recovered from Iron Age pits.

Household

SF 163. Key (lever-lock). Length 70 mm, diameter of loop 20 mm (Manning 1985, 94, pl. 42.60–62). Main House, Baulk 28/31/33, topsoil 1.

Objects of personal use

SF 100. Penannular brooch. Diameter 28 mm. Circular section with milled knobbed terminals, pin is wrapped around the ring. Fowler Type A2 (Butcher 2001, 65, fig. 26.143, lacks pin; Webster 1975a, 199, fig. 109.6). Barn, Trench β1, in baulk, Room 21. Late Iron Age to end of Roman period.

SF 417. Brooch. Length 52 mm, width 18 mm. Fibula brooch, ?Nauheim derivative (Price 2000, 33, fig. 2.1.3). Hall, Trench G8β, Layer 9, below slates outside end wall of building. Iron Age brooch 1st century BC–1st century AD (Fig. 106.1).

SF 521. Pin. Length 82 mm. Looped head, bent/hooked point (diameter 6 mm). Iron Age site, Iron Age Pit XV, Layer 3 (Fig. 106.2).

SF 601. Bracelet. Diameter 69 mm, width 3 mm. Fragment, rectangular section, fine notched decoration (Price 2000, 43, no.145, not illustrated). Main House? (Fig. 106.3).

146 THE FINDS

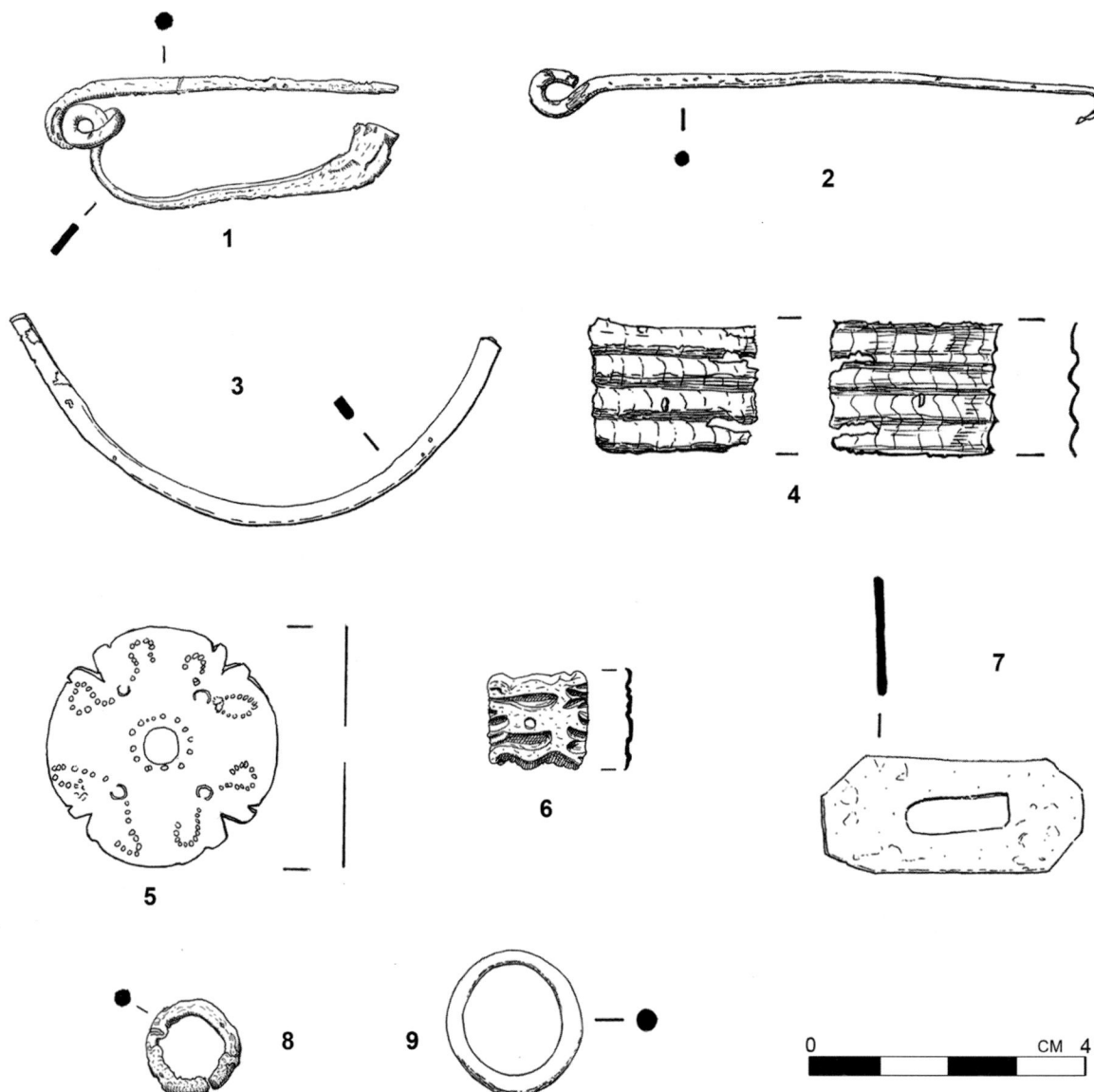

Fig 106 Small finds 1–9. Copper alloy

THE FINDS

Miscellaneous fragments and objects of unknown function

SF 73. Binding. Length 23 mm, width 18 mm. Fragment of corrugated strip, ornamental binding. Main House, Room 11, floor of hypocaust, final third of 3rd century (Fig. 106.4).

SF 21. Fitting. Length 36 mm, width 13 mm. Fragment of sheet with remains of rivet. AB II, west end, Trench 12. Room 14.

SF 173. Fitting. Disc (diameter 35 mm) with perforated centre (diameter 5 mm), 0.5 mm thick, serrated edge. Main House (Fig. 106.5).

SF 206. Fitting. Length 14 mm, width 13 mm. Perforated sheet/mount, decorated with ?repoussé. Iron Age site, trial Trench 6, Layer 2 or 4, Feature H (Fig. 106.6).

SF 547. Fitting. Length 38 mm, width 16 mm. Plate mount with rectangular perforation in centre. Iron Age site, Roman Pit XX, Layer 12 (Fig. 106.7).

SF 641. Ring. Diameter 12 mm. Small ring, broken or penannular in shape, circular section; chain link, or suspension ring (Hooley 2001, 104, fig. 42.174–6). Iron Age site, Iron Age Pit XV, top layer (4) (Fig. 106.8).

SF 20. Ring. Diameter 20 mm. Oval section (Redknap 1986, 108, fig. 73.103). Main House, Trench 6, topsoil. Room 5 (Fig. 106.9).

SF 59. Ring. Diameter 15 mm, width 1.5 mm. Rectangular section. AB II east end.

SF 155. Ring. Diameter 28 mm, width 2.5 mm. Bent, circular section, crude notching near terminal. Main House.

SF 434. Ring. Diameter 21 mm, width 1 mm. Decorated by bands of notching; ends make lap joint. AB II east end, Trench 28, Layer 2, in 'tumble', line of south wall.

SF 480. Ring. Diameter 18 mm, width 4 mm. Octagonal with simple inscribed decoration on the faces. Iron Age site, Ditch II, Layer 1, loose brown soil.

SF 431. Rod. Length 32 mm. Fragment, circular section, curved tapering to one end. Possibly part of a bracelet. Iron Age site, Iron Age Pit VIII.

SF 5. Strip. Length 26 mm, width 2.5 mm. Slight bend at end. AB II west end, Trench 3, under limestone slabs. Room 19.

SF 99. Wire. Length 220 mm. Bent. Circular section with diameter 1.5 mm. Hall, Trench 3.

SF 191. Fragment, possibly a shank. Length 14 mm. Hall, Trench 3, in black humus next to natural.

SF 192. Fragment. Length 20 mm. Hall, Trench 3, in black humus next to natural.

SF 429. Fragment. Length 13 mm. Iron Age site, Iron Age Pit VIII, in clay-with-flints.

SPFFP. Fragment. Length 9 mm. Provenance unknown.

The ironwork

Introduction

The majority of the ironwork has been badly affected by corrosion. A selection of objects were radiographed, which has assisted the process of identification, but many cannot be assigned to a category, other than that of miscellaneous. Consequently, the assemblage consists mainly of small and fragmentary objects; larger more complete pieces are generally absent, which may suggest that scrap iron was collected and recycled. In common with other Romano-British sites, there is a limited range of artefact types (Richards 2000, 360), and it is unsurprising that structural material is well represented. There are only a few objects associated with domestic use or personal adornment.

The metalwork is organised by category and each one is divided by sub-category (alphabetically). Objects that were only tentatively assigned to a category have been placed at the end of that particular group.

Agricultural implements

The agricultural tools include a plough coulter of unusual form, reaping hooks and goads. This is a small group, but the objects reflect a variety of tasks and both the number and range of objects is fairly typical for the Roman period. For example, at Silchester two pruning hooks, a scythe and a pair of ox goads were recovered (Richards 2000, 370), while from Wanborough there are six definite agricultural tools (Isaac 2001, 123–2).

SF 609. Goad. Length 41 mm. Single-turn implement with narrow spike and of square section (Richards 2000, 370, fig. 172.103; Manning 1984, 87, fig. 38.18). AB II west end (Fig. 107.10).

SF 472. Goad. Length 40 mm. Three-spiral implement (diameter across top spiral 12 mm.) with spiked shaft. For a similar example (two-spiral) see Redknap (1986, 118, fig. 79.261). AB II east end, Trench 28, Layer 9, above cobbling, below tile feature, line of south wall (Fig. 107.11).

SF 12. Plough coulter. Length 515 mm, width 159 mm, thickness 5 mm. Large socketed blade with remains of a rivet in the socket. Manning (1985, 44, pl. 18) cites examples from Great Witcombe (Gloucs.) and Coldham Common (Cambs.) that have long handles and triangular blades. Manning (*ibid*) describes these examples as typical, and it would appear that the Sparsholt example is a rare type. AB II west end, Trench A1, in chalk rubble from wall, Room 12. From its position it would have been either leaning against or hanging on the wall (Fig. 107.12).

SF 57. Reaping hook. Length 138 mm. A Manning Type 2 socketed reaping hook: handle of rectangular section and with a curved blade. These are fairly common implements: Manning provides a very similar artefact from Hod Hill (Dorset) of length 134 mm (Manning 1985, 53, pl. 22, F26), while another example is cited from Chilgrove 2 (Down 1979, 155, fig. 48.32). Such forms are found on both Iron Age and Roman sites, although the Roman pieces are more often tanged than socketed (Manning 1985, 53). AB II east end (Fig. 107.13).

SF 595. Reaping hook. Length 62 mm. A fragmentary reaping hook of Manning Type 1 with a socketed crescent-shaped blade. This is an Iron Age type and a comparable example can be cited from Hod Hill (Dorset) (Manning 1985, 53, pl. 22, F24). The Sparsholt example differs by having a horizontal rather than a curving blade. Iron Age site, Roman Pit XX, Layer 7 (Fig. 107.14).

Footwear

The footwear assemblage consists of both cleats and hobnails. The majority of the cleats were from the toe of a shoe or boot and tend to have an oval body with long tangs. Similar cleats were found at Neatham (see below). In addition, there is a pair of possible heel cleats. The examples with long tangs may have been staples for joining wood (Manning 1985, 131). Six single hobnails were found, plus two groups of hobnails.

SF 18. Cleat. Length 50 mm, width 13 mm. A cleat, or staple, for the toe of a boot or shoe: oval body and long tangs (Redknap 1986, 115, fig. 77.207). AB II east end, Trench 3, Room 17 a–b.

SF 52. Cleat. Length 26 mm, width 10 mm. A cleat, or staple, for toe of boot or shoe: oval body and long tangs. AB II east end, Trench 18, topsoil.

148 THE FINDS

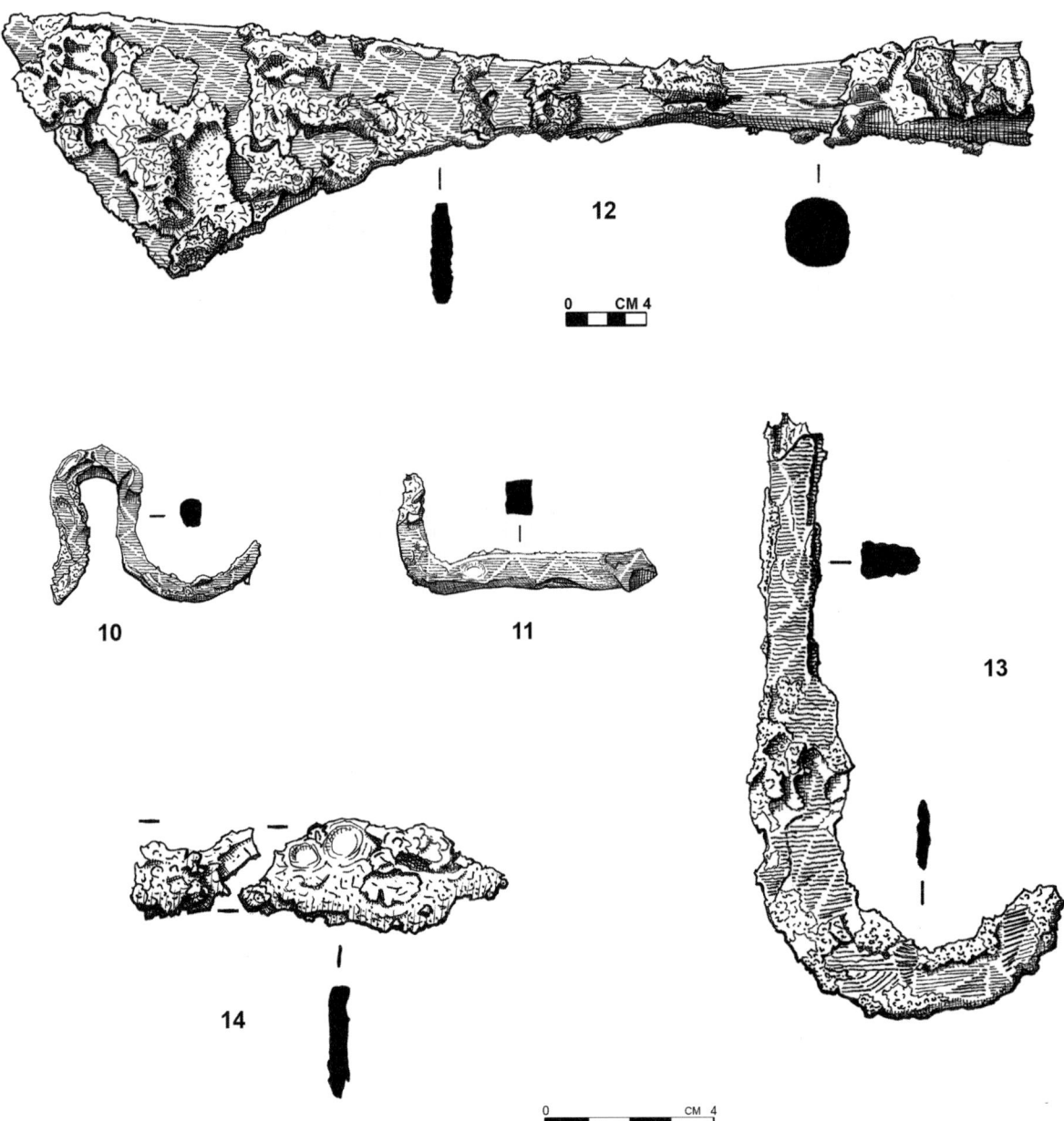

Fig 107   Small finds 10–14. Iron

SF 263. Cleat. Length 35 mm, width 85 mm. A cleat, or staple, for toe of boot or shoe with oval body (*ibid*, 115, fig. 77.205). Iron Age site, Trench 5/19 (upper pit fill), dark layer.

SF 356. Cleat. Length 41 mm, width 13 mm. A cleat, or staple, for toe of boot or shoe of oval body. AB II east end, Trench 26, Layer 2?, rubble tumble.

SF 459. Cleat. Length 25 mm, width 19 mm. Cleat, or staple, for toe of boot or shoe. AB II east end, Trench 25, edge of drain.

SF 539. Cleat. Length 95 mm. Cleat, or staple, for boot or shoe ?heel (*ibid*, 115, fig. 77.212; 119, fig. 80.271). AB II east end, Trench 28, Layer 9/9, line of south wall.

SF 346. ?Cleat. Length 25 mm, width 15 mm. Probable cleat for boot or shoe heel (*ibid*, 115, fig. 77.212). AB II east end, Trench 27, Layer 6, wall tumble.

SF 638. ?Cleat. Length 25 mm, width 16 mm. Fragmentary. Possible cleat for toe of boot or shoe heel. AB II east end, Layer 7, section through Room 18.

SF 408. Hobnails. Group of five boot or shoe nails. Hall, Trenches 2, 6 and 8, below rubble on floor.

SF 455. Hobnail. Length 16 mm. AB II east end, Trench 25, Layer 3.

SF 457. Group of 32½ hobnails. AB II east end, Trench 25, Layer 1 (south of south wall of AB II, 25 mm from plaster).

SF 527. Hobnail. Length 17 mm. Iron Age site.

SF 529. Hobnail. Length 14 mm. Iron Age site.

SF 531. Hobnail. Length 15 mm. Iron Age site.

SF 548. Hobnail. Length 20 mm. AB II east end, Trench 27, Layer 6e.

SF 640. Hobnail. Length 7 mm. AB II east end, section through Room 18.

Household fittings and items

Fragments of two possible bolts from barbed-spring padlocks were recovered. This was a common type and worked by pushing a bolt into the lock's case, while the springs, or barbs, of the bolt would lock it into place (Manning 1985, 95).

Vessels, such as buckets, are mainly represented by their metal fittings, e.g. hoops and handles, but it is possible that SF 57 is a binding from the upper edge of an iron-bound vessel.

Locks

SF 1. ?Lock. Length 104 mm. A possible bolt from a barb-spring padlock with parts of two springs (Down 1989, 208, fig. 27.10.30; Mould & Webster 2000, 132, fig. 4.19.187). Site E, Trench 3, clay with flints, Courtyard wall (Fig. 108.15).

SF 317. ?Lock. Length 84 mm. A possible bolt from a barb-spring padlock. Hall, Trench 3, unstratified.

Domestic utensils

SF 157. ?Binding. Length 63 mm, width 20 mm. Fragment with curved edge, possible vessel binding. Main House, Trench 33, topsoil 1, debris 3.

Knives and razors

There are a relatively large number of knives, although there are problems identifying the type because of wear to the blade and poor preservation, the latter being a particular problem. The dimensions (in order) relate to the length of the object, its width and (where an accurate measurement was possible) the thickness across the top of the blade.

SF 17. Knife. Length 78 mm, width 16 mm. The knife has a copper alloy hilt ring. Tang is missing, back angled down to point, blade slopes up to meet point. Manning Type 18B, although the angle of the back is more pronounced on the Sparsholt example (Manning 1985, 117, pl. 55, Q58). AB II west end, Trench 1, beneath rubble on tessellated floor. Room 12 or 19 (Fig. 108.16).

SF 15. Knife/razor. Length 80 mm, width 18 mm. Knife or razor with looped handle, back and cutting edge meet at the point. The shape of the blade corresponds to Manning's Type 11 (1985, 114, pl. Q12), but the handle differs in that it terminates in a vertical positioned loop. Main House, Trench 17, topsoil (Fig. 108.17).

SF 37. Knife/razor. Length 135 mm, width 21 mm. Fragmentary, long tang, square-section, L-shaped terminal to tang. Too little of the blade survives to identify type. Main House, Trench 28, outside wall. Room 3 (Fig. 108.18).

SF 98. Knife. Tang and fragment of blade. Length 110 mm, width 21 mm. Too little survives to identify type. Hall, Trench 3 (Fig. 108.19).

SF 264. Knife. Length 310 mm, width 35 mm. Fragment of long blade and tang, section is concave in shape. Tip of blade missing, unable to determine type. Hall, Trench 2, Layer 4 (Fig. 108.20).

SF 384. Knife handle. Length 94 mm. The knife has a bone handle, iron tang and copper alloy end plate (diameter 20 mm). The blade is missing. AB II west end, Trench βi. Room 13 (Fig. 108.21).

SF 656(7). Knife. Length 80 mm, width 22 mm. A fragment of blade and tang. Too little survives to identify type. Provenance unknown.

SPDGA. Knife. Length approx. 205 mm, width 25 mm, thickness 5 mm. The blade is bent at right angles to the tang. Does not appear to conform to a Manning type. Provenance unknown (Fig. 108.22).

SF 86. ?Knife. Length 35 mm, width 15 mm, thickness 10 mm. Possible blade tip: pointed end, triangular section. Too little survives to identify type. Hall, Trench 3.

SF 97. ?Knife. Length 44 mm. ?Knife tang of rectangular section. Too little survives to identify type. Hall, Trench 3?

SF 295. ?Knife. Length 115 mm, width 21 mm. The object has a diamond-shaped section (9 mm width) and is a possible knife or tool. Hall, Trench 3, Layer 7, humus in-fill.

SPDFY ?Knife. Length 84 mm, width 23 mm, thickness 5 mm. A possible tang and part of blade. Too little survives to identify type. Provenance unknown (Fig. 108.23).

SPDFHU. ?Knife. Length 95 mm, width 16 mm, thickness 4 mm. Possible blade. Manning Type 18B. Provenance unknown (Fig. 108.24).

Nails, studs and rivets

The examples from Sparsholt are classified using the types devised by Manning. Nails are the most common iron find from Romano-British sites, but the bulk belong to one of two types (Manning 1985, 134). Type 1 is the most frequently occurring nail, followed in a much smaller quantity by Type 2 (*ibid*). A variety of different nails were recovered from Sparsholt, and, as expected, the majority can be classified as Type 1. Several of the more interesting examples have been illustrated and are listed below. Thirty nails have not been included in the catalogue and details of these can be found in the archive.

SF 43. Head of nail/stud, diameter 25 mm. Bronze sheet, over iron domed head. Iron spiked shank. Closest to Manning Type 8 (Down 1979, 155, fig. 47.14). Trench 31 (topsoil outside Courtyard wall) (Fig. 108.25).

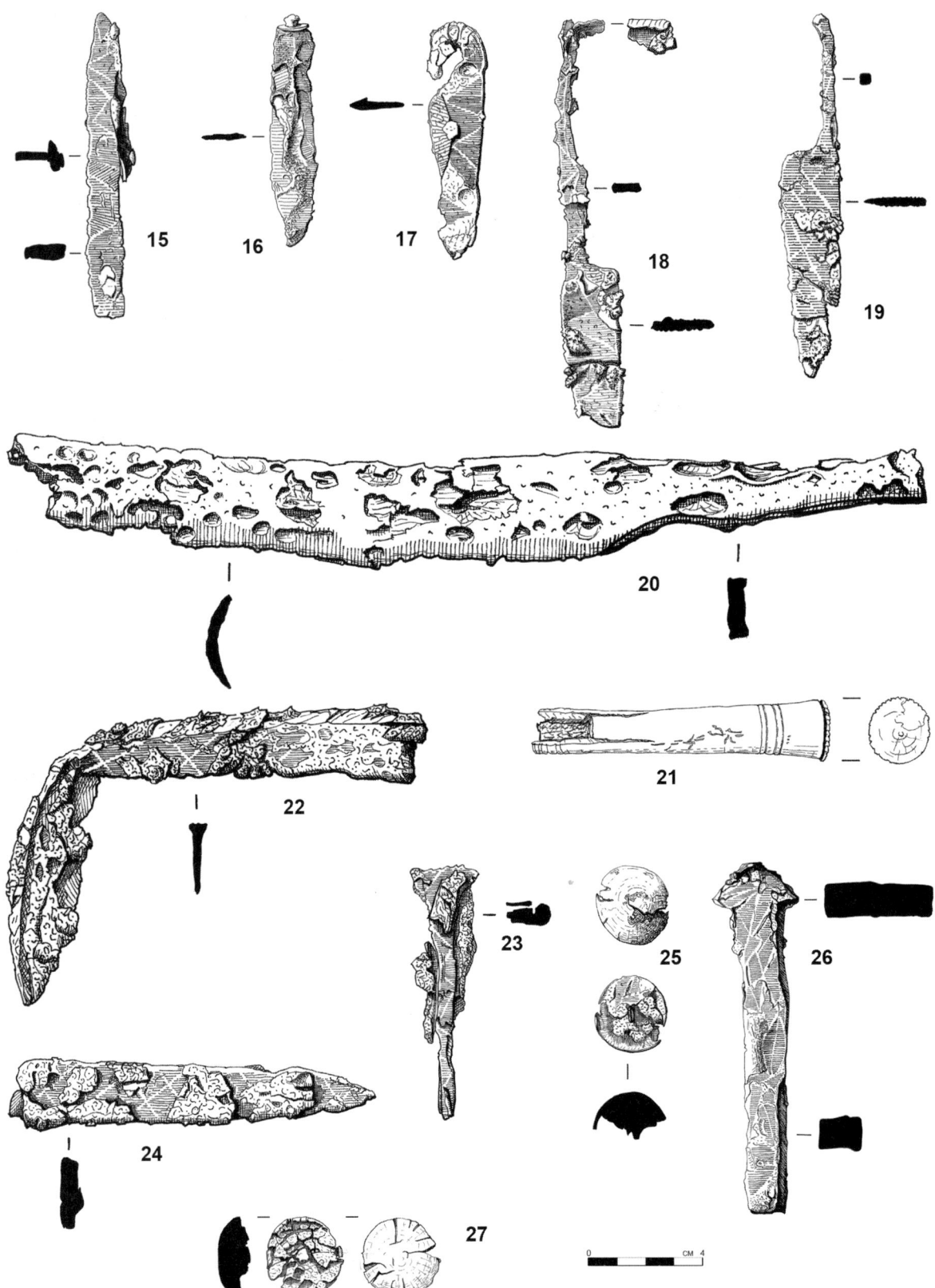

Fig 108   Small finds 15–27. Iron

SF 47. Nail. Length 118 mm (broken shaft). Rectangular section, head has been rounded by hammering. Manning Type 2. AB II east end, Trench 16, Room 19 (Fig. 108.26).

SF 352. Head of nail/stud, diameter 26 mm. Bronze sheet over iron domed head. Iron spiked shank, similar to SF 43. Closest to Manning Type 8. Hall, Trench 4, Layer 5, chalk packing in corner (Fig. 108.27).

Tools and objects of industrial use

A small group of objects was recovered that represent ironworking, while several other objects attest to the presence of other types of industrial activity.

Ironworking
Several tools were recovered that were probably the chisels or punches of the metalworker, but as Manning states (1985, 9–10), it can often prove very difficult to distinguish between these tools. This is compounded by the fact that most of the objects tentatively identified as chisels lack their heads, thus making a definite identification impossible.

SF 357. Chisel or punch. Length 83 mm. Fragmentary. Rectangular section, square head (width 18 mm) (Manning 1985, 10, pl. 5, A25). Punch (Down 1979, 155, fig. 47.13) or chisel (Isaac 2001, 121, fig. 50.1). AB II west end, Trench γF15, Layer 3, rubble layer north of wall. Room 19?

SF 597. Chisel or punch. Length 65 mm. Stout object, with flattened end, rectangular section, a punch, chisel or wedge (Manning 1985, 10, pl. 5, A.26). Iron Age site, Roman Pit XX, Layer 5.

SF 62. ?Chisel. Length 156 mm, width 14 mm. Object tapers to point, with two rivets. Rectangular section, possibly similar to Manning 1985 A30/33. AB II, Trench 5/8, Layer 4, Room 17.

SF 211. ?Chisel. Length 75 mm, width 0.8 mm Tapering, rectangular-section object, head missing, possibly a chisel (Richards 2000, 369, fig. 171.77; 370, fig. 171.93; Manning 1985, 9, pl. 5 A.22). Hall, Trench 3.

SF 319. Off-cut. Cube-shaped object, 19 mm³. AB II east end (unstratified).

SF 334. Slag. Hall, Trench 2.

Other industries
SF 298. Modelling tool or possibly stylus. Length 115 mm, width 7 mm. Square section, possibly double-ended implement (Manning 1985, 32, pl. 13, C12; Richards 2000, 370, fig. 171.94; Manning 1984, 85, fig. 37.9, single-ended example). Hall, Trench 3, unstratified.

SF 152. ?Modelling tool. Length 117 mm, width 35 mm (head). Square section, long shank, with spatulate head exhibiting teeth. A possible modelling tool, but does not conform to any of Manning's types. Main House (Fig. 109.28).

SF 158. ?Scraper. Length 161 mm, width 17 mm. Implement with rolled loop terminal and tapering shank. A possible scraper (Mould and Webster 2000, 131, fig. 4.15.159). Main House, Trench 33, topsoil.

Objects of personal use

This is a small, but disparate collection of objects, consisting of dress accessories and writing implements. All the styli from Sparsholt are of iron, which would probably have been the cheapest type available (Manning 1985, 85). There is also an iron ferrule that would have been fitted to either a staff or spear.

SF 355. Brooch. Length 45 mm, width 19 mm. Fibula brooch, pin missing, rectangular section. Hall, Trench 4, Layer 1, unstratified.

SF 405. ?Buckle. Three large fragments (originally 12 in total), largest is perforated and has a triangular-shaped terminal. One other fragment is a possible pin shaft. Possible buckle plate or armour plate (Richards 2000, 374, fig. 173, nos 162–3). Hall, Trench 8γ, Layer 4, beneath rubble in entrance.

SF 226. Ferrule. Length 95 mm. A hollow socketed ferrule for attachment to a wooden shaft of a staff or spear (Redknap 1986, 113, fig. 77.196). Hall, Trench 2, Layer 3.

SF 608. Strap fitting. Length 32 mm, width 17 mm. Narrow binding, possibly for knife sheath (Redknap 1986, 115, fig. 78.217). AB II west end (Fig. 109.29).

SF 536. Stylus. Length 94 mm. Square section to circular section with damaged eraser and broken point. Manning Type 3 (1985, 85). AB II east end, Trench 31 ext., Layer 2, above wall of AB I.

SF 456. Stylus. Length 120 mm. Circular section, intact eraser and point. Manning Type 3. AB II east end, Trench 28, Layer 5.

SF 610. ?Pin/stylus. Length 76 mm. Fragment, tapering to point, circular section, possibly a pin or stylus. Main House.

Miscellaneous fragments or objects of unknown function

The group contains several iron rings of varying diameters. Overall, rings are very common and come in a range of different sizes, which reflect a variety of functions (Manning 1985, 140). Many were associated with horse equipment, or served as general fastenings, but as Manning (*ibid*) states, rings could have been put to many other uses, such as finger rings or as part of a chain. There are numerous fragments of strips (n=21), which were probably bindings for boxes and structural woodwork (*ibid*, 142), but without further information it is impossible to give definite identifications, plus plates, rods etc. and iron fragments (n=42). These have not been included in the catalogue; details can be found in the archive.

SF 13. Plate. Length 57 mm, width 38 mm. Curved plate fragment with a lip at wider edge. Possibly part of a water pipe junction collar, or hub/nave lining (Manning 1985, 72, pl. 30, H35–6). Main House, Trench 17, topsoil.

SF 35. Plate with fragmentary shank (length 17 mm) and ?diamond-shaped head. ?Rivet. AB II west end, Trench 15, Layer 2, on rubble, Room 14 (Fig. 109.30).

SF 55. Ring. Diameter 50 mm, circular section. AB II east end, Layer 3, fall of roof with burnt material (Fig. 109.31).

SF 382. Ring. Diameter 43 mm. ?Square section. AB II west end, Trench β3, Layer 12. Room 12? (Fig. 109.32).

SF 401. Ring. Diameter 33 mm, circular section. Fragment of iron fused to the object. AB II west end, Trench E2, Layer 3, rubble. Room 23?

SF 127. Strip. Length 132 mm. U-shaped copper alloy binding over an iron inner core (originally 4 pieces). Possibly a bracket or binding for furniture or box (Price 2000, 61, fig. 2.16.406; Goodburn 1984, 53, fig. 21.185). Barn, Trench E2, Room 22 (Fig. 109.33).

SF 606. Strip. Length 120 mm, width 15 mm. Possibly part of SF 607. AB II east end (Fig. 109.34).

SF 607. Strip. Length 120 mm, width 15 mm. Fragment of binding or tool. Possibly part of SF 606. AB II east end (Fig. 109.35).

SF 629. Strip with separate socket. A possible hinge. Length 59 mm, width 27 mm. Diameter of socket 9 mm. Iron Age site.

SF 560. Tripod. Length 77 mm. A tripod-shaped object with four pointed legs. Possibly a head of a cauldron chain (Manning 1985, 100–2, pl. 46.P10). AB II east end, Trench 31, ext. 2 (Fig. 109.36).

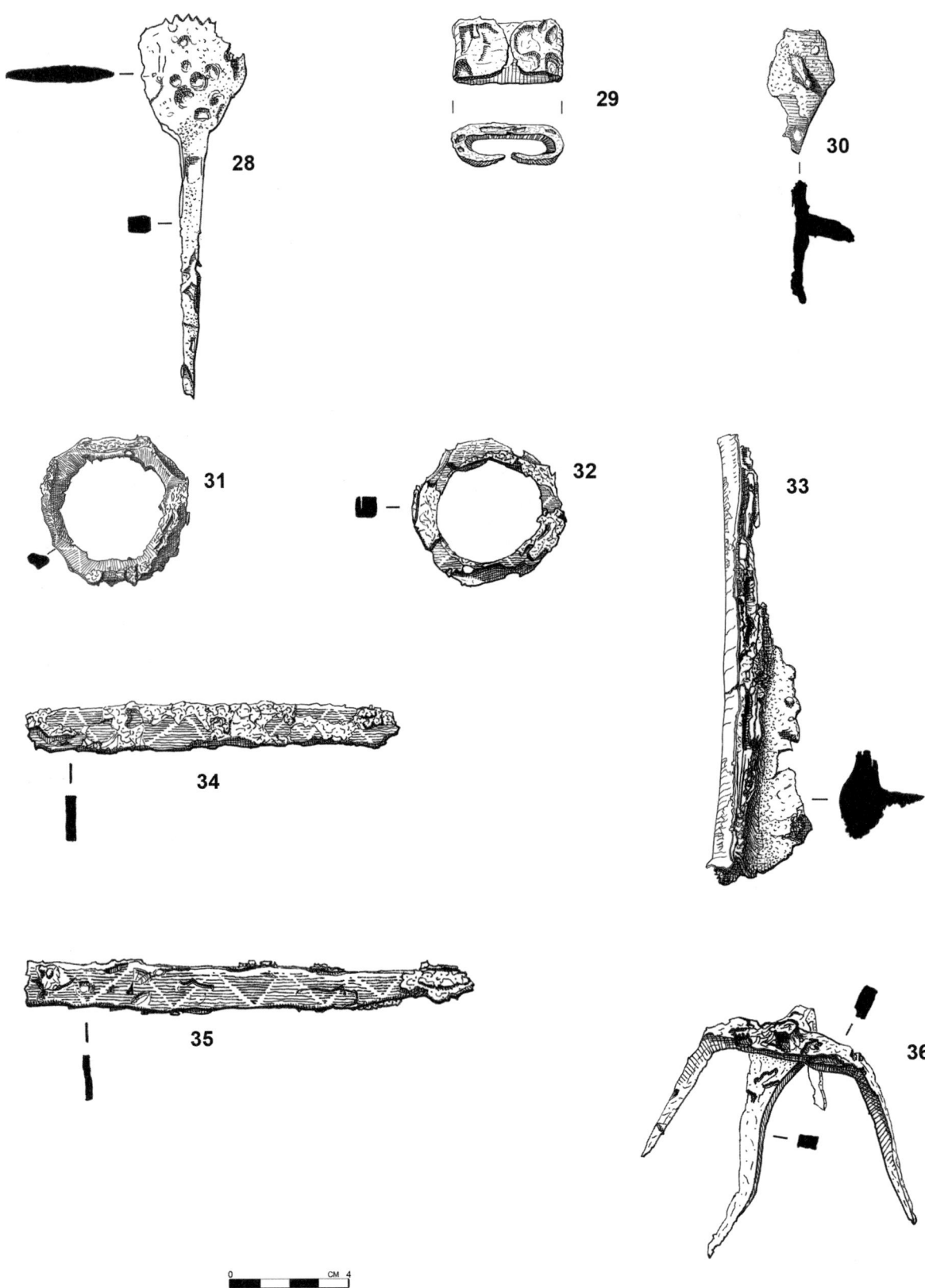

Fig 109 Small finds 28–36. Iron

SF 151. Plate. Length 50 mm, width 30 mm. Slightly curved, rivet hole, similar to SF 13. Main House.

SF 201. Rods. Two thin iron rods (length 85 mm and 100 mm) of circular section with copper alloy binding, possibly a handle. Hall, Trench 3, Layer 4, dark humus layer.

SF 302. Rod. Length 160 mm. A twisted rod of rectangular section, possibly a latch lifter or long bent pin (Price 2000, 71, fig. 3.3.86). Hall, Trench 2, unstratified.

SF 395. Rod/bar. Length 95 mm. Rectangular section. AB II east end, baulk, Layer 4, above wall feature.

SF 532. Object. Length 30 mm. Iron and wood. AB II east end, Room 17, plaster in-fill.

SF 582. Object. Length 80 mm. Square-sectioned (x-ray shows coiled terminal), possibly fragment of spiked loop (Manning 1985, pl. 61, R.39) or a figure-of-eight loop (*ibid*, pl. 64, S.14). AB II east end, Trench 30, Layer 5, in mortar, ovens/burnt area.

Structural fittings

This is one of the largest groups ranging from structural bindings, through various hooks to water pipe collars. Many of the artefacts (n=24) are undiagnostic and or fragmentary and have not been included in the catalogue. Details of these can be found in the archive.

SF 197. Binding. Length 41 mm, width 33 mm. Rectangular object of square section. Binding (Redknap 1986, 115, fig. 78.214). Hall, Trench 3, Layer 4, black humus above natural.

SF 199. Binding. Length 56 mm, width 15 mm. Rectangular section, possibly an angle binding (Manning 1985, 142, pl. 69.S110). Hall, Trench 3, Layer 4, black humus above natural.

SF 225. Binding. Length 54 mm, width 15 mm. Rivet hole. Hall, Trench 3.

SF 312. Binding. Length 65 mm, width 20 mm. Perforated. Hall, Trench 3, unstratified.

SF 51 ?Binding. Length 65 mm, width 28 mm. Two perforations, probably a binding (Price 2000, 81, fig. 3.8.314). AB II east end, Trench 18, Layer 2 (Fig. 110.37).

SF 625. ?Binding. Length 42 mm, width 28 mm. A rounded and perforated terminal (diameter 12 mm), possibly a fragment of a ?binding strap (Redknap 1986, 115, fig. 78.219), or bucket handle mount (Richards 2000, 370, fig. 172.109). Iron Age site, Trench I/II.

The group contains several wall hooks with spiked tangs that would have allowed them to be hammered into a wall, and had either a U- or L-shaped hook. In addition, there are two double-spiked hoops, which allowed a ring, for example, to be secured between the arms of the hoop (Manning 1985, 130), and one loop-headed spike.

SF 137. Hook. Length 58 mm. Square-section, U-shaped wall hook with attachment spike (Price 2000, 73, fig. 3.5.156). Main House, Trench 32, topsoil (Fig. 110.38).

SF 190. Hook. Length 67 mm. Rectangular section, U-shaped. AB II east end, Trench 25, Layer 14, below rubble layer. Baths?

SF 349. Spiked loop. Length 70 mm. Loop for suspension (Redknap 1986, 115, fig. 78.226; Webster 1975b, 242, fig. 130.231). AB II east end, Trench 27, Layer 6, hard-packed mortar layer (Fig. 110.39).

SF 540. Hook or clamp. Length 32 mm. Square section, L-Shaped. AB II east end, Trench 28, Layer 9/9a.

SF 546. Double-spiked loop. Length 50 mm. Iron Age site, Roman Pit XX, Layer 11 (Fig. 110.40).

SF 153. Fragment of double-spiked loop. Length 50 mm, width 34 mm (Redknap 1986, 115, fig. 79, 238). Main House (Fig. 110.41).

A number of pipe collars were recovered. These were used to join wooden water pipes; examples have been found from towns, such as Silchester, and villas, such as Fishbourne (Manning 1985, 128). Manning gives an average diameter for British examples of between 85 and 110 mm (*ibid*, 128–9); the Sparsholt examples conform to this range.

SF 265. Pipe collar. Diameter 108 mm, width 25 mm. Fragmentary water pipe junction collar, with stop ridge and traces of wood on interior and exterior of artefact. AB II east end, Trench 25, drain 21 (Down 1979, 158, fig. 51, nos 60 and 61; Manning 1984 99, fig. 43.112–115) (Fig. 110.42).

SF 341. Pipe collar. Diameter approx. 95 mm, width 25 mm. Fragmentary water pipe junction collar, with stop ridge and traces of wood on interior and exterior of artefact. AB II east end, Trench 25, Layer 21, drain 21.

SF 370. Pipe collar. Diameter 105 mm, width 25 mm. Water pipe junction collar with stop ridge. AB II east end, Trench 26, Layer 10, drain 10 (Fig. 110.43).

SF 389. Pipe collar. Diameter 95 mm, width 25 mm. Water pipe junction collar. AB II east end, Trench baulk 26/27, Layer 10, drain 10 (Fig. 110.44).

SF 27. Rod. Length 88 mm, width 13 mm. P-shaped with looped terminal (diameter of loop 34 mm), made from square-sectioned bar (Redknap 1986, 121, fig. 82.308). Main House, Trench 22. Room 1, Corridor (Fig. 110.45).

SF 207. Rod. Length 60 mm, width 11 mm. Of square section. Hall, Trench 3, Layer 4, black humus.

SF 380. Rod. Length 117 mm, width 68 mm. Bent, rectangular section, possible bracket. Sealed on floor and nailed onto surface. AB II west end, Trench β, Layer 5, floor surface, Room 13?

Staples are very common and represent one of the simplest ways of joining wood, with the U-shaped example being especially widespread (Manning 1985, 131). It is therefore notable that the majority of the pieces from Sparsholt are L-shaped.

SF 54. Staple. Length 66 mm, width 35 mm. L-shaped object, square section (Redknap 1986, 115, fig. 78.233–6). Traces of mortar on one surface. AB II east end, Trench baulk 6/7, fall of roofing material.

SF 67. Staple. Length 110 mm, width 52 mm. Fragment, L-shaped, square section. Main House, doorway from Room 9 to Corridor, against the wall.

SF 81. Staple. Length 85 mm, width 30 mm. Fragment, L-shaped, square section. Hall, Trench 3, Layer 4.

SF 120. Staple. Length 40 mm, width 24 mm. Fragment. Barn, Layer 3?, entrance to Room 21.

SF 209. Staple. Length 61 mm, width 30 mm. Fragment, L-shaped. Hall, Trench 3, Layer 4, black humus.

SF 353. Staple. Length 118 mm, width 46 mm. Fragment, L-shaped. Hall, Trench 4, debris west of building's wall (Fig. 110.46).

SF 392. Staple. Length 61 mm, width 28 mm. Fragment, L-shaped, rectangular section. AB II west end, Trench β4, Layer 3, rubble layer. Internal, ovens and burnt area (Fig. 110.47).

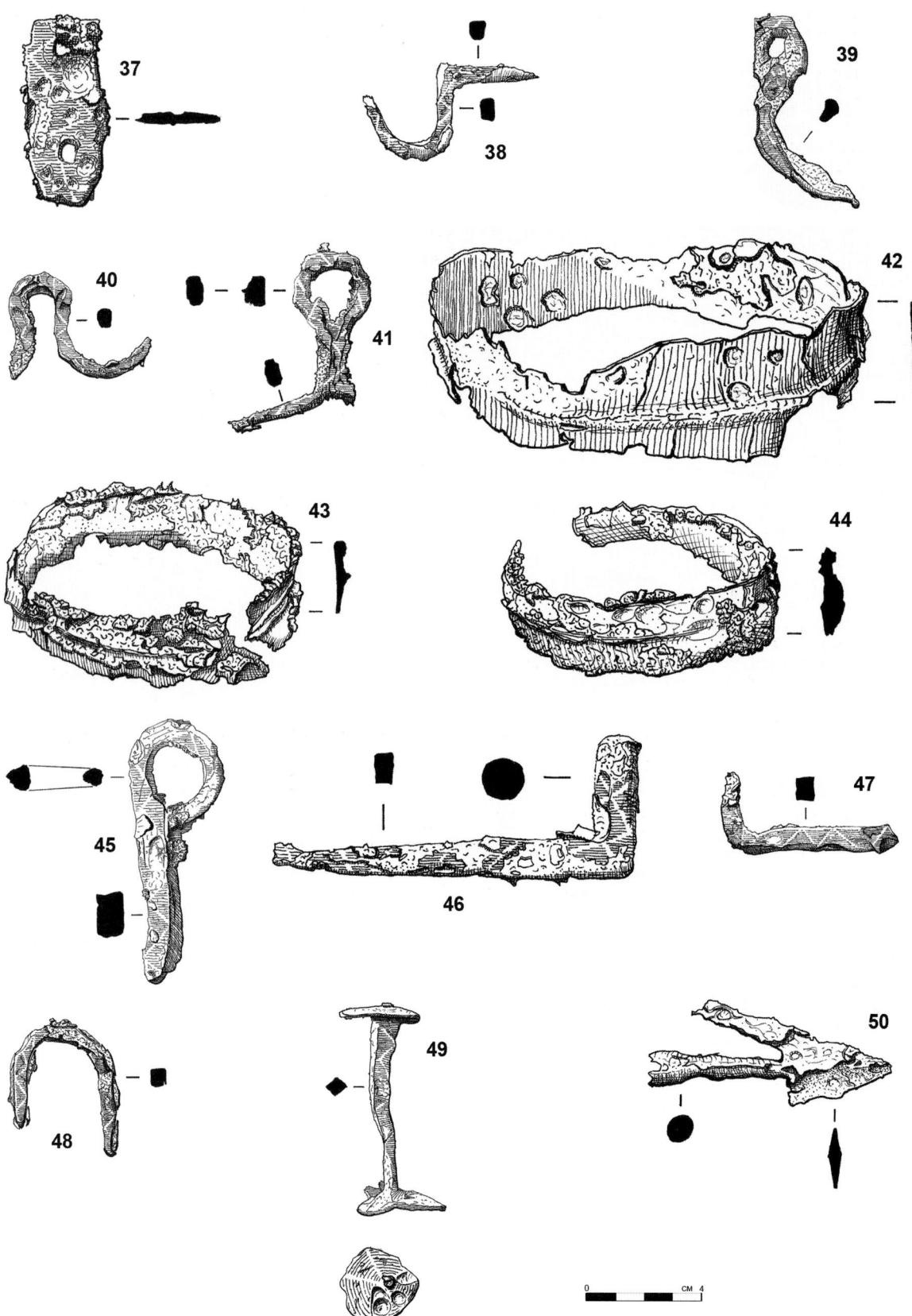

Fig 110 Small finds 37–50. Iron

SF 419. Staple. Length 31 mm, width 31 mm. Square section. Hall, Trench 2 (on floor level).

SF 422. Staple. U-shaped (diameter 26 mm), D-shaped section (Price 2000, 75, fig. 3.6.185). AB II west end, Trench β4, Layer 11 (south Courtyard wall). Internal, ovens and burnt area.

SF 465. Staple. Length 37 mm, width 40 mm. Fragment, L-shaped. AB II east end, Trench 28, Layer 9.

SF 554. Staple. Length 45 mm. Rectangular section. AB II east end (Fig. 110.48).

SF 616. Staple. Length 32 mm, width 18 mm. Iron Age site, Roman Pit XX.

SF 632. Staple. Length 45 mm, width 15 mm. Rectangular section. Iron Age site, Roman Pit XX, Layer 7.

SF 639. Staple. Length 50 mm, width 71 mm. Fragment, L-shaped. Iron Age site, Roman Pit XX, Layer 8.

SF 9. Tie/holdfast. Length 66 mm. Lozenge foot, circular head, shank of rectangular section. Employed when a nail was not considered to be sufficiently strong enough to join two timbers together (Manning 1985, 132–3, pl. 62, R80–1; Webster 1975, 242, fig. 129.228). AB II east end, Trench 1/2, in rubble, Room 15 (Fig. 110.49).

Transport

This is a small group consisting of horseshoes. Horseshoes were rarely used in Roman Britain, and most examples do not come from secure contexts, although a Roman date is accepted for an example from Portchester Castle (Webster 1975b, 235). Only SF 596 is stratified, and a Roman date has to be considered for this example.

SF 23. Horseshoe. Length approx. 110 mm, width 12 mm (one arm). Three rivet holes (1 circular, 2 rectangular). Main House, Trench 21, topsoil, Room 9a.

SF 328. Horseshoe. Fragment. Length 101 mm, width 31 mm (one arm). With three nails. Hall, Trench 3, topsoil.

SF 596. Horseshoe. Fragment. Length 77 mm, width 25 mm (one arm), with nail. AB II east end, above natural, south of foundation trench Building I.

Military objects

SF 387. Arrowhead. Length 77 mm. Barbed, one barb missing, diameter of socket 10 mm. Manning lists no examples from Roman Britain, and although barbed arrowheads are known from Fishbourne, Richborough and Shakenoak Farm, none seems to be securely stratified and a later date is possible (Manning 1984, 106). This would appear to be the case with the Sparsholt piece. AB II west end, Trench γ1, Layer 2, topsoil (Fig. 110.50).

Lead

Introduction

As at Silchester (Boon 2000, 357), a small quantity of lead was recovered, which comprised mainly scrap and the residues of industrial activity. The exception is SF 202, a lead perforated disc. Its function cannot be confirmed, but it may have been a weight, a token or a counter (Anderson 2001, 117).

SF 202. Disc. Diameter 30 mm, width 2 mm. Perforated (diameter 6 mm), rectangular section. Slightly smaller discs were found at Wanborough, although only one was perforated (Anderson 2001, 117). Hall, Trench 3, Layer 5.

Miscellaneous fragments of objects of unknown function

SF 67. Slag. Rod. Length 75 mm, width 27 mm. Iron Age site, Roman Pit XX, Layer 19.

SF 288. Perforated, roughly square sheet with rivet. Length not recorded. AB II east end, Trench 26, Layer 5, chalky earth.

SF 462. Lump. Length 34 mm, width 23 mm. AB II east end, Trench 28, Layer 6c.

SF 519. Slag. Length 29 mm. AB II east end, Trench 28, Layer 6e, burnt layer.

SF 543. Slag. Length 37 mm, width 27 mm. AB II east end, Trench 27, Layer 6e, burnt layer.

SF 611. Slag. Length 40 mm, width 28 mm. Main House.

SF 612. Slag. Rod. Length 58 mm, width 8 mm. AB II east end, Trench 12, top of foundation trench of AB II, south wall. Room 19.

SF 619. Slag. Rod. Length 65 mm, width 12 mm. AB II east end, Trench 27, rubble fill of stoke hole, AB I.

SF 624. ?Slag. Length 55 mm, width 14 mm. AB II east end, Trench 27, rubble fill of stoke hole, AB I.

SF 248. ?Slag. Length 56 mm. Curved object. AB II east end, Trench 25, Layer 19, below slate slabs. ?Baths.

ROMAN GLASS

by Denise Allen

The assemblage comprises a fragmentary cup and a further ten vessels which have been catalogued as worthy of note, although not all can be assigned with certainty to any specific vessel form. There are a further 15 fragments from blue-green bottles, 33 indeterminate blue-green fragments and 51 indeterminate colourless fragments, although it is possible that 29 of the latter may be from a single vessel, possible a cylindrical bottle of the late 2nd to 4th century AD. There is one indeterminate yellow-green fragment. This makes a total of 110 vessel fragments, which may represent up to 80 vessels. The two most finely decorated pieces are one vessel with fine facet-cutting (no 1), although the form is unknown. Another is decorated with a pinched-out point (no 2). Both these must have been from good-quality table ware.

In addition there are 33 window glass fragments, two glass tesserae, one bead and one rounded knob of glass which may be from a lid, a pin, or perhaps evidence of glass working.

Vessel glass

Fragmentary cup, SF 570 (Fig. 111)

A fragmentary cup of good-quality, thin-walled colourless glass, finely made and with only a few bubbles and blowing swirls within the metal. The rim is outflared, and would probably originally have been fire-rounded and thickened. Now, however, it is chipped quite evenly around its entire circumference. This is unlikely to have been caused by weathering or damage in the ground; its regularity suggests it was deliberate, possibly the result of cutting back (grozing) the rim edge to hide a larger, accidental chip. Beneath the rim are faint, horizontal wheel-incised lines. The body of the cup is hemispherical, and has been decorated whilst still warm and pliable with 12 short vertical ribs, formed by running a reamer up and down the glass. These alternate with vertical pairs of nipples, or horns, pinched out using a pair of pucellas. The base is slightly flattened, with usage scratches and a central pontil mark on the underside. Height approximately 62 mm; diameter of rim 84 mm.

The glass cup was found in Pit XX. It came from the primary silts (Layer 10), along with pottery, bronze and iron objects. The cup was found in a fragmentary condition, with some pieces missing, so it is only possible to conjecture as to whether it was dropped nearby, the pieces swept up and disposed of. Contextual dating evidence is provided by a barbarous radiate coin of *c* AD 270–95 in Layer 8, and also by two more barbarous radiates associated with the dumping of demolition rubble in the upper fill.

Hemispherical cups of this type have been discussed in detail by Dr Hilary Cool (1990). Their characteristics include an out-turned, fire-rounded rim, now missing in this instance. However, the presence of a pontil mark is a strong indication that this was the original rim form of the Sparsholt vessel. The pinched-out decoration can take a variety of forms, including pinched-up nipples or knobs and ribs as here, and/or larger lugs both with and without horns, sometimes alternating with indentations.

Parts of four cups of this type were included amongst grave-goods from the cemetery at Brougham, Cumbria, deposited between AD 220 and 270. The most complete of these provides a very close parallel for the Sparsholt cup (Price & Cool 1989, 3). It has a fire-rounded rim, and it seems almost certain that this was the original the rim form of the Sparsholt cup. The pontil mark on the cup base is a good indicator that the rim was originally finished by fire-rounding or folding, and the subsequent chipping or grozing around its entire circumference was presumably to hide some larger

Fig 111   Glass cup (SF 570)

chip or other damage. This was a device quite commonly employed in Roman times to ensure re-use of a broken vessel.

Other British parallels are missing the rim altogether. There is a fragmentary cup from Colliton Park, Dorchester, which has single-headed lugs alternating with double-headed lugs (Allen forthcoming, no.34), a fragment similar to the Sparsholt cup from South Shields (unpublished, Newcastle Museum of Antiquities accession. no. 1956.128.32.A), and a fragment from Verulamium with vertical rows of three, rather than two, nipples, again alternating with short ribs (unpublished, Verulamium Museum, accession. no. 81.2369).

Even smaller colourless fragments showing evidence of nipples or lugs are quite commonly found on British sites, and it seems likely that most of these belonged to hemispherical cups of the type under discussion. Other vessel forms were decorated in this way, including beakers (eg Wheeler 1936, 186–7, fig. 29:26 from Verulamium) and flasks (e.g. La Baume & Salomonson 1976, pl. 19:147 and 24: 178 from the Löffler Collection in Cologne), but these were much less common.

Dr Cool concludes that colourless hemispherical cups with fire-rounded rims and pinched-out decoration represent the commonest form of drinking vessel in the mid-3rd century. This would fill a hitherto unexplained gap in the record of common glass drinking vessels, between colourless cylindrical cups (Isings 85b), common during the later 2nd and earlier 3rd centuries, and truncated conical beakers and hemispherical cups with cracked off rims (Isings forms 96 and 106), which occur in large numbers in the 4th century. Difficulties in recognising small fragments, and the lack of close dating evidence, have prevented the identification from being made before. The Sparsholt vessel is therefore extremely valuable in reinforcing this conclusion.

The catalogues

Decorated body fragments, formed uncertain

1. SF 40 (Fig. 112.1)
Three fragments of colourless glass, fairly thick-walled, apparently blown, and all with wheel-cut decoration on one surface. One fragment has an apparently straight wheel-cut groove, with a wheel-cut line along each side of it. Most of one oval facet survives to one side of this, with a curved wheel-cut line partly framing it. The other two smaller fragments also have parts of oval facets extant – two on one and one, framed by a curved wheel-cut line on the other. The form of the vessel is not at all clear from these fragments, but all fragments have a curve suggesting a vessel diameter of about 80 mm (if the cut band is vertical).

The facet-cutting on these fragments is fairly typically Roman, forming a pattern of oval facets with broad cut lines. However, the straight, broad band is unusual, especially if, as the curvature suggests, this was vertical. They could represent a group of fairly thick-walled cups with a variety of facet-cut designs which were popular in the late 1st and earlier 2nd centuries AD (Price & Cottam 1998, 80–3, fig. 26) or they could be from a later vessel, since facet cutting was used on a variety of bowls over a long period of time (eg *ibid*, 97–9, 115–17, figs 37 and 47). Without a more accurate idea of the design it is impossible to say.

2. SF 256
Small fragment of colourless glass, with one small pinched-out point extant.

This is most likely to be from a convex cup with tooled decoration. An almost complete cup of this type was found in a pit during these excavations at Sparsholt Villa (see above). Hilary Cool has suggested that they are the commonest type of drinking vessel during the 3rd century in Britain (Cool 1990, 167–75), and a number of examples have been found on sites of this date (Price & Cottam 1998, 112–13, fig. 45). This type of decoration does occasionally occur on other vessels such as small flasks, so the identification as a cup is not certain.

Base fragments, forms uncertain

Two blue-green and three colourless fragments from the bases of vessels are catalogued below. All are common base types, and none can be assigned with certainty to specific forms, but no. 4 is likely to be cup, because of its size, and no. 6 is likely to be a bowl or plate.

3. SF 180 (Fig. 112.2)
Fragment from the tubular pushed-in base-ring of a vessel, form indeterminable, blue-green glass, diameter approximately 60 mm.

4. SF 189 (Fig. 112.3)
Fragment from the tubular pushed-in base-ring of a vessel, form indeterminable but probably a cup or beaker, blue-green glass, diameter 40 mm.

5. SF 482 (Fig. 112.4)
Fragment from the tubular pushed-in base-ring of a vessel, form indeterminable, colourless glass, diameter approximately 80 mm.

6. SF 221 (Fig. 112.5)
Fragment from the solid base-ring of a vessel, probably a bowl, of colourless glass, diameter 80 mm.

This appears to be an applied true base-ring, which is more commonly used on blue-green and coloured bowls with tubular rims, but is not unknown on colourless bowls (eg Harden *et al.* 1987, 98, no. 40, 4th-century bowl from Bonn).

7. SF 364 (Fig. 112.6)
Fragment from the flattened base of a rounded colourless vessel, form indeterminable. Base thickened, flattened, and with external usage scratches. Diameter of base *c* 30 mm.

Rim fragments

Three vessels are represented by rim fragments, one indeterminate, but two are of greenish colourless glass, and are bottle, jugs or flask. No. 9 is likely to be of 3rd- or 4th-century date. There are 29 colourless body fragments, all quite thin-walled and apparently from a cylindrical vessel, possibly the same one. These are listed below and marked *. They may all be from a cylindrical bottle, perhaps belonging to rim no. 9. This is by no means certain, but it is a possibility – two complete cylindrical greenish colourless bottles with looped handles, and a rim of this type, came from graves 35 and 38 at Lankhills cemetery, Winchester, dated AD 310–50, and there was a further fragmentary neck from grave 337, dated AD 330–50 (Harden 1979, 220, nos 20–1, 411, figs 27, 91).

8. SF 289
Tiny folded rim fragment of blue-green glass, just the very edge extant, diameter indeterminable, probably from a bowl or a jar.

9. SF 447 (Fig. 112.7)
Rim fragment of a bottle or flask of greenish colourless glass. Rim cracked off flat and ground smooth, bands of horizontal wheel-incised lines beneath. Diameter of rim *c* 3.5 mm.

There are several vessel forms which had rims like this during the 3rd and 4th centuries. One possibility is a globular flask with cylindrical neck (Price & Cottam 1998, 181, fig. 82) and another is a cylindrical bottle with looped handles (*ibid*, 206–7, fig. 94).

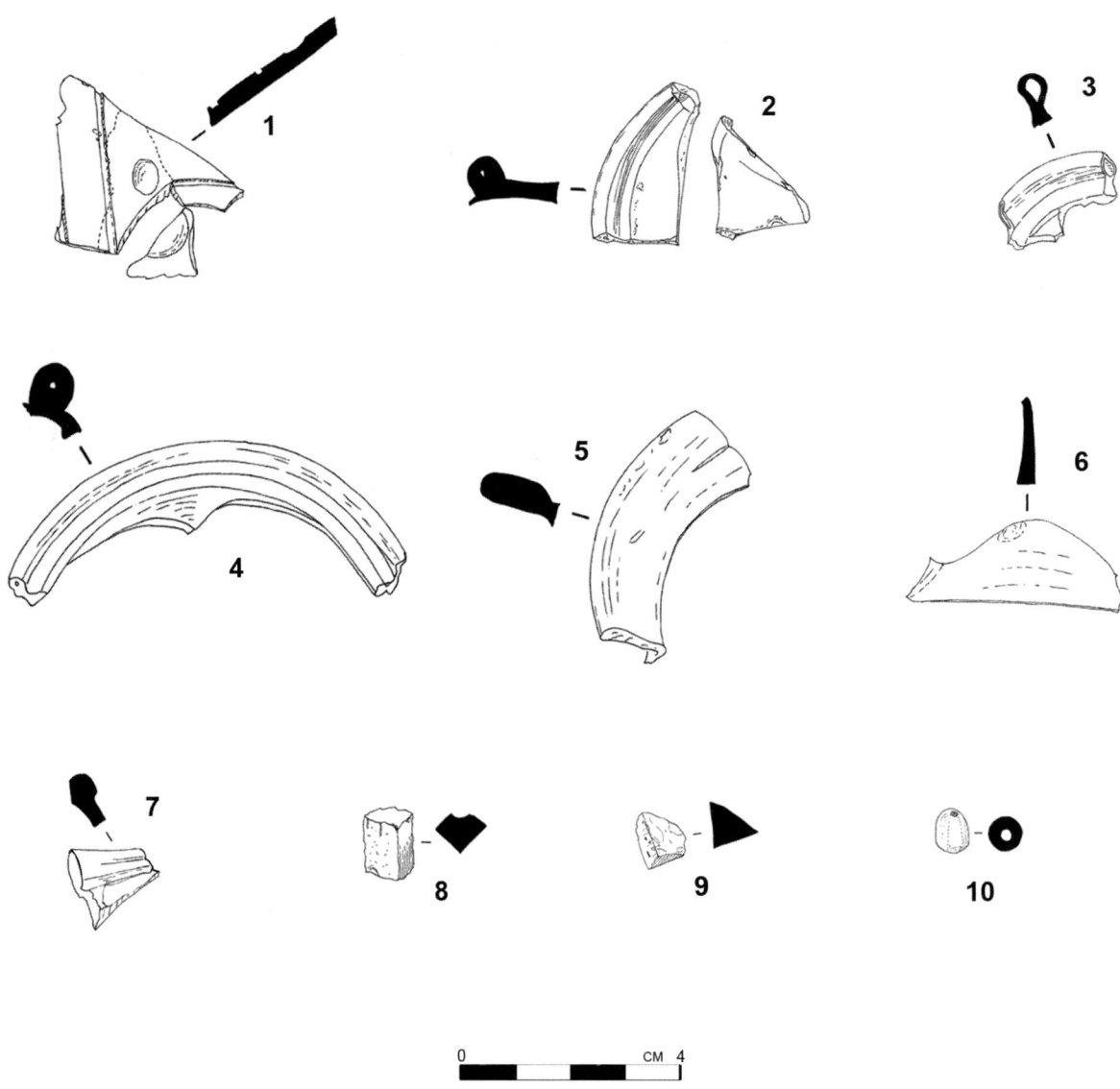

Fig 112   Small finds 1–10. Glass

THE FINDS

10. SF 484
Rim fragment of greenish colourless glass – edge of a folded lip, probably of a flask, jug or bottle, diameter *c* 40 mm.

Bottles

A total of 15 fragments most probably represent the very common blue-greeen bottles of the 1st and earlier 2nd century AD (Price & Cottam 1998, 191–8, figs 88–9). These include one rim and three neck fragments, which could be from bottles of any shape, and seven body fragments and a further four possible which are likely to be from square (or perhaps hexagonal) bottles.

SF 180	one body fragment, blue-green square bottle
SF 203	one bottle rim fragment – folded lip, blue-green
SF 438	one fragment, probably body of square bottle
SF 441	one body fragment, ? square/prismatic bottle, blue-green
SF 443	one body fragment, ? square/prismatic bottle, blue-green
SF 483	one blue-green fragment, possibly bottle body
SF 501	one blue-green fragment, possibly bottle body
SF 511	one blue-green lower neck fragment, jug, bottle or flask
SF 512	one blue-green fragment, possibly bottle body
SF 544	one blue-green lower neck fragment, probably bottle, possibly jug or flask
SF 552	one blue-green fragment, possibly bottle body
SF 556	one blue-green bottle body fragment, probably square
SF 564	one blue-green bottle body fragment, probably square
SF 579	one blue-green bottle neck fragment
SF 580	one blue-green bottle body fragment, probably square

Indeterminate vessel frags

Blue-green = 33 fragments

SF 121	one tiny indeterminate blue-green fragment
SF 138	one indeterminate blue-green fragment
SF 148	two fragments folded blue-green glass, distorted by fire; rim or base
SF 172	one indeterminate blue-green fragment
SF 239	four indeterminate blue-green fragments (same vessel)
SF 242	one indeterminate blue-green fragment
SF 243	one indeterminate blue-green fragment
SF 255	one indeterminate blue-green fragment
SF 258	one indeterminate blue-green fragment
SF 267	one indeterminate blue-green fragment
SF 273	one indeterminate blue-green fragment, horizontal wheel-incised line
SF 290	one small lump of melted glass, blue-green
SF 291	one indeterminate blue-green fragment
SF 348	one indeterminate blue-green fragment
SF 410	one indeterminate blue-green fragment
SF 442	one blue-green fragment, part of one rib extant
SF 444	one indeterminate blue-green fragment
SF 451	one indeterminate blue-green fragment
SF 467	one indeterminate blue-green fragment
SF 470	one indeterminate blue-green fragment
SF 495	one indeterminate blue-green fragment
SF 515	one indeterminate blue-green fragment
SF 516	one indeterminate blue-green fragment
SF 517	one indeterminate blue-green fragment
SF 545	one indeterminate blue-green fragment
SF 551	one indeterminate blue-green fragment
SF 555	one indeterminate blue-green fragment
SF 587	one indeterminate blue-green fragment
SF 630	one indeterminate blue-green fragment

Colourless = 51 (including 29 which may be from the same cylindrical bottle, marked *)

SF 142	one indeterminate colourless fragment
SF 176	one indeterminate colourless fragment
SF 232	one indeterminate colourless fragment
SF 241	one indeterminate colourless fragment
SF 250	one indeterminate colourless fragment
SF 251	one indeterminate colourless fragment
SF 252	one indeterminate colourless fragment
SF 294	one indeterminate colourless fragment
SF 377	one tiny indeterminate greenish colourless fragment
SF 388	one indeterminate colourless fragment
SF 407	one indeterminate colourless fragment
SF 415	one indeterminate colourless fragment
SF 445	one indeterminate colourless fragment, part of one rib extant
SF 449	one tiny indeterminate colourless fragment
SF 473	one indeterminate colourless fragment
*SF 490**	*one indeterminate colourless fragment*
*SF 491**	*one indeterminate colourless fragment*
*SF 492**	*11 indeterminate colourless fragments (same vessel)*
*SF 496**	*one indeterminate colourless fragment*
*SF 504**	*one indeterminate colourless fragment*
*SF 505**	*two indeterminate colourless fragment (same vessel)*
*SF 506**	*three indeterminate colourless fragments (same vessel)*
*SF 507**	*two indeterminate colourless fragments*
*SF 508**	*one indeterminate colourless fragment*
*SF 513**	*one indeterminate colourless fragment*
*SF 514**	*one indeterminate body fragment, one base or shoulder fragment, colourless*
SF 520	one indeterminate colourless fragment
*SF 534**	*4 indeterminate colourless frags*
SF 541	one indeterminate colourless fragment, part of fine self-coloured trail
SF 591	two indeterminate colourless fragments
SF 623	one indeterminate colourlcss fragment
SF 631	one indeterminate colourless fragment
SF 614	many tiny crumbled colourless frags, indeterminate

Yellow-green = one fragment

SF 557   one indeterminate yellow-green fragment

Window glass = 33 fragments

All of the window glass is of the 'cast' matt/glossy variety, which is thought to have been commonly made until at least AD 300 (Allen 2002).

SF ?103	one small fragment blue-green matt/glossy window glass
SF 141	one fragment blue-green matt/glossy window glass
SF 147	one fragment blue-green matt/glossy window glass
SF 156	one fragment blue-green matt/glossy window glass
SF 178	one fragment blue-green matt/glossy window glass
SF 181	one fragment blue-green matt/glossy window glass
SF 230	one fragment blue-green matt/glossy window glass
SF 259	one tiny fragment blue-green matt/glossy window glass
SF 344	one fragment blue-green matt/glossy window glass
SF 361	one fragment blue-green matt/glossy window glass
SF 378	one fragment blue-green matt/glossy window glass
SF 393	one fragment blue-green matt/glossy window glass
SF 394	one fragment blue-green matt/glossy window glass
SF 398	one fragment blue-green matt/glossy window glass, retouched edge
SF 400	one fragment blue-green matt/glossy window glass, thumb edge
SF 402	one fragment blue-green matt/glossy window glass
SF 404	one fragment blue-green matt/glossy window glass, thumb edge
SF 411	one fragment blue-green matt/glossy window glass, slightly fire-distorted
SF 413	one fragment blue-green matt/glossy window glass
SF 416	one fragment blue-green matt/glossy window glass
SF 423	one fragment blue-green matt/glossy window glass
SF 432	one fragment blue-green matt/glossy window glass
SF 436	one fragment blue-green matt/glossy window glass
SF 474	one fragment blue-green matt/glossy window glass
SF 478	one fragment blue-green matt/glossy window glass
SF 493	one fragment blue-green matt/glossy window glass
SF 497	one fragment blue-green matt/glossy window glass
SF 522	one fragment blue-green matt/glossy window glass, thumb edge
SF 523	one fragment blue-green matt/glossy window glass
SF 524	one fragment blue-green matt/glossy window glass
SF 572	one fragment blue-green matt/glossy window glass
SF 576	one fragment blue-green matt/glossy window glass

SF 617   one fragment blue-green matt/glossy window glass

Objects

12. SF 50 (Fig. 112.8)
Small, irregular green glass tessera; one rectangular face, 10 mm x 7 mm, the other irregular, max width 7 mm.

13. SF 635 (Fig. 112.9)
Small, irregular turquoise glass tessera, one nearly square face, 8 mm x 7 mm; max depth approximately 7 mm.

Glass tesserae such as these could be from a mosaic pavement – sometimes glass tesserae were used to pick out details in a floor otherwise made of stone. Alternatively, this could be evidence of the re-working of glass, since tesserae were a convenient form for transporting glass.

14. SF 613 (Fig. 112.10)
Small ovoid bead of blue-green glass, diameter 5 mm, length 8 mm.

This is common form of glass bead which cannot be closely dated.

15. SF 467
Rounded solid knob of blue-green glass, flattened on one side, and with a broken edge on the underside. Max diameter 22 mm, depth 17 mm.

It is just possible that this may be the knob of a jar lid – not common but occasionally occurring in burials of the 1st to 2nd centuries with glass cinerary urns (Price & Cottam 1998, 142–3, fig. 61). The flattened edge would be unusual in this case, however. Alternatively it may be the head of a glass pin. It may even be evidence of glass working, in that mis-shapen pieces such as this often seem to have been pulled from the furnace to test the viscosity of the glass prior to working it, or a by-product of other stages of glass working (Shepherd & Wardle 2009, 45–6).

Post-medieval = 16, some from the same vessels/window?
SF 2   post-medieval bottle fragment, pale green, inscribed (W.YOR etc)
SF 4   post-medieval bottle fragment, pale green
SF 6   post-medieval bottle fragment, pale green
SF 8   post-medieval bottle fragment, pale green
SF 41   post-medieval bottle fragment, pale green
SF 260   one blue-green fragment window glass, ?post-medieval
SF 261   one blue-green fragment window glass, ?post-medieval
SF 262   one blue-green fragment window glass, ?post-medieval
SF 345   post-medieval bottle fragment, dark green
SF 350   post-medieval fragment, dark green
SF 359   colourless facet cut fragment, modern
SF 362   post-medieval fragment, dark green
SF 366   post-medieval bottle fragment, dark green
SF 367   post-medieval bottle fragment, dark green
SF 369   post-medieval bottle fragment, dark green
SF 383   post-medieval bottle fragment, dark green

LOOMWEIGHT

by David E Johnston

655 Pit VII. Seven fragments, the largest is illustrated (Fig. 113). It is of soft, slightly gritted brown clay, crudely kneaded and disintegrating along the resulting fault-lines.

It appears to have been a roughly rectangular block, with one face carefully smoothed, the other roughly pressed down. Part of a third smoothed face might possibly be present. The single surviving perforation is c. 12 mm in diameter, consistent in width and showing faint striations.

It is impossible to reconstruct its original form with any certainty. Of the three forms found in this region from the Late Bronze Age and Iron Age (cylindrical, pyramidal and triangular) the triangular form predominates (Fasham 1985, 90). The apparently rectangular shape of this piece is therefore anomalous. It has been examined by Dr Elaine Morris (pers. comm.) who concludes that it is not briquetage and is probably a loomweight. In view of the perforation, the possibility that it is either daub or part of a fire-bar should probably be discounted.

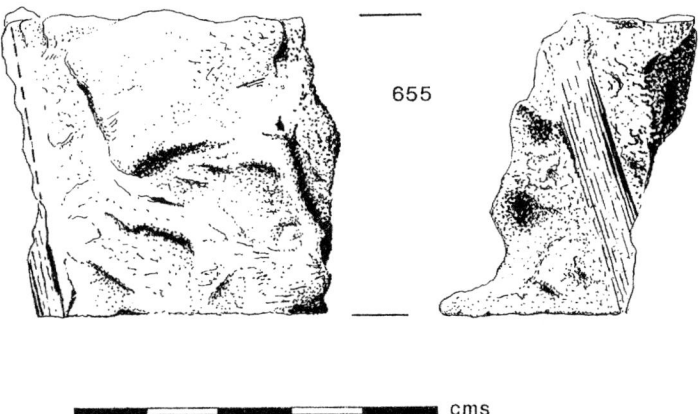

Fig 113   Loomweight (SF 655)

THE OBJECTS OF BONE

by Nick Stoodley

General introduction

In total there are 26 bone artefacts: two pieces of worked bone (in addition to another possibly worked bone fragment which has not been located and is not included in the total); four miscellaneous artefacts; three handles; and 17 pins. Each object has retained the unique small finds number that it was assigned on its discovery. The catalogue is organised by category of object. Measurements are given, which, unless otherwise stated, refer to maximum dimensions. The pins have been classified according to the types established by Crummy (1983). Contextual information relating to the site, trench and layer number is given for each artefact (where known). Comparisons are cited, but where there are multiple examples of the same type of object, they are only provided for the first example. Most of the pieces are chronologically undiagnostic and are unable to assist in dating.

Overall patterns and comparisons (Table 27)

Exactly half of the bone artefacts (13/50%) were retrieved from the Iron Age and Roman site (Site L), and all but one piece were stratified in various layers in Roman Pit XX, reflecting the deposition of these objects in rubbish. The exception was a pin that was found in a topsoil layer overlying Ditch II. Site F (AB II) produced the next largest total with seven (27%), while the remainder were distributed across the rest of the site. The Main House (Site D) only produced two artefacts: a pin from outside the structure and an unfinished piece of drilled bone from Room 11. The overall scarcity of bone objects is consistent with the picture provided by the metalwork and supports the idea that much of the portable material from the villa was removed in antiquity.

The majority of the artefacts belong to the category of objects of personal use and most of these pieces are simple bone hair pins. Where the head has survived, all the pins can be identified as belonging to Crummy's Type 3 (pins with a spherical head). Crummy subdivided the heads into four Groups (A–D) and all but one belong to her Group B, which demonstrate 'a semi-circular or elliptical lower half with a slightly conical or low convex upper half' (Crummy 1983, 21). The exception is SF 510 which has a lenticular head (Group C). All the specimens are undecorated; the incised marks on the head of SF 204 were made by turning the object against a knife. Only two of the pins are complete: SFs 11 and 403. At 112 mm in length the latter is just slightly longer than the maximum length (111 mm) identified at Colchester for these types (Crummy 1983, 22). Both of these pins were associated with buildings (AB II and the Hall), while unsurprisingly all the examples from Pit XX were fragmentary. Broken pins were, however, found during the excavation of the villa buildings, demonstrating that not all the damaged examples were collected up and disposed of. Crummy (1983, 22) discovered that although Type 3 pins occurred in the later 2nd and earlier 3rd century, the majority were in contexts dated to the later 3rd and 4th century – a date range which is consistent with Sparsholt generally.

Site	Pin	Handle	Worked bone	Misc.
A		1		
C	1			
D	1			1
F	4	1	1	1
G	2			
L	8	1	2	2

Table 27: Bone artefacts by site

There was more variation in the types of pin found at several of the villas investigated by the Danebury Environs Roman Project. At Grateley South ten pins were recovered, of which six could be indentified to type and of these Type 3 is the most common (no. = 3), followed by Types 6 (no. = 2) and 2 (no .= 1) (Cunliffe & Poole 2008b), while at Fullerton, the ten bone objects include four pins of which one is a Type 5, two are fragmentary and one is an unfinished piece (Cunliffe & Poole 2008d). The 14 bone objects from Houghton Down include three pins: one is a Type 6 and another, which is described as having a 'thistle head', is a probable Type 6 (Cunliffe & Poole 2008a). At Chilgrove I (West Sussex) the three pins are all Type 5, while at Chilgrove II the ornamental head of a pin was recovered (possibly a Type 4), and the remaining three examples can be classified as Type 3 (Down 1979). Although the unclassified examples from Sparsholt urge caution, it seems that the owners had very conservative tastes when it came to this type of hair fastener.

Three bone handles were recovered at Sparsholt, of which SF 384 furnished a knife and was decorated with a copper-alloy end plate. In addition to several pieces of worked bone, which probably attest to industrial activity on the site, the remainder of the artefacts consist of a decorated object that may be a bobbin and three pieces of bone inlay which probably furnished a wooden box or casket.

Catalogue

Objects of personal use

SF 11. Pin. Length 104 mm. Undecorated. Sub-circular section, width 4 mm; Group B head, width 8 mm. Crummy Type 3: Clausentum, deposit of the early 3rd century to late 4th century (Cotton and Gathercole 1958, 48); Fishbourne, Period 3 occupation-layers, 100–280 (Cunliffe 1971, 148). Site F, Trench F4 (Fig. 114.1).

SF 145. Fragmentary pin. Length 52 mm. Undecorated. Sub-circular section, width 3.5 mm. Site C, rubble.

SF 175. Fragmentary pin. Length 55 mm. Undecorated. Circular section, width 4 mm; Group B head, width 7 mm. Crummy Type 3. Site D, Trench 31/33, outside house.

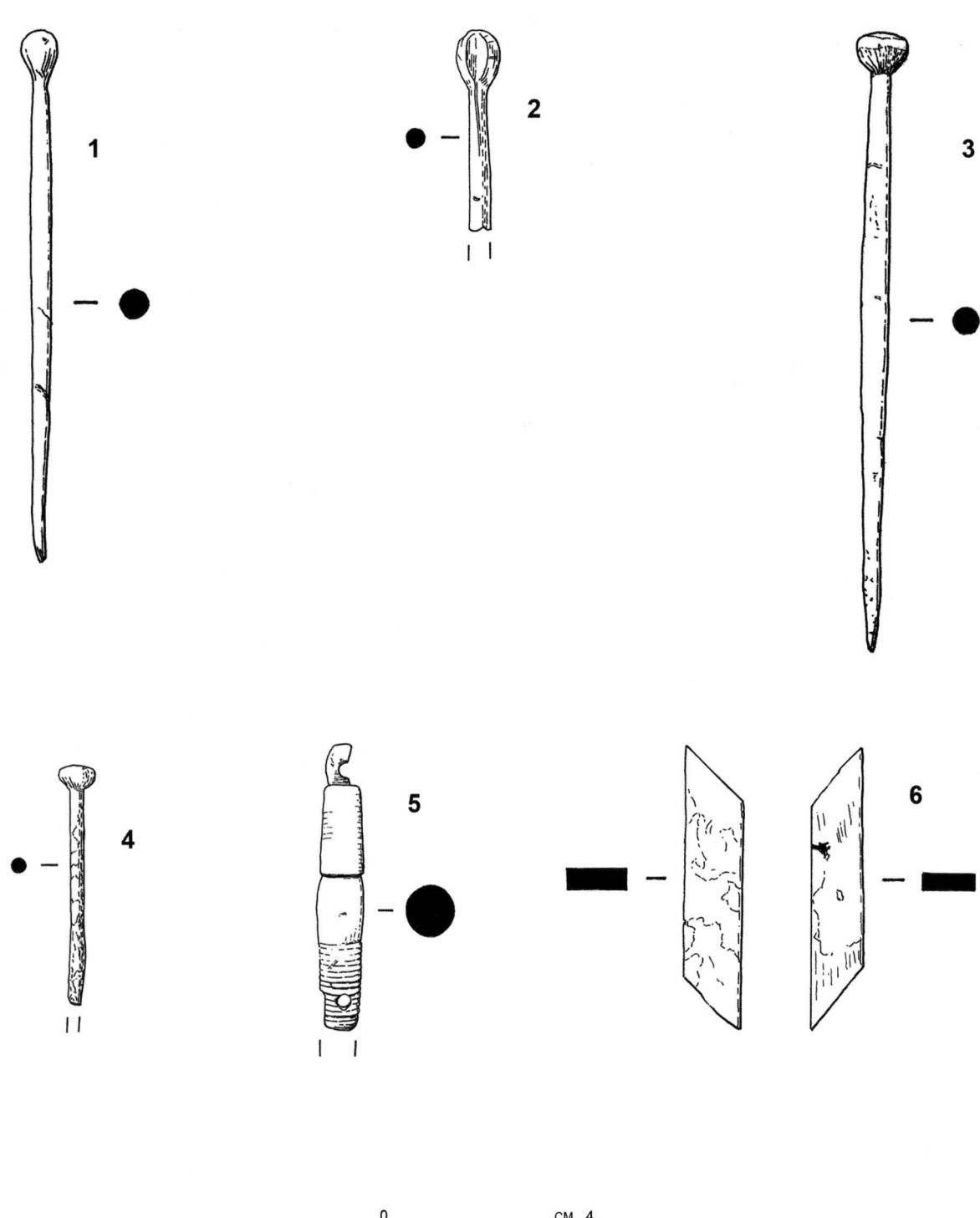

Fig 114   Small finds 1–6. Bone

SF 204. Fragmentary pin. Length 35 mm. Circular section, width 3.5 mm; Group B head with horizontal incised lines, width 8 mm. Crummy Type 3. Site G, Trench G3, Layer 4 (Fig. 114.2).

SF 374. Fragmentary pin (two connecting fragments). Combined length 34 mm. Undecorated. Circular section, width 3 mm. Site F, Trench 26, Layer 14.

SF 403. Pin. Length 112 mm. Undecorated. Sub-circular section, width 5 mm; Group B head, width 10 mm. Crummy Type 3. Site G, Trench G8, kiln (Fig. 114.3).

SF 452. Fragmentary pin. Length 22 mm. Undecorated. Sub-circular section, width 4 mm; Group B head, width 7 mm. Crummy Type 3. Site F, Trench 29, under topsoil.

SF 476. Fragmentary pin. Length 27 mm. Undecorated. Sub-circular section, width 4 mm. Site L, Pit XX, Layer 4.

SF 477. Fragmentary pin. Length 38 mm. Undecorated. Circular section, width 5 mm; Group B head, width 8 mm. Crummy Type 3. Site L, Pit XX, Layer 4.

SF 510. Fragmentary pin. Length 45 mm. Undecorated. Circular section, width 3 mm; Group C head, width 8 mm. Crummy Type 3. Site L, Ditch II, Layer 1 (topsoil) (Fig. 114.4).

SF 526. Fragmentary pin. Length 27 mm. Undecorated. Sub-circular section, width 5 mm. Site L, Pit XX, Layer 8.

SF 566. Fragmentary pin. Length 63 mm. Undecorated. Sub-rectangular section, width 3 mm; Group B head, width 5 mm. Crummy Type 3. Site L, Pit XX, Layer 19.

SF 583. Fragmentary pin. Length 70 mm. Undecorated. Sub-circular section, width 4 mm; Group B head, width 7 mm. Crummy Type 3. Site F, Trench 32, topsoil.

SF 585. Fragmentary pin. Length 26 mm. Undecorated. Sub-rectangular section, width 4 mm; Group B head, width 6 mm. Crummy Type 3. Site L, Pit XX, Layer 7.

SF 590. Fragmentary pin. Length 73 mm. Undecorated. Sub-circular section, width 3 mm. Site L, Pit XX, Layer 5.

SF 598. Fragmentary pin. Length 34 mm. Undecorated. Sub-circular section, width 3 mm; Group B head, width 9 mm. Crummy Type 3. Site L, Pit XX, Layer 5.

SF 599. Fragmentary pin. Length 52 mm. Undecorated. Circular section, width 4 mm. Part of SF 598.

SF 384. Bone knife handle with iron core and copper-alloy terminal. See iron catalogue (p.00). Site A, Trench B1.

SF 463. Fragment of handle or collar. Length 21 mm, width 20 mm. Decorated with four horizontal incised lines. Site F, Room 18, on chalk floor.

SF 573. Fragmentary bone handle. Length 85 mm, width 23 mm, diameter of perforation 18 mm. Undecorated. Site L, Pit XX, rubble.

Miscellaneous objects

The assemblage also contains three plain pieces of parallelogram-shaped bone inlay. Thin strips such as these were used as casings for wooden boxes or caskets, although they are usually decorated with incised geometric patterns (Crummy 1983, 82). The three examples were found in Pit XX (Site L).

SF 615. Fragmentary, probably parallelogram-shaped, bone inlay. Length 34 mm, width 10.5 mm, depth 5 mm. Undecorated. Site L, Pit XX, Layer 10 (bottom).

SF 66. Fragment of drilled bone (unfinished). Length 130 mm, width 20 mm. Width of drilled hole 18 mm x 20 mm (other side, more elongated). Cut marks along length of one side. Site D, Room 11.

SF 509. Fragmentary, possible bobbin, with vertical groove. Length 54 mm, width 9 mm. Decorated with horizontal incised lines. Lower section pierced (width of hole 3 mm); fragmentary pierced head (2 mm). Site F, Trench 30, Building 1, Layer 2 (Fig. 114.5).

SF 571. Two pieces of parallelogram-shaped bone inlay. Both with dimensions of: length 53 mm, width 10 mm, depth 5 mm. Undecorated. Site L, Pit XX, Layer 18 (Fig. 114.6).

Worked bone

SF 530. A fragment of possibly worked bone. Length 49 mm, width 13 mm. Site L, Pit XX, Layer 10.

SF 637. Fragment of rib with knife marks. Length 96 mm, width 24 mm. Site L, Pit XX, Layer 7.

THE QUERNS

by David E Johnston

Introduction

Fragments of 12 querns were found, all from upper stones, some of them very large examples with diameters up to about 0.90 m. All or most are of the characteristic late Roman form, with flat or slightly domed tops, generally rather thin and flat but with a variety of thicknesses and angles of the grinding surface. Many were well worn before being broken, and no. 9 had apparently been rejuvenated. Another (no. 7) had been re-used as a sharpening stone.

All were mere fragments, and at least one (no. 12) had been deliberately broken up, to judge from its small size and what looked like pick-marks, while two (nos. 3 and 4) were roughly squared as building stone. All but three were found in the rubble, suggesting (but not conclusively) that they had been used as building stone. One exception (no. 12) was in the rough flint floor of the Hall, the material being derived from ruined walls elsewhere on the site. Another (no. 1) had been used to fill up a natural cavity to support the foundations of the north (first) Courtyard Wall. The third exception (no. 2) had evidently been on the wooden floor of the Barn when the mortar rendering of the derelict building slipped off and sealed it below the collapse of the wall itself. This too was a mere fragment.

Their sources are varied, five being from the popular millstone grit that was exploited from deposits in either Derbyshire or Yorkshire; five were from the Greensand, four of them possibly from the Midhurst region in Sussex; another possibly came from the Purbeck limestones, as did the roof-slates. Only one was imported, of Niedermendig lava from the Mayen quarries of the Rhineland.

This report has been prepared with the help of Dr D. P. S. Peacock, of Southampton University.

Catalogue

1. **SF 643**. Three fragments of a quern, 0.04 m thick, diameter uncertain. Niedermendig lava. From the fill of a natural cavity below the foundations of the north Courtyard Wall (earlier wall associated with AB I).

2. **SF 104**. 0.06 m thick at the edge, diameter approximately 0.40 m. Upper Greensand, probably from the Midhurst region. A dark specimen. The Barn (Room 21), south-east corner, at the bottom of the mortar slip, practically on the natural.

3. **SF 2**. 0.09 m thick at the edge. Diameter uncertain: it was apparently squared off for use as building stone. As no. 2, but lighter. Main House (rubble).

4. **SF 103**. 0.09 m maximum thickness. The edge broken off and apparently squared as building stone. As no. 3. The Hall (rubble).

5. **SF 102**. Thickness 0.11 to 0.03 m at the feeder-hole. The upper surface shows the slot for the handle. As no. 3. The Hall (rubble).

6. **SF 19**. Maximum thickness 0.09 m, diameter approximately 0.80 m. Glaucolitic sandstone, with distinct fossils, probably from the Greensand (a fossiliferous horizon, but a different facies from no. 2). AB II (Site F, rubble).

7. **SF 25**. Maximum thickness 0.06 m, diameter uncertain but very large. The upper surface has been re-used as a sharpening stone. Slightly pink millstone grit. Main House (rubble).

8. **SF 644**. A small fragment, maximum thickness 0.05 m, diameter uncertain. Pinkish-grey millstone grit. AB II (Site F, unstratified probably rubble from Baths).

9. **SF 49**. A large fragment, maximum thickness 0.09 m, diameter approximately 0.80 m. The grinding surface shows two broad shallow radial grooves; 5 concentric rows of pecked dots at the outer edge probably represent rejuvenation. Millstone grit. AB II (Site F, rubble).

10. **SF 14**. A small fragment, 0.06 m thick with a flat top and a chamfer at the edge. Diameter approximately 0.70 m. Slightly pink millstone grit. Main House (rubble).

11. **SF 30**. Upper surface very rough, perhaps broken away. Maximum thickness 0.05 m, diameter uncertain but possibly about 0.90 m. Grey millstone grit. Main House (rubble).

12. **SF 642**. A very small fragment, deliberately broken in antiquity (3 large pick-marks are visible on one broken edge). The grinding surface is visible on one face. It is from a large specimen, at least 0.11 m thick. Diameter uncertain, but very large. Sandy limestone, probably Jurassic, possibly from the Purbeck region. The Hall (on the natural among flints making up a rough floor).

THE COLUMN

by Tom Blagg† (written in 1990, updated for this report)

SF 396. Miniature column (Fig. 115) found in rubble above the mosaic in Room 12 (AB II) with the top facing in towards the centre of the room.

Height, 0.77 m (capital, 0.26 m, base 0.205 m)

Diameters: shaft below capital mouldings, 0.179 m; mid-shaft, 0.265 m; shaft above base mouldings, 0.205 m; base torus, 0.305 m.

Fine-grained cream oolitic limestone.

The column has been turned on a lathe, as is clear from the horizontal rilling on the surface of the shaft and mouldings, from the narrow grooves on the neck and on the base torus, and from the small beads and fillets and the shallow profile of the mouldings. The dowel holes at the ends would have served for mounting it on a lathe. It is normal for column bases to have two torus mouldings. Examples with a single torus below a cavetto or cyma moulding are mainly restricted to Wessex, and datable to the 3rd and 4th centuries.

The bulbous profile of the shaft is unusual. It strongly suggests that the column was not intended to be used architecturally, but as a pedestal, to support a table top, for example. Columns used in this way have been found associated with table tops in Germany, and the suggestion has also been made for Britain (Solley 1979, 173–5), though not with the actual form of the column in mind; this is also significant, however. Recently, a column, a part column and a fragment of a chip-carved table were found at Fullerton (Durham 2008, 134). The Fullerton column is 0.84m and confirms the view that shorter single columns belong with table tops.

The small size of the Sparsholt example would tell against its architectural use, even as a veranda column standing on a low wall. Such 'dwarf' columns, e.g. those from the villa at Bignor, the Colliton Park house in Dorchester and the temple at Nettleton, are usually between 1.1 and 1.2 m high. The column from Sparsholt is, in fact, the smallest complete example known from Roman Britain. Two columns which, although now lacking their capitals, would not have been much larger when complete, are also similar in the bulbous profile of their shafts and likely to have been baluster supports: one from the villa at East Grimstead, Wiltshire (Sumner 1924, 26, with an inaccurate drawing), the other from Winchester (Cunliffe 1964, 92, fig. 26 and pl. Va). It seems significant that these baluster columns occur only in the area of distribution of chip-carved stone table tops (Solley 1979, fig.1).

Fig 115   Column

FLINT

by David E Johnston

A small quantity of flint waste, some of it exhibiting scraper retouch, was found throughout the villa site, either unstratified or in Roman contexts. The degree of patination varied considerably, as would be expected on a chalk site with pockets of clay with flints, and is not an indicator of age. The sample was too small to merit analysis: two stratified pieces, however, from Iron Age contexts are of interest (Fig. 116):

486 Flake in cloudy brownish flint, lightly patinated, with good platform and pronounced bulb. Crude and uneven retouch occupies some 60% of the edge. The wear is discussed below. Pit XVII, Layer 6.

489 Segment of a large flake in blue-grey flint, lightly patinated. The entire outline is formed by crude, almost vertical retouch. The wear (at both ends) is discussed below. Pit VIII, Layer 2.

These are essentially two versions of the same tool, designed to be held as in Fig. 116. In contrast to most Neolithic and Bronze Age scrapers the entire outline of these is retouched, not merely the working edge. Experiments have shown that an edge-scraper, made in seconds, lasts very little time before it is discarded in favour of a fresh one. Edge-wear is therefore seldom visible to the naked eye. These tools, on the other hand, are more laboriously made, for longer use. Use-wear is indeed clearly visible on no. 486, while the working edge of no. 489 is quite worn and polished at both ends. The sharp end of the latter seems to have been used for rubbing grooves rather than scraping, and it is suggested that these tools were made for working a more abrasive material than leather – pottery, for instance. Many other uses are, of course, possible, and in view of the evidence for Bronze Age activity in the area the date of these flakes and their subsequent retouch and use must remain uncertain.

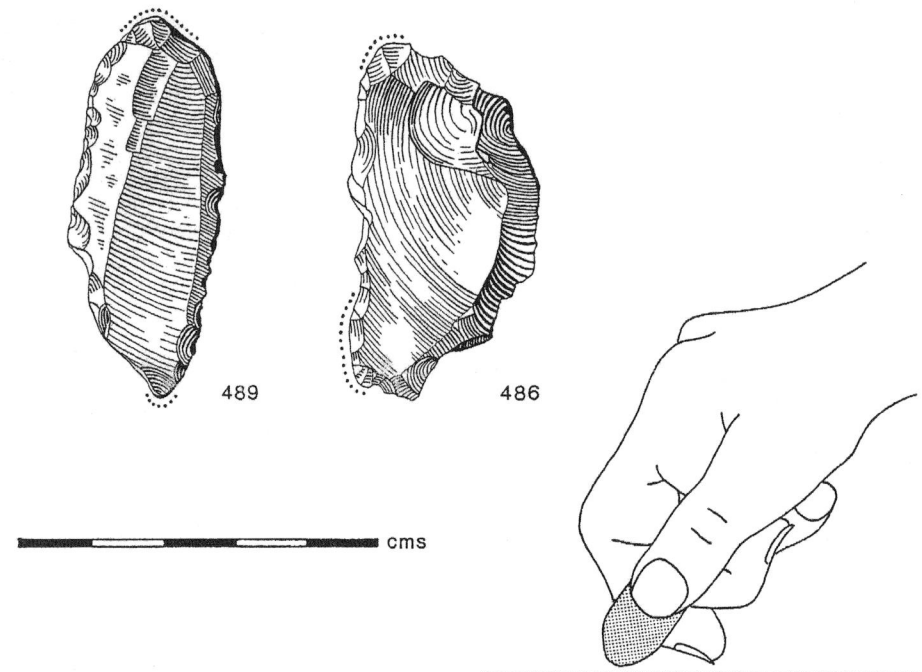

Fig 116   Flints 486 and 489

Chapter 16

Bone

The human skeletal remains

by Garrard Cole

Introduction

This report contains an assessment of the complete human skeletal remains assemblage from the excavations at Sparsholt Roman Villa. The paper archive refers to earlier works covering parts of the assemblage. Some infant remains were examined by Rosemary Powers and were described as full-term infants. Later, Tony Waldron produced a short report on several mixed deposits of infants (Samples H and L in Table 28). This unpublished report (Waldron undated) presented age and minimum number of individuals (MNI) estimates in the absence of contextual material.

Sample	Label	Type	C14 candidate
A	F27	Single inhumation	Y
B	SPAβBC	Residual	N
C	SPDEA	Residual	N
D	SPDES	Residual	N
E	SPDET	Residual	N
F	SPDFH	Single inhumation	Y
G	SPDIY	Residual	N
H	409, SPG2BF/U	Mixed deposit	Y
I	SPLDK, SPLEG	Animal bone	N
J	SPLEC	Residual	N
K	SPLOT/B, SPLEV	Single inhumation	Y
L	SPLGD, SPLGS/T	Mixed deposit	Y

Table 28: Initial assemblage summary

Material

The material considered in this report comprises 1288 fragments weighing 2432 g from a variety of deposits. They range from isolated residual material through disturbed deposits of individual or multiple skeletons to individual inhumation burials. The time span of deposits, as determined by radiocarbon dating of selected elements, ranges from the late Iron Age to the medieval period, with most material dated to the 3rd to 4th centuries AD in the Romano-British period. The material covered in this report is summarised in Table 28.

The material forming Sample I comprised three fragments of a young mammal skull thought by the excavators to be human. This material was extracted from the human remains assemblage and passed on to the faunal specialist for assessment. It is not considered any further in this report.

Methods

Standard osteological methods were used to determine age, sex and stature. The assemblage was dominated by neonatal and adult material. Neonatal age at death was determined using long bone length (Fazekas & Kóza 1978; Scheuer *et al.* 1980) supplemented by evidence from dental development (Al Qahtani 2008; Schour & Massler 1941) and metrics for the pars basilaris (Scheuer & MacLaughlin-Black 1994). Neonatal sex estimation was based on the morphology of the greater sciatic notch of the ilium (Waldron *et al.* 1999). Whilst there is no universally accepted method for determining the sex of neonatal remains, this method is an analogue of the established method used for determining the sex of adult remains. It has been validated using DNA sex determination for a number of individuals from several Romano-British villas in England.

For the adult material, sex determination was based on pelvic and skull morphology (Buikstra & Ubelaker 1994), along with metrics of the humerus and femoral head (Dittrick & Suchey 1986) and the radial head (Berrizbeitia 1989). Age determination was based on age-related changes of the auricular surface and pubic symphysis of the pelvis (Buikstra & Ubelaker 1994), along with dental wear (Miles 1962). The Miles method was developed for Anglo-Saxon material, with significant dental wear arising from the consumption of a coarse diet. This method has been applied to other populations with high levels of dental wear. Stature estimation was derived from measurements of the lengths of long bones in accordance with the method of Trotter and Gleser (1952; 1958).

A significant part of the assemblage consisted of mixed and disturbed material with commingled remains from multiple individuals. Data for all material, disturbed or otherwise, were recorded in an Access database, storing context, element, age, sex, length, condition, fragment count and weight as appropriate. The age and sex data for the individual elements were determined using the methods outlined above for complete inhumations. This allowed a MNI to be determined for each commingled group. The exact number of individuals is not known. It will be greater than or equal to the MNI value, with a highly unlikely theoretical maximum represented by the number of fragments found in each mixed context.

Dental terminology rather than anthropological terminology is used when referring to specific teeth in a dentition. This is primarily of relevance when discussing the deciduous dentition and premolars of the permanent dentition (Hillson 1996).

Dating information

Selected material from each significant context was submitted for radiocarbon dating. One date was obtained for each distinct inhumation. A further three dates were obtained for the two main mixed groups. One group had material with different context numbers thought to be from the same context. A date was obtained for each to check that hypothesis.

The data shown in Table 29 indicate that the material derives from three cultural periods – Late Iron Age (166 BC–AD 19, Sample K), Romano-British (early 3rd to late 4th century AD, Samples F, H and L) and medieval (15th to 17th century, Sample A). The material for these periods will be considered separately.

Iron Age period

Material

The Iron Age material (Sample K) labelled SPLOT, SPLOB, SPLEV and SPLOG was discovered in Ditch XXI but was not processed immediately after the completion of the original excavation. The bulk of the material was still encased in clay-rich soil which had to be removed prior to examination for this report. The material comprised three anatomically disjointed sections of an inhumation burial. The sections were a fragmented skull and the first two cervical vertebrae, an articulated torso and arms extending from the first thoracic vertebra to the pelvis, and a foot articulated with a short segment of distal tibia and fibula. Supernumerary material included an adult humerus head and a small fragment of the ramus of a right juvenile mandible. Other artefacts present included a sherd of Iron Age pottery and a small quantity of animal bone.

A photograph taken during excavation (see Fig.117) showed that the torso was oriented on its side with the right side down. The skull, not visible in the photograph, was reportedly found in an approximately correct anatomical position in relation to the torso. The intervening cervical vertebrae, C2 to C7, were not recovered. The photograph shows what appears to be a femoral head in close proximity to the acetabulum of the left side of the pelvis. This turned out to be a spheroidal flint nodule. The photograph does not show the distal leg and foot bones so their position in relation to the other elements is unknown.

The material was in a relatively poor condition, which was further complicated by the delay in cleaning it. The torso material was coated with PVA consolidant prior to block lifting. The skeleton appears to have been buried in or covered by a clay matrix. A clay coating was strongly adherent to the ribs and the pelvis. The uncleaned torso demonstrated that the intervertebral disk space was preserved.

Analysis

The presence of the strongly adherent dried clay coating on the pelvis prevented visualisation of the auricular surface. This meant age determination was limited to tooth wear. Wear on the mandible suggest an age of 30–35 years, whilst wear on the maxilla suggests an age of 40–45 years. Given the uncertainty in the applicability of Miles' method, the individual can only be confidently classified as adult.

Sex determination was primarily based on morphology of the pubic shape, sciatic notch, auricular surface and post-auricular space. These factors were supported by metrics based on measurements of the radial head and the glenoid cavity. The heavily fragmented and poorly represented skull limited observation to the mastoid process morphology. All of these factors, taken together, suggest the individual was probably female.

Lab ID	Sample	$\delta 13C$	Uncalibrated Date		Calibrated Date 95% Confidence Interval	
			Centre	SE	Lower	Upper
27058	A	−18.30	385	27	AD 1443	AD 1629
27059	F	−18.98	1736	29	AD 238	AD 387
27060	H	−18.92	1746	29	AD 230	AD 386
27061	H	−18.90	1735	29	AD 239	AD 387
27062	K	−20.04	2051	29	166 BC	AD 19
27063	L	−18.55	1755	29	AD 214	AD 385

Table 29: Radiocarbon dating summary

Fig 117: Sample K SPLOT inhumation (photographed 1972)

Stature could not be estimated as no intact and complete long bones were present in the recovered material.

The supernumerary juvenile mandible fragment exhibits a molar crypt estimated to be crown complete. It is not known if this represents the second or third molar. This suggests the individual may have had a developmental age between eight and 15 years (Al Qahtani 2008).

Skeletal indices

None of the primary skeletal indices – platymeric, platycnemic and cranial – could be measured for this individual.

Non-metrical traits

The right calcaneus had a divided anterior facet. This is a relatively common (33%) non-metrical normal variation (Brothwell 1981).

Dental pathology

The dental formula for the individual is shown in Table 30. The dentition exhibited three slight carious lesions on the mandibular dentition. A small lesion was noted on the distal occlusal surface of the right third molar, and a slight interstitial lesion was located close to the cemento-enamel junction of the

A	7	A	5	4	3	2	1	X	X	3	4	5	6	7	8
C	7	6	X	X	X	X	1	1	2	3	C	C	6	7	A

Table 30: Sample K SPLOT dental formula
(A – lost ante-mortem, X – not observable, C – caries)

distal side of the left second premolar and the mesial surface of the left first molar.

Slight deposits of calculus were observed on both the mandibular and maxillary dentitions. Mandibular calculus deposits were located on the buccal side of the right first to third molars and on the buccal side of the left first molar. For the maxillary dentition, calculus deposits covered the buccal, distal and lingual faces of the left third molar, the buccal surface of the left first premolar and the buccal surface of the right second molar.

The right first and third maxillary molars were lost ante-mortem as was the left third mandibular molar. The socket for the right third maxillary molar is partly resorbed, whilst the sockets for the other teeth lost ante-mortem are fully resorbed.

Several of the teeth in the maxilla exhibited signs of rotation from normal orientation. The right second incisor is rotated 45° anti-clockwise seen from occlusal, whilst the left first premolar is rotated about 30° clockwise.

All teeth exhibit a gap of about 4 mm between the alveolar margin and the cemento-enamel junction, the result of continuous eruption in the presence of long-term wear of the occlusal surface of the teeth.

Skeletal pathology

There is evidence for slight degenerative changes on some elements of the spine. The dens of the first cervical vertebra has slight lipping on the superior margin. There is slight compression of the lower margin of the lower facets of the thoracic vertebrae, from the second to the seventh inclusive. The seventh, eighth and ninth thoracic vertebrae exhibit slight marginal lipping on the anterior margin of the body. This lipping is more prominent on the right side for the seventh and eighth vertebrae. The three lumbar vertebrae present, the first to the third, exhibit slight marginal bilateral osteophytes on the intervertebral facets. The lower face of the first lumbar vertebra, both faces of the second and the upper face of the third lumbar vertebrae all have small bilateral Schmorl's nodes. These nodes may be the result of great stress being applied to the spine resulting in herniation of the intervertebral disk (Waldron 2009). In addition, the right acromio-clavicular joint exhibited slight marginal osteophytes.

The right ulna had a very prominent inter-osseous crest. There is also an encircled vascular channel anterior to the articulation for the radial head. The radial tuberosity has rounded marginal osteophytes on the medial side. The lateral and medial margins of the coranoid process of the ulna have prominent osteophytes, possibly the result of hyperextension of the right elbow.

Taphonomy

The right side of the mandible exhibits irregular linear crazed cracking suggesting the bone was directly exposed to the weather for some time in the past. Some skeletal elements had a firmly adherent clay coating, others exhibited slight surface dissolution and some skull fragments exhibited rounded margins suggestive of disturbance and redeposition.

The major missing elements are the left leg and foot, most of the right leg and the left forearm. Given that the individual was buried lying on her right side, some or all of these elements would be more exposed to disturbance caused by the mechanical excavator used in the early phase of the excavation. If the legs were in an extended position, both feet would be in close proximity, whereas if the legs were flexed to a greater or lesser degree the left leg could fall forward with respect to the right, as would the left foot. This latter case fits the recorded evidence better than the former so the individual was more likely to have been buried lying on the right side with legs flexed.

Summary

The human skeletal remains from the Iron Age Ditch XXI represent an MNI of three individuals. The major components represent one adult, probably female and probably aged 45 years or more, exhibiting slight spinal degeneration and slight dental disease. The spinal degeneration may be the result of normal ageing processes, activity or a combination of the two. Supernumerary material includes part of the right mandible of a juvenile, possibly aged eight to 15 years, and the humeral head of a second adult.

Romano-British period
Material

The material from this period represents one single inhumation (Sample F, context SPDFH) found in a grave against the wall of Room 5 in the Main House and two mixed disturbed deposits (Sample H recovered from a shallow grave by the wall of the Hall and Sample L found beneath the floor of Room 10 in the Main House) containing multiple individuals.

Analysis

The individual inhumation SPDFH was assessed for age and sex. The angle of the right sciatic notch was measured to be 28°, which falls between the male and female limits (Waldron *et al.* 1999). The sex is therefore indeterminate. Measurements of the diaphyseal lengths of the humerus, radius, clavicle, femur and tibia suggest a gestation age of 38–41 weeks. The metrics for the pars basilaris are shown in Table 31, along with the gestational age range suggested by data provided by Scheuer & MacLaughlin-Black (1994).

Sample	Label	SL mm	ML mm	W mm	Age
F	SPDFH	13.8	17.2	15.2	40 week – 1 month

Table 31: Sample F SPDFH, pars basilaris metrics
Note: 'week' – gestational development age; 'month' – developmental age after birth

The three maxillary and three mandibular incisors present are all crown complete. The left maxilla canine crown is half complete, as is the left mandibular first molar. Two cusps on the left mandibular second molar are fused. This corresponds to a developmental age of birth to 1.5 months (Al Qahtani 2008). Given the greater uncertainty and variability in the dental development and the pars basilaris data, the best estimate for the developmental age is the 38–41 weeks derived from long bone diaphyseal length data.

The material from Sample H (labels 409, SPG2BF and SPG2BU) and Sample L (labels SPLGD, SPLGS and SPLGT) was treated as commingled material as described above. This material was assessed by Tony Waldron. The concordance for his labels and the excavation labels is given in Table 32.

Lacking accurate contextual details, Waldron considered MNI values for each sample (2, 3, 4) separately and as one combined group. Neither of

Sample	Label	Waldron label
H	409	2
H	SPG2BF/U	4
L	SPLGD/S/T	3

Table 32: Waldron context concordance

Waldron's groupings represents the known archaeology but it is now understood that materials labelled 409 and SPG2BF/U come from the same context.

The material from both Samples H and L contained measurable long bones (humerus, ulna, radius, femur and tibia). Scapulae were also present, as were fragmented ribs. Skull fragments were present in Sample H, whilst mandible and vertebral fragments were present in L. Both samples lacked hand and foot bones along with fibulae. All material was of a similar developmental age.

MNI estimates shown in Table 33 are based on the maximum count of identified sided and sexed bones.

The metrics for the intact long bones in Sample H show a gestation age range of 35–39 weeks, whilst the gestation age range for Sample L is 36–38 weeks. The sex determination data is shown in Table 34.

Sample	Scapula	Clavicle	Humerus	Ulna	Radius	Pelvis	Femur	Tibia	MNI
H	2	0	5	3	2	2	3	2	5
L	1	1	2	1	2	1	1	1	2
Total	3	1	7	4	4	3	4	3	7

Table 33: Samples H and L MNI values

Sample	Label	Angle (°)	Sex
H	409	33	M
H	SPG2BF	24	F
L	SPLGD	28	Indeterminate

Table 34: Samples H and L sex determination

Skeletal indices

The primary skeletal indices – platymeric, platycnemic and cranial – are not applicable to neonatal material.

Non-metrical traits

No non-metrical traits were observed.

Dental pathology

The dental formula for skeleton SPDFH is shown in Table 35. No dental pathology was observed on the partially mineralised crowns of the surviving teeth.

P	P	P	P	1	1	2	3	P	P
P	P	P	2	1	P	2	P	4	5

Table 35: Sample F SPDFH dental formula
(P – lost post-mortem)

Skeletal pathology

No pathological changes were observed on the skeleton SPDFH. The normal physiological changes of the neonatal metaphyses of the long bones were present.

Taphonomy

Skeleton SPDFH was both well represented and well preserved. All skeletal elements were present to some degree with the exception of the feet. The bone surface was in excellent condition and showed little taphonomic change.

In contrast, the material from the mixed deposits is less well preserved, with a notable lack of almost all hand and foot bones, and a significant under-representation of vertebrae. In addition, the material labelled 409 and SPG2BF (see Fig. 71) exhibited variable taphonomic changes. In both cases, a dominant part of the assemblage, possibly representing a single individual, was better preserved than the smaller number of residual bones representing the other individuals forming the relevant MNI. This may mean that the different individuals forming the composite in each context had different taphonomic histories. This in turn may mean they had different burial histories. For example, the poorer material may have been buried before the better-preserved material. Given the fact that the hand and foot joints are the first to degrade during decomposition, the presence of hands and feet in anatomically consistent positions is the sign of an undisturbed primary inhumation (Duday 2009). The almost complete lack of hand, foot and vertebral bones, coupled with fragmented rib and skull elements, may be explained by incomplete recovery during excavation. Alternatively, it may mean that the material was originally buried elsewhere and then reburied in its final location in the villa at some later date. It is also possible that disturbance by burrowing animals may have played a part, though there is only slight evidence of rodent gnawing.

Summary

The material from the Romano-British contexts located close to structural elements (detailed in Table 36) of the villa buildings represents multiple individuals deposited as a single inhumation and two mixed disturbed deposits. The cause of death is not obvious for any of them. The individuals from the mixed disturbed deposits (409, SPG2BF and SPLGD) were all less than 39 weeks of gestational age. They either were stillborn or premature births shortly followed

Sample	Label	Location
F	SPDFH	Grave cut set against wall of Room 5 in the House
H	409 SPG2BF/U	Simple scoop of grave against a wall of the Hall
L	SPLGD PLGS/T	Beneath the earthen floor of Room 10

Table 36: Location of Romano-British material

by death from unknown causes not leaving skeletal traces. Waldron (undated) refers to embryotomy, a surgical procedure to remove a foetus from the womb in order to preserve the life of the mother. There is no evidence for such a procedure having been carried out for any member of this assemblage. The individual in the single inhumation (Sample F SPDFH) died at a slightly later age of 38–41 weeks, but again there is no clue as to why. This child may have died shortly after birth.

Medieval period

Material

Photographic evidence taken at the time of excavation appears to show that the context F27 material (Sample A from Table 28) came from a well-defined grave cut located just within the Courtyard next to the disturbed foundation trench of AB I (Fig. 118). The bones visible in the photograph suggest the material may not have been in anatomical position when recovered. The material was generally in very good to excellent condition, with almost complete skeletal representation.

Analysis

The angle of the right sciatic notch was measured to be 26° which falls within the female range (Waldron *et al.* 1999). Measurements of the diaphyseal lengths of the humerus, radius, clavicle, femur and tibia suggest a gestation age of 39–42 weeks. The metrics for the pars basilaris are shown in Table 37, along with the gestational age range suggested by data provided by Scheuer & MacLaughlin-Black (1994). The four mandibular deciduous premolars were all crown complete which corresponds to a developmental age of 1.5–4.5 months ± 3 months (Al Qahtani 2008). The best estimate for the developmental age is thought to be 39–42 weeks.

Sample	Label	SL mm	ML mm	W mm	Age
A	F27	13.8	17.3	15.9	40 week – 1 month

Table 37: Sample A F27 pars basilaris metrics

Note: 'week' – gestational development age; 'month' – developmental age after birth

Fig 118 Sample A F27 *in situ* (photographed 1972)

Skeletal indices

The primary skeletal indices – platymeric, platycnemic and cranial – are not applicable to neonatal material.

Non-metrical traits

No non-metrical traits were observed.

Dental pathology

The dental formula for F27 is shown in Table 38. No dental pathology was observed.

The peaks mesio-lingual and mesio-buccal cusps of the left and right first molars are distinctly darker in colouration than the rest of the crown. There are two fine foramina opening from the interior base of the crown into the mesio-buccal cusp of the left first molar.

X	P	P	X	X	P	P	P	P	P
5	4	P	P	P	P	P	X	4	5

Table 38: Sample A F27 dental formula
(P – lost post-mortem, X – not observable)

Skeletal pathology

The right orbit exhibits a band of fine linear porosity along the internal angle between orbital roof and the superior orbital margin. This condition is described as low-grade cribra orbitalia (Nathan & Haas 1966). This condition is of unknown aetiology and seems to be relatively common in archaeological material.

The skeleton showed widespread cortical thinning and porosity, mainly on the skull but also on the distal end of the ribs, the fossa superior to the spine of the scapulae and the lateral surface of the left and right ilium. Fine layers of periosteal new bone are present on this surface adjacent to the sciatic notch. The long bone shafts show no sign of porosity or periosteal new bone. Fine porosity is present at the metaphyses of the long bones. This latter porosity is probably the normal physiological pattern seen in neonatal material.

The porosity on the skull is mainly endocranial affecting the pars basilaris, the left and right pars lateralis of the occipital, the lower right margin and nuchal zone of the squamous part of the occipital bone, the basilar part and greater wings of the sphenoid and the posterior region of the petrous part of the temporal bones. There is also a small zone of porosity on the exterior of the squamous part of the temporal bone.

This pathology has expressed itself within the normal gestation period which suggests the cause must be some pathogen capable of crossing the placenta barrier. A small number of bacterial, viral and protozoan pathogens are capable of this and can cause skeletal lesions.

Toxoplasmosis is a parasitic pathogen whose primary host is the cat. The primary symptoms are microcephaly, mental retardation, hepatosplenomegaly with occasional cerebral calcifications.

Congenital syphilis indicated by skeletal changes has a high mortality, with most individuals affected dying before four years of age (Ortner 2003). Congenital syphilis is marked by the presence of dental malformations (Hutchinson's incisors and Mulberry or Moon's molars). The molars present in this case are normal, whilst the incisors were not recovered during excavation. The long bones show no sign of prolific bilateral periosteal new bone that is characteristic of treponemal disease.

Rubella can affect a newborn child if the mother becomes infected herself during the first three months of pregnancy. Skeletal changes take the form of developmental defects of the long bone metaphyses, primarily the distal femur and proximal tibia. The shafts of the long bones show no sign or periosteal new bone. The skull can also be affected, with changes manifesting as imperfect mineralisation and an enlarged frontal fontanel. Post-natal rubella infection does not induce skeletal changes.

Cytomegalovirus can also cross the placenta. The symptoms are similar to toxoplasmosis. Central nervous system defects may lead to blindness or deafness.

Both rubella and toxoplasmosis may induce skeletal lesions at the metaphyses of long bones, especially the distal femur and proximal tibia (Aufderheide & Rodriguez-Martin 2006) which may be distinguishable when viewed on x-ray. Given the evidence available, the differential diagnosis for the disease reduces to toxoplasmosis, rubella or cytomegalovirus. The congenital form of these conditions is typically marked by failure to thrive and subsequent death (Beeson et al. 1979).

Taphonomy

The skeletal material shows little taphonomic damage. The cortical bone is generally well preserved. The photograph of the in-situ material suggests the remains have been substantially disturbed after burial, possibly by rodent action or root growth from nearby bushes or trees.

Summary

F27 (Sample A) represents the remains of a single inhumation burial containing a neonate that died at the equivalent of 39–42 weeks' gestation. The skeletal remains were well preserved, showing evidence for some skeletal pathology that could manifest itself within the normal gestation period. One cause could be intrauterine rubella, with toxoplasmosis and cytomegalovirus as further possibilities.

Residual material

The residual material consists of 25 fragments of bone from six contexts weighing 98.2 g, summarised

Sample	Label	Fragments	Weight	Comment
B	SPAβBC	1	4.4	Adult skull fragment
C	SPDEA	2	1.9	Neonate radius fragments
D	SPDES	2	1.8	Neonate skull fragments
E	SPDET	13	1.5	Neonate ribs, humerus, vertebra fragments
G	SPDIY	3	33.9	Adult skull fragments
J	SPLEC	4	54.8	Adult pelvis fragments encased in clay
Total		**25**	**98.2**	

Table 39: Residual material

in Table 39. It was not possible to determine age, sex or stature data from this material, which comprises a mixture of adult skull and mixed neonatal material. The condition of the material is generally good to excellent with the exception of the pelvis fragments. These are encased in dried clay, are poorly preserved and very fragile. The actual bone weight will be much less than the 54.8 g listed for the whole specimen.

The contexts for the residual material are widely separated on the site, so it is reasonable to assume that the material derives from different individuals when calculating MNI figures.

Overall summary

The assemblage is summarised in Table 40 for MNI and age, whilst sex determination is detailed in Table 41.

The assemblage contains the remains of one adult inhumation from the late Iron Age period, one infant inhumation from the Romano-British period and one infant inhumation from the medieval period. The remaining material is mainly mixed disturbed neonatal material from the Romano-British period, supplemented by a small amount of residual material of unknown origin.

The presence of the Iron Age inhumation burial in a ditch disturbed by the mechanical excavator is intriguing. It is not clear from the limited archaeological data whether this burial was the result of a natural death or something darker. The presence of small amounts of intrusive human material from other individuals suggests other burials were made in the vicinity. It is impossible to say from the evidence whether or not these were contemporary with the main inhumation.

Moore (2009) provides a useful summary of explanations proposed for the burial of infants and neonates in Romano-British villas. The practice has been interpreted as evidence for infanticide, surreptitious burial, the disposal of unwanted babies and as an indicator of spirituality. Whatever the specific reason, burial in association with villa structures appears to be a favoured rite. The limited evidence from the Sparsholt material suggests another possibility to those listed above. There seems to be evidence for a re-deposition in a more propitious location of neonates and infants who died at various times prior to the construction of a particular phase of the villa. The low gestational ages, their relatively narrow range and the presence of both sexes seem to preclude infanticide.

The burial of the medieval infant, a female aged 39–42 weeks of gestation, seems to fit in with the idea of a surreptitious burial in a place both clearly marked by extant surviving walls and at the same time likely to remain undisturbed. This individual may have died as a result of intrauterine rubella shortly after birth.

Period	MNI	Neonate	Infant	Juvenile	Adult
Iron Age	3			1	2
Romano-British	8	8			
Medieval	1	1			
Residual	6	3			3
Total	**18**	**12**		**1**	**5**

Table 40: MNI summary by period

Period	Male	Female	Indeterminate
Iron Age		1	2
Romano-British	1	1	6
Medieval		1	
Residual			6
Total	**1**	**3**	**14**

Table 41: Sex determination by period

The faunal remains

by Richard Ward

The current collection of faunal remains totals 7,428 fragments of bone: 3,097 were identifiable to species and will form the basis of this study, while 531 of the remaining 4,331 unidentified bones were classed by size. The high frequency of unidentified remains was due mostly to small fragment size and/or lack of diagnostic indicators.

After the excavation the faunal remains were kept for a number of years within the Faunal Remains Unit (University of Southampton). A preliminary evaluation of the assemblage was undertaken, but no formal report was made. The remains were then returned to Winchester Museum Service. For the purpose of this report the bones were returned to Southampton University to undergo fresh analysis.

Methodology

Recovery

Most of the faunal remains were recovered by hand and because of this there is probably a bias towards larger skeletal elements, although a number of smaller sheep/goat bones and even juvenile cat remains were discovered. Remains of small birds, rodents and amphibians were also present, although they seem to have originated from soil samples. It is unknown how regularly this sampling was carried out but the Site Notebooks indicate that only areas of specific interest were sampled.

Identification

The remains were identified using osteological reference collections for comparisons as well as bone atlases, such as Schmid (1972) and Pales & Lambert (1971). Closely related species were distinguished as follows: sheep/goat (*Ovis aries*) and goats (*Capra hircus*) were identified according to the morphological differences outlined by Boessneck (1969), while criteria set forth by Lister (1996) were used to differentiate between red deer (*Cervus elaphus*) and fallow deer (*Dama dama*). Horse and donkey remains were recorded as equid, although patterns of enamel folds in their teeth were recorded as outlined by Eisenmann (1981). The morphology of the olecranon, scapula and metapodials was used to identify the difference between dogs (*Canis familiaris*) and foxes (*Vulpes vulpes*) following Wayne (1986), while bird species were identified to family using Cohen and Serjeantson (1972).

Wherever possible bones were identified to species. The exceptions are vertebrae (not including the axis and atlas) and ribs, which were assigned to one of two size classes, cattle/horse or sheep/goat/pig.

The data were entered into a Microsoft® Excel spreadsheet, which listed the provenance of the specimen within the archive, the part of the site it came from and the bag number with which it was labelled. Species, element, fusion and taphonomic processes such as gnawing, butchery, surface modification and burning were recorded according to a system of codes. Bones of uncertain origin were not recorded.

Quantification

All bones identified to species were recorded in full, while fragmentary bones that could not be identified were separated into individual bags and counted. Serjeantson's (1972) diagnostic zones were applied to the bones to illustrate possible overlaps in later quantification and potential patterns in the survival rates on site. Ribs were only recoded if zones 1–4 were present; the same criterion was also applied to ulnae of all mammals.

The MNI (Minimum Number of Individuals) was calculated using the sideable elements present for each of the major species by noting which element and individual zone was the most prevalent.

The NISP (Number of Identified Specimens) was used to calculate (by dividing by their total and multiplying by 100) the percentages of species, representation of elements and taphonomic processes. Similarly the percentages of bone survival were calculated by dividing the number of bones present by those that would be expected from the MNI and multiplying by 100.

Sexing

Sexing was positively recorded for pig canines following morphological differences noted in Schmid (1972, 80–1) and for galliform remains by the presence of a spur on the tasometatarus (Serjeantson 2009, 47). The sex of the main domesticates and deer was determined by pelvis morphology using reference collections. With cattle, however, it was also possible to use the distal metapodials. This method involves plotting the distal breadth of metatarsals or metacarpals against the depth of the medial trochlea (as outlined in Davis 1992). The measurements should form a bimodal distribution, the smaller group indicating females and the larger males (Svensson *et al.* 2008).

Ageing

The age of the main domesticate species was based on the mandibular deciduous and permanent 4th pre-molars (dP4 and P4), molars (M1–3), loose teeth and jaws. Wear stages were recorded for cattle, sheep/goat/goat and pig dentition and scored as outlined in Grant (1982). Co-ordination of the wear stages within the mandibles and their ontogenetic age were made using Payne (1973) for sheep/goat/goat, Legge (1981) for cattle and O'Connor (1988) for pigs.

The state of epiphyseal fusion was recorded where possible, both distal and proximal fusion recorded as unfused, fusing or fused. To determine age at death the data were compared to the rates of fusion as outlined in Reitz & Wing (2008, 72). These data, in combination with the evidence from the dentition, provide a general overview of the ages of the species. Since bird bones develop differently, lacking epiphyseal plates, a bone was recorded as juvenile only when a 'spongy' appearance was noted, which indicates that ossification was still occurring.

Measurements

Measurements were taken with a pair of Mitutyo Absolute Digimatic© digital callipers to the nearest 0.1mm following Von den Driesch (1976). To estimate the withers heights the following regression factors were used: Kiesewalter (1888) for horse, Matolcsi (1970) for cattle, Teichert (1975) for sheep/goat and pig, and Harcourt (1974) for dog.

Bone modification

For all recorded specimens the degree of burning, gnawing, surface modification and butchery was scored. Gnawing was recorded as resulting from a carnivore or rodent, in addition to whether the example had been digested. Butchery marks were examined with the naked eye and the location together with the type of mark (cut, chop or saw) noted. Burning was recorded in degrees as burnt, charred and calcified. Finally, surface modification such as erosion, abrasion and root etching was recorded if deemed notable.

Results

Taphonomy

The preservation of the remains was very good as a result of the chalk and clay soils. Of the bones that were identified only 11% exhibited surface modification; about a third had been damaged by root etching, and another third by erosion which could have been due to water or other factors within the soil. Considering Sparsholt's location within an area of woodland, the remains had not been badly affected by this environment. Poor packaging had, however, contributed to abrasion and further fragmentation. A small amount of gnawing was noted: 8% of the total number of bones. Of these, 91% were gnawed by carnivores, most likely dogs, indicating that remains were either fed to dogs or were opportunistic finds scavenged from kitchen waste. Rodent gnawing was recorded on 4% of affected bones, which suggests that there might have been an open area for dumping of waste. A further 1% exhibited gnawing by both canids and rodents, and the remaining 4% showed evidence of being digested.

Overall species representation

Domestic animals dominate, making up 86% of the assemblage, and include cattle, sheep/goat, pig, dog, cat, birds (mainly galliforms), and equids. Cattle and sheep/goat/goat are dominant (28% and just over 33% respectively); pig records just over 4% of the identified remains, comparable to the equids (Fig. 119). Of the sheep/goat only one bone was positively identified as goat; as there may be more bones within the sheep that are not morphologically different, they will be referred to as sheep/goat for the rest of the paper but most likely represent sheep. Wild species such as fox, red, roe and fallow deer, rabbit, hare and rodents (Table 42) make up the remaining 14%. Based on the calculated MNI (Table 43) there is a greater frequency of sheep/goat than cattle and a relatively small amount of other species. In spite of the predominance of sheep/goat, cattle probably provided most of the meat because of their larger size.

	Iron Age		Roman	
	NISP	%	NISP	%
Carnivore			7	0.3
Dog	201*	22.8	140	5.1
Fox			146*	5.4
Canid			10	0.4
Cat			22	0.8
Equid	10	1.1	124	4.6
Pig	24	2.7	105	3.9
Cervus	3	0.3	16	0.6
Roe Deer	24*	2.7	15	0.6
Fallow Deer			14	0.5
Red Deer	1	0.1	23	0.8
Red/Fallow deer	1	0.1	8	0.3
Cattle	107*	12.1	671	24.6
Sheep/Goat	139	15.8	772	28.3
Sheep			1	0.0
Goat	2	0.2		
Amphibian	1	0.1	3	0.1
Bird	3	0.3	36	1.3
Fish	1	0.1	8	0.3
Hare/Rabbit	3	0.3	7	0.3
Rabbit	3	0.3	92	3.4
Hare			3	0.1
Rodent	222*	25.2	69	2.5
Sheep/Pig-sized	59	6.7	213	7.8
Cow/Horse-sized	77	8.7	182	6.7
Domestic Fowl			28	1.0
Pheasant	1	0.1		
Duck, Mallard-sized			4	0.1
Wood Pigeon			2	0.1
Woodcock			1	0.0
Galliform			3	0.1
Totals:	882		2725	

Table 42: Summary of all species identified on site (*=includes articulating bone groups or, in the case of the fox, a complete individual is present)

Domesticates (Fig. 120)

Body part representation
A large percentage of the mandibles and skull fragments of cattle are present, followed by roughly equal

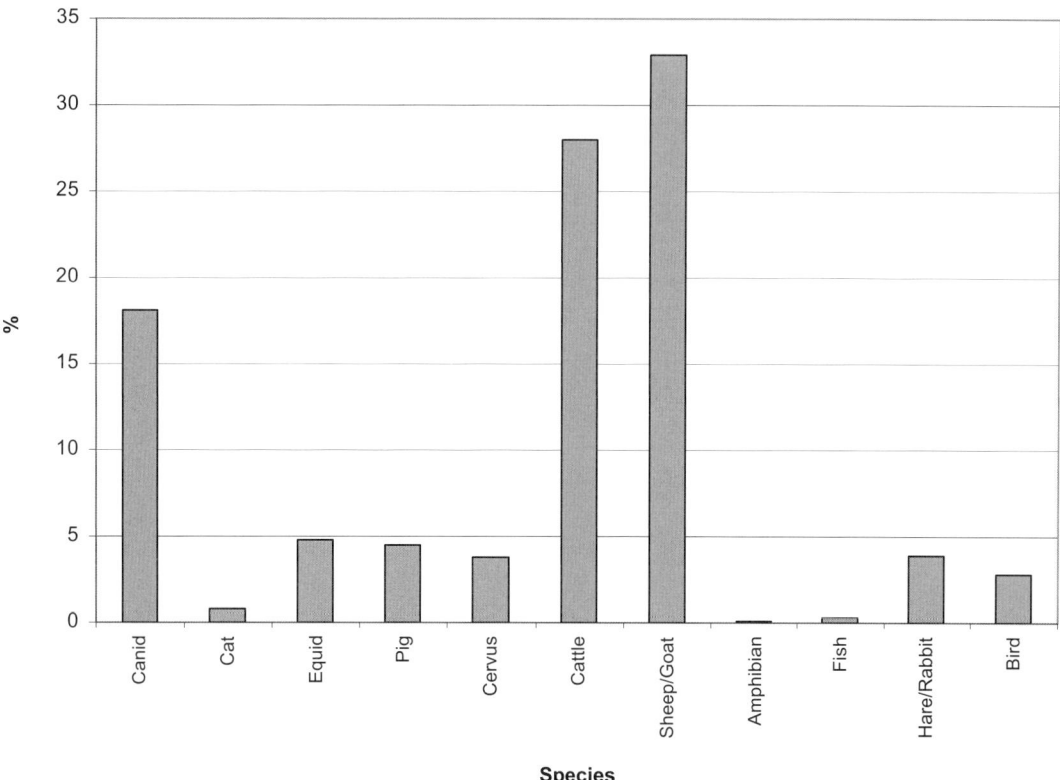

Fig 119 Overall species representation shown as percentages of the Number of Individual Specimens

Species	Overall MNI
Cattle	21
Sheep/Goat	29
Pig	6
Equid	5
Dog	6
Fox	3
Cat	2
Rabbit	8
Fallow Deer	2
Roe Deer	2
Red Deer	3

Table 43: Overall MNI for species on site

amounts of all the limb elements, including metapodials. The sheep/goat/goat remains are generally similar to the cattle, in particular the high proportion of mandibles. There is an equal distribution of bones from the forelimbs but a favouring of the lower hind limb bones. Pigs show a radically different distribution to that of the cattle or sheep/goat/goat: a high number of upper forelimbs compared to the hind limbs, along with a large number of mandibles, and more metatarsals than metacarpals. This distribution may indicate the arrival of pig meat on the bone, with shoulders being favoured over the legs. The proportion of metatarsals may indicate the use of trotters, although as pigs have more metatarsals per foot than the ungulates, only about 20% of what would be expected is present. There are a number of

pig skull and mandible fragments possibly derived from complete heads which were fragmented due to butchery processes or indeed the fragile nature of the skulls themselves. The large number of mandibles is also noted in the survivability graph: 67% of the mandibles expected, based on the overall MNI, are present. The range of equid bones shows that most elements are present, with the exception of some of the smaller bones. No horse burials were discovered and the small number of bones suggests that they may have been processed into smaller pieces to aid their disposal, eaten or discarded elsewhere.

Axial elements such as vertebrae and ribs were not identified to species but classed by size. Based on the relative frequencies of both species, bones of cattle/horse size should probably be identified as cattle. In comparison, the sheep/goat/pig-sized specimens show that there are more ribs of this size class, but a smaller proportion of vertebrae present; this pattern probably results from the use of ribs for meat.

Age
Cattle. Dental evidence indicates that a small number of cattle were killed around sub-adulthood (18–30 months; Fig. 121), but the majority were significantly older, around 3 to 10 years of age. The loose M3s (3rd molars, Fig. 121) exhibit a majority of wear stages also consistent with mainly older animals. Epiphyseal fusion (Fig. 123) demonstrates that a large number of cattle survived beyond 2 years of age, only dropping in any significant number

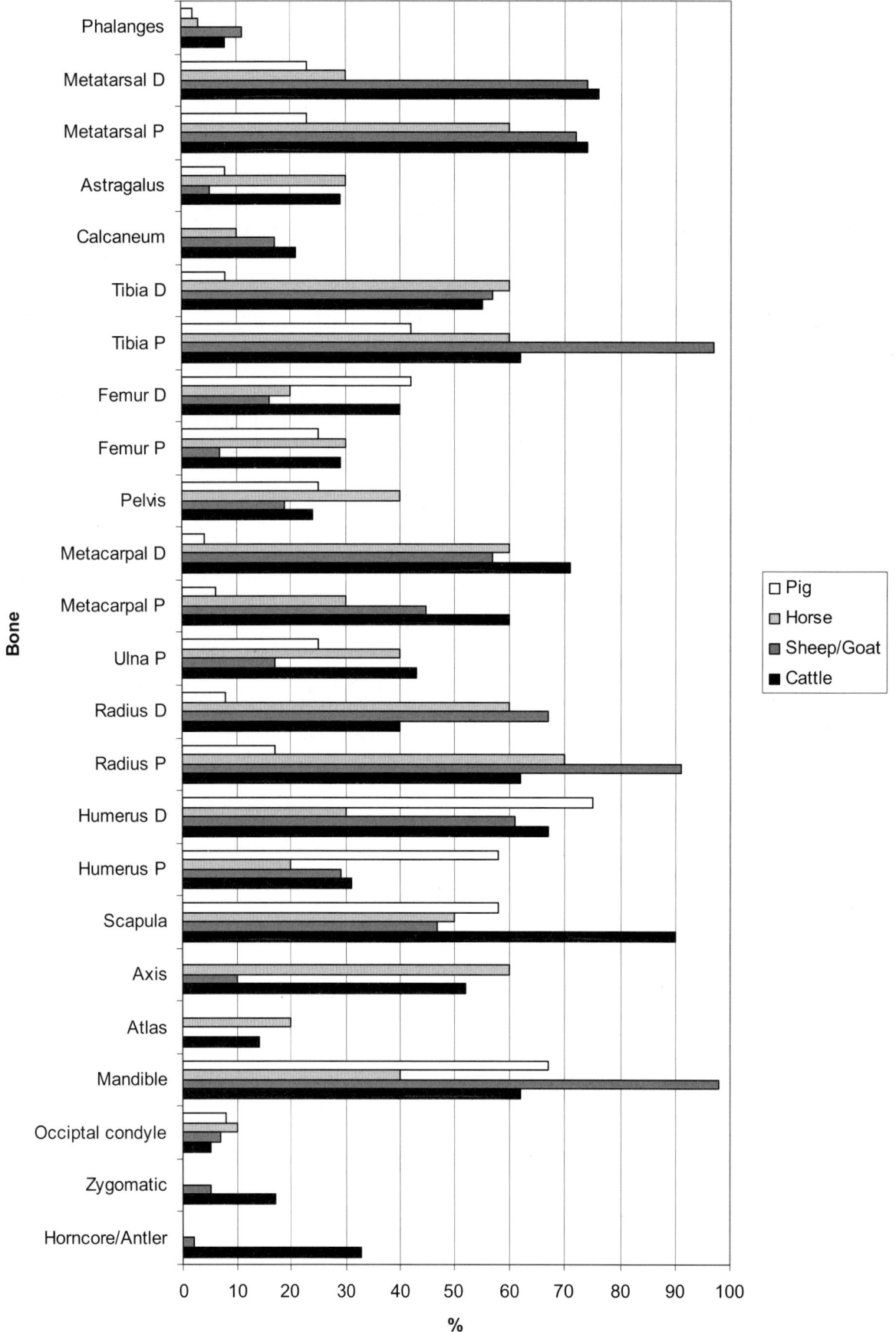

Fig 120 Percentage of bone survival for main domesticates based on overall MNI

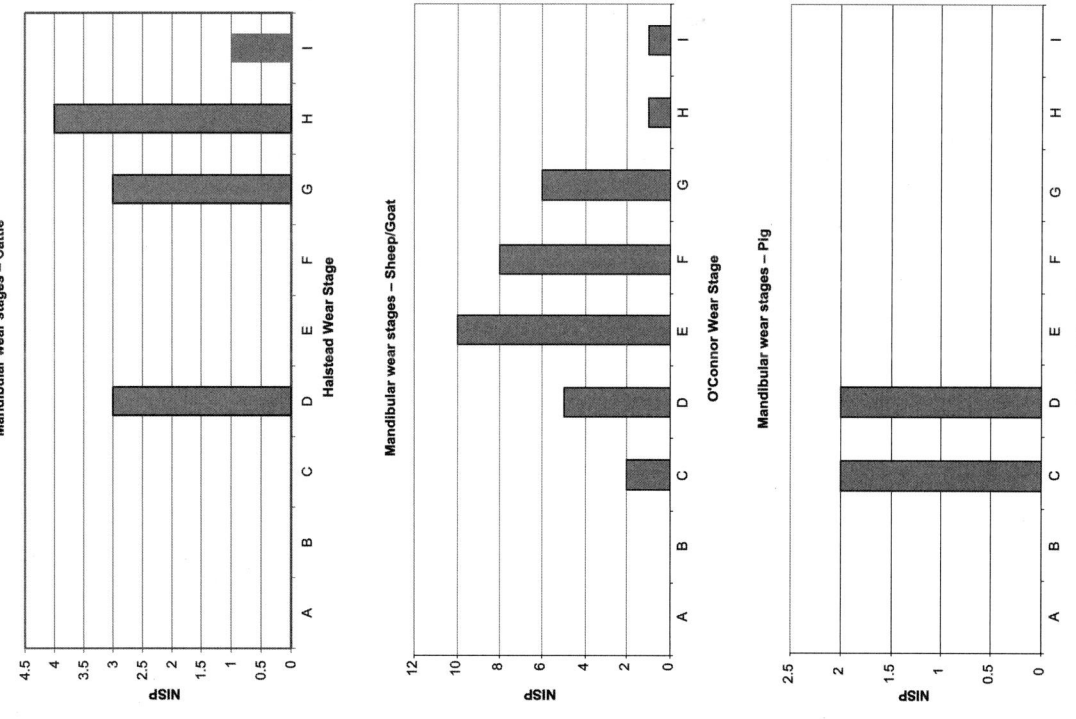

Fig 121 Age stages of domesticates determined from complete mandibles recovered

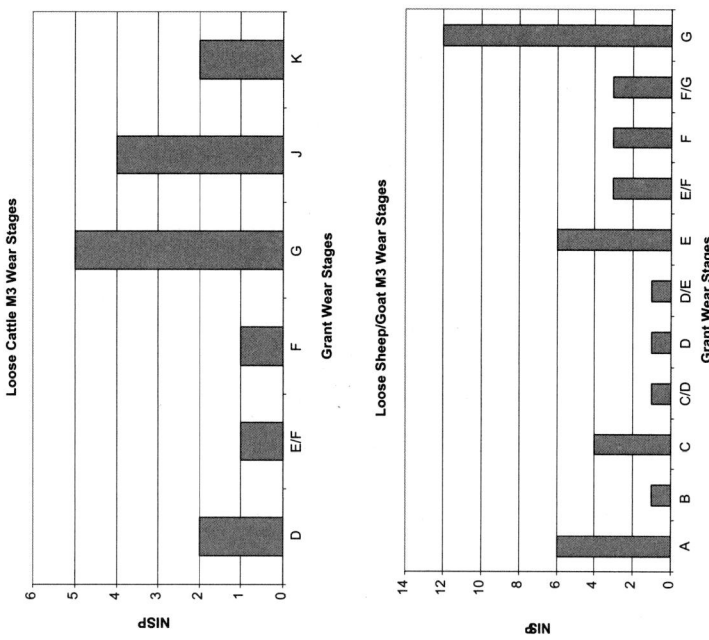

Fig 122 Wear stages of loose M3s for cattle and sheep/goat recovered

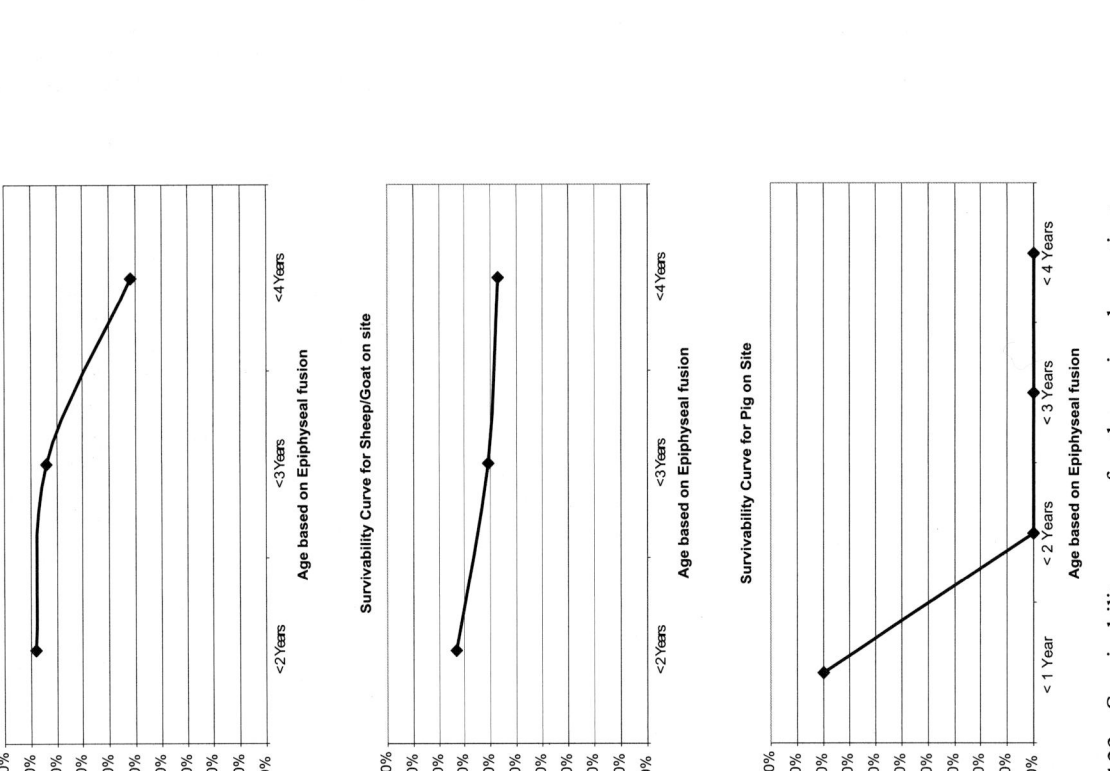

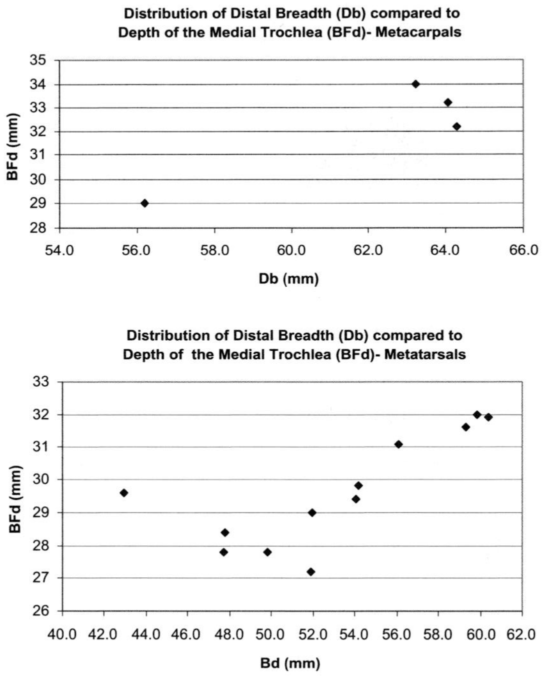

Fig 124 Sex plot for cattle metacarpals and metatarsals

Fig 123 Survivability curves for the major domesticates based on epiphyseal fusion noted from the remains

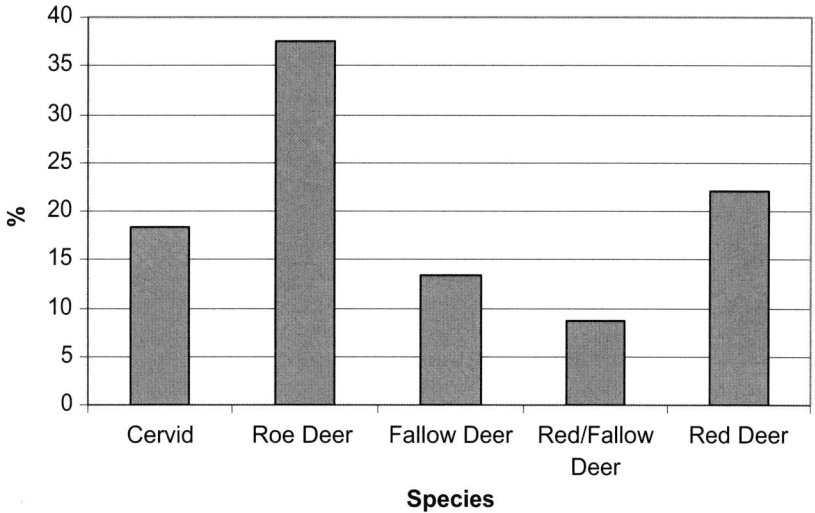

Fig 125 Distribution of deer species as NISP of total Cervus specimens

around the age of 4 years; 50% did not survive this age.

Sheep/goat. The calculated mandible year stages produce a curving pattern: a few sheep/goat are killed around 6 months to 2 years, with a peak at the 2- to 3-year Stage (E). A steady drop off follows, with a few animals kept beyond 6 years of age. The M3s present (Fig. 122) show a peak at Stage A which indicates a small number of animals were being killed earlier than the rest. Another peak correlates with a kill off at around 2–4 years, while the last one exhibits wear stages expected of adult sheep/goat between 3 and 8 years of age. The epiphyseal fusion data (Fig. 123) shows a similar pattern, 75% surviving beyond 2 years, followed by a gradual decrease. This evidence shows that 57% of the ovicaprines survived to 4 years and beyond, ie they survived into older age, as indicated by the mandibular evidence.

Pig. Only a small amount of data is available (Figs 121 and 123). The dental evidence indicates that these animals were killed after their first year, while epiphyseal fusion data show that none survived beyond their second year.

Size

A calculation of the withers height for cattle gives a range of 103.6–125.4 cm, with an average height of 115.7 cm (based on the ten greatest length measurements). Withers heights of the sheep/goat bones give a range of 52.8–78.2 cm and an average height of 65 cm. As a result of the highly fragmented state of the pig remains only one measurement (based on an astragalus) could be calculated and produced a height of 66.2 cm. Although it cannot be representative, it gives a rough idea of the size of the pigs kept at Sparsholt.

The equids have a withers height range of 126–137.5 cm and an average of 132.4 cm. It was based on eight specimens and was calculated using the horse factors outlined by Kiesewalter (1888). An examination of the enamel folds revealed that most of the remains were horse which would put them at only 12.1 and 13.2 hands height (average of 13 hands height by modern standards), thus classifying them as ponies.

Sex

Cattle. Few sexually dimorphic characteristics separate male and female cattle; consequently measurements of the metapodials are commonly used to determine their sex (Svensson *et al.* 2008). Both metacarpals and metatarsals were measured (Fig. 124). Metacarpals provide more reliable data, but only four comparable sets of measurements could be taken, of which one is a low outlier. The result could indicate a propensity of males, but with so few measurements no definitive conclusions can be drawn. Although the evidence from the metatarsals is less reliable (Svensson *et al.* 2008, 943), more measurements were achieved and an overall spread is displayed. Again, there is an outlier, plus three specimens that group at the higher end of the graph, most probably males; the central cluster is indicative of a (larger) female group. A small number of horn cores were recovered, but because of fragmentation it was not possible to distinguish the sexes of the animals that they derived from.

Sheep/goat. Similarly, preservation and low frequency of remains precluded the examination of horn cores to determine sex. A number of skull fragments, however, suggested that not all sheep/goat were horned, while some showed the beginnings of horns.

Pig. From the canines, five males and three females were identified revealing a slightly higher number of boars than sows.

Equid. Horse canines exhibit sexual dimorphism: presence is generally considered to be indicative of maleness. Three horse canines were identified, two rights and one left, demonstrating at least two males.

Pathologies/abnormalities

Only limited evidence for pathologies and abnormalities was discovered. This may not be an accurate representation of these conditions because not all illnesses are severe enough to affect the skeletal record.

Cattle. Pathological changes are age-related and given the generally higher age of the cattle some pathologies are expected, although only 31 specimens produced evidence. The majority take the form of articular surface lesions, mainly on the long bones, and present as Baker & Brothwell (1980, 110) Type 1 lesions, otherwise known as osteochondrosis (Ward 2009). The other abundant pathology is exostosis found around articular surfaces or shafts; this can be age-related and in some cases presents as osteoarthritis. Areas of reactive bone growth were also noted on a calcaneus, which could be due to wither irritation of the periosteum (layer of tissue in contact with the bone), injury or the infection of this area. Overall, the small amount of pathologies does not indicate that the stock suffered from any major diseases.

Sheep/goat. Only one sheep/goat bone showed pathological change: an abscess in the mandible at the point of the M1, causing the loss of the tooth and changes in the bone around the point.

Equid. Lesions on articular surfaces, similar to that of Type 1 (Baker & Brothwell 1980, 110), were noted on a radius, metatarsal, humerus and scapula, although most appear to have healed over, leaving only faint traces. There was also a case of exostosis noted on the distal end of a metacarpal, potentially a reaction to use rather than a discernible pathology.

Pig. No pathologies or abnormalities were noted.

Other mammals

Deer comprise only 4–5% of the identified bones, red, roe and fallow deer being represented. The majority of the specimens are roe deer (Fig. 125), although the group includes a large number of bones that appear to originate from a single juvenile specimen. Red deer are the second most numerous and are the only deer to exhibit signs of butchery, consisting mainly of cut marks.

Canids. Dog was present in almost every part of the site (Table 42), but the main concentrations were in AB II and the Iron Age settlement. The former seems to have contained the burial of a relatively complete dog, and although it is missing most of its skull, both mandibles are present. A similar deposit was also found, but with fewer bones. The two collections are assumed to belong to the same animal as they were recovered together. Site L contained a number of articulated remains: a juvenile dog, a set of articulating phalanges, a set of limb bones and two complete articulating skeletons, one missing a skull.

Shoulder heights were calculated from bones within four articulating groups, and an average height estimated for each animal. The results from separate groups seem to show the presence of two separate breeds, one smaller one, potentially a house or lap dog (Wh=35.8 cm), and another, much larger one (Wh=46.4–51.6 cm), possibly a hunting dog. Similar differences were noted by Harcourt (1974).

Fox. Two sets of articulating remains were recovered. A well-preserved animal came from (Roman) Pit XX (the top of Layer 8): the skull and limb bones were complete but it was missing some metapodials and caudal vertebrae. A number of ribs were fractured towards the proximal end but had healed. An ulna was also found to have a non-union break at its distal end. The second group was found in AB II and comprises a collection of limbs, vertebrae and skull fragments. The measurements from the limbs are fairly close, suggesting that these remains originated from the same animal.

Cat. The only evidence was a collection of kitten remains from AB II, along with a single adult humerus and a small number of metapodials. The juveniles were mainly represented by skull remains, with few limb bones surviving.

Lagomorphs. Evidence was found throughout the site, the majority identified as rabbit, while three specimens were found to be hare. As a result of the overall condition of the remains they could represent modern intrusions to the assemblage, especially given the site's position in woodland, although one specimen has knife cuts which may indicate that it was butchered during the Roman period. The uncertainty as to when rabbits were introduced into Britain makes the interpretation of such remains problematic (Yaldon 1999, 159).

Rodents. The evidence comes primarily from the Main House and the Iron Age settlement, with a few remains from AB II (the evidence is not included on Fig. 119 because the majority of it comes from a single deposit within the Iron Age settlement which greatly distorts the figures). Most the evidence came from the chalk fill at the base of Pit XVII and comprises 17 voles and three shrews, totalling 192 of the overall 253 remains (76%). Given the differing states of fusion on the remains and the description of the deposit this concentration is most likely a later intrusion, perhaps representing a nest that collapsed, trapping the voles.

Birds

Birds are poorly represented, especially in terms of the major species (Fig. 126). The majority of the remains could not be identified due to size or fragmentation. The most common species are domestic fowl (over 35%), which closely resemble bantams in size. It is known that domestic fowl were imported into Britain for food and were fairly small (Serjeantson 2009, 279–80). The other species include pheasant, wild duck, wood pigeon and woodcock.

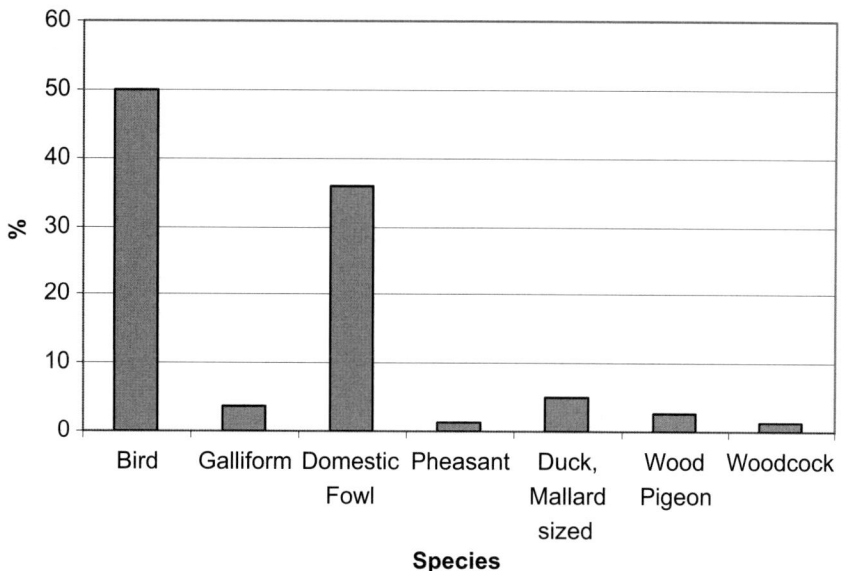

Fig 126   Distribution of different bird species found as percentage of total bird NISP

Fish and amphibians

The recovery methods probably explain why so few fish and amphibians were recovered (Table 42). No conclusions can be drawn.

Discussion

The discussion will interpret the evidence and also place it in context by assessing it against other local sites. It will look firstly at the Iron Age settlement and will draw on sites in the Somborne Valley and the Andover area, including examples investigated by the Danebury Environs Project (hereafter DEP), as comparative evidence. The majority of the section discusses the Roman villa and for comparison sites excavated as part of the Danebury Environs Roman Project (hereafter DERP) will be cited. Roman Sparsholt will also be compared to Winchester to check for contacts between the villa and its closest urban centre. Finally, an intra-site analysis will examine differences between the villa's buildings, which may yield information on the use of individual structures, or parts of structures.

The Iron Age settlement

The analysis of the Iron Age settlement affords an insight into the species reared and practices followed before the Roman occupation. Only a small quantity of bone was recovered from the Iron Age features (NISP=882), of which almost 200 are from the vole nest in Pit XVII and can be discounted. The farming system was focused on sheep/goat and cattle, with pig of lesser importance. It is a pattern mirrored at all the Iron Age settlements within the region; see for example the occupation sites investigated as part of DEP, such as New Buildings, Houghton Down and Suddern Farm (Hamilton 2000, 63–8).

At Sparsholt, sheep/goat were more numerous than cattle; this contrasts with the general findings from Hampshire, which show that more cattle were reared than sheep/goat (King 1991, 16). At New Buildings the proportion of cattle appears unusually high and might reflect seasonal activities as opposed to indicating a 'different economy' (Hamilton 2000, 63). The situation at Suddern Farm is complicated by the fact that it is unknown how representative the data is of the settlement, but it is considered to have a high proportion of cattle (*ibid*, 67-69). At Somborne Park Farm (Little Somborne) just over 80% of the identified remains are cattle (Harding 2010, 16), and the settlement at Houghton Down also records a relatively high proportion of cattle (Hamilton 2000, 66-67). At Little Somborne roughly similar numbers of cattle and sheep/goat bones were recovered (Neal 1980, 124) and the same is true of Knights Enham (Andover): cattle accounts for 48% and sheep/goat 52%. The greater quantity of sheep/goat at Sparsholt may simply reflect the fact that individually they do not produce the same amount of meat as cattle. Only a dramatic difference in the NISP would indicate a favouring of sheep/goat over cattle and this is not the case. Alternatively, the lower number of cattle could be explained by the apparent lack of a nearby water source (p.2), or that it was a relatively low status site which contrasts with the settlements at Houghton Down and Suddern Farm, for example, where the higher proportions of cattle may reflect a higher status (Hamilton 2000, 67-68). A small amount of pig was found at Sparsholt and this is consistent with the two Somborne sites mentioned above.

Lack of information means that a detailed analysis of husbandry practices at Sparsholt is not possible, although only adult cattle were present which demonstrates that breeding did not take place on site or at a location nearby. This is similar to Nettlebank Copse where the majority of cattle were mature. At

Little Somborne, although older animals predominated, there were some younger individuals, which is again the case at Somborne Park Farm. Moreover, the remains of neonatal cattle demonstrate that birthing took place at Houghton Down and Suddern Farm. The presence of unfused and juvenile sheep/goat bones indicates the rearing of sheep/goat at Sparsholt, while evidence for neonatal lambs was also recovered from Nettlebank Copse, Houghton Down and Suddern Farm, which contrasts with Little Somborne where the sheep/goat were mainly of adult age and New Buildings where no remains of neonatal lambs were found.

Iron Age storage pits are often associated with ritual behaviour, for example the 'special' deposits of animal and/or human remains in the basal fills after they were no longer used for the storage of grain (Hill 1995). Special deposits involving various species of animal were encountered at the DEP sites of New Buildings, Nettlebank Copse, Suddern Farm and Houghton Down. At Sparsholt an example was found in Pit XIII: the left hind leg of a cow had been deposited with the articulating bones from the tibia, foot and femur lying in line. Only the patella, one digit and a second phalanx were missing. Based on the epiphyseal fusion, the remains belonged to a cow of around 2–3 years of age, which would have stood at c. 1.03m tall. Another example of ritual deposition was that of a juvenile roe deer (Pit XIII). Apart from a fragment of mandible, it was missing its skull; perhaps it had been removed as part of the ritual, although the fragile and friable nature of juvenile skulls could explain its omission.

Iron Age/Roman comparison

To compare the Iron Age and Roman evidence the species were calculated in tri-plot form and assessed against the results obtained by King (1984; 1989) (Fig. 127). Various categories of Roman sites are displayed and both Iron Age and Roman Sparsholt are indicated. As already described, in the Iron Age there is a higher amount of sheep/goat/goat compared to cattle. In the Roman period cattle and sheep/goat/goat are roughly equal with fairly low amounts of pig which distinguishes Sparsholt from the other Roman sites and places it in the un-Romanised settlement category. This is also found when Sparsholt is compared to the raw data from King's study (Fig. 128): the Roman distribution falls below the general grouping.

There is no difference between the size of the Iron Age and Roman cattle at Sparsholt, which suggests that the Roman period did not result in improved husbandry practices or the importation of new breeding stock. At Houghton Down the cattle became larger during the Roman period (Hammon 2008, 78), possibly reflecting changes to husbandry, stock or perhaps the conditions in which the animals were kept (Applebaum 2002, 517).

The Roman villa

In general, a typical farming system based around cattle and sheep/goat/goat with lesser numbers of pig is observed at Roman Sparsholt. A very similar situation is found at other rural sites in Hampshire, for example at Monk Sherborne (Ingrem 2005, 102–05), Knights Enham and the DERP sites of Dunkirt Barn, Houghton Down, Thruxton, Grateley South and Fullerton (Hammon 2008, 77–9). At Sparsholt sheep/goat/goat slightly outnumber cattle but the latter provided more meat and would probably have made a greater contribution to the diet. Sheep/goat also dominated the assemblages at Houghton Down, Thruxton and Fullerton. The chalk downland on which Sparsholt was sited would have suited sheep/goat, while the lack of a ready supply of water may have discouraged the keeping of large herds of cattle.

Both cattle and sheep/goat were multi-purpose animals and along with their meat, wool/hide and dairy products could have been the main surpluses as evidenced from the kill off patterns. In addition, manure from sheep/goat was an important fertiliser (Hammon 2008, 77).

The remains of neonatal and foetal cattle, sheep/goat and pig were recovered at all the above mentioned DERP settlements, indicating that breeding took place on site or close by. At Sparsholt the foetal and juvenile animals indicate that a small flock of sheep/goat were bred and maintained, with most killed at around 2–4 years of age, that is, when the meat is both plentiful and easier to process (Bourdillon 1988 180). The age at which the sheep/goats were slaughtered at Grateley South and Fullerton also reveals that the majority of sheep/goats were reared for meat. At Sparsholt, however, the data shows that some survived into older age revealing a demand for secondary products, such as wool and milk. Britain's export of wool is mentioned in late Roman documents and King (1991, 18) has argued that this product may have been one of the key commodities produced by rural estates. A few sheep/goats appear to have been kept until they were old, possibly as breeding rams or castrates to provide fleece. The sheep/goats show a greater range of sizes and appear significantly larger on average than the Winchester animals (Maltby 2010, 138); they may be the larger hornless breed of sheep/goat noted in Hampshire in the later Roman period (Maltby 1994, 94), a suggestion supported by the relative lack of horn cores, or skulls exhibiting horns.

Only a small amount of evidence for foetal and juvenile cattle was recovered, which suggests that generally breeding was not taking place at Sparsholt. Compared to urban centres, such as Winchester, villas tend to produce a greater quantity of calf remains (Maltby 2010, 112–14). Although the bones of immature animals are more fragile and easily destroyed, some evidence would be expected. A preference for older animals is also supported by the evidence from sexing: a greater proportion of females are noted, while only a few bulls may have been kept

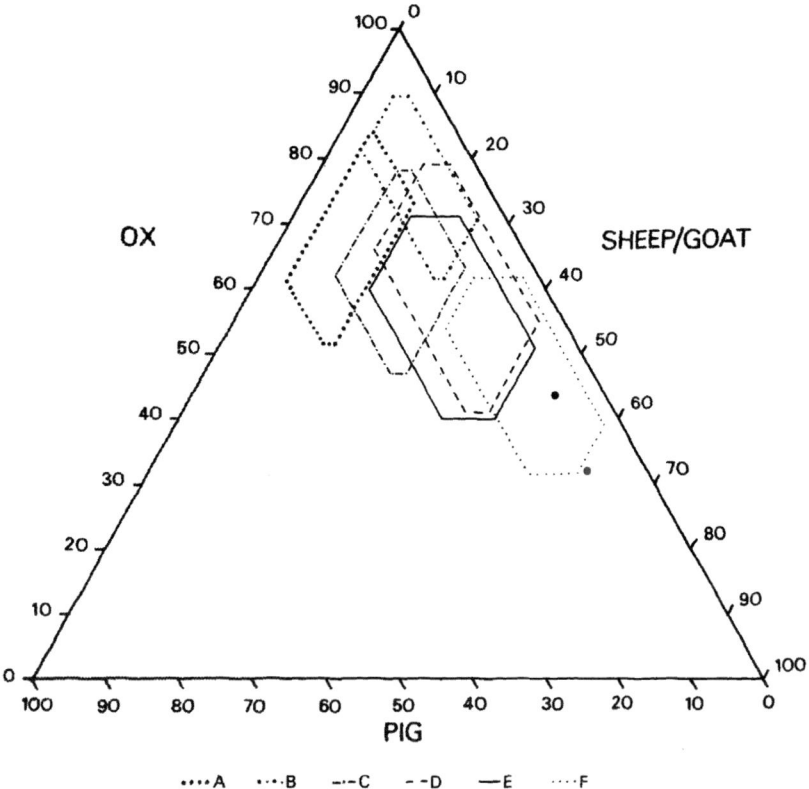

Fig 127 Tri-plot (ox, sheep/goat, pig) by King (1989) with Roman and Iron Age Sparsholt (grey spot). Key; A: Auxiliary sites; C: *coloniae* and Romanised towns; D: *vici* and Romanised settlements, E: villas; F: un-Romanised settlements

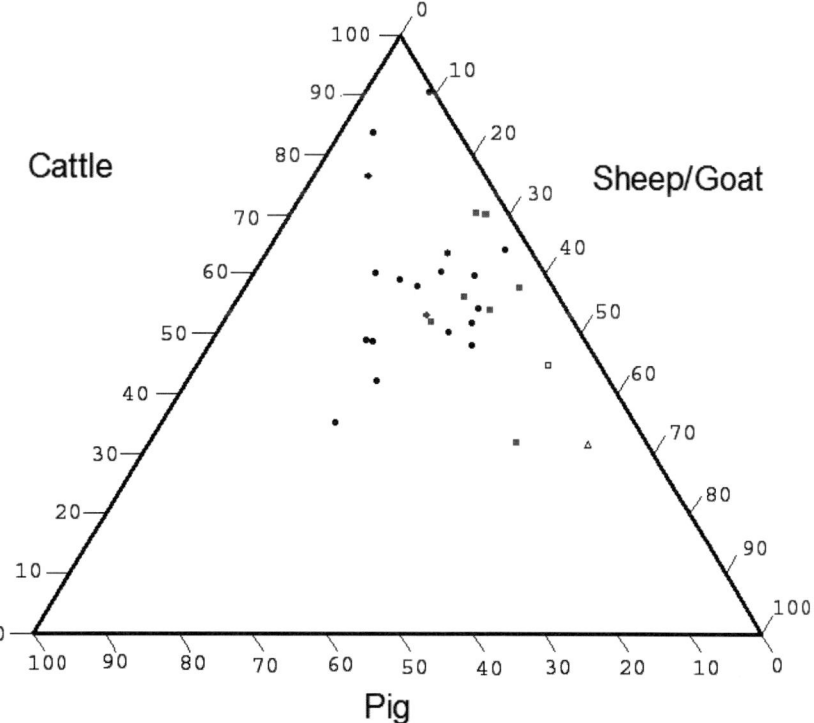

Fig 128 Tri-plot (ox, sheep/goat, pig) with King (1984) original data: Key; Roman Sparsholt (square); Iron Age Sparsholt (triangle); early Roman villas, 1st–2nd century AD (grey squares); late Roman villas, 3rd–4th century AD (black dots)

for breeding and traction. There was little variation in the size of the Sparsholt cattle, but the average size was almost identical to the cattle found in Winchester (*ibid*, 115), which may suggest that only the older animals used for traction were kept and any animals that were bred were traded. It was common to keep some elderly cattle in the Roman period; they would have been used for milk and traction rather than being a source of meat (Grant 2006, 381). Animals that were no longer useful for traction could have been consumed along with meat imported into the site. At Dunkirt Barn the cattle were reaching old age and were probably utilised for traction. Similar findings come from Houghton Down, Grateley South and Fullerton, although for the latter two the evidence is limited.

The next most numerous species at Sparsholt was pig. None of the pigs survived beyond their second year indicating that they were killed for their meat, i.e. when they had reached their maximum body weight, which is similar to the evidence from Dunkirt Barn, Grateley South and Fullerton. At Sparsholt, pigs were scarce which is interesting as a marginal increase in this species is taken to be a sign that a site was becoming more Romanised (King 1989, 54). Winchester, which must have been an important centre of Roman culture, was only 6 km away but does not appear to have influenced the diet of the Sparsholt residents. The lack of very young/foetal remains indicates that pigs were not being bred on site. According to Maltby (1994, 98; 2010,143) the absence of a rural pig-breeding tradition indicates that they were bred in the towns, or that urban sites acted as a focal point for trading smoked or salted joints imported from the continent. The recovery of meat bones, mainly the shoulder joint, trotters and skulls, supports the idea that these parts were brought to the site, perhaps having been acquired in Winchester.

The distribution of horse throughout the site appears to be *ad hoc*. There are no horse burials and from the butchery evidence it can be assumed that horse was eaten on site. This is a practice noted at Rudston villa (Chaplin & Barneston 1980), where it is believed that horses that had outlived their usefulness were consumed. At Sparsholt articular lesions on a number of the joints are likely to have caused lameness and could have led to the animals being slaughtered. The Winchester horses record a similar height to the Sparsholt examples, although more of a range is present.

The remains of red deer may have originated from hunting, which was a popular activity during the Roman period and it is possible that the larger of the Sparsholt dogs could have been used in the chase (Harcourt 1974, 168). The deer remains exhibit evidence of butchery, suggesting that they were consumed; deer were also found at Grateley South and Fullerton.

A small number of fish bones were collected, but no definitive conclusions about the species can be made. Oyster shells were, however, mentioned in the site books and Johnston (1972) suggests that fish could also have been imported to the villa from the rivers and coast.

Intra-site analysis

All the individual buildings conform to the general species pattern for the villa: the figures fluctuate slightly, but cattle and sheep/goat dominate. The other species exhibit greater variation, perhaps suggesting different functions for the individual buildings, or at least parts of them. If meat processing was common, and was accompanied by regular cleaning, then the evidence may reflect only the final phases of occupation, however.

The Aisled Building

This building produced the greatest quantity of faunal remains and there is evidence for how space within the structure was organised. The remains from the west end exhibit a similar frequency of cattle and sheep/goat meat bones. A grouping of certain joints, mainly the shoulder and lower hind limb, was also found. Cattle produced more metatarsals than tibiae, while in sheep/goat the reverse was recorded, a pattern that could have resulted from more cattle metapodials being used as stock bones or for gelatine extraction, while sheep/goat tibiae derived from butchery and related extraction processes. Both animals also recorded similar, but small, proportions of foot bones and phalanges. Meat bones and oyster shells were trodden into the floor and in fact many of the specimens may have originated from this floor, along with a large number of unidentified fragments (n=1250). This end of the building was probably domestic involved in the preparation of food – an idea supported by the ovens and hearth in Room 19.

A greater quantity of animal remains was found in the east end. Overall there is a similar pattern to the west end, although more body parts are represented. For example, the sheep/goat produced more radii and skull fragments, but fewer metapodials and carpals/tarsals, although a large number of 1st phalanges are present. The cattle remains are broadly comparable, although more metatarsals and phalanges are recorded. The presence of a significant amount of butchered remains is a probable indication that this end of the building was used for the preparation of meat, a theory supported by the cooking vessels and vessels associated with culinary activities found in this part of the building. The area could also have also been used to store dried meat as suggested by the presence of large storage vessels. Moreover, the area recorded over twice the amount of gnawed bone compared with the western end of the building. Remains from processing were either fed to domestic dogs or scavengers had access to refuse, perhaps from a midden that had been located outside the building.

The Main House

This structure exhibits the same species pattern as the Aisled Building, although with a slightly higher proportion of cattle. Pig and equine bones were present, plus wild deer (roe, fallow and red) and wood pigeon, mallard and domestic fowl. A large number of rodents are recorded, including a collection of vole remains from a feature in Room 6 and a group of (house) mouse bones from an unspecified location. The mice could have nested in the building, or were attracted to the midden located outside Room 2. Evidence of gnawing is again present, possibly suggesting scavengers raiding this midden or pets being fed scraps from the table. Most of the bones from the Main House could have derived from the midden, but without detailed contextual information this cannot be proven.

Compared to the Aisled Building, cattle remains show a higher frequency of meat-bearing joints, mainly the pelvis/femur and scapula/humerus, with very few non-meat bones of the phalanges, lower limbs and metapodials. There are also a large proportion of mandible fragments, which could be evidence of a specific meal, for example a jaw being served with cheek meat still attached or the bone being used in a soup; this may reflect a difference in status between the occupants of the Main House and the other buildings. A range of sheep/goat bones are present: radii, pelves and first phalanges are particularly abundant, while tibia and lower hind limbs outnumber femurs. The high proportion of phalanges suggests that they may have been attached to the metapodials before being cooked and then disposed of. The lack of any carpal or tarsal bones, including the astragalus and calcaneus, may be a further indication that limbs were being divided before arriving at the Main House. Alternatively, these small bones may have been overlooked by the excavators, although they were recovered from other areas of the site.

The Barn

A small number of animal remains were recovered from the Barn, consisting mainly of juvenile sheep/goat, various cattle bones and a large quantity of maxillary and mandibular sheep/goat teeth. The evidence indicates that little meat processing took place in the building, or that it was regularly cleaned. The teeth could have derived from the stabling of sheep/goats. Alternatively, the material could have come from a period of sporadic dumping during the later phases of the site, perhaps when the building's use changed as evidenced by the blocking off of the main room (Room 21).

The Hall

The hall produced few remains. Sheep/goat/goat and cattle were again the most abundant animals. Horse ranked third and there is very little evidence for any other species, although some fallow and red deer remains were collected, including a number of red deer antlers: two appear to have been collected, while the third was a sawn-off tine point. Cattle are largely represented by non-meat bones: a few tibiae, metapodials and mandibles. Scapulae are fairly abundant, but this is partly due to their high fragmentation.

The sheep/goat remains are represented by large numbers of scapula, mandible and lower hind limb bones that are relatively more complete than the corresponding remains from cattle. The evidence demonstrates a preference for shoulder and shin joints, in addition to the possibility of cheeks being consumed. An abundance of horse remains was recovered, but consists mainly of mandibular and maxillary teeth.

Roman features associated with the Iron Age settlement

The Iron Age site produced a scattering of Roman features and of these Pit XX and Ditch II provided a wealth of information. The former was a cess pit that probably served AB I and was infilled with rubble after the building was demolished. It can therefore provide important information about animal husbandry during the earliest phase of the villa and it is interesting that although the pit produced evidence for a large range of species, sheep/goat dominate followed by cattle. Butchery marks on cattle and sheep/goat bones demonstrate that the feature was used to dispose of waste from the preparation of food. Sheep/goats are also represented by non-meat bones, which suggests that these remains could have originated as waste after cooking. Pig shows a similar pattern, with a small number of metatarsals and phalanges, perhaps evidence of the occasional use of trotters.

A large number of canid remains were recovered. Dog is represented by a number of fragmentary limb bones, the remains of a puppy from the lower layers and two adult skulls. A complete fox had been deposited in the top layer of cess. This could have been a wild animal that was caught and deposited shortly before the pit was sealed. It may have been skinned; there is no evidence of butchery, but if the procedure was done carefully it would leave little or no trace. Alternatively, the animal may have been a pet. The broken, but healed, ribs and the unusual healed break in the ulna, perhaps caused by disciplining the animal, are common injuries recorded on domestic dogs from this time (MacKinnon 2010, 305–6). Moreover, the dentition supports the view that the fox was a pet which lived to an advanced age: a number of teeth are missing (M2 and M3 and several incisors) and the fact that alveolar reabsorption is present suggests that this happened during its life. In addition, the upper and lower M1s show signs of very heavy wear, also indicating an advanced age. Wild foxes seem only to live to around 5 years in the wild, though in captivity they are known to live to around 10 years or more (Southern 1964, 356), indicating that this particular fox could have been kept by the occupants of the villa.

Other than domestic fowl, the pit produced a wild mallard bone and an intact woodcock skull, birds that are known to have been eaten during the Roman period (Cool 2006, 115) and could have come from the local environment.

Ditch II produced fewer remains than Pit XX, but showed a difference in the evidence: mainly cattle and cattle/equid-sized bones consisting largely of hind limbs, skull and mandibles, similar to the evidence for sheep/goats. Limited evidence for butchery was noted, but compared to Pit XX there was more gnawing. Scavengers could easily have got access to such waste if it had been dumped into an open ditch.

Ditch IV and Pit V did not provide as many bones as the other features mentioned so will not be discussed in great detail. A few cattle and sheep/goat bones were recovered, comprising of a number of long bone, skull, mandible and metapodial fragments, indicating an *ad hoc* use of the features to dispose of probable food waste.

Conclusion

On the basis of the faunal remains, Roman Sparsholt was a typical rural site having much in common with surrounding settlements. All the major domesticates were exploited, although it seems limited breeding took place and it is probably only sheep/goat that were bred. In common with several of the DERP sites there may have been a reliance on sheep/goat, but cattle were probably more important to the diet. A small range of wild species were also present and it is interesting that along with dogs, a fox may also have been kept.

Winchester was only 6 km away and must have had a major impact on agricultural production within its hinterland with rural producer sites, such as Sparsholt and also Owlesbury, 7 km distant, modifying their practices in order to supply this urban market (Hammon 2008, 97). The cattle that Winchester consumed were adult animals of between 4 and 7 years that had not been used for milk or traction (*ibid*). The limited evidence from Sparsholt indicates a slight bias towards older males and it is just possible that it was supplying Winchester with younger female cows.

Not only would Winchester have administered the surrounding countryside, it would also have been a centre of Roman culture. The town did not appear to have had a significant influence on the Sparsholt diet, however. Only slight differences are found between the Iron Age and Roman phases. Sheep/goat remained an important species, while pig, which is taken as an indicator of Romanisation, was not at all prevalent. Certainly a pork-based diet, as found in rich and highly Romanised sites, such as Fishbourne Palace (West Sussex) (Hammon 2008, 85), was not adopted. Another indicator of status is domestic fowl (*ibid*, 88), but these remains were also scarce suggesting that Sparsholt was not a particularly wealthy establishment and was unable to acquire exotic species.

References

Adkins, L & Adkins, R 1986 *Under the Sludge, Beddington Roman Villa, Beddington*, Carshalton & Wallington Archaeological Society.

AHBR, Archaeology and Historic Buildings Record Search, http://historicenvironment.hants.gov.uk/AHBSearch.aspx.

Al Qahtani, S J 2008 *Atlas of Tooth Development and Eruption*, London.

Aldsworth, F G 1983 Excavations at Bignor Roman villa, *Sussex Archaeological Collections* **121**, 203–8.

Allen, D 2002 Roman window glass, in Aldhouse-Green, M & Webster, P (eds) *Artefacts and Archaeology, aspects of the Celtic and Roman World*, 102–11.

Allen, D forthcoming Colliton Park glass.

Anderson, A S 2001 Lead objects, in Fitzpatrick *et al.* 2001, 117–18.

Applebaum, S 2002 Animal husbandry, in Wacher, J S (ed.), *The Roman World*, Padstow, 504–26.

Aufderheide, A C & Rodriguez-Martin, C 2006 *The Cambridge Encyclopaedia of Human Palaeopathology*, Cambridge.

Baker, J & Brothwell, D 1980 *Animal Diseases in Archaeology*, London.

Beeson, P B, McDermott, W & Wyngaarden, J B 1979 *Cecil Textbook of Medicine*, 15th edition, Philadelphia.

Berrizbeitia, E L 1989 Sex determination with the head of the radius, *J Forensic Sci* **34**, 1206–13.

Biddulph, E 2006 What's in a name? Graffiti on funerary pottery, *Britannia* **37**, 355–9.

Black, E 2008 Pagan religion in rural south-east Britain: contexts, deities and belief, in Rudling, D (ed.), *Ritual Landscapes of Roman south-east Britain*, Oxford.

Boessneck, J 1969 Osteological differences between sheep (*Ovis Aries* Linné) and goat (*Capra Hircus* Linné), in Brothwell, D R & Higgs, E S (eds) *Science in Archaeology: a survey of progress and research* (2nd edn). New York, 331–58.

Boismier, W 1994 *The Evolution of the Hampshire Landscape. Archaeological Resources on County Council Owned Farm and Recreation Land*, Hampshire County Planning Department Archaeological Report **2**.

Boon, G C 2000 The objects of lead, in Fulford, M & Timby, J *Late Iron Age and Roman Silchester, Excavations on the Site of the Forum-Basilica 1977, 1980–86*, Britannia Monogr Series **15**, London, 357–9.

Booth, P 1991 Intersite comparisons between pottery assemblages in Roman Warwickshire: ceramic indicators of site status, *J Roman Pottery Studies* **4**, 1–10.

Bourdillon, J 1988 Countryside and town: the animal resources of Saxon Southampton, in Brooke, D (ed) *Anglo-Saxon Settlements.* Oxford, 177–95.

Bowen, H C & Fowler, P J 1966 Romano-British rural settlements in Dorset and Wiltshire, in Thomas, A C (ed.), *Rural Settlement in Roman Britain*, CBA Res Rep 7, London, 43–67.

Brodribb, G 1987 *Roman Brick and Tile*, Gloucester.

Brothwell, D 1981 *Digging Up Bones: the excavation, treatment and study of human skeletal remains*, Oxford.

Buikstra, J E & Ubelaker, D H 1994 *Standards for Data Collection from Human Skeletal Remains*, Fayetteville, Arkansas.

Butcher, S A 2001 The brooches, in Fitzpatrick *et al.* 2001, 41–69.

Chaplin, R E & Barneston, L P 1980 Animal bones, in Stead, I M (ed.), *Rudston Roman Villa*, Leeds, 149–55.

Chatwin, C P 1948 *British Regional Geology, The Hampshire Basin*, HMSO.

Cocks, A H 1920–21 A Romano-British homestead in the Hambleben Valley, Bucks, *Archaeologia* **71**, 141–198.

Cohen, A & Serjeantson, D 1996 *A Manual for the Identification of Bird Bones from Archaeological Sites*, London.

Cole, G H 1988 A Romano-British bath house at Wyck near Alton, Hampshire, *Proc Hampshire Field Club* **44**, 25–39.

Collingwood, R G & Richmond, I A 1969 *The Archaeology of Roman Britain*, London.

Collis, J R 1977 A Roman burial from Crab Wood, Sparsholt, Hants, *Proc Hants Fld Club Archaeol Soc* **33**, 69–72.

Cooke, N, McKinley, J I & Seager Smith, R H in prep *A Roman Settlement to the South-east of Amesbury and its Cemeteries: volume I the settlement*, Wessex Archaeology monogr.

Cool, H E M 1990 The problem of 3rd century drinking vessels in Britain, *Annales de 11e Congrès de l'Association Internationale pour l'Histoire du Verre* (Basel 1988), 167–75.

Cool, H E M 2006 *Eating and Drinking in Roman Britain,* Cambridge.

Cosh, S R 2012 The Central Southern Group, *Mosaic* **39**, 7–17.

Cosh, S R & Neal, D S 2005 *Roman Mosaics of Britain. Vol II South-West Britain,* Soc. Antiq. Monogr.

Cotton, M A & Gathercole, P W 1958 *Excavations at Clausentum, Southampton, 1951–54,* Ministry of Works Archaeological Reports 2, London.

Courtney, F M & Trudgill, S T 1984 *The Soil,* London.

Crawford, O G S & Keiller, A 1928 *Wessex from the Air,* Oxford.

Crummy, N 1983 *The Roman Small Finds from Excavation in Colchester 1971–79,* Colchester Archaeological Report 2, Colchester.

Cunliffe, B W 1964 *Winchester Excavations, 1949–60, Vol. 1.* Winchester.

Cunliffe, B W 1971 *Excavations at Fishbourne 1961–1969, Volume 1: the site,* Soc Antiq Res Rep 26, London.

Cunliffe, B W 1975 *Excavations at Portchester Castle, Volume 1: Roman,* Soc Antiq Res Rep 32, London.

Cunliffe, B W 1983 *Danebury: anatomy of an Iron Age hillfort,* Frome and London.

Cunliffe, B W 1984 *Danebury: an Iron Age hillfort in Hampshire volume 2: the finds,* CBA Res Rep **52b**, London.

Cunliffe, B W 1987 *Hengistbury Head, Dorset, Volume 1,* OUCA Monogr **13**, 205–321.

Cunliffe, B W 1992 Pits, preconceptions and propitiation in the British Iron Age, *Oxford J Archaeol* **11.1**, 69–83.

Cunliffe, B W 1993 *Wessex to AD 1000,* London.

Cunliffe, B W 2000 *The Danebury Environs Project. The Prehistory of a Wessex Landscape. Volume 1: introduction,* English Heritage and OUCA Monogr **48**, Oxford.

Cunliffe, B W 2005 *Iron Age Communities in Britain,* Abingdon.

Cunliffe, B W 2008 *The Danebury Environs Roman Programme. A Wessex Landscape during the Roman Era, Vol. 1 Overview,* English Heritage and OUCA Monogr **70**, Oxford.

Cunliffe, B W & Brown, L 1987 The Later Prehistoric and Roman Pottery, in Cunliffe, 1987, 205–321.

Cunliffe, B W & Poole, C 2008a *The Danebury Environs Roman Programme: a Wessex landscape during the Roman Era, vol 2 – part 1, Houghton Down, Longstock, Hants, 1997,* English Heritage and Oxford University School of Archaeology, Monogr **71**, Oxford.

Cunliffe, B W & Poole, C 2008b *The Danebury Environs Roman Programme: a Wessex landscape during the Roman Era, vol 2 – part 2, Grateley South, Grateley, Hants, 1998 and 1999,* English Heritage and Oxford University School of Archaeology, Monogr **71**, Oxford.

Cunliffe, B W & Poole, C 2008c *The Danebury Environs Roman Programme: a Wessex landscape during the Roman Era, vol 2 – part 7, Dunkirt Barn, Abbotts Ann, Hants, 2006 and 2007,* English Heritage and Oxford University School of Archaeology, Monogr **71**, Oxford.

Cunliffe, B W & Poole, C 2008d *The Danebury Environs Roman Programme: a Wessex landscape during the Roman Era, vol 2 – part 3, Fullerton, Hants, 2000 and 2001,* Oxford, English Heritage and Oxford University School of Archaeology, Monogr **71**, Oxford.

Cunliffe, B W & Poole, C 2008e *The Danebury Environs Roman Programme: a Wessex landscape during the Roman Era, vol 2 – part 4, Thruxton, Hants 2002,* English Heritage and Oxford University School of Archaeology, Monogr **71**, Oxford.

Dark, K & Dark, P 1997 *The Landscape of Roman Britain,* London.

Darling, M J 1994 Guidelines for the Archiving of Roman Pottery, Study Group for Roman Pottery Guideline Advisory Document **1**.

Davies, S M 1981 Excavations at Old Down Farm, Andover, part II: prehistoric and Roman, *Proc Hants Fld Club Archaeol Soc* **37**, 81–163.

Davey, N 1945 Examination of the materials of construction from the Park Street villa, appendix to O'Neil, H E The Roman villa at Park Street, near St Albans, Herts: report on the Excavations 1943–45, *Archaeol J* **CII**, 21.

Davey, N 1961 *A History of Building Materials,* London.

Davey, N & Ling, R 1982 *Wall Painting in Roman Britain,* Britannia Monogr Ser **3**, Norwich.

Davis, S J M 1992 *A Rapid Method for Recording Information about Mammal Bones from Archaeological Sites,* Ancient Monuments Laboratory Report **19/92**.

Dicks, J 2009 The Rowlands Castle Romano-British pottery industry, *J Roman Pottery Studies* **14**, 51.

Dicks, J 2010 *Warblington Romano-British Villa.*

Dittrick, J & Suchey, J M 1986 Sex determination of prehistoric central California skeletal remains using discriminant analysis of the femur and humerus, *American J Physical Anthropology* **70**, 3–9.

Down, A 1979 *Chichester Excavations 4: the Roman villas at Chilgrove and Up Marden,* Chichester.

Down, A 1989 *Chichester Excavations 6,* Chichester.

Duday, H 2009 *The Archaeology of the Dead: lectures in archaeothanatology,* Oxford.

Durham, E 2008 Reports on the Roman pottery, ceramic building material and small finds, in Cunliffe & Poole 2008d.

Eisenmann, V 1981 Étude des Dents Jugales Inférieures des Equus (Mammalia, Perissodactyla) actuels et Fossiles, *Palæovertebrata* **10** (3–4), 130–226.

Esmonde Cleary, A S 2012 *Chedworth Roman Villa,* Stroud.

Evans, J 1987 Graffiti and the evidence of literacy and pottery use in Roman Britain, *Archaeol J* **144**, 191–204.

Fasham, P J 1985 *The Prehistoric Settlement at Winnall Down, Winchester*, Hants Fld Club Archaeol Soc Monog **2**, Gloucester

Fasham, P J 1987 *A 'Banjo' Enclosure in Micheldever Wood, Hampshire*, Hants Fld Club Archaeol Soc Monog **5**, Gloucester.

Fasham, P J, Farwell, D E & Whinney, R J B 1989 *The Archaeological Site at Easton Lane, Winchester*, Hants Fld Club Archaeol Soc Monogr **6**, Gloucester.

Fazekas, I G & Kóza, F 1978 *Forensic Fetal Osteology*, Budapest.

Fitzpatrick, A F, Wacher, J & Anderson, A S 2001 *The Romano-British 'Small Town' at Wanborough, Wiltshire*, Britannia Monogr Series **19**, London.

Foot, R in archive *Roman Ceramic Building Material from The Brooks*, Winchester Museums Service Archive, site BR.

Frere, S S 1982 The Bignor Roman Villa, *Britannia* **13**, 135–95.

Fulford, M G 1975 *New Forest Roman Pottery*, BAR Brit Ser **17**, London.

Gerrard, J 2010 Finding the fifth century: a late fourth- and early fifth-century pottery fabric from south-east Dorset, *Britannia* **41**, 293–312.

Gibson, A 2002 *Prehistoric Pottery in Britain and Ireland*, Stroud.

Gibson, C & Knight, S 2007 A middle Iron Age settlement at Weston Down Cottages, Weston Colley, near Winchester, Hampshire, *Proc Hants Fld Club Archaeol Soc* **62**, 1–34.

Godwin, G N 1924 Roman Antiquities at Sparsholt, *Hampshire Notes and Queries*, **5**, 75.

Going, C J 1987 *The Mansio and other Sites in the South-Eastern Sector of Caesaromagus: the Roman pottery*, CBA Res Rep **62**, London.

Goodburn, R 1984 The non-ferrous metal objects, in Frere, S *Verulamium Excavations III*, Oxford, 19–68.

Grant, A 1982 The use of tooth wear as a guide to the age of domestic ungulates, in Wilson, B, Grigson, C & Payne, S (eds), *Ageing and Sexing Animal Bones from Archaeological Sites*, BAR Brit Ser **109**, Oxford, 91–108.

Grant, A 2006 Domestic animals and their uses, in Todd, M (ed.), *A Companion to Roman Britain*, Oxford, 371–94.

Green, M J 1976 *The Religions of Civilian Roman Britain*, BAR Brit Ser **24**, Oxford.

Grinsell, L 1938–40 Hampshire barrows, parts 1–3, *Proc Hants Fld Club Archaeol Soc* **14** (1–3), 9–40, 195–230, 346–66.

Hadman, J 1978 Aisled buildings in Roman Britain, in Todd, M (ed.) *Studies in the Romano-British Villa*, Leicester, 187–96.

Hambleton, E 1999 *Animal Husbandry Regimes in Iron Age Britain. A Comparative Study of Faunal Assemblages from British Iron Age Sites*, BAR Brit Ser **282**, Oxford.

Hamilton, J 2000 Animal husbandry: the evidence from the animal bones, in Cunliffe 2000, 59–76.

Hammon, A 2008 Animal Husbandry: an overview of the evidence from the animal bones, in Cunliffe 2008, 74–100.

Harcourt, R A 1974 The dog in prehistoric and early historic Britain, *Journal of Archaeological Science* **1**, 151–76.

Harden, D B 1979 Glass vessels in Clarke, G *The Roman Cemetery at Lankhills. Winchester Stud 3: Pre-Roman and Roman Winchester*, Part 2, Oxford, 209–20.

Harden, D B, Painter, K S, Pinder-Wilson, R H & Tait, H 1968 *Masterpieces of Glass*, The British Museum.

Harden, D B, Hellenkemper, H, Painter, K & Whitehouse, D 1987 *Glass of the Caesars*, Milan.

Harding, P 2010 An Iron Age farmstead at Somborne Park Farm, Little Somborne, *Proc Hants Fld Club Archaeol Soc* **65**, 7–22.

Hartley, K 2012 Note on Sparsholt Mortaria, unpublished.

Hatch, F W, Rastall, R H & Greensmith, J T 1965 *Petrology of the Sedimentary Rocks* (4th edition), London.

Headworth, H G 1970 The selection of root constants for the calculation of actual evaporation and infiltration for chalk catchments, *J Instit Water Engineers* **24**, 431–46.

Henig, M & Booth, P 2000 *Roman Oxfordshire*, Stroud.

Hill, J D 1995 *Ritual and Rubbish in the Iron Age of Wessex: a study on the formation of a specific archaeological record*, BAR Brit Ser **242**, Oxford.

Hillson, S 1996 *Dental Anthropology*, Cambridge.

Holbrook, N & Bidwell, P 1991 *Roman Finds from Exeter*, Exeter Archaeological Reports **4**.

Hooley, A D 2001 Copper alloy and silver objects, in Fitzpatrick *et al.* 2001, 75–116.

Hooley, R 1928 Excavation of an early Iron Age Village on Worthy Down, Winchester, *Proc Hants Fld Club Archaeol Soc* **10**, Part 2, 178–92.

Hostetter, E & Howe, T N (eds) 1997 *The Romano-British Villa at Castle Copse, Great Bedwyn*, Indiana.

Idorn, G M 1959 *The History of Concrete Technology – Through a Microscope*, Beton-Tek, **25** (4), 119.

Ingrem, C 2005 Faunal remains, in Teague 2005, 102–115.

Isaac, A 2001 Iron objects, in Fitzpatrick *et al.* 2001, 121–39.

Isings, C 1957 *Roman Glass from Dated Finds*, Archaeologica Traiectina, Groningen.

Jacob, W H 1895 The Roman Structure at Westwood, Sparsholt, *Proc Hants Fld Club Archaeol Soc* **iii**, 201–05.

Johnston, D E 1965 The Roman villa at Sparsholt, *Proc Hants Fld Club Archaeol Soc* **23** (1964–66), 46–47.

Johnston, D E 1972 *The Sparsholt Roman Villa: summary of excavations 1965–1972*, University of Southampton.

Johnston, D E 1977 The central southern group of mosaicists, in Munby, J & Henig, M *Roman Life and Art in Britain*, BAR Brit Ser **41**(i), Oxford, 315–27.

Johnston, D E 1978 Villas of Hampshire and the Isle of Wight, in Todd, M (ed.) *Studies in the Romano-British Villa*, Leicester, 71–92.

Johnston, D E 1981 The Roman Villa, in Knowles, C (ed.) *A History of Sparsholt and Lainston*, Phillimore, 113–22.

Johnston, D E 2004 *Roman Villas*, Aylesbury.

Jones, G P 2011 Romano-British Pottery, in Powell, A B *An Iron Age Enclosure and Romano-British Features at High Post, near Salisbury*, Wessex Archaeology Monogr, 57–62.

Kiesewalter, L 1888 *Skelettmessungen an Pferden als Bietrag zur Theoretischen Beurteilungslehre des Pferdes*, University of Leipzig Dissertation.

King, A C 1984 Animal bones and the dietary identity of military and civilian groups in Roman Britain, Germany and Gaul, in Blagg, T F C & King, A C (eds) *Military and Civilian in Roman Britain: cultural relationships in a frontier province*, BAR Brit Ser **136**, Oxford, 187–218.

King, A C 1989 Villas and animal bones, in Branigan, K & Miles, D (eds) *The Economies of Romano-British Villas*, Sheffield, 51–59.

King, A C 1991 Food production and consumption – meat, in Jones, R F J (ed.) *Britain in the Roman Period: recent trends*, Sheffield, 21–8.

King, A C 1996 The south-east facade of Meonstoke aisled building, in Johnson, P (ed.) *Architecture in Roman Britain*, CBA Res Rep **94**, Halifax, 56–69.

King, A C 2006 Rural settlement in southern Britain: a regional survey, in Todd, M (ed.) *A Companion to Roman Britain*, Oxford, 349–70.

La Baume, P & Salomonson, J W 1976 Romische Kleinkunst, Sammlung Karl Loffler, *Wissenschaftliche Kataloge des Romisch-Germanischen Museums*, Koln III.

Lea, F M 1970 *The Chemistry of Cement and Concrete* (3rd edition), London.

Legge, A J 1981 Aspects of cattle husbandry, in Mercer, R J (ed.) *Farming Practice in British Prehistory*, Edinburgh, 169–81.

Lister, A M 1996 The morphological distinction between bones and teeth of Fallow Deer (Dama dama) and Red Deer (Cervus elaphus), *International Journal of Osteoarchaeology* **6**, 119–43.

Lyne, M A B & Jefferies, R S 1979 *The Alice Holt/Farnham Roman Pottery Industry*, CBA Res Rep **30**, London.

MacKinnon, M 2010 'Sick as a dog': zooarchaeological evidence for pet dog health and welfare in the Roman world, *World Archaeology* **42** (2), 290–309.

Malinowski, A, Slatkine, R & Ben Yair, M 1962 Durability of Roman mortars and concretes for hydraulic structures at Caesarea and Tiberias, RILEM *International Symposium on the Durability of Concrete, Praha 1961*, Czechoslovak Academy of Science, Praha, 531.

Maltby, M 1994 The meat supply in Roman Dorchester and Winchester, in Hall, A R & Kenward, H K (eds) *Urban-rural Connexions: perspectives from environmental archaeology*, Symposia of the Association for Environmental Archaeology **12**, 85–102.

Maltby, M 2010 Faunal remains from contexts of the mid-2nd–late 4th/early 5th centuries in the northern suburb and on the city defences, in Maltby, M (ed.) *Feeding a Roman Town: environmental evidence from excavations in Winchester, 1972–1985*, Winchester.

Mann, M D 1963 *The Roman Villa at Woodchester*.

Manning, W H 1984 Objects of iron, in Frere, S *Verulamium Excavations III*, Oxford, 83–106.

Manning, W H 1985 *Catalogue of the Romano-British Iron Tools, Fittings, and Weapons in the British Museum*, London.

Margary, I D 1967 *Roman Roads in Britain*, 3rd rev. edn, London.

Matolcsi, J 1970 Historische Erforschung der Körpergrösse des Rindes aufgrund von ungarischen Knochenmaterial, *Zeitschrift für Tierzüchtg u Züchtungsbiol* **87**, 89–137.

Meaney, A 1964 *A Gazetteer of Early Anglo-Saxon Burial Sites*, London.

Miles, A E W 1962 Assessment of the ages of a population of Anglo-Saxons from their dentition, *Proceedings of the Royal Society of Medicine* **55**, 881–6.

Mills, A D 1993 *A Dictionary of English Place-Names*, Oxford.

Moore, A 2009 Hearth and home: the burial of infants within Romano-British domestic contexts, *Childhood in the Past: an international journal* **2**, 33–54.

Moorhead, S & Stuttard, D 2012 *The Romans Who Shaped Britain*, London.

Moray-Williams, A 1909 The Romano-British Establishment at Stroud, *Archaeol J* **LXVI**, 33–52.

Morris, P 1979 *Agricultural Buildings in Roman Britain*, BAR Brit Ser **70**, Oxford.

Moss, E 1993 A Survey of Roman Villas in Hampshire, unpublished typescript, Winchester.

Mould, Q & Webster, G 2000 The small finds, in Ellis, P (ed.) *The Roman Baths and Macellum at Wroxeter, excavations by Graham Webster (1955–85)*, English Heritage Archaeological Report **9**, London, 108–42.

Nathan, H & Haas, N 1966 Cribra orbitalia. A bone condition of the orbit of unknown nature, *Israel J Medical Sci* **2**, 171–91.

Neal, D S 1980 Bronze Age, Iron Age and Roman settlement sites at Little Somborne and Ashley, Hampshire, *Proc Hants Fld Club Archaeol Soc* **36**, 91–143.

Neal, D S 1981 *Roman Mosaics in Britain*, London.

Neal, D S & Cosh, S R 2009 *Roman Mosaics of Britain. Vol III South-East Britain*, London.

O'Connor, T 1988 *Bones from the General Accident Site, Tanner Row, The Archaeology of York* **15/2**. London.

Ortner, D J 2003 *Identification of Pathological Conditions in Human Skeletal Remains*, 2nd edition, New York.

Pales, L & Lambert, C 1971 *Atlas Ostéotogique pour servir à L'identification des Mammiféres Du quaternaire 1. Membres Herbivors*, Edition du Centre Mational de la Recherche Scientifique.

Payne, S 1973 Kill-off patterns in sheep and goats: the mandibles from Aşvan Kale, *Anatolian Studies* **23**, 281–303.

Peacock, D P S 1969 A contribution to the study of Glastonbury ware from south-western Britain, *Antiq J* **49**, 41–61.

Peacock, D P S 1971 Roman amphorae in pre-Roman Britain, in Jesson, M & Hill, D (ed.) *The Iron Age and its Hill Forts*, Southampton, 169–88.

Peacock, D P S & Williams, D F 1986 *Amphorae and the Roman Economy: an introductory guide*, London.

Percival, J 1976 *The Roman Villa*, London.

Perring, D 2002 *The Roman House in Britain*, Abingdon.

Price, E G 2000 *Frocester, A Romano-British Settlement and its Antecedents and Successors*, Gloucester.

Price, J & Cool, H E M 1989 The Romano-British glass project, *The Glass Cone* **21**, 3–5.

Price, J & Cottam, S 1998 Romano-British Glass Vessels: a handbook, *CBA Practical Handbook in Archaeology* **14**.

Rawlings, M & Fitzpatrick, A P 1996 Prehistoric sites and a Romano-British settlement at Butterfield Down, Amesbury, Wiltshire, *Archaeol and Nat Hist Magazine* **89**, 1–43.

Redknap, M 1986 The small finds, in Millett, M & Graham, D *Excavations on the Romano-British Small Town at Neatham, Hampshire, 1969–1979*, Hants Fld Club Archaeol Soc Monog **3**, Gloucester, 101–39.

Reece, R 1991 *Roman Coins From 140 Sites in Britain*, Cotswold Studies, Cirencester.

Rees, H, Crummy, N, Ottaway, P & Dunn, G 2008 *Artefacts and Society in Roman and Medieval Winchester: small finds from the suburbs and defences, 1971–1986*, Winchester.

Reitz, E & Wing, E 2008 *Zooarchaeology*. Cambridge.

Richards, D 2000 The iron work, in Fulford, M and Timby, J *Late Iron Age and Roman Silchester, Excavations on the Site of the Forum-Basilica 1977, 1980–86*, Britannia Monogr Series **15**, London, 360–79.

Ross, A 1968 Shafts, pits, wells – sanctuaries of the Belgic Britons? in Coles, J M & Simpson, D D A (eds), *Studies in Ancient Europe: essays presented to Stuart Piggott*, Leicester, 255–85.

Scheuer, L & MacLaughlin-Black, S 1994 Age estimation from the pars basilaris of the fetal and juvenile occipital bone, *International J Osteoarchaeol* **4**, 377–80.

Scheuer, L, Musgrave, J H & Evans, S P 1980 The estimation of late fetal and perinatal age from limb bone length by linear and logarithmic regression, *Growth* **92**, 173–88.

Schmid, E 1972 *Atlas of Animal Bones for Prehistorians, Archaeologists and Quaternary Geologists*, Amsterdam.

Schour, I & Massler, M 1941 The development of the human dentition, *J American Dental Association* **28**, 1153–60.

Scott, E 1990 Romano-British villas and the social construction of space, in Samson, R (ed.) *The Social Archaeology of Houses*, Edinburgh, 149–72.

Scott, E 1993 *A Survey of Romano-British Villas in Britain*, Leicester.

Seager Smith, R H & Davies, S M 1993 Roman Pottery, in Woodward, P J, Davies, S M & Graham, A H *Excavations at the Old Methodist Chapel and Greyhound Yard, Dorchester, 1982–1984*, Dorset Nat Hist and Archaeol Soc. Monogr **12**, 202–89.

Seager Smith, R, Marter Brown, K & Mills, J M 2011 The pottery from Springhead, in Biddulph, E, Seager Smith, S & Schuster, J *Settling the Ebbsfleet Valley: High Speed 1 excavations at Springhead and Northfleet, Kent, the Late Iron Age, Roman, Saxon and medieval landscape: Vol. 2, Late Iron Age to Roman Finds Reports*, Oxford, 1–134.

Seager Smith, R H in prep Later prehistoric and Romano-British pottery, in Andrews, P, Booth, P, Fitzpatrick, A, Walsh, K, Brady, K, Good, O, Powell, J & Thacker, D *Different Landscapes and Changing Land Use: a transect across the south of Thanet. The Archaeology of The East Kent Access (Phase II)*, Wessex Archaeology Monogr.

Serjeantson, D 1972 The animal bones, in Needham, S & Spence, T (eds), *Runnymede Bridge Research Excavations. Vol. 2 Refuse and Disposal at Area 16 East, Runnymede*, London, 194–223.

Serjeantson, D 2009 *Birds*, Cambridge.

Shepherd, J & Wardle, A 2009 *The Glass Workers of Roman London*, Museum of London.

Smith, D J 1969 The mosaic pavements, in Rivet, A L F (ed.) *The Roman Villa in Britain*, London, 75–125

Smith, D J 1978 Regional aspects of winged corridor villas in Britain, in Todd, M (ed.) *Studies in the Romano-British Villa*, Leicester, 117–48.

Smith, J T 1964 Romano-British aisled houses, *Archaeol J* **120**, 1–30.

Smith, J T 1997 *Roman Villas: a study in social structures*, London.

Solley, T W J 1979 Romano-British side-tables and chip carving, *Britannia* **10**, 169–77.

Southern, H N 1964 *The Handbook of British Mammals*, Oxford.

Stoodley, N 2013 *The Archaeology of Andover: excavations of Andover Archaeological Society 1964–89*, Stevenage.

Sumner, H 1924 *Excavations at East Grimstead, Wiltshire: being a record of the discovery of a Roman villa*, London.

Svensson, E M, Götherström, A & Vretemark, M 2008 A DNA test for sex identification in cattle confirms osteometric results, *Journal of Archaeological Science* **35**, 942–6.

Symonds, R 1992 *Rhenish Wares: fine dark coloured pottery from Gaul and Germany*, Oxford University Committee for Archaeology, Monogr **23**.

Taylor, M 2007 The samian, in Bennett, P, Couldrey, P & Macpherson-Grant, N *Highstead near Chislet, Kent Excavations 1975–1977*, The Archaeology of Canterbury New Series **4**, 242–4.

Teague, S 2005 Manor Farm, Monk Sherborne, Hampshire: archaeological investigations in 1996, *Proc Hants Fld Club Archaeol Soc* **60**, 64–135.

Teichert, M 1975 Osteometrische Untersuchungen zur Berechnung der Widerristhöhe bei Schafen in Clason, A T (ed.) *Archaeozoological Studies*, Amsterdam, 51–69.

Tomalin, D & Hanworth, R 1998 *A Guide to The Roman Villa at Brading, Isle of Wight*, Orglander Roman Trust.

Tomber, R & Dore, J 1998 *The National Roman Fabric Reference Collection*, MoLAS Monogr **2**.

Trotter, M & Gleser, G C 1952 Estimation of stature from long bones of American whites and Negroes, *American J Physical Anthropology* **10**, 463–514.

Trotter, M & Gleser, G C 1958 A re-evaluation of estimation based on measurements of stature taken during life and of long bones after death, *American J Physical Anthropology* **16**, 79–123.

Tyers, P 1996 *Roman Pottery in Britain*, London.

Van Deman, E B 1912 Methods of determining the date of Roman concrete monuments, *American J Archaeol* **XVI** (2), 230.

van der Veen, M 1989 Charred grain assemblages from Roman-Period corn driers, *Archaeol J* **146**, 302–19.

Von den Driesch, A 1976 *A Guide to the Measurement of Animal Bones from Archaeological Sites*, Peabody Museum Bulletin **1**, Cambridge Mass.

Vitruvius (translated by Granger, F) 1955 *De Architectura*, London.

Wade Martins, S 2004 *Farmers, Landlords and Landscapes*, Macclesfield.

Waldron, T nd The Human Bones from Sparsholt, unpublished.

Waldron, T 2009 *Palaeopathology*, Cambridge.

Waldron, T, Taylor, G M & Rudling, D 1999 Sexing of Romano-British baby burials from the Beddingham and Bignor villas, *Sussex Archaeological Collections* **137**, 71–9.

Ward, R 2009 Osteochondrosis in Cattle from the Scottish Isles: causes and implications when analysing animal assemblages, Cardiff University dissertation.

Warry, P 2006 *Tegulae: manufacture, typology and use in Roman Britain*, BAR Brit Ser **417**, Oxford.

Warry, P 2008 Liss roofing material, in Annelay, G *Liss Roman Villa, Liss, Hampshire*, Liss Archaeological Group, unpublished.

Warry, P 2010 Legionary tile production in Britain, *Britannia* **41**, 127–47.

Warry, P 2012 The Silchester tile industry in Fulford, M *Silchester and the Study of Romano-British Urbanism*, J Roman Archaeol Monogr, 49–75.

Warry, P 2013 An assessment of the tegulae and imbrices, and ceramic building material and stone tile, in Cunliffe, B *The Roman Villa at Brading, Isle of Wight: the excavations of 2008–10*, Oxford University School of Archaeology Monogr **77**, 148–54.

Watson, A 1999 *Aurelian and the Third Century*, London.

Wayne, R K 1986 Limb morphology of domestic and wild canids: the influence of development on morphologic change, *Journal of Morphology* **187** (3), 301–19.

Webster, J 1975a Bronze and silver, in Cunliffe 1975, 198–215.

Webster, J 1975b Iron, in Cunliffe 1975, 233–47.

Wells, A F 1962 *Structural Inorganic Chemistry* (3rd edition), Oxford.

Wessex Archaeology, 2011 MoD Headquarters, High Street, Durrington, Wiltshire, archaeological evaluation report (Phase 2), unpublished client report ref. 74410.04, Salisbury.

Wheeler, R E M 1936 *Verulamium: a Belgic and two Roman cities*, Soc Antiq Res Rep **XI**, Oxford.

Williams, D F 2005 Analyses petrographiques, in Cunliffe, B W & Galliou, P *Les Fouilles du Yaudet en Ploulec'h, Cotes-d'Armor. Volume. 2: Le site de la Prehistoire a la fin de l'Empire gaulois*, Oxford Sch. Arch. Monogr **63**, Annexes, 98–101.

Williams, D F & Keay, S J 2006 Roman Amphorae: a digital resource, http://ads.ahds.ac.uk/catalogue/archive/amphora_ahrb_2005/index.cfm.

Williams-Freeman, J P 1933 Ashley Roman Camp, *Proc Hants Fld Club Archaeol Soc* **33**, 209–10.

Wilson, D R 1966 Roman Britain in 1965: sites explored, *Journal of Roman Studies* **56**.

Wilson, D R 1967 Roman Britain in 1966: sites explored, *Journal of Roman Studies* **57**.

Wilson, D R 1970 Roman Britain in 1969: sites explored, *Britannia* **1**.

Yaldon, D 1999 *The History of British Mammals*, London.

Young, C J 1977 *The Roman Pottery Industry of the Oxford Region*, BAR Brit Ser **43**, London.

Index

There is no entry for 'Sparsholt villa', as it forms the main subject of this report

Agricultural estate 87
Aisled Buildings (sites A and F) 10, **20–40**, 77, 103–04, 186, Figs 8, 13
Aisled Building I 10, **20–24**, 77, 79, 80, 84, 86, 123, 128, 132, 143, 187
  foundations and walls 20–22;
  bath-suite **22**, 131, Figs 15, 16;
  date 22–24
Aisled Building II 10, 20, **24–40**, 72–73, 79, 80, 84, 86, 87, 123, 128, 129, 132, 134, 136, 138, 143, 144, 161, 165, 182, Figs 17, 18
  bath-suite (rooms 15–18) **32–38**, 40, 84, 86, 130, 131, Fig 29, 30, 31, 32, 33, 34, 35;
  foundations and walls **24–26**, Figs 19, 20, 21;
  roof **26**, 40, Fig 22;
  room 12 **26**, 130, Fig 23, 98, 99;
  room 13 **26**, 130, Fig 24;
  room 14 **26–30**, 130;
  room 19 **30–31**, Fig 25, 26;
  room 23 **31–32**, Fig 28
Alchester, Oxon, 122
Amesbury, Wilts, 106
Anglo-Saxon 6
Animal bones 55, 57, 59, 63, 64–68, 77, **175–88**, Fig 119, 120, 121, 122, 123, 124, 125, 126 Table 42, 43
  Iron Age **183–84**;
  Iron-Age – Roman comparison **184**, Fig 127, 128;
  Roman **184–88**
Animal husbandry 18–19, 82
Ashley Camp, Hants, 2, 5

Bannister, E 6
Balksbury, Hants, 84
Barn 5, 10, 11, **59–63**, 71, 77, 79, 84, 104–05, 145, 164, 187, Fig 59, 60
  floors 59;
  foundations and walls **59**, Fig 61, 62, 63;
  roof 59;
  room 20 **59**;
  room 21 **59**, Fig 61, 64;
  room 22 **59**, Fig 62
Beddington, London, 20
Belgae 19, 84
Bembridge limestone 24, 71
Bignor, West Sussex, 58, 73, 74, 87, 113

Binsted, Hants, 73
Bone objects 55, **161–63**, Fig 114, Table 27
Brading, Isle of Wight, 68, 84, 86, 123, 124, 126, 127
Bramdean, Hants, 114, 117
Bronze Age barrows 2
Brougham, Cumbria, 156
Burnt flint 15
Burials
  Medieval 22, Fig 14, 118;
  Iron Age 12, 82, Fig 117;
  Roman 6, 45, 49, 64, 86, Fig 45, 71

Carausius and Allectus 87
Carisbrooke, Isle of Wight, 117
Castle Copse, Wilts, 20, 86, 114, 117
Ceramic building material **121–127**, Fig 100, 101, 102, 103, 104, 105, Table 10, 11, 12;
  brick 33, 49, 54, 64, 72, **122**;
  box flue 32, 35, 38, 45, 54, **122**, Fig 55
  imbrex 11, 26, 38, 40, 41, 59, **121–22**;
  signatures **125–27**;
  tegula 11, 26, 29–30, 33, 38, 50, 14, 45, 49, 59, **121–22, 123–2**
Chedworth, Gloucs, 87
Chichester, Sussex, 88
Chilgrove villas, West Sussex, 60, 73, 77, 84, 86, 88, 114, 117, 142, 161
Chronology **77–80**
Clanville, Hants, 84, 86, 87
Coins 6, 22–24, 26, 30, 40, 42, 43, 45, 47, 49, 54, 55, 57–8, 59, 63, 64, 70, 73, 75, 80, **139–40**, 156, Fig 86, 87
Colliton Park, Dorset, 157
Column 26, **165**, Fig 115
Combley, Isle of Wight, 86, 117
Concrete, composition of **132–138**
Constantine I 88
Constantius II 88
Corn-drier **33**, 40, 86, Fig 31
Courtyard 7, 10, 20, 26, 40, 59, 63, 70, **71–81**, 174, Fig 72, 77, 82, 83
Courtyard walls 8, 10, 20, 26, 38, 63, **71–73**, 79, 80, 86, 88, 164, Fig 72, 73, 74, 75, 76, 77
Crab Wood, Hants, 2, 6
Crookhorn, Hants, 123, 126, 127

Crop processing 82, 86, 88, 144

Danebury, Hants, 90, 91
Danebury Environs Project 18
Daub 20
Dinnington, Som, 117
Ditches
  Iron Age *see* Iron Age (Site L);
  Roman 47, 57, 73, 161, 187, 188, Fig 10, Fig 11, 56, 58;
  Undated 57
Downton, Wilts, 117
Drainage 38, Fig 29, 77
Dunkirt Barn, Abbotts Ann, Hants, 20, 33, 60, 84, 86, 88, 184, 186

East Grimstead, Wilts, 165
Easton Lane, Winchester Hants, 90, 91
Economy 18, 77, 86, 87
Entrance **73–75**, 79, 80, 84, 87, Fig 77, 78, 79, 80
Excavation techniques **7, 82**
Exeter 103

Farley Mount, Hants, 1, 2
Field systems 5
Fifehead Neville, Dorset, 118
Fireplace **45**, Fig 44
Fishbourne Palace, Sussex, 188
Flint tools **166**, Fig 116
Forestry Commission 6, 8
Frocester, Gloucs, 76–77
Frampton, Dorset, 118
Fullerton, Hants, 87, 142, 161, 165, 184, 186

Geology 2
Glass 5, 22, 55, 77, **156–160**, Fig 111, 112
Grateley South 33, 84, 88, 142, 161, 186
Great Casterton, Rutland, 84, 86
Great Up Somborne Wood, Hants, 5, 87

Hall 10, 11, **64–70**, 77, 80, 88, 101, 105, 143, 145, 164, 170, 187, Fig 65, 66, 69, 70, 71
  floor 64;
  foundations and walls **64**, Fig 67, 68;
  roof 64
Hampshire Field Club 6, 114
Hampshire County Council 6
Hampshire Notes and Queries 75
Hearths **30, 32,** 40, 49, **64,** 86, 87, 88, 123, Fig 25, 28, 50, 51, 52, 68
Hemsworth, Dorset, 118
Hinton St Mary, Dorset, 118
Houghton Down, Hants, 84, 86, 87, 88, 161, 183, 184, 186
Human bone **167–75**, Table 28, 29, 39, 40, 41
  Iron Age **168–170**, Fig 117, Table 30;
  Roman **170–172**, Table 31, 33, 34, 35, 36;
  Medieval **172–174**, Fig 118, Table 37, 38
Hunting 186
Hypocausts
  Aisled Building II **32–38**, Fig 33;
  Main House 10, **47–54**, 80, 86

Itchen Abbas, Hants, 114, 117

Jacob, W H 6
Johnston, D E **xii**, 1, 6–7, 10, 74, 82, 117, 186, **Fig xiii**

King's Somborne, Hants, 6
Kirton Farm, Hants, 2–5
Knight's Enham, Andover, 183, 184

Landscape 82
Langton, Yorks, 84, 86
Lainston House, Hants, 2
Littlecote, Wilts, 122
Little Somborne, Hants, 2, 6, 183, 184
Loomweight **160**, Fig 113
Lydney, Gloucs, 106
Lynchets 2

Magnentius 88
Main House 10, **41–58**, 71–71, 77, 79, 80, 84, 86, 87, 105, 128, 129, 132, 134, 136, 138, 145, 161, 170, 182, 187, Fig 36, 37, 93
  foundations and walls **41**, Fig 38, 39, 76;
  room 1 (corridor) **41–42**, 45, 47, 49, 58, 84, Fig 40, 41, 95;
  room 2 **42–45**, 129, Fig 42, 43, 94;
  room 3 **45**, 131;
  room 4 **45**, 129, Fig 44;
  room 5 **45**, 129, Fig 45, 46;
  room 6 **45**, Fig 46, 47;
  room 7 **45**, 84–86, 87, 129, 131, Fig 47, 96;
  room 8 **47**, 58, 129–130;
  room 9 **47**, 130;
  rooms 9a and 10 **47–49**, Fig 49, 50;
  room 11, 58, 86, 130, Fig 49, 53, 54, 55, Fig 97;
  roof **41**
Meonstoke, Hants, 86
Mesolithic-Neolithic 2
Metalwork **141–55**, Table 21, 22, 23, 24
  copper alloy 18, 55, **145–47**, Fig 106;
  Iron 38, 47, 55, 63, 68, **147–155**, Fig 107, 108, 109, 110, Table 25, 26;
  lead **155**
Micheldever Wood, Hants, 90, 91
Middens 49, **57–58**
Ministry of Public Buildings and Works 6, 114
Monk Sherborne, Hants, 142, 184
Mosaics **113–120**
  Aisled Building II 12, 87, **114**, Fig 23, 98, 99;
  Main House 8, 10, 40, 42, 45, 49, 58, 80, 86, 87, **113–114**, Fig 40, 41, 93, 94, 95, 96, 97
Mussel shells 30

Neatham, Hants, 142
Nettlebank Copse, Hants, 183, 184
New Buildings, Hants, 183, 184
Newport, Isle of Wight, 86, 117, 122
Nisbett, N C 6

Old Down Farm, Andover Hants, 90, 91
Ovens **30–31**, 40, **64**, 86, 88, Fig 26, 27, 69, 70

Owlesbury, Hants, 188
Oyster shells 30

Palaeolithic 2
Pitney, Som, 84, 86
Pits (Roman) **55–57**, 77, 105–06, 132, 156, 161, 182, 187, 188, Fig 56, 57
Place-name (Sparsholt) 2, 6
Portchester, Hants, 121, 142
Private/public space 86, 87
Pottery
    Iron Age 5, 12, 15, 18, 20, 57, **90–94**, Fig 88, Table 2, 3, 4:
        decoration **91**;
        fabrics **90–91**;
        forms **91**;
        flint-tempered 12, 15, 57, **90–91**;
        Glastonbury ware **92**;
        manufacture and use **91–92**;
        sand-tempered 15, **90–91**;
        shell-tempered 15, **90–91**;
    Roman 22, 24, 26, 30, 31, 32, 33, 35, 38, 42, 45–47, 49, 54–55, 57–58, 63, 64, 70, 74, 75, 77, **94–112**, Fig 32, 89, 90, 91, 92 Table 5, 6, 7:
        Alice Holt industry 101;
        amphorae 92, 94;
        Coarsewares 24, 30, 31, 32, 33, 35, 45, 47, 49, 54, 55, 57, 88, **101–103**;
        Finewares 2 2, 24, 30, 31, 33, 38, 49, 54, 57, 74, 75 **95–101**;
        graffiti 57, **102**;
        imports 22, 24, 35, 57, 59, 75, **95–96**;
        Nene Valley colour-coated ware 95, 101;
        Overwey/Tilford wares 101;
        Rowlands Castle industry 101;
        samian 63

Querns **164**

Ritual behaviour 19, 64, 82, 105, 106
Robbing 80
Rockbourne, Hants, 84
Roman roads 1, 2, 5, 68, 82, Fig 2, 3
Rudston, Yorks, 186

Shore, T W 6
Silchester, Hants, 117
Site L (Iron Age) 7, **12–19**, 82–84, 105–06, 143, Fig 6, Fig 9, 84
    animal bone 15, 182, **183–84**;
    burials 12, 168;
    date **18**;
    ditches 12, 15, 18, 57, 168, Fig 9, 10, 11, 58;
    features elsewhere **20**, 47;
    phasing **12**;
    pits **12–18**, 19, 182, 184, Fig 9, Fig 12, Table 1, Table 2;
    pottery 12, 15, 18, 20
Social status 40, 73, 74, 77, 80, 86, 87, 188
Somborne Park Farm, Hants, 2, 183, 184
South Shields, Tyne and Wear, 157
Sparsholt, Hants, 1, 5, 6, Fig 1
Springhead, Kent, 106
St Catherine's hillfort, Hants, 5
Stroud, Hants, 59, 73, 74
Suddern Farm, Hants, 183, 184

Taxes 87–88
Teg Down, Hants, 5
Tessellated floor 13, 42, 45, 47, Fig 42, 43
Thruxton, Hants, 84, 86, 87, 117, 142, 184
Tiles (roof) 26–30, 59, 64, 80, **121–22**
Tool marks 15
Trade 18, 84, 92, 95
Turner, R C 6
Twyford, Hants, 84

University of Southampton 6

Verulamium, St Albans Herts, 157

Wall plaster 32, 38, 40, 45, 47, 55, **128–31**
    composition **128–129**;
    colour **129**;
    paint **129**;
    petrographic examination **130–31**, Table 13, 14
Warblington, Hants, 84
Well 10, 38, 40, 71, **75**, 76, 79, 82, 84, 86, 88, Fig 81
West Dean, Hants, 117
West Meon, Hants, 117
West Wood, Hants, 2
Winchester Museum Service 1, 114
Winchester
    Venta Belgarum 1, 5, 84, 87, 113, 117, 121, 122, 157, 165, 184, 186, 187;
    Oram's Arbour 5, 84
Winnall Down, Hants, 90, 91
Wool 184
Woodchester, Gloucs, 87
Worthy Down, Hants, 18